Modelling and Assessing
Second Language Acquisition

Multilingual Matters

1. "Bilingualism: Basic Principles"
   HUGO BAETENS BEARDSMORE
2. "Evaluating Bilingual Education: A Canadian Case Study"
   MERRILL SWAIN AND SHARON LAPKIN
3. "Bilingual Children: Guidance for the Family"
   GEORGE SAUNDERS
4. "Language Attitudes Among Arabic-French Bilinguals in Morocco"
   ABDELÂLI BENTAHILA
5. "Conflict and Language Planning in Quebec"
   RICHARD Y. BOURHIS (ed.)
6. "Bilingualism and Special Education"
   JIM CUMMINS
7. "Bilingualism or Not: The Education of Minorities"
   TOVE SKUTNABB-KANGAS
8. "An Ethnographic/Sociolinguistic Approach to Language Proficiency Assessment"
   CHARLENE RIVERA (ed.)
9. "Communicative Competence Approaches to Language Proficiency Assessment:
   Research and Application"
   CHARLENE RIVERA (ed.)
10. "Language Proficiency and Academic Achievement"
    CHARLENE RIVERA (ed.)
11. "Pluralism: Cultural Maintenance and Evolution"
    BRIAN BULLIVANT
12. "Placement Procedures in Bilingual Education: Education and Policy Issues"
    CHARLENE RIVERA (ed.)
13. "The Education of Linguistic and Cultural Minorities in the OECD Countries"
    STACY CHURCHILL
14. "Learner Language and Language Learning"
    CLAUS FAERCH, KIRSTEN HAASTRUP AND ROBERT PHILLIPSON
15. "Bilingual and Multicultural Education: Canadian Perspectives"
    STAN SHAPSON AND VINCENT D'OYLEY (eds)
16. "Multiculturalism: The Changing Australian Paradigm"
    LOIS FOSTER AND DAVID STOCKLEY
17. "Language Acquisition of a Bilingual Child"
    ALVINO FANTINI
18. "Modelling and Assessing Second Language Acquisition"
    KENNETH HYLTENSTAM AND MANFRED PIENEMANN (eds)
19. "Aspects of Bilingualism in Wales"
    COLIN BAKER

Please contact us for the latest information on recent and forthcoming books in the series.

Derrick Sharp, General Editor, Multilingual Matters, Bank House, 8a Hill Road, Clevedon, Avon BS21 7HH, England.

MULTILINGUAL MATTERS 18

Modelling and Assessing Second Language Acquisition

Edited by
Kenneth Hyltenstam and
Manfred Pienemann

MULTILINGUAL
MATTERS LTD

British Library Cataloguing in Publication Data

Hyltenstam, Kenneth
  Modelling and assessing second language
  acquisition.—(Multilingual matters; 18)
  1. Language and languages—Study and teaching
  2. Language acquisition
  I. Title   II. Pienemann, Manfred
  401'.9   P53

  ISBN 0–905028–42–2
  ISBN 0–905028–41–4 Pbk

Multilingual Matters Ltd
Bank House, 8a Hill Road,
Clevedon, Avon BS21 7HH,
England.

Typeset by Photo·Graphics, Honiton, Devon
Printed and bound in Great Britain by
Short Run Press Ltd, Exeter EX2 7LW

Contents

PART II

PART I

1 Introduction

KENNETH HYLTENSTAM & MANFRED PIENEMANN

Over the last fifteen years or so, the study of L2 acquisition has become a vital area of research. The amount of published results has been immense, especially if we consider the short time span during which the field has developed. Scientific periodicals, monographs, readers and textbooks have appeared in increasing quantities, and the number of scholars engaged in this type of research in various parts of the world is increasing steadily. Although the emphasis in the field has been on *second language acquisition* in its narrow sense, i.e. the acquisition of an L2 in the target language environment, rather than on *foreign language learning*, i.e. the formal classroom learning of an L2 (typically the learning of English, French, German, or Spanish at school throughout the world), a fair amount of research has focused on this latter situation (see e.g. Felix, 1981; Hahn, 1982; Lightbown, 1983; Seliger & Long, 1983; Faerch *et al.*, 1983). Research on second language acquisition, it should be noted, has been concerned with both untutored — or "natural" — language acquisition, and situations where the learner has been supported by formal teaching.

However, despite the intensity of L2 acquisition research, the knowledge gained has not yet influenced the language teaching profession or the language classroom very much. Of course, differences in degree of influence exist between countries, as well as between language teaching settings. Various factors have been important in this respect, such as whether there are personal promoters engaged in the diffusion of results, and whether there is a structural readiness for certain types educational changes. From the second language researcher's point of view, it is generally felt that knowledge about the nature of L2 acquisition should make up part of what needs to be taken into account in language teaching, although there is of course no obvious, uniquely identifiable "teaching method" implied in this knowledge.

3

The planning of this volume started out in response to the question: What are the implications of second language acquisition research for language teaching? The aim of the book is therefore to give this question an in-depth consideration from various points of view. The discussion centres around issues such as whether and how teaching, teaching materials and testing can be planned and executed in ways that are more favourable for the individual learners, if known facts about second language acquisition are taken into account. As the title of the book suggests, it is divided into two parts. Part I deals with those factors which concern syllabus design, teaching materials, and teaching itself. Part II is concerned with assessment testing.

L2 acquisition research: An overview

At this point, as a background for the discussion in the book, a brief review of the field of second language acquisition research is in order. Of necessity, we cannot go into any kind of detail as regards the empirical work that has been carried out in the area. In particular, we will not consider research methodologies *per se*, since we feel these questions cannot be adequately dealt with within the framework of a short introduction. Rather, we shall touch upon those questions which have been addressed as main issues and discuss why, i.e. we will try to give an idea of what influences have been important for the development of the field. This discussion also seeks to articulate the various relationships existing between second language acquisition research and other research areas. Individual results from second language acquisition research are given detailed treatment in the various contributions in this volume.

In this overview, the notion of second language acquisition is used in a broad sense covering all sorts of L2 acquisition or learning.

The emergence of empirical second language acquisition research

In 1945, Charles Fries published a book under the title *Teaching and Learning English as a Foreign Language*. In one of the first pages, Fries wrote the following:

> "The most efficient materials are those that are based upon a scientific description of the language to be learned, carefully compared with a parallel description of the native language of the learner." (p.9)

This view was one reflection of the common observation that a second language learner's first language influenced the second, and of the assumption that the learner's problems with the new language arose due to differences between the two languages. This contention is even more clearly expressed by Robert Lado in *Linguistics across Cultures*, published in 1957:

> "We will assume that the student who comes in contact with a foreign language will find some features of it quite easy and others extremely difficult. Those elements that are similar to his native language will be simple for him, and those elements that are different will be difficult."
> (p. 2)

These books by Fries and Lado, which were written for language teachers, together with work by Haugen (1953) and especially Weinrech (1953) at a more descriptive and linguistically theoretical level, constituted the incentive for the concentration on contrastive analysis in the 50's and 60's. The so-called strong claim of contrastive analysis (Wardhaugh, 1970) implies that all "errors" a second language learner may make can be explained by reference to the nature of the first language. This view presupposes a mechanistic learning theoretical orientation, and such an orientation was of course the main trend during the behaviouristic era (cf. Skinner, 1957).

At the shift from mechanistic to mentalistic ideas about learning during the 60's (where Chomsky's critique of Skinner (Chomsky, 1959) was instrumental in precipitating the rise of the mentalistic conviction in language learning or language acquisition research), it was only natural to question the strong claim of contrastive analysis. Furthermore, practice showed that the predictions of contrastive analysis were not always borne out, i.e. differences between L1 and L2 did not always cause difficulties, and, similarly, where the two languages were alike, the difficulties were not always absent.

In 1968, it can be noted, Georgetown University's Annual Round Table Meeting on Linguistics and Language Studies (Alatis, 1968) was devoted to contrastive linguistics and its pedagogical implications. The participants of this meeting, which included many of those who had worked practically within the contrastive analysis framework (for example Lado, Stockwell, Moulton, Di Pietro, and Rivers), discussed the limitations and the values of contrastive analysis. Interestingly, some kind of consensus concerning the predictive role of contrastive analysis can be discerned in the different contributions to the meeting. This agreement seems to be a reflection of the attitudinal shift in learning theory mentioned above. In cognitive learning theories, the manifestation of learning problems may have other causes than influences from earlier established stimulus-response links. The main idea at the meeting was that the nature of the mother tongue cannot be considered more than but one of many possible causes of learning problems. This view is what Wardhaugh (1970) later labelled the weak claim of contrastive analysis.

Even if the Georgetown Round Table Meeting in 1968 was important as an indication of the fact that a theoretical shift had indeed taken place in the area of second language learning, its impact on the development which followed seems to have been limited. More important were the programmatic articles that were written more or less independently — so it seems — by a number of scholars in the late 60's and early 70's. Corder (1967, 1971), Selinker (1969, 1972) Nemser (1971), and Richards (1971a, 1972) are among the articles that were referred to during the 70's in virtually every study within the field of second language acquisition — or *interlanguage studies*, to use the term introduced by Selinker in 1969. In slightly different ways, these authors expressed more or less the same idea, viz. that the learner actively constructs his grammar for the new language in a way similar to a child acquiring his first language. As a basis for the construction of a grammar for L2, the second language *input* (or rather the part of the input which the learner can competently handle in perception, the *intake* in Corder's terminology (Corder, 1967)) is used. Input, however, is only one kind of data for the learner. There are also other sources available, such as the structure of the mother tongue or other languages that are known to the learner, general communication and learning strategies, and strategies for simplification of communication and learning. This view is based on the idea that the human mind is endowed with an innate predisposition for language acquisition and that this innate ability to learn languages remains even after the first language is acquired (see especially Selinker, 1972). Corder (1967) proposes "as a working hypothesis that some at least of the *strategies* adopted by the learner of a second language are substantially the same as those by which a first language is acquired."

All these authors strongly called for the need for empirical research concentrating on the language of the second language learner. The last fifteen years of research in the field of second language acquisition attests to the fact that this call was indeed heeded.

Empirical work

Error analysis. One of the early empirical approaches was the analysis of second or foreign language learners' errors. This branch of research, known as *error analysis*, can be seen as an immediate response to the dissatisfaction with contrastive analysis and the predictions that could be made on this basis. If a constrastive analysis could not correctly predict what errors a learner with a particular L1/L2 constellation would make, a necessary step seemed to be to make an inventory of what errors actually did occur and then discuss their possible backgrounds. This strongly data-driven type of research resulted in various error taxonomies (e.g. Richards, 1971a, 1971b; Selinker, 1972), which, in summary, contain main categories such as *interlingual errors*, i.e. errors due to language transfer, *intralingual or developmental errors,* comprising overgeneralizations related to second language simplifying strategies and other kinds of false hypotheses made by the learner, as well as errors due to communication simplifying strategies. A third category was *teaching induced errors*.

As mentioned by Corder (1978), error analysis can be seen as having two aims, one being immediately pedagogical — in that it points out for teachers what errors can be expected of a certain learner — and the other being theoretical — in that it addresses the question of the nature of the learner's interlanguage competence. The insufficiency of error analysis for this second purpose was however pointed out early (Hammarberg, 1973; Schachter, 1974), and the claim was made that a more complete picture of the learner's interlanguage could only be gained through investigations of the learner's total performance and a consideration of what parts of the target language the learner might have avoided using altogether. The claim that observational data, which generally were used in error analyses, must be combined with experimental data was also made during this period (e.g. Corder, 1973). For an overview of the error analysis approach, see Corder (1978).

Morpheme studies. Another early approach was what has been labelled *the morpheme studies*. Influenced both methodologically and analytically by studies in the area of first language acquisition of English, particularly those by Brown (1973) and de Villiers & de Villiers (1973), this approach set out to investigate second language learners' acquisition of a number of grammatical morphemes, such as the Progressive *-ing*, the Plural *-s*, the Article *a/the* etc. (Dulay & Burt, 1973 and later studies). The aim was to identify whether an invariant order of morpheme acquisition parallel to what had been found in the first language context (Brown, 1973) actually existed for second language learners as well. Dulay & Burt, and a number of other scholars who were influenced by them, studied various learner groups differing in background factors such as first language, age, and language instruction. Both oral and written production were investigated. The results showed a uniform patterning as regarded the degree of correctness to which each morpheme was supplied in obligatory contexts by all these different groups of learners. Dulay & Burt concluded that there was a unique order of acquisition for L2 learners, although different from the order that was found for L1 learners.

Due to a number of methodological difficulties, there have been many controversies about the interpretation of the results of the morpheme studies. Since the methodology has been cross-sectional, and since the analytical approach is one where group results rather than individual results can be studied, it seems premature to regard the patternings, that undoubtedly do exist in the data, as *acquisition orders*. One might refer to them as *accuracy orders* or *difficulty orders* (Larsen-Freeman, 1975). Andersen (1977, 1978) has suggested that analytical methods be applied to the data where both group patterns and individual patterns can be observed, and Rosansky (1976) has pointed to the possibility that the uniformity of results in various studies could partly be an effect of their use of the same or similar elicitation instruments. Andersen (1977) has also drawn attention to the difficulties involved in the delimitation of linguistic categories in the morpheme studies. For summaries and overviews of the morpheme studies, see Krashen (1977), Burt & Dulay (1980), and Hatch (1978a).

Studies dealing with the development of particular structural areas. If the morpheme studies have aimed at identifying the acquisitional sequences that might exist among various grammatical morphemes, another main trend has been to characterize how interlanguage development proceeds *within* particular structural areas. The studies typical of this approach have been longitudinal, but cross-sectional methods have also been used. The choice of what linguistic phenomena should be studied has of course partly been governed by knowledge of what structures of a particular L2 turn out to be particularly hard to learn. Thus, in many cases, linguistic areas that are problematic for L2 learners with various L1's have been chosen. Since the areas of negation and interrogation are difficult in many L2's, these phenomena are without doubt the ones that have been most studied cross-linguistically (Ravem, 1968, 1974: Norwegian L1/English L2; Cazden *et al.*, 1975; Schumann, 1978a, 1979; Stauble, 1978: Spanish L1/English L2; Felix, 1978, 1982; Wode, 1981a: English and German L1/English and German L2; Hyltenstam, 1978a: various L1's/Swedish L2; Lightbown, 1980: French L1/English L2; Trévise & Noyau, 1984: Spanish L1/French L2; Clahsen *et al.*, 1983: Spanish-Italian-Portuguese L1/German L2).

In German L2, since word order is one of the outstanding difficulties for second language learners, acquisitional sequences within this area have been a focus of study in the ZISA group (Clahsen *et al.*, 1983; Pienemann, 1981). Of course, a number of other areas have also been dealt with, especially in work that has aimed at a more comprehensive description of the second language development of one learner (e.g. Hakuta, 1976;

Huebner, 1983), or a group of learners (e.g. Andersen, 1977; Klein & Dittmar, 1979; Pienemann, 1981; Clahsen *et al.*, 1983). This is also the case with the studies of L2 immersion students in Canada (e.g. Harley & Swain, 1977). Particular syntactic areas have also been utilized to throw light on questions such as whether first and second language development are parallel or not (e.g. Cook, 1973; Ervin-Tripp, 1974), although the investigation of the linguistic patterning as such has not been the focus of interest in these cases.

It is certainly the case that syntactic and morphological areas have been studied more extensively in second language acquisition research than phonology or lexicon. Phonological studies, however, have been conducted during the entire period we are dealing with. But probably because the amount of research has been considerably smaller, its influence seems to have been generally weaker; indeed, in an overview in 1978, Tarone characterized the area as largely ignored. There have been at least two very interesting foci in the phonological L2 research, one of which concerns the concept of variability. Dickerson (1975) pointed to the degree of systematicity that can be found in the L2 learner's variable pronunciation of certain segmental units, and concluded that this patterned behaviour could throw new light on the phonological development of L2 learners. This area will be further dealt with below in the section of variability analysis.

The other focus has been that of comparing the phonological development/behaviour of learners with different L1's acquiring the same L2. The aim here has been to discern general, non-L1-specific characteristics and the interplay between these general developmental features and features that are due to transfer. A common framework for this direction has been the universalist approach (see below). An early publication within this branch was Johansson (1973). See also Wode (1980) and Bannert (1983).

Studies of lexicon or vocabulary learning have been rarer, which is unfortunate but explainable in terms of lack of workable theoretical frameworks for lexical analysis. The studies of interlanguage vocabulary are often linked to the concept of communicative strategies, but also, from a different perspective, to universals of lexico-semantic organization (Levenston & Blum, 1977; Blum-Kulka & Levenston, 1983; Kotsinas, 1984).

Variability analysis. The apparent inconsistency of the second language learner's output, i.e. features of variation, has attracted a considerable amount of attention in second language acquisition research, since it has been felt that this variation, as mentioned above, gives information about the changes that are taking place in the learner's interlanguage competence (e.g. Dickerson, 1975; Dickerson, 1976; Hyltenstam, 1977; Andersen, 1978; Tarone, 1982). In methodology and aims, these studies were strongly influenced by studies in sociolinguistics and dialectology (e.g. Labov, 1969; Trudgill, 1974), where, likewise, features of variation were used for gaining insights into the wider systematicity in the speech community. To simplify grossly, younger speakers use innovative features with greater frequency than older ones. This insight could then be used for making conclusions about ongoing language changes (see also Weinreich et al., 1968 on this point). In particular, the so-called wave model for linguistic change (Bailey, 1973) and the notion of linguistic continua, as developed in creole studies (Bickerton, 1975), have been influencial, as theoretical frameworks. The method of implicational scaling (DeCamp, 1971) has been a useful · tool in sorting out and displaying large amounts of data showing group and individual patternings simultaneously (in addition to the second language acquisition studies mentioned above, see also Hyltenstam, 1978b; Dittmar, 1980; Pienemann, 1981; Meisel et al., 1981; Clahsen et al., 1983).

Pidginization, simplification and individual variation. One characteristic of second language learners' performance is the fact that in initial phases of acquisition or in fossilization, it contains certain structural features that are typical for different kinds of simple registers. The parallel between pidgins and, particularly, fossilized learners' interlanguage has been taken to mean that the same processes are at work in pidginization and second language acquisition (Heidelberger Forschungsprojekt "Pidgin-Deutsch" 1975; Schumann, 1978a, 1982; Andersen, 1981). As mentioned above, creole studies, especially those viewing the spectrum of creole varieties in a speech community as constituting a continuum, have provided the framework for some studies (e.g. Stauble, 1978).

Linked to the observation that certain L2 learners fossilize in initial "pidgin-like" phases of acquisition, while others develop further towards the target, are a number of discussions about individual differences among learners and the factors that may determine whether a learner will fossilize or develop further (e.g. Schumann, 1978a, 1978b). The ZISA studies point to the fact that socio-psychological factors do not just determine how far a certain learner will reach in a unilinearly organized L2 development: such factors also determine qualitative features in the learner's interlanguage. Therefore, different *learner types* can be discerned by correlating on the one hand social and psychological factors for certain learners and on the other hand these learners' linguistic characteristics (Meisel et al., 1981; Pienemann, 1981; Clahsen et al., 1983; Nicholas, 1982).

Individual differences among L2 learners can of course be looked at from other aspects than the ones we have noted here. Wong-Fillmore (1979), for example, observed that various communicative styles were typical of different L2 learning children. Wong-Fillmore discusses possible correlations between such communicative styles and success in L2 development.

Language typology and second language acquisition. Another field of linguistic research where parallels of patterning to second language acquisition can be observed is that of language typology and language universals. The notion of *markedness*, which has played an important role in universals studies, has also been employed in second language acquisition studies (Eckman, 1977; Gass, 1979; Hyltenstam, 1984; Wode, 1981a; Rutherford, 1982; Zobl, 1983; for an overview, see Hyltenstam, 1982). The notions of markedness and language universals have been employed particularly in attempts to qualify the predictions about transfer in particular L1/L2 constellations on the one hand and acquisitional orderings in particular L2's on the other, as well as to discover the interplay between transfer and intralingually determined developmental sequences.

Transfer. The notion of *transfer*, which, as we have seen, was central to contrastive analysis, has been dealt with extensively in recent years within a broader framework of linguistic, and especially psycholinguistic, theoretical reasoning. In this work, transfer has been largely dissociated from its behaviouristic base, and what is discussed instead is how and why the learner draws on some — but not all — of his knowledge from L1 in the use of an L2. Thus, the notion of transfer is redefined within a mentalistic perspective. In particular Kellerman and Jordens (see e.g. Kellerman, 1980, 1983; Jordens & Kellerman, 1981) have outlined the view that predictions of transfer must be based not only on the structural properties of L1 and L2, but also on insights into how the structures of L1 are perceived intuitively by the learner as being either transferable or non-transferable into a particular L2 at a specific phase of acquisition. The conditions of transferability are thus dependent on the structural distance between L1 and L2 and how the learner perceives this distance (Ringbom, 1978; Sjöholm, 1979). For analyses of the notion of transfer, see also Sharwood Smith (1979) and Meisel (1983).

Discourse analysis. Since the mid 70's, a growing field of interest in second language acquisition research has been that of *discourse analysis* (for an overview, see Hatch & Long, 1980). This development is parallel to what has happened in linguistics generally, and, in particular, in the field of first language acquisition studies. There, the focus of interest has shifted from a concentration on the child's utterances to the communicative interaction between child and caretaker. The concentration on the child's utterances was a reflection of the Chomskian view that the child constructed his grammar on the basis of innate ability and exposure to the language of the environment, i.e. the *input*. The quality of this input was not considered in detail, since it was regarded as a sufficient explanation for the child's language development to refer to innateness. A dissatisfaction with this explanatory level resulted in a shift of attention, first to the child's input, i.e. the mother's or caretaker's speech (cf. the notions of *motherese*, *caretakerese*!), and then to the communicative interaction between the child and the adult.

Similarly, in L2 research, *input studies* developed into a particular branch of research (for overviews, see Hatch, 1979 and Long, 1983). The input provided by the language teacher has been of particular interest for natural reasons (Henzl, 1979; Gaies, 1977; Chaudron, 1978; Håkansson, 1982; Long & Sato, 1983). But other native speaker input has also been studied (e.g. Long, 1983).

In studying the communicative interaction between the L2 learner and the native speaker, one of the aims has been to investigate the degree of interdependence between structural language development and the communicative involvement of the learner (Hatch, 1978b; Wong-Fillmore, 1979; Wagner, 1983).

Related to the field of input studies, as it were, is the particular area of *"foreigner talk" studies* (Ferguson, 1975; Meisel, 1977). These studies, however, originated within research on speech registers, while the input studies derived from the anti-Chomskian research into L1 acquisition. Foreigner talk is characterized by deviations from the target language norm which are purportedly simplificatory. Long (1983) has made a terminological distinction between *ungrammatical foreigner talk* containing such deviations and *grammatical foreigner talk*, which is structurally simple and tuned to the learner's level of competence without being deviant, thus extending the notion of foreigner talk to cover also this latter situation.

Three recent volumes give an idea of what the vast field of discourse analysis in second language acquisition comprises: Larsen-Freeman (1980; Richards & Schmidt (1983); Sajavaara & Lehtonen (1980).

Communicative strategies. Closely linked to the field of discourse analysis are the studies of *communicative strategies*. Communicative strategies can broadly be characterized as the ways the language learner solves perceived communicative problems when using his interlanguage (cf. Faerch &

Kasper, 1983a). Various taxonomies of such strategies have been suggested, one often cited being that developed by Tarone (1977). The articles in a collection by Faerch & Kasper (1983b) give a comprehensive picture and various views and research approaches in the study of communicative strategies.

Instruction and second language acquisition research: The aim and structure of this volume

As we outlined above, the present volume is an attempt to ulilize existing findings from L2 acquisition research for practical purposes, i.e. teaching and assessment. In this attempt, the contributors share to some extent the conviction that findings from L2 acquisition are relevant to the formal instruction of language. This is, of course, an opinion not shared by all scholars. Some researchers maintain, for example, that formal L2 acquisition may be an acquisitional type *sui generis*, and that the processes of language instruction and formal learning may be substantially different from natural L2 development (cf. Bausch & König, 1983). Consequently, what is a learning barrier in natural acquisition, does not in their view have to be one in formal acquisition.

The present volume does not primarily address this fundamental and general issue. Rather, the majority of its authors take the view that there are some principles which apply to both formal and natural acquisition (which does, of course, not mean that the two are identical).

Apart from this general point of agreement, the articles in this book express a number of — sometimes conflicting — viewpoints. Suggestions as to how available knowledge on L2 development might be utilized for practice are highly dependent on the researcher's opinion concerning the nature of the processes of language learning and instruction.

As the editors, we are glad that this controversy is openly discussed in the following collection of interrelated articles. The reason is as follows: On the one hand we think that we have gathered enough data and hypotheses on L2 development, which are often closely related to issues of L2 instruction, to start to communicate with the "second/foreign language teaching public". If we do not communicate with each other, practitioneers might not be able to appreciate genuine psycholinguistic solutions to problems of instruction even when we one day might be capable of providing them. On the other hand, we feel that a controversial discussion is an appropriate way of representing the fact that there is not to date *one* single and genuine solution to instructional problems, and that we have to work towards a more comprehensive approach in co-operation.

Thus the intention of this volume is not to argue for a specific approach to instruction or assessment. The co-existence of several competing approaches to the two cases of application on which this book concentrates is meant to counteract the emergence of a "psycholinguistic" or "developmental" method for foreign/second language teaching. We think practitioneers have often enough experienced the emergence of dogmatic new approaches which have claimed too much.

However, we do think there are a number of issues in L2 instruction which have so far only been treated intuitively, and that we should continually try to replace intuition by insights into language learning mechanisms.

For the better understanding of the individual articles, a note on the internal structure of the book might be helpful. As mentioned above, the volume consists of two parts, each of which concentrates on one instance of applying L2 research to practice. The papers by Pienemann, Ingram and Clahsen were distributed to all contributors before the other articles were written, since they contain specific proposals on their respective topics, which are then discussed by other authors. The other articles were sent out to all contributors when a draft was ready. Thus there are a number of cross-references in this volume. The order in which the articles appear in the book is intended to reflect these cross-references (within each section); the articles are ordered so that what is mentioned first appears first.

Part I contains a variety of proposals for the application of L2 research to teaching. These proposals are all made "from one direction", namely from scholars who have long been involved in L2 research themselves and who acknowledge the importance of their research for practice. Partly as a reaction to the position paper (Pienemann), a number of contributions deal explicitly with syllabus construction (Long, Lightbown, Pica). In this discussion the reader will be provided with a wide range of findings from research into the relation of natural and formal (classroom) L2 acquisition and about decisively different ways to implement findings on learning processes into syllabus construction.

A special obstacle in this implementation is indicated by Nicholas, who claims that what is learnable for one learner does not have to be learnable for another. Hammarberg also addresses the notion of learnability, and concludes that teaching might benefit from taking various factors into account which influence the learnability of a certain structure or unit.

Further, Clyne reports on a school experiment which investigates the effect of the presence and absence of an explicit linguistic syllabus on the children's L2.

Another type of proposal for application (Hyltenstam) utilizes knowledge from L2 research for the revision of general concepts of L2 instruction.

Part II is devoted to L2 testing. In this domain, indirect tests were dominant in the past. This volume contains three different approaches to direct testing. Ingram, who also gives a broad overview of the field in his article, advocates a proficiency-*rating*-approach. Lapkin outlines a task-solving (communicative) approach developed at the Ontario Institute for Studies in Education. Finally, Clahsen develops a profile analysis for L2 acquisition based on findings from research into natural L2 development. The approaches by Clahsen and Ingram are evaluated in Fried's article on the validity of L2 tests.

However, determining the optimal test procedure (for a certain purpose) is not the only major problem in this field. A more delicate one is the mis-use of language proficiency tests as a decision-making instrument in "streaming" learners into different classes and in immigration policy. Stölting, in his article, stresses the informants' competence and right to participate in the evaluation of their L2 skills.

Many researchers have experienced that the term "language proficiency" is a chameleon, and in this volume, the notion of proficiency is itself the topic of Hulstijn's contribution. The differences in the above-mentioned three approaches to direct L2 testing originate to a considerable extent in what the authors intend to measure. At first glance, Ingram, Clahsen and Lapkin all investigate proficiency. They do, however, refer to rather different concepts. Clahsen clearly relates his analysis to the *developmental* stage (and the specific path) of the learners. Ingram and Lapkin refer to the communicative task that the testees are able to perform — and they test them in fairly different ways. Thus the question "how much have they learned?" can be asked from entirely different perspectives:

- How correct is their interlanguage compared to the last test and to the target language? (as partly implied in Lapkin's approach)
- How many communicative tasks can the testee perform? (Ingram)

– How far has the learner proceeded on the developmental path? (Clahsen)

These different perspectives certainly do not match. It has been shown that "correctness" does not directly correlate with the stage of development (cf. Meisel *et al.*, 1981; Huebner, 1983). It has further been shown that individual learners can to a highly varying degree exploit the structures which are at their disposal as a given stage of acquisition.

An example may illustrate why "communicative proficiency" and "developmental stage" are conceptually different. In their work on German word order and phrase structure, the ZISA group identified a stage at which the learners are able to produce auxiliaries but not the "verb separation rule"[1] which is obligatorily required in German as soon as auxiliaries are inserted. The interesting aspect for the interaction of communicative competence and the acquisition of morpho-syntactic phenomena is that in the data, there are (at least) two different learner types: one who uses the auxiliary at the expense of target correctness, thus being able to use a device for referring to the past (i.e. present perfect; cf. Wode, 1981b; Meisel, 1982). The other learner type does not make use of the auxiliary at this stage, thus being "correct" but communicatively disadvantaged.

From these theoretical considerations, we might expect that communicative proficiency and developmental stage can never completely overlap. A preliminary study by Brindley & Singh (1982) indicates, however, that there is a rough correlation between the two. We certainly need more research to explore the precise relationship between these concepts of proficiency.

Notes to Chapter 1

1. The effect of this rule is that the main verb is moved into sentence final position (e.g. Subject + *Aux* + Object + *Verb*). Examples are given in the chapters by Clahsen and by Pienemann in this volume.

References

Alatis, J. E. (ed.) 1968, *Contrastive Linguistics and Its Pedagogical Implications. 19th Annual Round Table.* Monograph Series on Languages and Linguistics. Washington D.C.: Georgetown University Press.
Andersen, R. W. 1977, The impoverished state of cross-sectional morpheme acquisition/accuracy methodology (or: The leftovers are more nourishing than

the main course). *Working Papers on Bilingualism*, 14, 47–82.
—1978, An implicational model for second language research. *Language Learning*, 28, 221–82.
—1981, Two perspectives on pidginization as second language acquisition. In R. W. Andersen (ed.), *New Dimensions in Second Language Acquisition Research*. Rowley, Mass.: Newbury House.
Bailey, C.-J. N. 1973, *Variation and Linguistic Theory*. Arlington: Center for Applied Linguistics.
Bannert, R. 1983, Phonological variation and language teaching. In S. W. Felix & H. Wode (eds), *Language Development at the Crossroads*. Papers from the Interdisciplinary conference on Language Acquisition at Passau. Tübingen: Gunter Narr.
Bausch, K. R. & König, F. G. 1983, 'Lernt' oder 'erwirbt' man Fremdsprachen im Unterricht? Zum Verhältnis von Sprachlehrforschung und Zweitsprachenerwerbsforschung. *Die Neueren Sprachen* 82/4, 308–36.
Bickerton, D. 1975, *Dynamics of a Creole System*. London: Cambridge University Press.
Blum-Kulka, S. & Levenston, E. A. 1983, Universals of lexical simplification. In C. Faerch & G. Kasper (eds), *Strategies in Interlanguage Communication*. London: Longman.
Brindley, G. & Singh, K. 1982, The use of second language learning research in E.S.L. proficiency assessment. *Australian Review of Applied Linguistics* 5/1, 84–111.
Brown, H. D., Yorio, C. A. & Crymes, R. H. (eds) 1977, *On TESOL '77: Teaching and Learning English as a Second Language*. Washington D. C.: TESOL.
Brown, R. 1973, *A First Language*. Harmondsworth: Penguin Education 1976.
Burt, M. K. & Dulay, H. C. 1980, On acquisition orders. In S. W. Felix (ed.), *Second Language Development. Trends and Issues*. Tübingen: Gunter Narr.
Cazden, C. B., Cancino, H., Rosansky, E. & Schumann, J. H. 1975, *Second Language Acquisition Sequences in Children, Adolescents, and Adults*. U.S. Department of Health, Education and Welfare, National Institute of Education, Office of Research Grants. Final Report Project No. 730744, Grant No. NE–6–00–3–0014.
Chaudron, C. 1978, English as the Medium of Instruction in ESL Classes: An Initial Report of a Pilot Study of the Complexity of Teachers' Speech. Modern Language Centre, Ontario Institute for Studies in Education.
Chomsky, N. 1959, Review of Skinner 1957. *Language*, 35, 26–58.
Clahsen, H., Meisel, J. M. & Pienemann, M. 1983, *Deutsch als Zweitsprache. Der Spracherwerb ausländischer Arbeiter*. Tübingen: Gunter Narr.
Cook, V. J. 1973, The comparison of language development in native children and foreign adults. *IRAL*, 11, 13–28.
Corder, S. P. 1967, The significance of learners' errors, *IRAL*, 5, 161–70.
—1971, Idiosyncratic dialects and error analysis. *IRAL*, 9, 147–60.
—1973, The elicitation of interlanguage. In J. Svartvik (ed.), *Errata. Papers in Error Analaysis*. Lund: CWK Gleerup.
—1978, Error analysis, interlanguage and second language acquisition. In V. Kinsella (ed.), *Language Teaching and Linguistics: Surveys*. Centre for Information on Language Teaching and Research and English Teaching Information Centre of the British Council. Cambridge: Cambridge University Press.
Corder, S. P. & Roulet, E. 1977 (eds) *The Notions of Simplification, Interlan-*

guages, and Pidgins and their Relation to Second Language Pedagogy. Genève: Droz.

DeCamp, D. 1971, Towards a generative analysis of a post-creole speech continuum. In D. Hymes (ed.), *Pidginization and Creolization of Languages*. London: Cambridge University Press.

Dickerson, L. J. 1975, The learner's interlanguage as a system of variable rules. *TESOL Quarterly*, 9, 401–07.

Dickerson, W. 1976, The psycholinguistic unity of language learning and language change. *Language Learning*, 26, 215–31.

Dittmar, N. 1980, Ordering adult learners according to language abilities. In S. W. Felix (ed.), *Second Language Development. Trends and Issues*. Tübingen: Gunter Narr.

Dulay, H. & Burt, M. 1973, Should we teach children syntax? *Language Learning*, 23, 245–58.

Eckman, F. R. 1977, Markedness and the contrastive analysis hypothesis. *Language Learning*, 27, 315–30.

Ervin-Tripp, S.M. 1974, Is second language learning like first? *TESOL Quarterly*, 8, 111–27.

Faerch, C., Haastrup, K. & Phillipson, R. 1983, *Learner Language and Language Learning*. Clevedon, Avon: Multilingual Matters.

Faerch, C. & Kasper, G. 1983a, Introduction. In C. Faerch & G. Kasper (eds) *Strategies in Interlanguage Communication*. London: Longman.

—(eds) 1983b, *Strategies in Interlanguage Communication*. London: Longman.

Felix, S. W. 1978, *Linguistische Untersuchungen zum Zweitsprachenerwerb*. München: Fink.

—(ed.) 1980 *Second Language Development. Trends and Issues*. Tübingen: Gunter Narr.

—1981, The effect of formal instruction on second language acquisition. *Language Learning*, 31, 87–112.

—1982, *Psycholinguistische Aspekte des Zweitsprachenerwerbs*. Tübingen: Gunter Narr.

Felix, S. W. & Wode, H. (eds) 1983, *Language Development at the Crossroads. Papers from the Interdisciplinary Conference on Language Acquisition at Passau*. Tübingen: Gunter Narr.

Ferguson, C. A. 1975, Towards a characterization of English foreigner talk. *Anthropological Linguistics*, 17, 1–14.

Fries, C. C. 1945, *Teaching and Learning English as a Foreign Language*. Ann Arbor: The University of Michigan Press.

Gaies, S. J. 1977, The nature of linguistic input in formal second language learning: Linguistic and communicative strategies in ESL teachers' classroom language. In H. D. Brown, C. A. Yorio & R. H. Crymes (eds), *On TESOL '77: Teaching and Learning English as a Second Language*. Washington, D. C.: TESOL.

Gass, S. 1979, Language transfer and universal grammatical relations. *Language Learning*, 29, 327–44.

Hahn, A. 1982, *Fremdsprachenunterricht und Spracherwerb*. Diss. University of Passau.

Håkansson, G. 1982, Quantitative studies of teacher talk. *Scandinavian Working Papers on Bilingualism* 1, 52–72.

Hakuta, K. 1976, A case study of a Japanese child learning English as a second language. *Language Learning*, 26, 321–51.

Hammarberg, B. 1973, The insufficiency of error analaysis. In J. Svartvik (ed.),

Errata. Papers in Error Analysis. Lund: CWK Gleerup.

Harley, B. & Swain, M. 1977, An analysis of verb form and function in the speech of French immersion pupils. *Working Papers on Bilingualism*, 14, 33–46.

Hatch, E. 1978a, Acquisition of syntax in a second language. In J. C. Richards (ed.), *Understanding Second and Foreign Language Learning. Issues and Approaches.* Rowley, Mass: Newbury House.

—1978b, Discourse analysis and second language acquisition. In E.M. Hatch (ed.), *Second Language Acquisition. A Book of Readings.* Rowley, Mass.: Newbury House.

—1979, Simplified input and second language acquisition. In R.W. Andersen (ed.) *Pidginization and Creolization as Language Acquisition.* Rowley, Mass.: Newbury House.

Hatch, E. & Long, M.H. 1980, Discourse analaysis, what's that? In D. Larsen-Freeman (ed.), *Discourse Analysis in Second Language Research.* Rowley, Mass.: Newbury House.

Haugen, E. 1953, *The Norwegian Language in America. A Study in Bilingual Behavior.* Philadelphia: University of Pennsylvania Press.

Heidelberger Forschungsprojekt "Pidgin-Deutsch" 1975, *Sprache und Kommunikation ausländischer Arbeiter. Analysen, Berichte, Materialen.* Kronberg/Ts.: Scriptor Verlag.

Henzl, V. 1979, Foreign talk in the classroom. *IRAL*, 17, 159–67.

Huebner, T. 1983, *A Longitudinal Analysis of the Acquisition of English.* Ann Arbor: Karoma.

Hyltenstam, K 1977, Implicational patterns in interlanguage syntax variation. *Language Learning*, 27, 383–411.

—1978a, Variation in interlanguage syntax. *Working Papers*, 18. Department of General Linguistics, Lund University.

—1978b, A framework for the study of interlanguage continua. *Working Papers*, 16, 65–86. Department of General Linguistics, Lund University.

—1982, Markedness, language universals, language typology and second language acquisition. Paper presented at the 2nd European North American Workshop on Cross-Linguistic Second Language Acquisition Research, Jagdschloss Göhrde, West Germany, Aug. 22–29, 1982. In C. Pfaff (ed.), *Cross Linguistic Studies of Language Acquisition Processes.* Rowley, Mass.: Newbury House.

—1984, The use of typological markedness as predictor in second language acquisition: the case of pronominal copies in relative clauses. Paper presented at the European North American Workshop on Cross-Linguistic Second Language Acquisition Research, Lake Arrowhead, Los Angeles, September 7–14, 1981. In R. W. Andersen (ed.), *Second Languages.* Rowley, Mass.: Newbury House.

Johansson, F. A. 1973, *Immigrant Swedish Phonology. A Study in Multiple Contact Analysis.* Lund: CWK Gleerup.

Jordens, P. & Kellerman, E. 1981, Investigations into the "transfer strategy" in second language learning. In J. -G. Savard & L. Laforge (eds), *Actes du 5ᵉ congrès de l'Association Internationale de Linguistique Appliquée.* Québec: Les Presses de l'Université Laval.

Kellerman, E. 1980, Transfer and non-transfer: Where are we now? *Studies in Second Language Acquisition* 2/1, 37–58.

—1983, Now you see it, now you don't. In S. Gass & L. Selinker (eds), *Language Transfer in Language Learning.* Rowley, Mass.: Newbury House.

Klein, W. & Dittmar, N. 1979, *Developing Grammars. The Acquisition of German Syntax by Foreign Workers.* Berlin: Springer-Verlag.

Kotsinas, U. -B. 1984, Semantic over-extension and lexical over-use in immigrant Swedish. *Scandinavian Working Papers on Bilingualism*, 2, 23–42.
Krashen, S. D. 1977, Some issues relating to the monitor model. In H. D. Brown, C. A. Yorio & R. H. Crymes (eds), *On TESOL '77: Teaching and Learning English as a Second Language*. Washington, D. C.: TESOL.
Labov, W. 1969, Contraction, deletion and inherent variability of the English copula. *Language*, 45, 715–62.
Lado, R. 1957, *Linguistics across Cultures. Applied Linguistics for Language Teachers*. Ann Arbor: The University of Michigan Press.
Larsen-Freeman, D. 1975, The acquisition of grammatical morphemes by adult ESL students. *TESOL Quarterly*, 9, 409–19.
—(ed.) 1980, *Discourse Analysis in Second Language Research*. Rowley, Mass.: Newbury House.
Levenston, E. A. & Blum, S. 1977, Aspects of lexical simplification in the speech and writing of advanced adult learners. In S. P. Corder & E. Roulet (eds), *The Notions of Simplification, Interlanguages, and Pidgins and their Relation to Second Language Pedagogy*. Genève: Droz.
Lightbown, P. M. 1980, The acquisition and use of questions by French L2 learners. In S. W. Felix (ed.), *Second Language Development. Trends and Issues*. Tübingen: Gunter Narr.
—1983, Acquiring English L2 in Quebec classrooms. In S. W. Felix & H. Wode (eds), *Language Development at the Crossroads*. Papers from the Interdisciplinary Conference on Language Acquisition at Passau. Tübingen: Gunter Narr.
Long, M. H. 1983, Linguistic and conversational adjustment to non-native speakers. *Studies in Second Language Acquisition* 5/2, 177–93.
Long, M. H. & Sato, C. J. 1983, Classroom foreigner talk discourse: forms and functions of teachers' questions. In H. W. Seliger & M. H. Long, (eds), *Classroom-Oriented Research on Second Language Acquisition*. Rowley, Mass: Newbury House.
Meisel, J. M. 1977, Linguistic simplification: A study of immigrant workers' speech and foreigner talk. In S. P. Corder & E. Roulet (eds), *The Notions of simplification, Interlanguages, and Pidgins and their Relation to Second Language Pedagogy*. Geneve: Droz.
—1982, Reference to past events and actions in the development of natural second language acquisition. Paper presented at the 2nd European North American Workshop on Cross-Linguistic Second Language 1982. In C. Pfaff (ed.), *Cross Linguistic Studies of Language Acquisition Processes*. Rowley, Mass.: Newbury House.
—1983, The rôle of transfer as a strategy of natural second language acquisition/ processing. *Language and Communication*, 3, 11–46.
Meisel, J. M., Clahsen, H. & Pienemann, M. 1981, On determining developmental stages in natural second language acquisition. *Studies in Second Language Acquisition*, 3/2, 109–35.
Nemser, W. 1971, Approximative systems of foreign language learners. *IRAL*, 9, 115–23.
Nicholas, H. R. 1982, Contextually defined queries: Evidence for variation in orientations to second language acquisition processes? Paper presented at the 2nd European North American Workshop on Cross-Linguistic Second Language Acquisition Research, Jagdschloss Göhrde, West Germany, Aug. 22–29, 1982.

In C. Pfaff (ed.), *Cross Linguistic Studies of Language Acquisition Processes*. Rowley, Mass.: Newbury House.

Pienemann, M. 1981, *Der Zweitspracherwerb ausländischer Arbeiterkinder*. Bonn: Bouvier.

Ravem, R. 1968, Second language acquisition in a second language environment. *IRAL*, 6, 175–85.

—1974, The development of wh-questions in first and second language learners. In J. C. Richards (ed.), *Error Analysis. Perspectives on Second Language Acquisition*. London: Longmans.

Richards, J. C. 1971a, A non-contrastive approach to error analysis. *English Language Teaching*, 25, 204–19.

—1971b, Error analysis and second language strategies. *Language Sciences*, 17, 12–22.

—1972, Social factors, interlanguage, and language learning. *Language Learning*, 22, 159–88.

—(ed.) 1978, *Understanding Second and Foreign Language Learning. Issues and Approaches*. Rowley, Mass.: Newbury House.

Richards, J. C. & Schmidt, R. W. 1983, *Language and Communication*. Harlow, Essex: Longman.

Ringbom, H. 1978, On learning related and unrelated languages. *Moderna språk*, 72, 21–25.

Rosansky, E. 1976, Methods and morphemes in second language acquisition research. *Language Learning*, 26, 409–25.

Rutherford, W. E. 1982, Markedness in second language acquisition. *Language Learning*, 32, 85–108.

Sajavaara, K. & Lehtonen, J. (eds) 1980, *Papers in Discourse and Contrastive Discourse Analysis*. Jyväskylä Contrastive Studies 5. Department of English, University of Jyväskylä.

Schachter, J. 1974, An error in error analysis. *Language Learning*, 26, 205–14.

Schumann, J. H. 1978a, *The Pidginization Process. A Model for Second Language Acquisition*. Rowley, Mass.: Newbury House.

—1978b, Social and psychological factors in second language acquisition. In J. C. Richards (ed.), *Understanding Second and Foreign Language Learning. Issues and Approaches*. Rowley, Mass.: Newbury House.

—1979, The acquisition of English negation by speakers of Spanish: a review of the literature. In R. W. Andersen (ed.), *The Acquisition and Use of Spanish and English as First and Second Languages*. Rowley, Mass.: Newbury House.

—1982, Simplification, transfer, and relexification as aspects of pidginization and early second language acquisition. *Language Learning*, 32, 337–66.

Seliger, H. W. & Long, M. H. (eds) 1983, *Classroom-Oriented Research on Second Language Acquisition*. Rowley, Mass.: Newbury House.

Selinker, L. 1969, Language transfer. *General Linguistics*, 9, 67–92.

—1972, Interlanguage. *IRAL*, 10, 209–31.

Sharwood Smith, M. 1979, Strategies, language transfer and the simulation of the second language learner's mental operations. *Language Learning* 29, 345–61.

Sjöholm, K. 1979, Do Finns and Swedish-speaking Finns use different strategies in the learning of English as a foreign language? In R. Palmberg (ed.), *Perception and Production of English: Papers on Interlanguage*, AFTIL 6. Department of English, Abo Akademi.

Skinner, B. F. 1957, *Verbal Bahavior*. New York: Appleton-Century-Crofts.
Stauble, A. -M. E. 1978, The process of decreolization: A model for second language development. *Language Learning*, 28, 29–54.
Tarone, E. 1977, Conscious communication strategies in interlanguage: a progress report. In H. D. Brown, C. A. Yorio & R. H. Crymes (eds), *On TESOL '77: Teaching and Learning English as a second Language*. Washington, D.C.: TESOL.
—1978, The phonology of interlanguage. In J. C. Richards (ed.), *Understanding Second and Foreign Language Learning. Issues and Approaches*. Rowley, Mass.: Newbury House.
—1982, On the variability of interlanguage systems. Paper presented at Milwaukee Symposium on Linguistics, March 1982.
Trévise, A. & Noyau, C. 1984, Adult Spanish speakers and the acquisition of French negation forms: Individual variation and Linguistic Awareness. Paper presented at the European North American Workshop on Cross-Linguistic Second Language Acquisition Research, Lake Arrowhead, Los Angeles, September 7–14, 1981. In Andersen, R. W. (ed.), *Second Languages*. Rowley, Mass.: Newbury House.
Trudgill, P. J. 1974, *The Social Differentiation of English in Norwich*. Cambridge: Cambridge University Press.
de Villiers, J. & de Villiers, P. 1973, A cross-sectional study of the acquisition of grammatical morphemes in child speech. *Journal of Psycholinguistic Research*, 2, 267–78.
Wagner, J. 1983, *Kommunikation und Spracherwerb im Fremdsprachenunterricht*. Tübingen: Gunter Narr.
Wardhaugh, R. 1970, The constrastive analysis hypothesis. *TESOL Quarterly*, 4, 123–30.
Weinreich, U. 1953, *Languages in Contact. Findings and Problems*. New York: Publications of the Linguistic Circle of New York 1.
Weinreich, U., Labov, W. & Herzog, M.I. 1968, Empirical foundations for a theory of language change. In W.P. Lehmann, & Y. Malkiel, (eds), *Directions for Historical Linguistics*. Austin: University of Texas Press.
Wode, H. 1980, Phonology in L2 acquisition. In S.W. Felix (ed.), *Second Language Development. Trends and issues*. Tübingen: Gunter Narr.
—1981a, *Learning a Second Language. 1. An Integrated View of Language Acquisition*. Tübingen: Gunter Narr.
—1981b, The emergence of reference to the past in language acquisition: L1, L2, re-learning in a cross-linguistic perspective. MS, University of Kiel.
Wong-Fillmore, L. 1979, Individual differences in second language acquisition. In C. J. Fillmore, D. Kempler & W. S. -Y. Wang (eds), *Individual Differences in Language Ability and Language Behavior*. New York: Academic Press.
Zobl, H. 1983, Markedness and the projection problem. *Language Learning*, 33, 293–314.

2 Learnability and syllabus construction

MANFRED PIENEMANN

University of Sydney, Australia

Introduction

The most apparent characteristic of tutored (or formal) second language development (foreign language learning) is that it is tutored by the way the linguistic learning problems are presented. It is an almost self-evident tenet of foreign/second language instruction that the teaching objectives must be graded in a way which appears learnable by the student. Thus the *syllabus* (i.e. the selection and grading of linguistic teaching objectives) is regarded as the basic motor of L2 tutoring. Corder (1973a:295f) figuratively compares its role to production engineering in industrial processes, the problem of which is

> " ... to specify the most efficient and economical way of organizing ... processes (which consist of different sub-components and sub-processes. MP) in time and space, so that components are ready when needed for sub-assembly and ultimately for final assembly in the finished product."

So, as is generally accepted by foreign language teachers – basic principles of syllabus construction are (i) that new structures have to be built up on known structures and (ii) that simple structures be taught before the complex. Plausible though the latter principle is at first glance, it has always been difficult to define what is simple. There were various linguistic measures, which, however, do not relate to psychological learning processes. And, of course, the language teacher has usually developed some intuitions about learning difficulties. Still, this basic principle of grading has always remained ambiguous.

The aim of this paper is to provide the syllabus designer with more precise principles for grading teaching material which are related to simplicity as defined within the framework of language learning. To attain this goal I will draw on research into second language development.

This research is relevant for foreign language teaching for obvious reasons: The first and clearest case where results are relevant is the mixed L2 learning environment which is the dominant learning context in immigrants' L2 learning in Europe, North America and Australia. Here the learner develops a second language in a natural context according to the principles of natural L2 acquisition. Simultaneously, instruction attempts to promote the second language development. Instruction can be adjusted to natural acquisition by building up on the regularities entailed in natural second language development. This allows us to assess the learners' linguistic competence in a systematic and generalizable way and to predict the order of learning problems to come.

The second case is the purely formal learning context (thus traditional foreign language classes). For this type of formal language learning too, the simplicity criteria derived from language acquisition may serve as less ambiguous principles for psychologically valid grading of teaching material than have so far been applied.

However, the solution of the grading problem is not as straightforward as it might now appear, as the findings from L2 acquisition research provide no obvious guidelines from which to derive principles for grading. Therefore, as a first step, some specific properties of *formal* second language instruction have to be taken into account:

(1) There are various types of syllabuses. Do we have to decide on a specific type on the basis of findings from L2 acquisition? If not, can the principles for grading be incorporated into the different syllabus types?
(2) Is formal second language learning an acquisitional type *sui generis*, so that there may be more efficient principles for grading than those derived from natural L2 acquisition?

Besides this, the possible consequences of concrete proposals for principles of grading on language development have to be evaluated, before they can be put into practice.

These questions describe the course the arguments will take in this paper. In the following section the main types of syllabuses will be outlined, attempting to answer question (1). The second section will be dealing with answering question (2), and in the third section different proposals for the application of L2 acquisition research to syllabus

construction will be sketched and critically evaluated for possible consequences. The final section will be devoted to elaborating a concrete
proposal for the implementation of grading principles into syllabus design.

Syllabus construction

Wilkins (1976) differentiates between two major types of approaches
to syllabus design. The *synthetic approach* is the one which we know from
the grammer-translation-method (although it is not bound to a specific
teaching method!).Its main characteristic is that items from the target
language are graded according to aspects of their grammatcial structure;
for instance, "affirmative sentences before questions, before negated
sentences etc.". Wilkins calls this procedure "synthetic", since it is the
learner's task to synthetize the different bits of information about the L2
grammar into meaningful utterances.

Within this approach some further tenets for grading are (as mentioned above) (i) that new structures have to be built up on old structures,
(ii) that simple structures be instructed before the complex and (iii) that
the linguistic interaction between certain structures (e.g. "do-insertion"
and "negation") are respected so that the corresponding structures may be
introduced successively (cf. Wienold, 1976). Still, these principles are seen
to leave open a rich variety of options for different paths of grading.

The other type of approach to syllabus design as differentiated by
Wilkins is labelled *analytic*. The corresponding syllabuses

" ... are organized in terms of the *purposes* for which people are
learning and the kinds of language performance that are
necessary to meet those purposes" (Wilkins, 1976:13; my
emphasis, MP).

This type of approach starts out from the actual speech behaviour and
regards content as being more important than linguistic form. Since any
linguistic content can be expressed in a variety of forms it is characteristic
of this approach not to isolate linguistic forms for instruction in advance
and make them the subject of instruction, but rather to provide the learner
with a variety of forms for a certain content which is at the focus of
instruction. Thus the term "analytic" indicates that the learner is given the
possibility to analyse the conventionalized relation between structures and
the corresponding contents.

There are various sub-types of this approach which are outlined, for
instance, in Wilkins (1976) or Johnson (1982). What is of special interest

for the topic of this paper is the role of grading. In the literature on analytic ("communicative") syllabuses we find both the opinion, that (1) there should be no structural grading at all (cf. Piepho, 1979; Terrell, 1977; Krashen, 1982; for discussion see Knapp – Potthoff & Knapp, 1982) and that (2) there should be grading, which, however, must be only secondarily dependent on structural principles (cf. Littlewood, 1981; Wilkins, 1973). This means that the syllabus designer or teacher *first* has to anticipate the learners' linguistic needs in terms of notions (e.g. "time", "cause" etc.) and then to select morpho-syntactic means for these notions, which should be graded (for an example see Cross, 1982).

Krashen (1982) raises two types of arguments against structural grading: One is that grading is not necessary, because the relevant input to the classroom learner will be graded (i.e. "tuned") automatically. I will deal with this argument later (see pp. 41–54). The second argument is the following: if the input is graded (even according to secondary principles) the focus of teaching is not really on meaning but on form (structure); consequently this type of input is bound to be less interesting (Krashen, 1982:69). We may respond that (1) the degree of motivation is difficult to measure, and has not *proved* to be higher without structural grading, and (2) even if motivation decreases through structural grading, the latter may be an absolute necessity for formal L2 learning. (This will be examined in the following two sections.)

Except for the first of the two arguments mentioned above, the debate about grading (and the syllabus in general) was scarcely related to problems of learnability or principles of language learning. The following remarks are intended to illustrate some of the reasons for changes in syllabus construction and, more significantly, to indicate that there is a serious lack of arguments from a learning theoretical point of view.

When contrasting the two approaches summarized above, it should be borne in mind that both are borrowings from linguistic theories. The grammatical syllabus orginates in structuralism and partly even in traditional grammar, whereas the communicative syllabus was motivated by the "communicative shift" in the late 60's/early 70's. This shift was evidenced by a number of linguistic sub-disciplines such as the ethnography of speaking, sociolinguistics, discourse-analysis etc. The grammatical is therefore the older approach, and was meant to be replaced by the communicative.

One basic line of argument in favour of the new approach against the old goes as follows: Communication consists of more than just the sum of grammatical rules. Since each grammatical rule may express a variety of meanings, there are language-specific conventions that relate the linguistic form of an utterance to its actual communicative effect. Therefore, foreign language instruction can only teach successful communication if it includes these conventions.

Leaving aside theoretical implications of the priority of semantics over syntax, this objection is certainly correct as far as teaching objectives are concerned. However, it is not a falsification of the grammatical syllabus *per se*. This is the point where the theoretical dependency of language teaching on "mother disciplines" becomes apparent: In linguistics the "communicative shift" was motivated by internal linguistic and sociological arguments which cannot in any simple manner be transferred onto the *learning* of language. If we can state — as we did above — that there are important items missing in the grammatical approach which are more semantic in nature, we can only conclude that they have to be included in the syllabus. But the fact that the missing items are semantic is not a sufficient argument that the syllabus can only start out from meaning. Theoretically, teaching can start from both ends. The superiority of one for the learning process has to be shown within a *psychological* framework.

The analytic approaches are further claimed to be superior to the synthetic, because the first are said to be in accordance with the *learner's communicative needs* (and thus more *motivating*), while the latter only provide a collection of linguistic forms, without specifying the semanto-pragmatic functions they can be used for. The logic of the argument is the following: Since a content (or a speaker's intention) is the starting point of an utterance, and since communicative syllabuses are designed starting from contents/intentions, they systematically provide the learners with instruments for their communicative needs. Such instruments are defined first of all within a notional or functional framework, referring to units like "asking", "informing", rather than in structural units like "sentence", "subject" etc.

However, it is the syllabus designer who has to assess the learner's actual needs and the instruments necessary to satisfy them. This assessment has to be done on the basis of certain semantic notions and pragmatic functions and the morpho-syntactic structures which are needed for these notions and functions. Of course, there are plausibility arguments for the selection and grading of notions and functions, and these may be related to sociological theories of the integration into a foreign society. But the selection and *grading* of the grammatical "instruments" rely on (hopefully) good guesses as to what is processable and learnable, rather than being related to the learners' actual state of L2 development. So the factors inside the language learner are excluded in this approach, despite its intended learner-orientation. The reason for this is that the semantically oriented approach underlying this type of syllabus has been over-interpreted as a psychological model of speech processing.

Thus the arguments for the communicative and against the structural syllabus were not related to language learning, and the structural syllabus is not based on a theory of language learning either. In the past the various approaches to syllabus construction did not leave open any other possibility than to decide on grading in a very intuitive manner; or to put it another way: properties of language learning were neglected in material grading, although grading is regarded as the basic motor for tutoring the learning processes.

Consequently, what I will elaborate in this chapter is not a new approach to syllabus construction, but psychological principles of grading, which can be implemented in any type of syllabus, provided it implies that teaching material be graded: Apparently, the grammatical syllabus can easily can be adjusted to psychological grading principles, if these are formulated in linguistic terms. In the notional approach, the grammatical means which carry the respective notions/functions may also be graded (cf. Littlewood, 1981; Wilkins, 1973), so that psychological grading principles can be applied (cf. also Ingram, 1982 for a detailed communicative syllabus with implicit structural grading).

The effect of formal instruction on L2 development

As I indicated above principles of grading cannot naively be derived from the regularities of *natural* L2 development. The considerations that have to be taken into account next are related to properties of *formal* L2 development. If we were to propose that formal L2 instruction should follow the stages of natural L2 development (as has been proposed by several authors, cf. pp. 41–54), the instruction would be structured according to psychological simple-complex principles underlying the natural development. But one might question whether these are the most efficient grading principles. One reason for this objection might be that copying the natural stages would imply that deviant L2 forms which will appear in the learners' language would have to be taught.

If one looks at this proposal from a perspective which views deviant L2 forms as indicators of erroneous learning, natural L2 development really does not appear to be the most propitious way. So it is not surprising that from this perspective development of more efficient principles of grading is attempted.

The fundamental question that has to be answered in this context is "what is the nature of formal L2 development?" This question is crucial in mixed as well as in purely formal acquisition environments. The mixed setting implies a stronger internal argument for adjusting teaching to regularities of natural acquisition, since here *natural* acquisition is a significant source of L2 development, which has to be respected systematically in instruction. Still, it might be considered that instruction might so powerfully tutor L2 development that the natural side of the process can even be improved. Below we will see how empirical research has thrown light on this question.

Does instruction make a difference?

In formal L2 instruction the learning process has traditionally been assumed to be primarily dependent on external factors. In this tradition it was thus implicitly taken for granted that formal L2 development could be tutored in any way which seemed desirable from the pedagogical perspective.

Recent research into the relation between formal and natural acquisition has reversed this perspective. Since the principles underlying natural acquisition turned out to be persistent in various types of acquisition and across different L1 backgrounds and age spans, it has been questioned whether instruction can rule them out. Going a step further, some studies investigate whether there is a set of principles for language acquisition which is the same for the natural and the formal type (cf. Felix, 1977) thus bringing about certain constraints which cannot be overcome by formal instruction.

In what follows in this section, I shall give a rough review of such research into the relation of formal and natural L2 acquisition. The underlying question of one main line of investigation is, which of the two possible sources for the development of a second language in a formal content actually has an influence on formal learning: (a) the structure of formal input (i.e. teacher talk and learning material) or (b) the principles of natural acquisition. Practically, this means that the question "does instruction make a difference?" (cf. Long, 1983) will be answered "yes" if the interlanguage structure attained through formal instruction is different from naturally acquired interlanguages and it is answered "no" if the two are similar.

Research into the role of input in formal acquisition/learning obviously is related to input studies in the natural context. Here it was investigated which influences the different degrees of simplification in the speech addressed to the learner have on the acquisition process (cf. Long, 1981). Again, this research is related to a view of first language acquisition which investigates the role of the mother's speech adjustments to the child's speech in the acquisition process (cf. Snow & Ferguson, 1977). Proponents of an "input view" claim that systematic aspects in the learner's speech development may reflect the structure of the linguistic input rather than linguistic learning principles (Larsen-Freeman, 1976a & b).

Accuracy-based studies

One type of research within this line of investigation was reviewed by Long(1983). The method applied in the 13 studies which Long reviewed was to test the L2 proficiency of learners with different learning environments (with respect to extent of exposure and amount of instruction) and to compare groups of learners with different learning environments for their level of L2 proficiency. So the proficiency level of learners with exposure only, for instance, was compared to the level of learners with the same degree of exposure *plus* instruction. The findings from these studies were ambiguous. Seven showed a positive effect of instruction, three a negative and three were unclear.

I think that the ambiguity of these results originates in the type of available data and in the research methods applied (for a similar criticism cf. also Pica, 1982a). The majority of informants had acquired English in a mixed setting, thereby reflecting the general situation of bilingualism in North America. Thus the main obstacle of these studies was to isolate the effect of formal learning from other factors. The method used in the attempt to bring this about was to compare some aspects of the interlanguagues among learners who had a varying amount of instruction. The comparison involved different kinds of proficiency tests or the counting of grammatical "errors" in the learner's speech, i.e. some kind of measure of correctness.

There are three major problems with this approach:

1. Since all informants in these studies had some degree of exposure to the "natural acquisition context" we cannot exclude that natural acquisition processes have been mixed with formal learning. Consequently, the differences in the results cannot be unambiguously explained by differences in learning contexts.
2. The measure for what is "the same extent of exposure" (as applied in several of the corresponding studies) is arbitrary since rating scales for the intensity of contact, as well as the

pure time of exposure by no means guarantee that in the respective comparisons the natural part of the learning/acquisition process was the same for the two groups under comparison. We know that the rate of acquisition may vary considerably between individuals, irrespective of the time and intensity of exposure (cf. Clahsen *et al.*, 1983).

3. Measuring L2 proficiency by the correctness of the target language use has the severest consequences for the validity of the research results. First, a well known criticism which has been levelled against error analysis and morpheme order studies alike is that correctness does not describe the creative aspects of the learner's language (cf. Meisel *et al.*, 1981; Andersen, 1977; Rosansky, 1976). It has been shown quite unambiguously in recent research (cf. Clahsen *et al.*, 1983) that high correctness may just as well appear (in different learner types) at a low level, whereas low correctness may (in other learner types) appear at the different levels, too. Secondly, the possibly different nature of learning and acquisition cannot be determined by a correctness measure, since the latter cannot describe the inherent structure of the developing linguistic systems (for more detail of the argument cf. Meisel *et al.*, 1981; Hatch, 1978).

Thus, the above 13 studies have tackled a very specific interpretation of the question as to whether teaching makes a difference, namely whether teaching can raise the degree of correctness in the use of the L2 structures. Keeping the limited scope of interpretation implied in this approach in mind, the above-mentioned results still have to be considered. I will return to this point below when further results are summarized.

Morpheme order studies

Another type of research within the main line of investigation presently discussed is (among others) reviewed by Pica (1982a). These are studies conducted in the tradition of "morpheme order studies". Thus, the attempt is made to isolate the effect of instruction by comparing rank orders of morpheme acquisition, rather than the accuracy of usage.

Krashen *et al.*, (1976) found no significant differences in the rank order of morpheme accuracy between learners from formal and natural learning contexts. This result is interpreted in correspondence with the *data elicitation techniques*, which (in this study) did not encourage conscious monitoring. According to Krashen's (1981) hypothesis, learned structures (as opposed to acquired) should have no influence on the acquired system if there is no time for monitoring. Krashen *et al.* interpret their finding as evidence in support of Krashen's hypothesis.

Further evidence of similarities between formal and natural L2 acquisition is provided by Fathman's (1978) comparison of rank orders of morpheme accuracy between learners of EFL AND ESL.

Makino (1979) found strong correlations between the rank order of accuracy in juvenile Japanese learners of ESL (in Japan) and the "natural" order obtained by Bailey *et al.*, (1974) and Dulay & Burt (1973, 1974). The data were taken from written tests with plenty of response time. Makino's findings seem to be in favour of the view that the same principles underlie the two types of L2 development. But this is disconfirming evidence for Krashen's prediction (above) for monitor use.

To blur the picture still further, Sajavaara's (1981) findings are in contradiction with Makino's, since the rank order of morpheme accuracy in Finnish learners of ESL (in Finland) did *not* correlate significantly with the "natural order" (with the BSM as elicitation measure). This seems to indicate that the nature of learning is *different* from acquisition.

Lightbown's study (in press) is devoted to determining the influence of both formal input and acquisition principles on formal L2 development. Her research into formal input was motivated by the debate on natural input. For instance, Larsen-Freeman (1976a) had suggested that natural sequences in morpheme acquisition might be determined by the frequency with which the corresponding morphemes occur in the input. For classroom L2 learning Larsen-Freeman (1976b) found positive correlations between the rank order of frequency of items in teacher talk and the accuracy of ESL learners. Lightbown (in press) points out, however, that there are some salient differences between the concrete rank order of frequency in teacher talk and the accuracy order of ESL learners in Larsen-Freeman's study. On the basis of longitudinal observation, Lightbown, compared the rank order of frequency of structures in the speech addressed to her 36 informants to the order of accuracy in the informants' speech. The amount of exposure to L2 communication was extremely low. The result was that

> " ... there is no direct relationship between the frequency with which certain forms appear in the classroom and the frequency or accuracy of use of these forms in the learners' language at the same point in time." (Lightbown, in press: 37).

As far as natural sequences are concerned Lightbown found no correlation with ESL accuracy order either. She explains this finding by showing that the informants from her classroom study were exposed to a distorted version of the English language in the instruction.

Summing up, this branch of research also leaves us with contradictory findings. These will be evaluated at the end of this section. Before we proceed to a second main line of investigation let me hint at a general weakness in this research:

As mentioned above, proficiency measures based on accuracy only presuppose that L2 development is equivalent to a gradual increase of the target language correctness. This assumption, however, does not comply with findings from longitudinal studies (cf. Meisel et al., 1981).

Evidently, establishing *rank orders* of accuracy as an index of L2 development implies an even more rigid presupposition, namely that this rank order remains constant throughout the various stages of L2 development; in the above studies, rank orders of accuracy were established on the basis of mean scores through the accuracy of a set of interlanguage features obtained in cross-sectional or longitudinal observations.[1] Empirical studies have shown that this presupposition cannot be upheld (cf. Clahsen et al., 1983).

Because of these strong reservations it is questionable whether the above comparisons of the two types of L2 development can validly reveal properties of the nature of formal and natural L2 development.

A universalist perspective

The assumption underlying a second main line of research is *one particular* manifestation of the general view that *all instances of language-learning, -change, -loss etc. might be determined by a set of shared principles*. A research perspective of this kind has been worked out by several scholars from different theoretical points of view (esp. Wode, 1981; Slobin 1973, 1975). The number of studies which have been conducted within this framework (with particular reference to formal L2 development) is relatively small. Leaving aside theoretical differences in the explanation of acquisition processes for the moment (for discussion see esp. Berman, 1982; Clahsen, 1982; Felix, 1982) we can differentiate two approaches (within this branch).

One of them is represented by the work of Felix (1978, 1982), Hahn (1982), Wode (1981), Pica (1982b) and Turner (1979). This research has primarily been conducted within the "integrated perspective of language acquisition" (cf. Wode, 1981).

Felix (1981) and Felix & Simmet (1981) compared the structures of utterances which appear under conditions of formal instruction with the type of structures known from natural acquisition. In this research they found a considerable number of structural parallels and similar learning strategies, although the learners had been exposed to an input sequenced in contradiction to findings from natural L2 acquisition. As these structural similarities appear in the two different types of language development (although the input was substantially different) the authors have a relatively strong empirical basis for concluding that the principles underlying natural acquisition also apply to the formal learning of a language.

On the basis of her longitudinal study of EFL development in a purely formal context, Hahn (1982) was able to show that the EFL learners produced the same sort of interlanguage "deviation" as in the natural acquisition of ESL, although apparently these structures can only have been created by the EFL learners themselves. She could also show, however, that there are learning strategies in EFL which do not exist in the natural L2 development. This is evidence for the assumption that formal and natural L2 development do not share *all* principles.

A similar study to the one by Hahn (1982) was conducted by Turner (1979) who compared the order of presentation of L2 items with the order of acquisition and found no correlation between them. Rather, structures emerged which had not been taught. However, since Turner's informants also had natural exposure the influence of instruction and natural acquisition cannot definitely be sorted out.

In comparing the frequency of interlanguage substitutions for English phonemes and consonant clusters in children acquiring English either in a formal or in a natural setting, Wode (1981) found considerable similarities in the phonological interlanguage systems of the two groups of learners.

Further evidence for common principles of formal and natural L2 development is provided by Pica (1982b) who established a consistent implicational scale for the acquisition of the English indefinite article in different linguistic contexts. The scale is based on the interlanguage of 18 adult informants, six from a naturalistic setting, six from a mixed and a further six from a formal setting. Since the implicational scale is consistent for all three contexts of acquisition, the indefinite article is acquired in the same order in the different linguistic contexts by the different learner groups.

Another subgroup of research postulating common principles for language development is characterized by the method which is more experimental than those discussed in the above studies. These are the studies by Dietrich *et al.*, (1979), Schumann (1978) and Pienemann (1984).

Dietrich *et al.* tried to isolate the influence of instruction by analysing the informants' interlanguage before and after a period of instruction. Since the items under instruction were mostly acquired *in principle* before the instruction (although they were not applied 100% correctly), and since, moreover, the percentage of correct usage did not unequivocally increase, the results cannot be interpreted unambiguously: on the one hand it may be that the failure of teaching is due to the particular type of instruction; on the other hand it may also be that a promotion of the acquisition process through instruction was not possible in principle.

Another experiment was conducted by Schumann (1978) as an additional part of an investigation into natural L2 acquisition. Schumann attempted to teach English negation to a "fossilized" adult learner of ESL in a naturalistic setting. The result was that the informant performed well in formal instruction tasks but he did not transfer this formal knowledge to natural communication.

The teachability hypothesis

Since the position I take in this paper for the evaluation of proposals in the "application debate" will strongly be influenced by the research on learnability/teachability which I conducted myself[2] (Pienemann, 1984), I shall take the liberty of ending this review with an outline of those results. The method was similar to that used by Dietrich *et al.* (1979); i.e. interlanguage samples from natural acquirers of German as a second language were gathered before and after an instructional experiment. In contrast to the study by Dietrich *et al.*, the informants were selected according to the actual stage of their L2 acquisition as measured in terms of acquisition of German word order rules.

This measure is based on an acquisitional sequence as was found in a number of cross-sectional and longitudinal studies for the acquisition of GSL (cf. Clahsen, 1980; Pienemann, 1980, 1981; Meisel *et al.*, 1981; Clahsen *et al.*, 1983). In this context, the relevant section of the acquisitional sequence (which consists of six distinct stages) is the following (cf. also Clahsen, this volume, Chapter 12):

X = "adverb-preposing"
    example: *da kinder spielen*   (Concetta)
      ("there children play")[3]

This preposing rule is optional in German. But once this rule is applied, Standard German requires a word order like "*there play children" (i.e. "inversion"). Before this stage, the adverb is always in final position.

X + 1 = "verb separation" (PARTICLE, cf. Clahsen & Meisel, 1979)
           example: *alle kinder muß die pause machen*   (Concetta)
           ("all children *must* the break *have*")

"Verb separation" is a typical obligatory Standard German rule. Before this stage, the word order with complex verbal groups is the same as in sentences with main verbs only, thus the same as in English: "*all children must have the break*"

X + 2 = "inversion"
           example: *dann hat sie wieder die knoche gebringt*   (Eva)
           ("then *has she* again the bone bringed")

In Standard German subject and inflected verbal element have to be inverted after preposing of elements.

From 100 Italian elementary school children who learned German as a second language in a natural context 10 informants were selected, who were either at stage X or X + 1 in their L2 development. In the experiment the attempt was made to teach the informants the structure from stage X + 2, i.e. "inversion". To this end, the informants were instructed as a separate class using teaching material which had been designed for this special purpose.

The result was that the learners from both stages (X and X + 1) mastered the formal learning tasks in the instruction, but only learners from stage X + 1 transferred this "knowledge" to their actual speech production.[4] Since the instruction was identical for both types of learners, the differing effect of instruction on the interlanguage system was concluded to have been due to the current stage of the informants' interlanguages.

The teachability hypothesis, which is intended to explain these results, can very roughly be summarized as follows: The processing prerequisites required for the above-mentioned structures concern primarily the reordering of underlying linguistic units. With additional reference to mnemonical investigations it could be shown that structure X is the simplest of the three to process, since no sentence internal rearrangements of underlying structures are necessary, while for X + 1 and X + 2 reorderings are required. It could be shown that the processing procedure underlying X + 1 is also required for X + 2, but for the latter structure an additional procedure has to be applied. With reference to such a type of implicational interrelation among different stages of acquisition, it was possible to demonstrate that the relevant acquisitional stages are interrelated in such a way that *at each stage the processing prerequisites for the following stage are developed* (for details see Pienemann, 1984). Thus structures from X + 2 cannot be processed by the learner of stage X without prior learning of X + 1, since a necessary processing prerequisite would be missing in the learners' interlanguage speech-processing mechanism.

Furthermore it could be shown that the processing prerequisites which determine the stages X to X + 2 also underly the development of a number of further structures cf. Table 4. Consequently, it was to be expected that the learners who developed from X + 1 to X + 2 through instruction also developed other structures which were not instructed. This, in fact, turned out to be correct.

The teachability hypothesis predicts that instruction can only promote language acquisition if the interlanguage is close to the point when the structure to be taught is acquired in the natural setting (so that sufficient processing prerequisites are developed). This hypothesis, of course, only holds if the successive emergence of processing prerequisites can be shown to apply to the acquisitional sequence under study. For instance, if it can be shown that sentence types (like "copula structures", "main verb structures" etc.) require different, not interrelated processing prerequisites, there would be no reason to suppose that the order of acquisition could be not reversed by instruction.

There are some further aspects which prove that the teachability hypothesis does by no means predict that instruction has no influence on acquisition whatsoever. For instance, we were able to show that — provided the learner is at the appropriate acquisitional stage — instruction can improve acquisition with respect to (a) the speed of acquisition, (b) the frequency of rule application and (c) the different linguistic contexts in which the rule has to be applied. For *variable features* (as opposed to developmental cf. Clahsen, this volume and Nicholas, this volume) – like the insertion of the copula — there is evidence that instruction has a drastic influence on L2 speech production. A similar experiment to that for the

above-mentioned developmental features was conducted for investigating
the teachability of variable features. The result for one informant is given
in Table 1. As can be seen the correct use of copula insertion increased
signficantly after the instruction of copula.

TABLE I   *Instructional Experiment: variational feature – omission of copula*

Carmine I

interview I	INSTRUCTION: copula	interview II (*recorded when inst. ended*)	interview III (*one week later*)
0.7		0.13	0.18

This is in complete agreement with the teachability hypothesis, since the
processing prerequisites for variable features like the copula are already
acquired when the given feature is applied with a higher probability than
zero, *since then it can, in principle, be processed.* Only for reasons of
simplification or/and effectiveness the learners' strategies may lead to a low
accuracy of a later stage (cf. Clahsen *et al.*, 1983). Thus for variable
interlanguage features, the type of learning barrier implied in the teachability hypothesis is not present.

As variable features are assumed to be dependent on external factors
(e.g. the degree of acculturation) (cf. Clahsen *et al.*, 1983; Schumann,
1978), however, we may expect that such learning success is not resistent to
the dynamics implied in the influence of external factors on the individual's
use of L2 strategies. Indeed, with the above informant the accuracy of
copula insertion decreased again some days after the instruction (cf. Table
1).

A pause for reflection

Let us return to the question from which our review of research
started out: does instruction have an effect on L2 development? We have
sketched two main lines of research. The results within the first were

contradictory. The second provided strong evidence for a set of principles which apply to formal as well as to natural L2 development and which limit the possible margin within which instruction may have an effect on L2 development. Do these findings fit together?

The teachability hypothesis is a potential framework for explaining the seemingly contradictory findings, since – in line with the bi-dimensional model of L2 acquisition (cf. Meisel *et al.*, 1981) – it differentiates between developmental and variational features of L2 development. It has been shown that teaching developmental features is subject to certain processing constraints which do not apply to variational features once they are acquired. The accuracy of usage of structures which are acquired in principle is a typical variational feature of interlanguages (cf. Clahsen *et al.*, 1983).

The studies which produced the contradictory findings were based on either the accuracy or the rank-order of accuracy in the usage of structures which were, in principle, acquired by the informants. Thus, they were based on variational features. In line with the teachability hypothesis (which is supported by empirical evidence) tutoring such features through instruction is not blocked by learnability constraints once they have been applied to a minimal percentage.

Since instruction may have an effect on these features, why did some studies produce negative results? There are two possible reasons:

1. The corresponding studies did not check carefully enough whether instruction was successful for the corresponding linguistic items from the teacher's perspective. In other words, the results might be negative simply because the instruction was bad.
2. The second reason can be that the influence of natural acquisition on L2 development was not carefully controlled. Since the application of variational features depends on learner-external factors which are partly rooted in the learning situation, the influence of instruction may be superimposed by the dynamics of variation in natural L2 acquisition.

In summary, there is good evidence that independently of the way the input is presented, classroom L2 learners produce the same type of (partly "deviant") interlanguage structures as observed in natural acquisition. Form this we may conclude that there is a set of developmental principles which apply to formal as well as to natural L2 development.

To stress this again: this is not to say that both types of L2 development are all the same. Quite obviously, formal and natural L2 development have very different external factors. However, the crucial question in the present context is whether there is a set of principles which is the same for formal and natural L2 development *despite* these differences in the external factors. As shown above, this is clearly the case. But this does not exclude influence of external factors altogether. Rather, as in natural language development, external factors might have an influence on the learning process within the margin determined by the constraining principles of L2 development.

In natural L2 acquisition such principles have been specified with reference to memory and procedures of speech processing. It has been shown that stages of acquisition are determined by the procedures necessary for processing the items to be learned (cf. Clahsen *et al.*, 1984; cf. also Pienemann, 1983). The mechanism underlying a number of acquisitional stages is that at each stage the learner develops processing prerequisites which are required at the subsequent stage and which are structurally built on the processing procedures developed earlier.

This explains why stages of acquisition cannot be reversed or skipped through the influence of instruction: as one of the processing prerequisites for structures of stage $X + 2$ is also the prerequisite for $X + 1$, the learner would automatically be in the position to process $X + 1$ as soon as he/she can handle the procedures underlying $X + 2$. Thus $X + 2$ cannot be introduced without simultaneously introducing the crucial processing prerequisite for $X + 1$ (cf. Pienemann, 1984). And this constraint of L2 development is rooted so deeply in human language processing it cannot be overcome by any type of input.

One thing has to be emphasized, however: this specific evidence for learnability/teachability constraints is so far only related to *children*. Since the cognitive structure in adults and their memory capacity is quite different from that of children, instruction might have a different effect on the former (although the underlying processing mechanisms may be the same).

From these findings we may derive some general tenets for syllabus construction:

- The principles of L2 development are not only a more reliable background for psychologically plausible simple-
- complex criteria in material grading than the present intuitive procedures, but they are a *necessary* background for grading, since formal L2 learning is subject to a set of

learning principles which are shared by formal and natural L2 development. Thus, teaching is only possible within the margin determined by these principles.

- As a consequence, any learning task which contradicts these principles is *not-learnable*; it would ask too much of the learner.

As mentioned above these tenets do not imply practical conclusions for syllabus construction. Rather, they may serve as the starting point for very different concrete proposals. Before I deal with developing a sketch of grading principles for an example language (German), I shall evaluate some (more theoretical) proposals which have been discussed in the past.

Discussing proposals for application

The basic proposals for basing foreign/second language instruction on findings from second language acquisition research had already been anticipated before there were any systematic findings from L2 development available. To illustrate this, a brief look at what has gone before might be elucidating.

We will remember that the decline of behaviourist approaches to language teaching had two types of consequences:

1. As a reaction against the receptive role the learner played in audio-lingual instruction and the predominant focus on form, attention was paid to what the learner might wish to say (meaning) (cf. Oller, 1971) and to more learner-oriented ways of practising the foreign language. These attempts are now elaborated in various types of communicative language teaching and approaches to learner-oriented teaching.

2. The other consequence had a stronger affinity to language acquisition. Since the behaviourist view of language acquisition was regarded as being falsified (cf. Reibel, 1971), applied linguists reconsidered what had been discussed before (cf. Sweet, 1899; Jespersen, 1904; Palmer, 1922), namely that second language acquisition (in the adult) may be the product of similar processes to those in first language acquisition (cf. Corder, 1967).

Once this step was taken it was only a short step to proposing that L2 learners may develop communicative skills in the second language without formal presentation of teaching material but through communicating in the second language (cf. Newmark, 1971).

This is, in fact, one of the two basic proposals which I shall label "abandon teaching".

The basic idea of the second proposal is also based on the hypothesis that in the language-acquiring adult there may be internal language learning mechanisms. From this hypothesis Corder (1973b) speculated that learning may be unsuccessful if the learner is taught what he is not ready for. From this it is natural to conclude that the order of acquisition determines the order of presentation. I will call this proposal "follow natural order".

Abandoning teaching & following "natural order"

These two types of proposals were later based on the early morpheme order studies and especially on the strong universalist claim implied in these studies, which says that the order of morpheme acquisition is always the same whatever the source language or the learning context.

From this perspective the two contrasting conclusions mentioned above have indeed been drawn: (1) Dulay & Burt (1973) suggested that with children the instruction of syntax can be abandoned since all learners pass through the same "natural order" anyway. (2) In a similar way as suggested for L1 acquisition (cf. McNeill, 1965), Krashen et al., (1975) proposed that the second language should be taught along the line of the natural order.

Quite obviously, both proposals fundamentally contradict the general tenets of current foreign/second language pedagogy. For this reason criticism of these innovative views may bring forth a number of arguments for more coherent proposals of application.

In the light of the preceding section it is apparent that at the time when the two proposals were made, almost no research into the relation between formal and natural L2 acquisition had been conducted. So in both cases a straight-forward position with regard to the effect of formal instruction was presupposed, without providing any evidence other than comparing the order of morpheme acquisition of learners from different contexts — a procedure which was criticized above.

It has been mentioned before that the natural order hypothesis, as implied in the morpheme order studies, has been strongly questioned on empirical, theoretical and methodological grounds. Thus one argument against the above proposals might be derived from questioning the critical hypothesis on which they are based (cf. Hatch, 1978). However, massive evidence for *invariant stages* in L2 acquisition which is based on broad longitudinal and cross-sectional studies of interlanguage development has been found in the meantime. This research, which is not subject to the same criticism as the morpheme studies, might be the basis of similar proposals. However, it is not the natural order whatever the theoretical implications which is the question here, but rather the inherent logic of the above proposals.

The most serious logical shortcoming of the "abandon-teaching proposal" is that it assumes that all learners of a second language automatically arrive at the same target point in their L2 acquisition. However, in contrast to first language acquisition it is a salient characteristic of L2 development that this is *not* the case. First, as illustrated by the L2 development of migrant workers in Europe or of socially disadvantaged immigrants in the States, second language acquisition may fossilize at early stages (cf. Clahsen *et al.*, 1983; Schumann, 1978; Klein & Dittmar, 1979). Secondly, even at higher stages of acquisition learners vary considerably in the extent to which they simplify the L2 (cf. Clahsen *et al.*, 1983; Meisel *et al.*, 1981; Pienemann, 1981).

Thus, abandoning teaching would mean not caring about these stigmatized paths of L2 development. Of course, for the time being, we cannot describe exactly how these fossilizing processes can most effectively be dealt with. But if teaching were abandoned we would not even try to deal with them. Since it was found that at least variational features of acquisition are not constrained by processing factors, instruction may have some effect on these processes.

So a positive effect of teaching is not an *a priori* impossibility. We may even discern the general direction in which a constructive proposal can be developed: socio-psychological factors are decisive in this aspect of L2 development, and thus should be in focus if instruction is intended to counteract the emergence of stigmatized interlanguage varieties (for some approaches cf. Januschek & Stölting, 1982).

However, from a psycholinguistic perspective such an approach has to remain a distant "utopia" for quite a while, since the necessary background information cannot yet be drawn from L2 research: although a wide range of research has shown that acculturation, social contact, learning style etc. all have an influence on the concrete route through the invariant stages which the individual learner takes, at the present time we cannot predict which set of socio-psychological variables determines which route of acquisition (cf. Wong-Fillmore, 1976; Schumann, 1978; Klein & Dittmar, 1979; Clahsen *et al.*, 1983; Meisel *et al.*, 1981; Pienemann, 1981).

Consequently, possibilities of counteracting the stigmatized effect of socio-psychological factors should be explored more intensively rather than ignoring this problem by abandoning instruction completely.

The second proposal, to teach syntax along the lines of the natural order, was implicitly based on the assumption that the order of acquisition cannot be reversed by instruction. As has been shown in the preceding section, the basic underpinnings of this assumption have in fact turned out to be correct. So, on the one hand there is some post-festum plausibility in this proposal, on the other hand this assumption was by no means coherently justified at the time it was published.[5]

Furthermore, it implies another shortcoming which did not become apparent because it was only based on morpheme studies — and these do not investigate the underlying regularities of "deviant" interlanguage systems. If this proposal is applied to interlanguage studies, then the teaching sequence has to contain all the "deviant" structures entailed in the development of the interlanguage.

This would require a much more dramatic change in the syllabus than the original proposal implied, since Krashen's natural order of target morphemes seems to be already very much in line with the teaching sequence in most ESL teaching materials (cf. Hatch, 1978). Findings from the natural development of German as a second language, however, — as I will show below — contradict the grading in teaching materials that are presently available. And more significantly, the interlanguage contains a large number of deviant though regular L2 forms, which — according to the proposal – have to be part of the teaching sequence.

Obviously, such a teaching procedure is bound to arouse vehement opposition among traditional language teachers, since it contradicts a number of his/her most fundamental tenets, like "improve erroneous speech". In fact, the consequences of such procedures are at present unknown. So, it would be wise to explore them before seriously proposing that this procedure be put to practice. One type of negative consequence might be the following. As Valdman (1978) has noticed highly simplified versions of L2 which (according to this proposal) would have to be taught at early stages evoke negative reactions on the part of the native-speaker.

This is not to say that teaching should stay the way it was before, because the fact that formal instruction is not the exclusive motor of L2 development in the classroom but that L2 learning is subject to specific learnability constraints demands that the teaching procedure be built up systematically on these constraints. For this task Krashen *et al.*'s proposal is the most straight-forward solution, which is certainly unrealistic in view of the present situation of foreign language instruction in schools. Consequently, a more acceptable solution has to be found.

Natural approach & optimal input

From the perspective of communicative language teaching, Terrell (1977) has proposed a "natural approach" to second language instruction. The logic of this proposal is the following: The primary goal of FLI should be communicative competence. Grammatical correctness as implied in traditional approaches to FLI impedes the development of the communicative skills. Since even at the earliest stages contents can be communicated with simplified morpho-syntactic means in natural L2 development, communicative competence can be attained when (1) focussing on function rather than on form — as implied in the communicative approach — and (2) when furthermore allowing for grammatical "incorrectness".

Thus, instruction is no longer seen as a process of grammatically tutoring L2 development but as providing linguistic input for acquisition in the classroom.

On the basis of his "monitor hypothesis" (cf. Krashen, 1981), Krashen (1982) has made this proposal more explicit. Krashen differentiates between (conscious) learning and (subconscious) acquisition. Learning (of linguistic structures) is only possible after puberty, and learned structures are stored in the "monitor". Actual speech production – which is based on the acquired systems – can be monitored according to the stored "knowledge" if certain conditions are met (sufficient time, focus on form, knowledge of the rule).

As far as instruction is concerned, its function in Krashen's work is primarily to support acquisition by providing optimal input (and to some extent to support learning for preplanned monitor use). For the acquisition, the "input hypothesis" is the crucial component in Krashen's work. It says that

1. it relates only to acquisition
2. the L2 acquirer proceeds in his/her L2 development by *understanding* structures $(i + 1)$ which are a little beyond the current stage of acquisition $(= 1)$. The cues for understanding $i + 1$ are drawn from the context.
3. when communication is sucessful, $i + 1$ will be provided automatically in the input.

Krashen further assumes that instruction promotes acquisition if it provides enough input containing i + 1. Consequently, one feature of "optimal input" is that it is comprehensible; i.e. that it provides contextual cues or refers to the background knowledge so that i + 1 can be understood.

I will not outline all the details of Krashen's work here but concentrate instead on what is related to research into developmental psycholinguistics. In this context there is one further feature of "optimal input" of immediate interest in our discussion: the input to classroom L2 learners should *not be grammatically sequenced*. Obviously, this is a drastic change in Krashen's position since 1976, when he proposed to sequence the input along the line of the "natural order". Krashen (1982) gives the following reasons for his revised position:

1. Since in a class not all learners will be at the same stage of acquisition, the instruction which is based on the natural order will – by chance – only fit some of the learners, whereas
    " ... unsequenced but natural input, ..., will contain a rich variety of structure – if it is comprehensible, there will be *i + 1* for everybody as long as there is *enough* input" (Krashen, 1982: 68f)
2. In grammatically sequenced instruction, structures to be learned only appear once and this may be missed by the learner for various reasons, whereas natural input will always provide the learner with the appropriate structures.
3. There is *no need* for a (natural) or other syllabus, since natural input *automatically* provides the right structures for all learners, because natural input is — due to general mechanism of simplification — roughly tuned to the learner's level of acquisition.
4. The grammatical syllabus — even if it is based on the "natural order" — distorts real communication in the classroom, because the focus will be on form rather than on function. (This is one of the standard arguments against the grammatical syllabus which was mentioned above.)

In summary, there are two essential components present in the natural approach. One consists of the tenets which were taken over from communicative language teaching. The other is the application of a certain part of L2 research into practice. As a whole, this approach has essentially the same practical consequences as the proposal of Dulay & Burt; namely to abandon teaching in the sense that the input will not be pre-structured from a didactic perspective. However, Krashen adds an elaborated hypothesis which guards the natural approach against the crucial criticism directed at Dulay & Burt's proposal; namely that L2 acquisition does not *automatically* arrive at the target norm. This is the input hypothesis, which views natural (and comprehensible) input as the motor of natural and formal L2 development.

My criticism of this approach consists of three parts: the first will be levelled against the input hypothesis, which is the central theoretical basis of the approach, the second will be directed at some weak points in the logic of Krashen's position towards the syllabus; and the third concentrates on one serious negative consequence of the approach.

1. The input hypothesis is highly speculative: It is not supported by any direct empirical evidence; it cannot even be operationalized or tested since the stages of acquisition to which it is related are left undefined in Krashen's work. He even admits that they have not sufficiently been explored. The hypothesis (that input containing i + 1 promotes language acquisition) is derived from the assumed learning-aid-effect of tuned input to the language learning child. This indirect evidence, however, has not proved to be reliable, since it is questionable whether care-taker talk is in fact tuned to the level of the child's L1 production. Krashen writes that

> " ... we see positive, but not strikingly high correlations
> between linguistic input complexity and linguistic competence
> in children (Newport, Gleitmann & Gleitmann, 1977; Cross,
> 1977)" (Krashen, 1981:2).

However, these positive correlations listed in Krashen's book (1981:126) are selected from a larger number of almost equally distributed *negative and positive* or zero correlations in the above author's studies.

Even if it could be shown that the linguistic input to the L2 learner is tuned to the current stage of the learner's performance, it still needs to be demonstrated (I) that understanding tuned input is the motor of natural acquisition and (II) that this motor also works for formal environments.

Furthermore, the input hypothesis implies an interrelation of the two sides of speech processing, comprehension and production. But this interrelation cannot be taken for granted: the acquisition-by-comprehension claim as implied in the input hypothesis only makes sense if it is implicitly assumed that comprehension and production develop as mirror-images of each other.

However, findings from language processing (cf. Bever, 1981; Forster, 1979) show that very different procedures underlie these two aspects of speech processing. There is also evidence from language acquisition that comprehension and production develop as separate abilities. Comprehension does not necessarily have to precede production. Rather, it is possible that children *produce* items first and only at a later stage understand them (cf. Bloom & Lahey, 1978).

2. Since at the present time the status of the input hypothesis is only speculative, one of the seemingly strong arguments against the syllabus is built on weak foundations. This is the claim that there is *no need* for a syllabus, since comprehensible input provides the acquisition promoting i + 1 for everyone at every time. Up to now, we do not have much evidence that there will be this abundance of fitting i + 1 and especially whether this will promote acquisition.

The heterogeneity of learner groups is not a severe objection against natural syllabuses, since learners can be grouped according to stages of acquisition and the instruction can be differentiated according to these groups. Detecting stages of acquisition in classroom learners is a topic which will be discussed in Part II of this volume.

Contrary to Krashen's assumption, it would not be a necessary feature of the natural syllabus that the structures to be learned appear once only. Rather, they would be in focus *at the right point* in the learners' L2 development, and naturally they would continue to appear in the speech addressed to the learner.

3. The most serious reservation about the natural approach is that it may lead to highly simplified versions of the target language. The reason for this has been sketched before when I criticized the abandon-teaching claim. Here it will be elaborated a bit more: It is correctly assumed in the natural approach that communication is possible in simplified interlanguage systems. But one might wonder why the learner should proceed in the L2 development when the simplified structures he/she has acquired convey all the necessary information.

It is a basic finding of sociolinguistics that besides providing means for message transmission, a person's language also contains means to express his/her social identity (cf. Haugen, 1956). Pidgin languages dramatically demonstrate that if there is no social identity to be expressed in the "second language", message transmission can function with an enormously reduced linguistic system (cf. Todd, 1974; Valdman, 1977).

Slobin (1973, 1975) has discussed two competing strategies in language acquisition. One is to be communicatively effective, the other is to be expressive. The first leads to effective exploitation of the available linguistic means and thus to a simplification of the target structures; the second requires an increase in complexity, since stylistic means, redundancy etc. are necessary in order to express role-relations, social meanings etc.

While in first language acquisition the child usually integrates into the "target" society, this is not necessarily the case in the second language acquisition. In the latter acquisitional type it has systematically been observed that owing to factors in the socio-psychological background, learners show – independent of the *stage* of acquisition – simplification strategies which resemble similarities to pidginization (cf. Clahsen *et al.*, 1983; Pienemann, 1981). It should be stressed here that in this simplified learner type L2 development does not simply stop at an early point. Rather, despite progress in acquisition, the learner may apply "effectivity strategies" which simplify the interlanguage to a much larger extent than would be necessary from a processing point of view (cf. Clahsen *et al.*, 1983; Meisel *et al.*, 1981; Meisel, 1980).

All this indicates that mere information transmission does not require a fully-fledged language, especially if the types of information to be conveyed are drastically restricted as is the case in many contexts of L2 acquisition.

Therefore, if FLI exclusively concentrates on message transmission as implied in the natural approach, the development of forms which carry social, rather than "content" information is left to the dynamics of natural or formal acquisition. This implies that a highly deviant and stigmatized interlanguage system may emerge which in a natural context

" ... condemns him (the learner, MP) to depreciated social status" (Valdman, 1975:424).

This is, of course, the contrary of what is generally expected of FLI.

In summary, the natural approach comes down to the same psycholinguistic core as Dulay & Burt's "abandon teaching" proposal, only it implies that the promotion of acquisition is guaranteed if the learner is provided with natural, comprehensible input. However, I have indicated that the motor-function of natural input cannot be taken for granted and that there is the serious danger that the natural approach — especially in mixed contexts — allows, or might even elicit, stigmatized L2 varieties.

Further contributions to syllabus discussion

Many of the arguments which have been raised in the past decade on applying L2 research to language instruction were sketched in the preceding sections. Still there are numerous further contributions. But to my knowledge all of them can be placed somewhere on the continuum represented by the two fundamental positions discussed above, i.e. "abandon teaching" or "follow the natural order".

In this section I will outline further approaches to this issue. Owing to the policy of this paper, some related research areas will not be represented here, since they are not concerned with the developmental perspective of L2 acquisition. This is (1) research into "the good language learner" (cf. Cohan & Aphek, 1981; Ruben, 1975; Stern, 1972), (2) studies into individualized (learner-oriented) L2 learning (cf. Allwright, 1978; Rodgers, 1978; Papilia, 1976) and (3) research into the teaching-learning process (cf. KIS, 1983).

Almost ten years ago Valdman (1974) provided empirical evidence for the assumption that learning is successful if the teaching material is graded in line with the stages of acquisition. In an experiment where the different types of French WH-questions were instructed, he found the following:

"Teaching materials avoid PRONOMINALIZATION and SIMPLE FRONTING because they are often qualified as "incorrect" by native speakers. I observed that beginning learners of French, who had been exposed only to the EST-CE QUE and INVERSION types made extensive use of SIMPLE FRONTING. (Valdman 1974, MP) Thus in terms of contents of course materials these cases constituted errors. The materials were modified so that the first interrogative structure taught was SIMPLE FRONTING. Surprisingly, learners exposed to the revised materials produced fewer SIMPLE FRONTING questions than the previous group and generalized the EST-CE QUE type which was selected as the primary construction for oral practice. I hypothesize from this experiment that SIMPLE FRONTING[6] constitutes for the learner the simplest construction his first approximate system (= interlanguage, MP) can handle and a facilitative intermediate step in the acquisition of the target EST-CE QUE type." (Valdman, 1975:425)

Judging from recent findings in L2 acquisition research, SIMPLE FRONTING in fact is a good candidate for a structure to be learned very early, since it does not disrupt any associated elements in the sentence as the other three rules would do (cf. Slobin, 1973; Bever, 1970; Clahsen, 1982; Meisel, 1980). Thus it appears that learning the developmentally earlier structure first facilitates the learning of the more complex structures.

At this time it was impossible to construct a natural syllabus, due primarily to a lack of valid findings from second language development. A few years later, Valdman (1978) suggested that, given the lack of knowledge about L2 acquisition, one promising direction for psychologically based syllabuses, would be to identify *universal principles* of L2 acquisition. As "pidginization" was claimed to be the underlying process of early L2 acquisition (cf. Schumann, 1974, 1978) Valdman discussed whether this process could be used as a model for grading teaching material. In a similar way to that of the natural approach it might seem at first glance that using pidginization as a model for grading meets in a unique way the requirements of communicative language teaching, for the "little" language provided in such an instruction would be a functioning communicative system from the very beginning, rather than a mere collection of unrelated linguistic items. The reservations Valdman has levelled against such a procedure may already be obvious from the above discussion of the "abandon teaching" proposal: pidginized varieties are stigmatized by the L2 society and teaching them may lead to the fossilization of L2 development (cf. Valdman, 1977).

To counter these reservations Valdman proposes the following model of application (called the "Focus Approach"):

1. The learners are allowed to use reduced and deviant forms in communicative activities.
2. However, these forms will not be brought into focus in the syllabus.
3. The learners are exposed to a
   " ... fully formed input filtered only by the application of pedagogical norms" (Valdman, 1977:68)
   (The latter is the order in which alternative morphosyntactic means serving the same function are introduced.)
4. The syllabus will be graded according to what is easy to acquire.

Thus, Valdman combines the positive aspects of the two basic proposals discussed above. On the one hand there is the possibility to use the "little language" even in a deviant form to meet the needs of communication. On the other hand tendencies of fossilization and pidginization are counteracted and the instruction is attempted to be organized in such a way that it does not contradict learnability constraints.

The weak point of this model is, of course, point (4), because the natural syllabus is not inferred from regularities of L2 development but from general principles of reduction in linguistic structures as present in pidginization and learner's errors. An attempt to make up for this deficit by relying on results of L2 research together with a further elaboration of the model will be presented in the last section of this chapter.

Recently, Ingram (1982) has made an elaborated proposal for a communicatively and developmentally oriented syllabus, which was designed for ESL instruction to migrants in Australia.

The syllabus is organized according to macroskills (speaking, listening etc.), specific function, syntax and lexis. Thus a structural grading is incorporated in a communicative framework as was suggested by theorists of communicative language teaching (cf. Littlewood, 1981; Wilkins, 1974). The interesting aspect of this proposal in the light of the topic discussed in the present paper is that the structural grading was derived from the paths of proficiency development in ESL as found in research with the Australian Second Language Proficiency Ratings (ASLPR) (Ingram, 1983).

To evaluate this contribution to syllabus construction the character of the ASLPR needs to be sketched:

"The ASLPR defines levels of second language proficiency at nine (potentially twelve) points along the path from zero to native-like proficiency. The definitions provide detailed descriptions of language behaviour in all four macroskills and allow the syllabus developer to perceive how a course at any level fits into the total pattern of proficiency development." (Ingram, 1982:66)

The descriptions of the respective proficiency levels are in fact very detailed in the different areas of linguistic analysis (cf. Ingram, 1983). However, in the context of the present discussion of adjusting the syllabus to principles of language learning, the crucial question is how reliable a description of natural L2 development the ASLPR levels are. This question is important because, in accordance with the teachability hypothesis a minimal requirement[7] of the principles of language learning is that a learning sequence may not contradict the natural sequence of acquisition.

The ASLPR is a very explicit nine-stage proficiency rating scale (with supplementary tests for reading and writing proficiency), which has proved to be *reliable* when tested by 36 raters (cf. Ingram, 1983). The description of these stages was drawn from the FSI Scale (cf. Ingram, 1983) and the researchers' experience in foreign and second language teaching. In addition the scale is reported to be assessed against the findings of developmental psycholinguistics. Since this assessment is not made explicit, the validity of the scale as a background frame for adjusting the syllabus to principles of language learning has to remain an unresolved problem for the time being.

Another pause for reflection

We have now discussed two major types of proposals for applying L2 research to language teaching. One was the "abandoning teaching" since — especially in the light of Krashen's "input hypothesis" — it seems to imply a psycholinguistic justification of the type of communicative language teaching which allows the learner to *use* his/her "little" language right from the beginning.

The arguments levelled against this approach were not directed against allowing the learner to have this special L2 experience. Rather, they are directed against the assumption that developing the basis for "successful communication" (through "optimal input") guarantees the development of a sufficient second language competence. I have argued that focussing on mere "information transmission" (which excludes the social, attitudinal etc. functions of language) allows for the development of a stigmatized L2 variety which may result in social disadvantages for the speaker. This appears to be reason enough to rule the first proposal out.

The apparent disadvantage of the "follow-natural-order" proposal is that, when interpreted in a straight-forward manner, it implies that the stages of interlanguage development containing all the "deviant" forms are the underlying pattern of formal input in classroom L2 learning. As mentioned above, we do not precisely know which negative consequences such a procedure might have. Maybe they have none. But since this is unknown, we should expect that learners, under the impact of the school's institutional authority, will not realize the stigmatization of certain simplified forms. We should further ensure that the simplified and restricted input implied by this proposal does not *impede* language acquisition for reasons such as too little "triggering experience" with the second language; for this is hypothesized to elicit progress in language development (within the given principles).[8]

However, when applying principles of L2 development to syllabus design we do not have to immerse ourselves in these difficulties, since there is no reason why the *whole* input to formal L2 learners should be equivalent to the structure of the corresponding interlanguage.

If the production system is intended to be emphasized then the input to the comprehension system does not have to be adjusted to the level of complexity of the production learning task since there are different types of processing procedures in the two systems. Rather, the instruction might focus on the learning problem in question.

Because learners at the stage "adverb-preposing", for instance, (= stage X) can semantically decode sentences with "inversion" (= X + 2) there is no reason why — in accordance with the structure of the corresponding interlanguage — "adverb-preposing" should be presented without "inversion" as would be suggested by the straight-forward interpretation of "follow-natural-order".

So, as Valdman (1978) implies, the presentation of "ill-formed" input structures can be avoided while the grading of L2 objectives may still be in line with the principles of L2 development. This can be done if the instructional input is not generally adjusted to the corresponding stage of L2 development, but is instead focussed on the crucial structure which the learner is prepared for to learn. The final section is devoted to making this proposal more explicit.

Elaborating a proposal

Some reservations about hasty application

One type of reservation about applying research into second language learning and acquisition to foreign language teaching has so far been dealt with only in outline, although it is of utmost importance for any application. In recent years many L2 researchers, when asked for proposals of application, would carefully indicate that our knowledge of L2 development is too thin and eclectic to serve as a valid basis for application to practise.

I fully agree with this position as far as *teaching methods* are concerned. But this paper is dealing with a special aspect of second language instruction to which — as I shall show below – L2 research can contribute at least as much as intuition has contributed in the past. For the developmental psycholinguist, the crucial difference between teaching methods and the grading of teaching material is the following:

Apart from certain practical requirements, which were roughly illustrated by Corder's comparison to production engineering, the basic problem of psychologically valid grading is to define *which items of the L2 are learnable* in which order (or in other words: what is simple and what is complex). As previously illustrated (see pp. 28–41) this basic problem can, in principle, be solved by developmental psycholinguistics.

The basic question in teaching methods is different. Here' the question is not *which* items of the L2 are learnable at what point in the L2 development, but *how* the respective items are optimally learnable. To be able to answer this question we need some very specific information about the formal learning process, above all how the "knowledge" (of whatever type, conscious or unconscious) obtained in formal instruction is transmitted to the unconscious system of speech processing and how (or whether) this transmission can be facilitated by formal means. At the present state of L2 research these are simply blank spots on the map of language acquisition.

Returning to "natural grading": in line with the argument developed earlier, one reservation about applying findings from L2 research to grading was that our knowledge of natural L2 development is too sparse to cover a syllabus for a relevant period of time in L2 learning (cf. Hatch, 1978).

Firstly, morpheme order studies in particular refer to a small set of L2 items only. This is apparent in Table 2, which shows on the left hand side a "natural order" of morpheme acquisition. Secondly, Hatch (1978) points out that this natural order would only require minor changes in the grading of presently available teaching material. These changes are indicated by arrows in Table 2 as they are discussed by Hatch. From this she concludes:

> "...the suggestions (= "follow natural order", MP) may sound innovative but in reality they aren't. While the leaps in logic may be dangerous in other ways, the resulting curriculum would not be different enough to make the application especially outlandish or dangerous." (Hatch, 1978:126)

TABLE 2   *Comparing "natural order" and textbook grading*

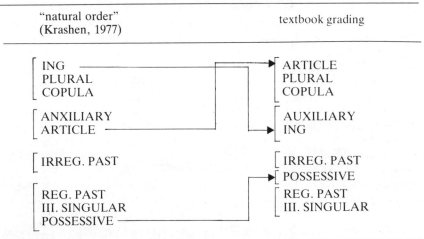

"natural order" (Krashen, 1977)	textbook grading
ING PLURAL COPULA	ARTICLE PLURAL COPULA
ANXILIARY ARTICLE	AUXILIARY ING
IRREG. PAST	IRREG. PAST POSSESSIVE
REG. PAST III. SINGULAR POSSESSIVE	REG. PAST III. SINGULAR

(According to Hatch, 1978: 126)

Any proposal for application should therefore be based on a sufficiently broad description of L2 development. Meanwhile there are, in fact, research results from ESL (e.g. Huebner, 1983; Pica, 1982b; Wode, 1981; Wong-Fillmore, 1976) which would allow us to work out a much more specific grading for EFL than is possible within the boundaries of the proposals discussed above.

In what follows I shall sketch a proposal for grading material according to the tenets developed in the preceding section. I shall concentrate on German as a Second Language (GSL). The course of arguments will be as follows: firstly, research into GSL development will be sketched very roughly in order to indicate the basis upon which the proposal is constructed. From this research, two sub-sets of findings will be selected and outlined for illustration. In a second step this will be compared to the grading of a current textbook for GSL, in order to illustrate that there is a need for reorganizing grading. Thirdly, for some structural domains a natural grading will be outlined—according to the above tenets. In a further step I shall show how this grading may be implemented in a communicative syllabus. Finally, some open questions will be discussed.

A rough sketch of research into GSL

A comprehensive overview of research in this area is given by Nicholas & Meisel (1983). Individual presentations of the various approaches current in West Germany are given in the collection of essays edited by Felix (1980) and partly in Studies in Second Language Acquisition (Volume 3, No. 2, 1981).

We cannot go into details of data-gathering procedure, acquisition criterion, linguistic analysis, framework of interpretation etc. even though all of these are relevant issues. What is of interest in the present context is to draw a very rough map of the linguistic domains in which consistent regularities of L2 development have been found.

As can be seen from Table 3 there is more than just a small set of morphemes which have been investigated for the development of German as a second language. Obviously, it would far exceed the available space to discuss even on a purely descriptive level details of findings. There are at least five volumes (cf. Felix, 1978; Klein & Dittmar, 1979; Orlović, 1978; Clahsen et al., 1983; Pienemann, 1981) and a wealth of essays which would have to be referred to in detail. In this context it may suffice to indicate that

TABLE 3 Research into German as a second language

Researchers	Source Language	Phonology	Syntax							Morphology		Lexico-semantics	Functions	Discourse & Gesture
			interrogation	negation	sentence struc.	word order	expansion (NP, VP, PP)	deletion	interlearner variation	NP	VP		temporal reference	
Felix	English		X	X	X									
Nicholas	English				X				X					
H.P.D.*	Span./Ital.	X	X	X				X		X	X			
Orlović	Jugos.									X	X	X		
ZISA**	Span./It./Port.		X	X	X	X	X	X			X		X	
Pfaff & Portz	Greek/Turk.			X		X		X		X				
Pienemann	Ital.					X	X	X						
Rehbein	Turk.													X

* cf. Klein & Dittmar, 1979
** cf. Clahsen et al., 1983; Meisel, 1982

(source: Nicholas & Meisel 1983)

a broad range of German morpho-syntax and aspects of a semantic and functional analysis are covered by recent research.

In order to be able to develop the following arguments, I shall select two smaller sub-sets of findings from GSL research. One is the—by now well-known—development of German word order. The other is the acquisition of devices for expressing the speech act "asking".

TABLE 4   *The development of word order in GSL*

Stages	V	PP	NP	Neg.
I	SVO	'adverb-prep.'	–	Neg + V
II	'verb-sep.'	–	TOP I	Neg – End
III	'inversion'	'ADV–VP'	–	–
IV	'V-End'	–	–	–

(*Sources:* Clahsen *et al.*, 1983; Clahsen, 1981; Pienemann, 1983)

Table 4 summarizes the development of the major German word order rules. Stages I-IV correspond to both (a) the temporal order of acquisition[9] and (b) the processing complexity of the rules. "Adverb-preposing", "verb-separation" and "inversion" have been mentioned before. SVO refers to the canonical word order in the first stage. ADV-VP refers to an optional permutation which moves a PP into a position right of the finite verbal element. TOPI stands for another optional permutation which moves an object-NP into initial position. Neg + V is an "unacceptable" interlanguage structure in German. The other Neg-rule moves the Neg-element into final position. V-End refers to the Standard German position of the verb in subordinate clauses, which is the final position. (For detailed information see Clahsen *et al.*, 1983.)

When the description of the emerging interrogation system of GSL is not restricted to the sentence type "question" a number of different devices for expressing the speech act "asking" can be observed in the interlanguages[10] (for references cf. Felix, 1978; Clahsen *et al.*, 1983):

1. In line with the simple structure of the very first stage of GSL
   development, the first questions are either *ellipses*, which only appear in
   certain dialogue contexts as the following example illustrates:

   A: da ist der spielplatz ("the play ground is over there")
   B: *wo?*[11]   ("where") (Luigina)

   or they are "prefabricated sentences" (Hakuta, 1974), which are
   learned by rote memory. They typically have a structure like:

   Was/Wer is N?   (What/Who is N?)

2. When sentences with lexically varied main verbs and one or more
   complements are produced (cf. Table 4, = stage I) questions are formed
   by the means available to the learner at that point in time. Consequently, yes/no-questions have the same syntactic surface structure as
   affirmative sentences. However, they are marked by a raising intonation (= German question intonation):

   L: *ich schreibe da*   ("I write there") (Luigina)

   Thus these structures are "deviant" in that subject and verb are not
   inverted as required in Standard German. This is also the case with
   wh-question

   A: *Warum du nicht deutsche sprechen?*(Antonio S)
       ("Why you no German speak"? = Why don't you speak German?)

3. Logically, the interrogation system in main clauses will conform to the
   target norms as soon as "inversion" is acquired:

   L: *Warum hast du auch eine nase?* (Luigina)
       ("Why have you also a nose?" = Why do you have a nose, too?
   L: *gehst du noch in der schule?* (Luigina)
   ("*Go you* still to school?" = do you still go to school?)

4. Since indirect questions are bound to subordinate clauses the interlanguage will be "deviant" with respect to word order (= SVO in subordinate
clauses) as long as "V-End" is not acquired. The correct structure appears
as soon as "V-End" is acquired.

As these two sub-sets of findings demonstrate, the different structural domains of the developing interlanguage systems are not isolated sub-systems, but they are structurally interrelated. Further interrelations appear in various domains, e.g. verbal morphology and word order or verbal elements and word order etc. (cf. Pienemann, 1981; Clahsen *et al.*, 1983). This will have to be taken into consideration in the planning of the natural grading.

Another important aspect of L2 research is that scholars have begun investigating L2 development from a perspective which is highly profitable for communicative language teaching. In a similar way to that outlined for the development of devices for expressing the speech act "asking", researchers have started to look at L2 development from a functional perspective. Thus the research question is no longer restricted to "how does a grammatical system X emerge?" but it is extended to "by which devices is a semantic function X expressed in the course of L2 develop-ment?". Leaving aside whether this approach will contribute to a more coherent *explanation* of L2 development, it certainly enables one to observe L2 development which would have been obscured if the focus had been entirely on the structural aspects.

The development of devices for establishing reference to the past is an example of this. As shown by Meisel (1982), it is not an item from the verbal morphology, such as "present perfect" (the usual means for this function in spoken German) which emerges as the first device. Rather, at least adult acquirers start out referring to past events, actions etc. by using adverbs and adverbials with an implicit perfective meaning:

mein man *gestern* geh arbeiten
("my husband *yesterday* go work" =
my husband went to work yesterday)

Similar cases can be observed in the early stages of the development of questions. Of course, some of the structures created by the learner are deviant or even stigmatized. It was discussed why such structures should not be taught. But the learner also develops structures which only have a "slightly deviant" degree of acceptability. For instance, yes/no-questions which are only marked by intonation (and not — additionally — by "inversion") are not salient deviations from the target norm. In certain contexts they might also appear in spoken German. Elliptic questions and question patterns are fully acceptable ways of asking questions.

Thus these interlanguage structures may be exploited for communica-tive language teaching. It is apparent that migrants will have to ask a lot of things right from the beginning of their acquisitional career. (The same is true for other learners as well.) On the one hand they will — in some textbooks — be provided with the structural means for asking questions (i.e. wh-pronouns and "inversion") at an early stage. However, at such an early period learners are not able to process these structures. On the other hand we cannot wait for the prerequisites of "inversion" to develop, since the learner would have to supress his/her questions for a period of approximately one year. So, introducing non-deviant interlanguage structures into the syllabus may contribute to solving the conflict between the learners' need to be expressive and the tenet not to support stigmatized forms.

Grading of a textbook

To illustrate the discrepancy between what is learnable and what the students are expected to learn in a language course, the natural stages of acquisition which were sketched above will be compared to the grading of the corresponding items in a current textbook. I would like to emphasize that this is an *illustration* of the above-mentioned discrepancy between learnability and current teaching, rather than an exhaustive comparison. The latter would, of course, have to take into account a broader section of the developing L2 grammar (and functions) and a representative number of textbooks. Obviously, this would exceed the available space of this volume.

The textbook I refer to (Gradewald, 1971), is currently used in the instruction of German as a foreign/second language for migrant children in Germany as well as in GFL abroad. It is built up according to a grammatical syllabus. The analysis of the textbook will differentiate between two aspects of the linguistic input, namely (1) the structures which appear in the exercises and which are expected to be (re-) produced by the learners and (2) those structures which are in focus in the instruction (learning objectives).

As can be seen from Table 5, the learning objectives and the structure of the general input are not identical for the two areas investigated. According to what we discussed about how comprehension and production develop, this differentiation may, in fact, be useful to cope with the differences in the development of the two aspects of speech processing. Difficulties will arise, however, if the teacher demands learning processes which are not possible at the time these appear in the textbook. And this is very likely to occur in the present context if the teacher insists on correct (re-) production of the general input, since it contains from the beginning (with respect to word order) two major structures which can only be processed at a later stage.

TABLE 5   *Grading in a textbook* ('Wir sind dabei', Gradewald, 1971)

A. *WORD ORDER*

chapter	general input, exercises	learning objectives
1	SVO inversion verb separation	*SVO*
4	SVO inversion verb separation adverb preposing	*adverb-preposing* *inversion*
8	see above	*modal verbs* (without verb separation!)
10	see above	*inversion* with *Mod+V*
12	see above	*inversion* (implicitly: verb separation)

B. *INTERROGATION*

chapter	general input, exercises	learning objectives
1	yes/no-question with inversion wh-questions with inv.	*yes/no-question* (with inversion)
2	see above	*wh-question* (with inv.)
3	see above	*yes/no- and wh-question*
4	see above	*inversion*

A more serious problem is implied in the grading of teaching objectives in both structural areas in question. In interrogation the textbook starts out (chapter 1!) with the structure which appears almost at the end of the natural acquisition process. This is brought about by two factors: (1) the orientation towards the dialogue structures (implying numerous questions) and (2) the idea of target-norm-correctness which — as in all traditional approaches – underlies the textbook. So the above-mentioned alternative structures which may serve the same function ("asking") were neglected altogether. Since inversion, which is acquired relatively late (cf. Table 4), is further implied in the learning objective of the very first chapter (yes/no-question), teaching and learnability are really adjusted in an extremely poor way.

The situation in the grading of word order rules is not quite as hopeless, since at least the first two structures are in line with learnability constraints. But inversion (chapter 4) is (1) much too early; it is (2) introduced simultaneously with adverb-preposing; and (3) verb-separation, which should precede inversion, is missing from the list of teaching objectives altogether (except for an implicit introduction in the last chapter).

Let me emphasize that this book is not a black sheep among GSL textbooks. Rather, with respect to word order it contains some fairly good guesses – in other textbooks this learning problem is not a focus at all.

"Natural grading"

The general guide-lines for grading which we developed in the course of this paper may be summarized as follows:

1. Do not demand a learning process which is impossible at a given stage (i.e. order of teaching objectives be in line with stages of acquisition).
2. But do *not* introduce deviant forms.
3. The general input may contain structures which were not introduced for production.

Table 6 illustrates how these guide-lines may be applied to the two developmental sequences which were above used as examples of regular-ities in GSL development. The main problem in this application is to avoid a conflict between tenets (1) and (2). This is apparent in the case of adverb-preposing and inversion. As was shown in previous sections, in Standard German, the preposing of adverbs obligatorily requires inver-sion. So, when adverb-preposing is introduced, we have two choices:

(A) On the one hand, we might follow tenet (1), and not introduce inversion at this point, in order to avoid demanding a learning process

TABLE 6 *"Natural grading"*

General input		teaching objectives		
word order	*"asking"*	*word order*	*"asking"*	*verbal elements*
SVO	elliptic questions/ question patterns	–	elliptic questions/ question patterns	V
SVO	elliptic qu./qu. patterns inton. qu.	SVO	intonation qu. (yes/no)	
SVO, adverb-preposing, *inversion*	see above	adverb-preposing	–	
SVO, adv.-prep., inversion. *verb-separation*	see above	–	–	Modal/auxiliary
see above	see above	verb separation	–	
see above	wh-qu., yes/no qu. with *inversion*	inversion	wh-qu., yes/no-qu. with *inversion*	

which the learner is not ready for. However, since adverb-preposing *obligatorily* requires inversion, this might lead to introducing a deviant form, thus contradicting principle (2). (B) On the other hand, following principle (2) only (i.e. introducing inversion simultaneously with adverb-preposing and thus conforming to standard norms), would have the consequence that one of the two teaching objectives (inversion) is not learnable.

A way out of this dilemma is shown in Table 6. As in the textbook analysis, teaching objectives are differentiated from the general input (i.e. those structures addressed to the learner which are not in focus of instruction). When adverb-preposing is in focus, inversion is applied simultaneously in the general input since this is required in the target language. But inversion is neither instructed at this point nor would I suggest reacting e.g. by "correction" to the corresponding "deviant" interlanguage forms which are bound to appear at this stage.

Thus, the input to the learners is not deviant but the learners are allowed to produce deviant forms as long as they have not developed the necessary processing prerequisites. Consequently, the missing structures are introduced as learning objectives as soon as the learner has developed these prerequisites (cf. Table 6).

Further structures are introduced in the same manner. Since the use of modals or auxiliaries requires "verb separation", the general input contains both types of structures once modals (or auxiliaries) are introduced, while "verb-separation" is a teaching objective only in the next step. Consequently, the teaching objectives are ordered parallel to the order of acquisition, whereas the general input also contains all the necessary "structural consequences".

In the grading of the other acquisitional sequence, which has been established from a more semantic or pragmatic perspective, another strategy for adjusting grading to L2 development can be exemplified: When considering the ordering of teaching objectives under the heading "asking" (cf. Table 6) we see that it is identical to the stages of acquisition, except that the markedly deviant from of wh-questions without inversion is not included.

Besides this negative selection (cf. principle (2)) forms are implemented into the syllabus, which emerge in L2 development but which were not included in the above textbook: elliptic questions, intonationally marked yes/no-questions and question patterns. These are all devices which allow the learner to fulfil a certain semantic function at a much earlier point in his/her L2 development than would be possible with the devices introduced in the textbook.

Implementation in a communicative syllabus

Because its structure is grammatical, the type of grading outlined above can easily be implemented into a grammatical syllabus. The difficult case is the communicative syllabus. As has been shown in the previous sections there are two opinions: (1) that there should be no structural grading behind the syllabus and (2) that the L2 items may be graded according to structural aspects, if the learners' linguistic needs are *first* anticipated and the morpho-syntactic, phonological etc. means, which are required to fulfill these needs, are selected afterwards.

My own position in the grading issue is influenced from the learning perspective. As I have argued throughout this chapter, foreign language teaching has to conform to the constraints of learnability/teachability. My proposal for implementing the above grading procedure in a communicative syllabus is therefore based on assumption (2).

Table 7 illustrates this implementation.[12] The syllabus is split into two parts: the general input (to the left in Table 7) and the learning objectives (the right). According to the tenets of communicative syllabus construction, the learning objectives are systematized in notional/functional terms ("asking", "temporal reference" etc.). The structural devices to fulfill these notions/functions are taken from the developing interlanguage system in line with the principles developed in the preceding sub-section.

Going from the top to the bottom of Table 7 represents the chronological axis of both the interlanguage development and the progress in formal instruction.

The items which have to be enclosed in the general input follow logically from what is introduced as a learning objective and from the "structural consequences" which are caused by these items. For instance, when structural means are selected for expressing temporal reference we might come to the "present perfect". The point at which this can be introduced is determined by the interlanguage-box in Table 7. There are three structural requirements for "present perfect": (1) the auxiliary, (2) the corresponding verbal morphology and (3) the resulting word order. So (1) and (2) may be in focus while (3) is in the first round — like in natural L2 development — only enclosed in the general input. It will be in focus only in the second round.

TABLE 7 *Communicative syllabus and interlanguage development*

GENERAL INPUT

the general input contains the learning objectives *plus* the 'structural consequences'

DEVELOPING INTERLANGUAGE

structure		functions	
word order	*morphol.*	*questions*	*etc.*
—	—	ellip. questions Wh + x	—
—	—	intonat. marked qu.	—
verb-sep.	ge+V+t	Wh-quest. without INV	—
INV	—	Wh-quest. with INV	—
—	—	—	—

LEARNING OBJECTIVES

questions	temporal reference (past act.)	etc.
ellptic questions Wh + x	—	—
intonat. marked qu.	connectives	—
0	—	—
Wh-quest. with INV	pres. perf. (+ verb-sep.)	—
—	—	—

Thus the developing interlanguage system together with our above grading principles serves as the structural source for the syllabus. The advantages of this procedure are the following:

1. L2 items are focused on in the order they are learnable.
2. L2 forms are introduced which have proved to be communicatively effective in natural L2 development.
3. The focus on meaning can be maintained in the instruction, while the required L2 items are selected and graded according to the above principles.

Final remarks

In this chapter I have attempted to outline one specific type of constructive contribution to language teaching which I have derived from research on natural and formal second language development. The topic of this contribution was a *general framework* for a psychologically valid grading of teaching material, which may replace former *intuitive* grading principles.

This general framework is not itself a syllabus. Rather, it contains the principles for constructing learnable syllabuses for different target languages, which will have to be worked out on the basis of the available findings about the development fo the corresponding L2s.

Thus there are two major aspects in my proposal which are open to further discussion. One is the framework for constructing learnable syllabuses. The other is whether the available research findings are sufficient in a language x.

Quite obviously, there are only very few languages which have been investigated with regard to L2 development. And for those few which have been researched, there are different bodies of findings. It is also certain that we are light years away from having a complete description (not to mention explanation) of any developing second language.

But what are we to expect? Even generations of linguists have not been able to describe a single language completely. What we have to compare our bodies of L2 findings to, is not the complete system of the L2 but just those tiny pieces of it which are usually included in second language syllabuses. From this aspect, I think we are well off at least for the first one or two years in the use of at least one language, German.

As can be seen from Table 3 (above p. 57), the development of German as L2 has been described in a relatively broad range of linguistic domains. Most of the items contained in the textbook which was analysed above are covered in L2 research. As was shown in the textbook analysis some items which would be covered in "natural grading" were even missing from the traditional syllabus. Thus there is a basis on which the actual effect of "natural grading" on classroom L2 development can be investigated.

Research of this kind may also be profitable for the less well investigated languages as well, because research on the "example language" may reveal insights into the teachability of L2s. This, in turn, may be decisive in reaching further decisions in syllabus construction and L2 research.

I do not, of course, think that constructing "learnable syllabuses" will solve all problems in foreign/second language teaching. We all know that such factors as, for instance, poor motivation may invalidate the possible effect of a neatly constructed syllabus. But I think replacing intuitively derived syllabuses by learnable syllabuses is a *necessary*, though by no means sufficient, step in improving language teaching. Apart from this, syllabus construction is only one component of what is needed for L2 teaching. However, it is the area to which — I think — research into L2 development can at the present stage make a constructive contribution, while other areas, such as teaching methods, still have to be speculated about.

Notes to Chapter 2

1. Another way of obtaining morpheme orders more clearly related to acquisition orders, is to set a criterion for "acquired" and to state in an individualized longitudinal study which order the different morphemes are acquired in. This, however, was not the case in the above studies.
2. This research was supported by a grant from the Cornelsen-Foundation.
3. All example sentences are translated literally in order to demonstrate the word order phenomena under discussion.
4. In my paper from 1984 I analysed one informant only from each respective stage. Since then it has been possible to state the results for further informants.
5. Besides the well-known reservations against the morpheme-order-studies, the teachability hypothesis can only be applied to the "natural order of morpheme acquisition", if it can be shown that the stages are interrelated in the way already described.
6. The original source reads " ... SIMPLE *INVERSION* constitutes ..." (my emphasis). But obviously this is a misprint.
7 .The additional requirement is that the processing mechanisms underlying the respective natural stages be interrelated in such a way that processing prerequisites for a stage x are developed on stage x-1 (cf. Pienemann, 1984).

8. Note that this possible function of input does not interfere with the position that no input of whatever type may surmount the learning constraints set by principles of speech processing.
9. It may be, however, that structures from different columns of Table 4 which appear at the same stage are not acquired simultaneously but successively. The table is neutral with respect to the temporal interrelation between the different columns.
10. The following list of devices is chronologically ordered but it is not exhaustive.
11. All examples from Eva and Luigina are taken from Pienemann (1981). The other examples are taken from Clahsen et al., (1983).
12. Note that Table 7 only illustrates the *general idea* of a naturally graded communicative syllabus. A comprehensive elaboration of such a syllabus would, of course, have to be based on a broad description of L2 development.

References

Allwright, D. 1978, Abdication and Responsibility in Language Teaching. *Studies in Second Language Acquisition*, 2, 1 73–97.
Andersen, R. 1977, The impoverished state of cross-sectional morpheme acquisition/accuracy morphology. In C. Henning (ed.), Proceedings of the Los Angeles Second Language Research Forum. UCLA. 308–20.
—— (ed.) 1979, *The acquisition and use of Spanish and English as first and second languages*. Washington, D.C.: TESOL.
Bailey, N.C., Madden, C. & Krashen, S.D. 1974, Is there a natural sequence in adult second language learning? *Language Learning*, 27, 235–44.
Berman, R. 1982, Cognitive principles and language acquisition. Paper presented at the 'Second European – North American Workshop on Cross-Linguistic Second Language Acquisition Research', Göhrde, West Germany 1982.
Bever, T. 1970, The cognitive basis for linguistic structures. In J. Hayes, (ed.), *Cognition and the development of language*. New York, 279–363.
Bever, Th. 1981, Normal Acquisition processes explain the critical period for language learning. In K.C. Diller (ed.), *Individual differences and universals in language learning aptitude*. Rowley, Mass.: Newbury House. 176–98.
Bloom, L. & Lahey, M. 1978, *Language development and language disorders*. New York: Wiley.
Burt, M. & Dulay, H. (eds) 1975, *Second language learning, teaching and bilingual education*. Washington: TESOL.
Clahsen, H. 1980, Psycholinguistic aspects of L2-acquisition: word order phenomena in foreign workers' interlanguage. In S.W. Felix (ed.), *Second Language Development Trends and Issues*. Tübingen: Narr.
—— 1981, The acquisition of German word order: a test case for cognitive approaches to L2 development. Paper presented at the European – North American Workshop on Cross-Linguistic Second Acquisition Research, Lake Arrowhead, Sept. 1981.
—— 1982, Autonomy and interaction in (second) language acquisition: evidence for an integrativist position. Paper presented at the 'Second European – North American Workshop on Cross-Linguistic Second Language Acquisition Research', Göhrde, West Germany 1982.

Clahsen, H. & Meisel, J.M. 1979, Eine psycholinguistische Rechtfertigung von Wortstellungsregeln. *Papiere zur Linguistik*, 21.

Clahsen, H., Meisel, J.M. & Pienemann, M. 1983, Deutsch als Zweitsprache. *Der Spracherwerb ausländischer Arbeiter*. Tübingen: Narr.

Cohan, A. & Aphek, E. 1981, Easifying second language learning. *Studies in Second Language Acquisition 1981*, Vol. 3, Nr. 2.

Corder, P. 1967, The significance of learner's errors. *IRAL*, 5, 161–70.

Corder, S.P. 1973a, *Introducing applied linguistics*. Harmondsworth: Penguin.

—— 1973b (unpublished paper) cited according to a quotation in Valdman, A. (1975), P. 423.

Cross, D. 1982, Compact courses, a curricular innovation: structure and content in practice. ERic, Centre for Applied Linguistics; U.S. Department of Education, Washington D.C.

Cross, T. 1977, Mother's speech adjustments: the contribution of selected child listener variables. In C. Snow & C. Ferguson (eds), *Talking to children*. Cambridge: Cambridge University Press. 151–88.

Dietrich, R. (ed.) 1976, Aspekte des Fremdsprachenerwerbs, Kronberg/Ts.

Dietrich, R., Kaufmann, T. & Storch, G. 1979, Beobachtungen zum gesteuerten Fremdsprachenerwerb. *Linguistische Bericht*, 64, 56–81.

Diller, K.C. (ed.) 1981, *Individual differences and universals in language learning aptitude*. Rowley, Mass.: Newbury House.

Dulay, H. & Burt, M. 1973, Should we teach children syntax? *Language Learning*, 23, 245–58.

—— 1974, Natural sequences in child second language acquisition. *Language Learning*, 24, 37–53.

Fathman, A. 1978, ESL and EFL learning: Similar or dissimilar? In C. Blatchford & J. Schacter (eds), *On TESOL '78': EFL Policies, Programs, Practices*. Washington, D.C.: TESOL.

Felix, S.W. 1977, Natürlicher Zweitsprachenerwerb und Fremdsprachenunterricht, *Linguistik und Didaktik*, 31, 231–47.

—— 1978, *Linguistische Untersuchungen zum natürlichen Zweitsprachenerwerb*. München: W. Fink..

—— (ed.) 1980, *Second Language development. Trends and issues*. Tübingen: Narr.

—— 1981, The effect of formal instruction on second language acquisition. *Language Learning*, 31, No 1, 87–112.

—— 1982, *Psycholinguistische Aspekte des Zweitsprachenerwerbs*. Tübingen: Narr.

Felix, S.W. & Simmet, A. 1981, Der Erwerb der Personalpronomina im Fremdsprachenunterricht. *Neusprachliche Mitteilungen*, 3, 132–44.

Felix, S.W. & Wode, H. (eds) 1983, Language development at the crossroads. Papers from the Interdisciplinary Conference of Language Acquisition at Passau. Tübingen: Narr.

Forster, K.I. 1979, Levels of processing and the structure of the language processor. In W. Cooper & E. Walker (eds), *Sentence Processing: psycholinguistic studies presented to Merril Garrett*. New York: Halsted. 27–85.

Gradewald, J. 1971, 'Wir sind dabei'. Ein deutsches Übungsbuch. München: Hueber.

Hahn, A. 1982, Fremdsprachenunterricht und Spracherwerb. Ph.D. Dissertation University of Passau.

Hakuta, K. 1974, A preliminary report of the development of grammatical morphemes in a Japanese girl learning English as a second language. *Working Paper on Bilingualism*, 14, 33–46.

Hatch, E. 1978, Apply with caution. *Studies in Second Language Acquisition*, Vol. 2, No. 2, 123–43.

Haugen, E. 1956, *Bilingualism in the Americas*. Alabama: Drawer.

Huebner, Th. 1983, *A longitudinal analysis of the acquisition of English*. Ann Arbor: Karoma Publishers.

Ingram, D.E. 1982, Developing a language programme. *RELC Journal*, Vol. 13, No. 1, 64–86.

—— 1983, Report on the formal trialling of the Australian Second Language Proficiency Ratings (ASLPR). MS Brisbane.

Januschek, F. & Stölting, W. (eds) 1982, Handlungsorientierung im Zweitspracherwerb. *Osnabrücker Beiträge zur Sprachtheorie*, 22.

Jespersen, O. 1904, *How to teach a foreign language*. London: Allen & Unwin (Reprinted 1956).

Johnson, K. 1982, *Communicative syllabus. Design and methodology*. Oxford: Pergamon.

KIS (=Koordinierungsgremium im DGF-Schwerpunkt 'Sprachlehrforschung') · (ed.) 1983, Sprachlehr- und Sprachlernforschung: Begründung einer Disziplin. Tübingen: Narr.

Klein, W. & Dittmar, N. 1979, *Developing grammars. The acquisition of German by foreign workers*, Heidelberg: Springer.

Knapp-Potthoff, A. & Knapp, K. 1982, *Fremdsprachenlernen und -lehren*. Stuttgart: Kohlhammer.

Krashen, S.D. 1977, Some issues relating to the monitor model: In H.D. Brown, C. Yorio & R. Crymes, (eds), *On TESOL '77: Teaching and Learning English as a Second Language*. Washington D.C.: TESOL.

—— 1981, *Second language acquisition and second language learning*. Oxford: Pergamon.

—— 1982, *Principles and practice in second language acquisition*. Oxford: Pergamon.

Krashen, S.D., Madden, C. & Bailey, N. 1975, Theoretical aspects of grammatical sequencing. In M. Burt & H. Dulay (eds), *Second language learning, teaching and bilingual education*. Washington: TESOL. 44–54.

Krashen, S. Sferlazza, V. Feldman, L. & Fathman, A. 1976, Adult performance on the SLOPE test: More evidence for a natural sequence in adult second language acquisition. *Language Learning*, 26, 145–51.

Larsen-Freeman, D. 1976a, An explanation for the morpheme acquisition order of second language learners. *Language Learning*, 26, 125–34.

—— 1976b, ESL teacher speech as input to the ESL learner. *Workpapers in Teaching English as a Second Language*, X, 45–50.

Lightbown, P. in press, Exploring relationships between developmental and instructional sequences in L2 acquisition. In H. Seliger & M. Long (eds), *Classroom language acquisition and use. New perspectives*. Rowley, Mass.: Newbury House.

Littlewood, W. 1981, *Communicative language teaching. An introduction*. Cambridge: Cambridge University Press.

Long, M.H. 1981, Input, interaction and second language acquisition. In H. Winitz (ed.), *Native language and foreign language acquisition*. Annals of the New York Academy of Science 379, p. 259–78.

—— 1982, Foreigner talk and early interlanguage: a cross-linguistic study. Paper presented at the 'Second European-North American Workshop on Cross-Linguistic Second Language Acquisition Research', Göhrde, West-Germany 1982.

—— 1983, Does second language instruction make a difference? A review of research. *TESOL Quarterly*, 17, 359–82.

Makino, T. 1979, English morpheme acquisition order of Japanese secondary school students. *TESOL Quarterly*, 13, 428.

McNeill, D. 1965, Some thoughts on first and second language acquisition. MS Harvard.

Meisel, J.M. 1980, Strategies of second language acquisition. In R.W. Andersen (ed.), *Pidginization, Creolization and Language Acquisition*. Rowley, Mass.: Newbury House.

—— 1982, Reference to past events and actions in the development of natural second language acquisition. MS Hamburg.

Meisel, J.M., Clahsen, H. & Pienemann, M. 1981, On determining developmental stages in natural second language acquisition. *Studies in Second Language Acquisition 1981*, Vol. 3, No. 2, 109–35.

Newmark, L.D. 1971, A minimal language teaching program. In P. Pimsleur & T. Quinn (eds), Papers from the Second International Congress on Applied Linguistics Cambridge, 1969.

Newport, E., Gleitman, H. & Gleitman, L. 1977, Mother, I'd rather do it myself: some effects and non-effects of maternal speech style. In C. Snow & C. Ferguson (eds), *Talking to children*. Cambridge. University Press 109–49.

Nicholas, H. 1981, 'to be' or not 'to be'; is that really the question? Developmental sequences and the role of the copula in the acquisition of German as a second language. Paper presented at the 'European – North American Workshop on Cross-Linguistic Second Language Acquisition Research', Lake Arrowhead, September 1981.

Nicholas, H. & Meisel, J. 1983, Second language acquisition: The state of the art. In S.W. Felix & H. Wode (eds), Papers from the Interdisciplinary Conference on Language Acqusition at Passau. Tübingen: Narr.

Oller, J.W.Jr. 1971, Language communication and second language learning. In P. Pimsleur & T. Quinn (eds), Papers from the Second International Congress on Applied Linguistics. Cambridge 1969.

Orlović, M. 1978, Zum Gastarbeiterdeutsch jugoslawischer Arbeiter im Rhein-Main Gebiet: Empirische Untersuchungen zur Morphologie und zum ungesteuerten Erwerb durch Erwachsene. Wiesbaden: Steiner.

Palmer, H.E. 1922, *The principles of language study*. London: Harrap.

Papilia, A. 1976, *Learner-centered language teaching: Methods and materials*. Rowley, Mass.: Newbury House.

Pica, T. 1982a, The role of language context in second language acquisition. Review article MS.

—— 1982b, The role of the English indefinite article. MS.

Pienemann, M. 1980, The second language acquisition of immigrant children. In S.W. Felix (ed.), *Second Language Development. Trends and Issues*. Tübingen: Narr.

—— 1981, *Der Zweitspracherwerb ausländischer Arbeiterkinder*. Bonn: Bouvier.

—— 1984, Psychological constraints on the teachability of languages. *Studies in Second Language Acquisition*, 6, 186–214.

Piepho, H.-E. 1979, *Kommunikative Didaktik des Englischunterrichts.* Limburg.
Reibel, D.A. 1971, Language Learning Strategies for the adult. In P. Pimsleur & T. Quinn (eds), Papers from the Second International Congress on Applied Linguistics. Cambridge 1969.
Rodgers, T.S. 1978, Towards a model of learner variation in autonomous foreign language learning. *Studies in Second Language Acquisition*, Vol. 2, No. 1, 73–97.
Rosansky, E. 1976, Methods and morphemes in second language acquisition research. *Language Learning*, 26, 409–25.
Ruben, J. 1975, What the 'Good Language Learner' can teach us. *TESOL Quarterly*, Vol. 9, No. 1, 41–51.
Sajavaara, K. 1981, The nature of first language transfer: English as L2 in a foreign language setting. Paper presented at the 'First European – North American Workshop on Second Language Acquisition Research', Lake Arrowhead, California.
Schumann, J.H. 1974, The implication of interlanguage, pidginization and creolization for the study adult second language acquisition. *TESOL quarterly 8.*, 145–52.
—— 1978, *The pidginization process: a model for second language acquisition.* Rowley, Mass.: Newbury House.
Slobin, D. 1973, Cognitive pre-requisites for the acquisition of grammar. In C. Ferguson & D. Slobin (eds), *Studies of child language development.* New York, 175–208.
—— 1975, Language change in childhood and history. Working Papers of the Language Behavior Research Laboratory, No.41. University of California, Berkeley.
Snow, C. & C. Ferguson (eds) 1977, *Talking to children.* Cambridge: Cambridge University Press.
Stern, H. 1972, What can we learn from the good language learner? *The Canadian Modern Language review*, 1974/75 31, 304–18.
Sweet, H. 1899, *The practical study of languages: a guide for teachers and learners.* London: Dent.
Terrell, T. 1977, A natural approach to second language acquisition and learning. *Modern Language Journal*, 6; 325–37.
Todd, L. 1974, *Pidgins and creoles.* London: Routledge & Kegan Paul.
Turner, D. 1979, The effect of instruction on second language learning and second language acquisition. In R. Andersen (ed.) The Acquisition and Use of Spanish and English as First and Second Languages. Washington, D.C.: TESOL.
Valdman, A. 1974, Error analysis and pedagogical ordering. Paper reproduced by L.A.U.T. (Linguistic Agency University at Trier).
—— 1975, Error analysis and grading in the preparation of teaching materials. *The Modern Language Journal*, 59, 422–26.
—— (ed.) 1977, *Pidgin and creole linguistics.* Bloomington: Indiana University Press.
—— 1978, Pidginization and the elaboration of learner-based syllabi in FL instruction. *Studies in Second Language Acquisition*, Vol.2, No.1, 59–72.
Wienold, G. 1976, Zur 'Progression' von Lehrmaterial im Fremdsprachenunterricht. In R. Dietrich (ed.), *Aspekte des Zweitsprachenerwerbs.* Tübingen: Narr. 15–33.

Wilkins, D.A. 1973, Notional analysis and the concept of a minimum adequate grammar. In S.P. Corder & E. Roulet (eds), *Linguistic insights in applied linguistics*. Brussels-Paris: AIMAV-Didier.

Wilkins, D.A. 1974, Second language learning and teaching. London: Dilling & Sons Ltd.

—— 1976, *Notional syllabuses. A taxonomy and its relevance to foreign language curriculum development*. Oxford: Oxford University Press.

Wode, H. 1981, Learning a second language. Vol.1, An integrated view of language acquisition. Tübingen: Narr.

Wong-Fillmore, L. 1976, The second time around: Cognitive and social strategies in second language acquisition. Ph.D. dissertation, Stanford.

3 A role for instruction in second language acquisition: Task-based language teaching

MICHAEL H. LONG

University of Hawaii at Manoa, U.S.A.

Program design

It is customary and quite natural to think of language teaching as having two principal components: language and teaching. Hence, when designing a language teaching programme, curriculum developers make sure the curriculum includes statements about *what* is to be taught, and *how*. These statements typically take the form of choices in syllabus type and teaching method, respectively. These, in turn, are realized at the classroom level through the materials adopted or written for the courses.

Needless to say, things are not quite so simple, as any practitioner will attest. There are, for example, numerous potential conflicts between choices in syllabus type and teaching method, as well as some happy marriages. Thus, while structural syllabuses and the audiolingual method were made for each other, the same can hardly be said for audiolingualism and notional-functional syllabuses. And some language teaching methods, such as the Natural Approach, seem to preclude syllabus design altogether, at least as a separate stage in programme development.

Quite apart from the obvious tensions that can arise between syllabus and method, however, it is arguable that there are several other problems inherent in this approach to programme planning. For example, syllabuses are supposed to determine both what is to be taught (selection) and the order in which this will be done (grading, or sequencing). Yet opting for a particular *type* of syllabus (structural, notional-functional, situational, etc.) says nothing about either selection or grading. A choice of syllabus type is nothing more than a decision about the *unit of analysis* to be employed in determining content and sequencing. Some syllabus types, such as structural and notional-functional, employ overtly linguistic units (structures, speech acts, etc.) for this purpose; others, such as topical and situational, choose covertly linguistic units — where the language will be used, what it will be used to talk about, and so on.

If selection and grading are handled systematically at all, it is at some other stage in programme planning: selection through some kind of learner needs analysis — if time permits and the requisite expertize is available — and grading through recourse to materials writers' intuitions about such matters as simplicity, frequency and valency. Even a cursory study of commercially published ESL materials shows, however, that needs analyses are rarely conducted, and that writers' intuitions differ alarmingly.

Programme design is in no better shape where teaching method is concerned. The two most widely used are still grammar translation and the audiolingual method — or worse, in some parts of the world, a ghoulish hybrid, often known locally as "the eclectic method" (*sic*). The former never had a basis in learning theory; the latter did (neo-behaviourism), but one long since discredited where language learning in normal populations is concerned.

The vacuum created by this state of affairs has led to the appearance of a variety of so-called "unconventional" methods in recent years: the Silent Way, Suggestopoedia, Counseling Learning/Community Language Learning, Total Physical Response (TPR) and the Natural Approach, to name but a few. Of these, only TPR has been subjected to controlled classroom testing. The Natural Approach does have an explicit theoretical base ("Extended Standard Monitor Theory"), but one that is, to say the least, controversial (see, e.g. McLaughlin, 1978; Pienemann, this volume Chapter 2). Several of the methods are offered by their advocates as the solution to all the language teacher's (or program designer's) problems, i.e. as incidentally circumventing thorny syllabus issues. Yet not one has anything to say about *what* will be taught through its use, and only one, TPR, comes accompanied by teaching materials.

Fortunately, just as syllabuses of one type or another are not the solution to the "what" in language teaching, so methods seem to be a red herring where the "how" is concerned. It is well known, for instance, that many apparently different teaching methods share much in common when implemented in the classroom, and also that teachers rarely stick to one method for very long in any case. In fact, for many teachers, "method" has been shown to be too abstract a level at which to conceptualize what they do (Swaffer *et al.*, 1982). And teachers trained in one ("communicative") approach to language teaching have been observed teaching lessons of which teachers in another (audiolingual) tradition would be proud (Long & Sato, 1983).

Another problem with the traditional approach to programme design is that, to date, most proposals for both syllabus design and teaching method have been made in a psycholinguistic vacuum. Syllabuses generally consist of inventories of items drawn not from any understanding of how a second language is learned, but from linguists' (partial) descriptions of the language itself and/or sociolinguists' (to date even more fragmentary) descriptions of the ways it is used. It is *assumed* that the same linguistic or sociolinguistic units — sentence patterns, grammatical constructions, speech acts, etc. — that were employed in analyzing the full, native speaker form or use of the language are also meaningful segments in which to teach it and in which to hope learners will acquire it. Sequencing of these segments, too, is generally uninformed by research on interlanguage development. As previously noted, it is based instead on materials writers' intuitions about such factors as the simplicity, frequency and valency of (target) forms and uses.

There is, of course, no reason to assume that acquisition proceeds in one step from zero proficiency to full target form or use, either of the whole code or of pieces of it (structures, notions, functions) presented one at a time in linear, additive fashion. Indeed, for both naturalistic and instructed second language acquisition (SLA), there is a wealth of evidence to the contrary. (For review, see, e.g. Andersen, 1983; Felix, 1981; Gass, 1983; Hatch, 1978; Meisel, 1982; Pica, 1983; Schumann, 1978; Wode, 1981.)

Where methodology is concerned, there is also no reason to assume that presenting the target language as a series of discrete linguistic or sociolinguistic teaching points is the best, or even *a* way to get learners to synthesize the parts into a coherent whole. In other words, there is no reason to believe that eventual performance units make viable acquisition units. However, with a few notable exceptions (e.g. TPR and the Natural Approach), this is exactly what most teaching methods do assume. It is reflected — in methods as *apparently* different as grammar translation, audiolingualism and the Silent Way — in the demand for immediate, forced production by the learner of native-like sentences from the very earliest stages of instruction, and the prescription of teacher "correction" for anything less.

To summarize, the design of language teaching programmes usually consists of statements about preferred syllabus types, on the one hand, and preferred teaching method, on the other. At best, choices made *separately* in each area will be compatible. They may conflict, however, as when a particular syllabus type presents the target language as discrete units of native speaker performance, but the method chosen rejects the overt focus on form (or function) that this would imply in the pedagogy.

Part of the problem derives, no doubt, from the practice of independent decision-making in the intrinsically related domains of syllabus and method. However, were this rectified, there would still be the problem that few current options in syllabus design and teaching method have any basis in SLA theory or research. Hence, any serious attempt to deal with one or more issues in programme planning from a psycholinguistic perspective is to be welcomed. Pienemann's proposal (this volume, Chapter 2) is such an attempt, and therefore worthy of careful study. By the same token, as long as the proposal concerns (or purports to concern) just one aspect of programme design, it is likely to be of limited validity, unless the decisions it implies or entails in other areas also have a defensible psycholinguistic basis.

Pienemann's proposal for sequencing

The psycholinguistic rationale for Pienemann's proposal (this volume) for sequencing in SL teaching derives from German research on the acquisition of GSL word order. This work provides strong motivation for positing four stages in GSL word order development: (1) (the canonical) SVO, (2) verb-separation, (3) inversion, and (4) (the target) verb-end, with rules from all preceeding stages persisting with the new rule marking each new stage. It also suggests that passage through *each* stage, in the order specified, is necessary for any learner who ultimately attains the fourth (target) stage.

The evidence consists primarily of a series of longitudinal and cross-sectional studies conducted by the ZISA group and others of both child and adult naturalistic and instructed acquirers from a variety of first language backgrounds. (See, e.g. Meisel *et al.*, 1981; Nicholas & Meisel 1983; and Pienemann, this volume, for review.) In addition, however, there is convergent validation for the empirically established temporal order in the form of an analysis of the processing complexity of each stage (Clahsen, 1984; Pienemann, 1984). This analysis predicts the same order, showing that attainment of any stage in the sequence depends upon mastery of the processing prerequisites of each preceding stage.

These findings are especially interesting both for SLA researchers and for those concerned with designing SL teaching programmes. There are two reasons why this is so. First, the word order data concern more than simply a *statistically* discernable "natural order" of accurate suppliance in obligatory contexts, as has been claimed for a group of often unrelated free and bound, NP and VP morphemes (see, e.g. Krashen, 1977). The GSL data argue for an apparently *inviolable* sequence of *linguistically and psycholinguistically related* syntactic constructions. Second, the GSL data come accompanied by a study documenting the failure of instruction (at least with children) to "beat the order" by skipping a stage (Pienemann, 1984), although the same study did show that instruction can (1) accelerate passage through the sequence, (2) increase the frequency of rule application, and (3) broaden the range of linguistic contexts in which the rule governing a stage is applied.

Pienemann interprets these findings as showing that the increased processing complexity of constructions at each stage determines their *learnability*, and that this, in turn, determines their *teachability*. Therefore, as a general principle, he advocates respects for learnability in SL teaching: "Do not demand a learning process which is impossible at a given stage" (Pienemann, this volume, p.63). The first part of his proposal (paraphrased) for a psycholinguistically grounded approach to sequencing in SL syllabus design follows directly from this principle:

1. Sequence the introduction of *learning objectives*, i.e. structures the learner is expected to comprehend and produce accurately, according to the established natural order for their acquisition.

Concern that rigid implementation of this proposal could occasionally lead to the teaching of socially stigmatized, non-target forms leads Pienemann to qualify the first principle (again paraphrased) thus:

2. Where (1) would involve presenting *deviant* interlingual forms, accept learner production of these as an inevitable part of interlanguage development, but do not teach such forms. Instead, switch to the next *grammatical* form in the sequence in the "general input" (teacher speech, textbook language), be it a transitional (interlingual) or target language form. Make the latter the learning objective (pedagogic focus of instruction) only when the learners show they are ready for it, as by the frequency of their production of the deviant form at the preceding stage.

Critique of Pienemann's proposal

Pienemann's proposal illustrates the *interdependence* of decisions in programme design. In this case, the proposal for *sequencing* in syllabus design entails certain methodological procedures. Thus, both parts, (1) and (2), above, imply, for example, that the classroom teacher will respect the validity in acquisitional terms of non-target forms in the learners' speech. This also means that the teacher will abstain from "correcting" any resulting errors which arise from discrepancies between the learners' current acquisitional stage and the full target form, unless the former be the penultimate stage in an acquisitional sequence and the latter the current learning objective.

Both of these last two procedures would be endorsed by Krashen and Terrell's Natural Approach. The Natural Approach goes further, however, in advocating that learner production even of interlingual forms not be forced, and also that *no* learner errors be corrected. Pienemann, however, explicitly rejects the Natural Approach, along with the theory of SLA upon which it is based. It is here that other more basic assumptions underlying the sequencing proposal become apparent. These concern general methodological and syllabus design issues, not just sequencing, and illustrate the problems inherent in attempting to deal with either the "what" or "how" of SL teaching in isolation.

While explicitly restricting his proposal to "any type of syllabus (which) implies that teaching material be graded" (p.28), Pienemann clearly makes certain assumptions about syllabus design in general, and about teaching methodology. These include the belief that a focus on form facilitates SL learning (a methodological issue). Indeed, he offers his 1984 study as evidence of this. That assumption, in turn, entails faith in what Wilkins (1976) calls "synthetic" syllabuses, i.e. those which, as Pienemann notes (p.25), present the target language as a series of discrete items and assume that the learner will be capable of synthesizing them when called upon to communicate. The fact that the discrete items in Pienemann's syllabus would be derived from analyses of interlanguage development, not just of the target language, does not alter this. Lastly, the particular types of discrete items that Pienemann apparently favours include linguistic structures, a choice which he attempts to defend by a rebuttal (pp.45–49) of Krashen's (1982) criticisms of structural syllabuses.

Krashen (1982 and elsewhere) offers four main criticisms of structural syllabuses, which are merely summarized here.

1. A pedagogic focus on one "structure of the day" will inevitably be *in*appropriate input for many (even all) learners, given that they are

rarely, if ever, at exactly the same stage of interlanguage development.

2. Structural grading allows learners only one shot at acquiring a new structure. If they miss it, perhaps because they are not ready for it, they have to wait until it appears in the syllabus again. This may never happen, or only long after the learners *are* ready for it.

3. The natural "rough tuning" in teacher speech obviates the need for overt structural grading, indeed obviates the need for an imposed syllabus altogether.

4. A focus on form, which is entailed by a structural syllabus, distorts real communication in the classroom, thereby limiting access for learners to the appropriately (naturally) tuned input. (Krashen also argues that conscious knowledge of a language, which a focus on form could produce, is in any case unusable in normal communication.) Krashen goes on to claim that, freed from the constraints of a structural syllabus, the natural speech adjustments teachers make in communicating in the classroom will be sufficient to provide what he considers the crucial factor in SLA: *comprehensible input*. This, plus a (vaguely defined) "low affective filter" to "let the input penetrate the relevant brain areas", Krashen holds, is necessary and sufficient for SLA.

Pienemann's attempted rebuttal of Krashen's position is in three parts.

1. There is inadequate evidence for the "input hypothesis". First, not even caretaker speech always shows the "tuning" Krashen says it does. Second, there is insufficient evidence to support the claim that caretaker speech or its SL equivalent, foreigner talk, promote first or second language acquisition. Third, Krashen's position assumes that comprehension precedes production, whereas work by Bever (1981) and Forster (1979) shows that "very different *procedures* underlie these two aspects of *speech processing*" (pp.47f, emphasis added). Finally, some child language research suggests that production sometimes precedes comprehension.

2. Krashen's position is characterized by faulty logic. First, (again) it has yet to be shown that comprehensible input promotes acquisition. Second, the fact that isolated structures *may* only be presented once does not mean that they *must* be. Third, learners can be grouped by acquisitional stage, so that one can be confident that the structure presented will be appropriate for them.

3. "Natural" language teaching of the sort advocated by Krashen and Terrell can have the unfortunate side effect of leading to early fossilization of a simplified code. This may be adequate for referential communication, but not for expressive or other social functions, as

illustrated by many of the world's pidgins. (Pienemann claims that the early fossilization is due to certain kinds of learners having poor social-psychological profiles, but notes that *all* learners show this tendency to simplify.)

My own position is that certain of both Krashen's *and* Pienemann's arguments are flawed. I will first comment briefly on Pienemann's rebuttal of Krashen's position.

Empirical support for the "input hypothesis"

Elsewhere (Long, 1981, 1983a, b), I have reviewed evidence consistent with the claim that comprehensible input promotes SLA, and have also attempted to deal with some *apparent* counter-evidence. (The latter comes chiefly from studies of language acquisition by children with restricted input, such as hearing children of deaf adults.) The relevant literature is far too extensive to review again here. Suffice to say that studies of naturalistic and instructed, child and adult, first and second language acquisition in normal and abnormal populations are consistent with the following three generalizations:

(i)   access to comprehensible input is a characteristic of all cases of successful (first or second) language acquisition,

(ii) greater quantities of comprehensible input seem to result in better (or at least faster) acquisition, and, crucially,

(iii) lack of access to comprehensible input (as distinct from *in*comprehensible, not any, input) results in little or no acquisition. (For example, hearing children of deaf adults who watch television a great deal learn only a few high frequency vocabulary items and some advertizing jingles.)

While it is true, as Pienemann points out, that not all studies have found caretaker/native speaker "tuning", many have, including studies of SL teachers' classroom speech (e.g. Gaies, 1977; and see Gaies 1983, for review). I have argued elsewhere, however (Long, 1981, 1982, 1983c), that this is irrelevant. More important than the *linguistic* tuning (of the input itself) are the *conversational* adjustments caretakers and native speakers seem always to perform, which make the input *comprehensible*, whether "tuned"/"simplified" or not. The *conversational* adjustments are pervasive, and have been found in all studies which have looked for them using comparable (adult native speaker/native speaker) baseline data. (See Long, 1983d, for review.)

Pienemann is correct in pointing out the lack, as yet, of *direct* evidence for a relationship between speech modifications and SLA.

Nevertheless, the literature referred to above strongly suggests that such a relationship exists. Moreover, in an earlier paper (Long 1983d), I have outlined an alternative route to establishing a causal relationship of this nature. Put simply, if it can be shown that linguistic and/or conversational adjustments promote comprehensibility, and that comprehensibility promotes acquisition, it can be *deduced* that the adjustments promote acquisition.

At least two recent studies provide evidence for the first (adjustment — comprehensibility) relationship, Chaudron (1983) showing an effect for topic restatements, and Long (1983e) for global foreigner talk modifications of a 15-minute lecturette. Since, in my opinion, there already exists good evidence for the second (comprehensibility — acquisition) relationship, as indicated above, I consider that there *is* sufficient reason to posit a causal role for comprehensible input in SLA. Whether or not comprehensible input is *sufficient* to guarantee acquisition is still an open question, of course. Further, acceptance of a causal role for comprehensible input in SLA does not entail belief that instruction cannot have beneficial effects, such as by increasing the rate of learning (see Long, 1983f, for review), or on the acquisitional processes involved (Pica, 1983).

The last of Pienemann's arguments against the input hypothesis concerns the possible independent development and/or functioning, once developed, of comprehension and production capacities. While it is true that some have claimed that different *procedures* underlie these two abilities, there is, to my knowledge, no claim that the linguistic *knowledge* underlying the two sets of procedures is different. Thus, Bever (1981), for example, explicitly posits the existence of what he calls a "psychogrammar" (p.184) which, during language development, at least, underlies and mediates between the two *performance capacities*. He does go on to claim that the psychogrammar falls into disuse in linguistically mature adults, and also that comprehension and production function independently. This is not, however, the same as a claim that the knowledge underlying the two systems (apparently akin to performance grammars) is learned separately or twice.

The fact that children sometimes produce forms they do not comprehend is also not, as I see it, an argument against the "input hypothesis". The child data are entirely consistent with the idea that production is limited by the degree of comprehension at any point in time. No one has yet claimed that children (or adult SL learners) use forms they do not understand in a target-like manner, except accidentally when a transitional form happens to be the target form, as in the often cited *went – goed – went/hoped* sequence many English-speaking children exhibit. And Pienemann has been prominent among those SL researchers who have drawn attention to the fallacy of thinking that *appearance* of a form in an interlanguage implies *acquisition* of anything else than the form itself. (See, e.g. Meisel *et al.*, 1981.)

The "faulty logic" of Krashen's position

Pienemann is obviously right in saying that isolated structures *need* not be presented once only. So-called "spiral" and "cyclical" syllabuses attest to this. This does not, however, invalidate Krashen's claim that whether or not their (single or multiple) occurrence is appropriate for particular learners' stages of interlanguage development will be a "hit-or-miss" affair. Pienemann's proposal for better timing of presentations and/or recycling of structures really amounts to a claim that we can increase the chances of "hits". But as Krashen argues, I think quite correctly, why not provide *constant* opportunities for acquisition through the rough tuning that accompanies communication with non-native speakers?

I would also dispute Pienemann's claim that learners can be grouped by acquisitional stage for the purpose of instruction. Quite apart from the logistical problems involved (teacher expertize in recognizing stages, sufficient numbers of classes/groups into which to divide students, etc.), which are not problems with the proposal itself, the claim rests on a faulty assumption. This is that learners who are at the same acquisitional stage for one structure will be at the same, or at least nearly the same stage in other aspects of their interlanguage development.

At first sight, Stauble (1981) appears to provide evidence that this might indeed be the case, finding a relationship between ESL negation stage – (1) *no* V, (2) *don't* V, (3) aux. neg., (4) analyzed *don't* – and VP morphology in the interlanguages of six Japanese and six Spanish fossilized naturalistic acquirers. However, even if we assume (and I would not) that all grammatical sub-systems fossilize simultaneously — and, hence, that the 12 subjects' final attainment reflected previous parallel development of those subsystems — the result is limited in generalizability by the fact that English negation and aux. development (part of the VP morphology) are inevitably inter-related. Moreover, in a subsequent study, Lamotte *et al.* (1982) re-examined Stauble's data, along with data from six instructed Vietnamese learners, this time looking at negation stages and all 18 subjects' NP morphology (definite article, indefinite article, plural and possessive). A relationship between negation stage and NP morphology was found for the Spanish speakers only. In general, significant variation within stages, across stages and across languages indicated serious problems for a unidimensional SL continuum with negation as the single predictor.

The risk of premature fossilization after "natural" language teaching

Pienemann's third objection to Krashen's position *may* turn out to be valid, although he offers no evidence to support it, basing his claims on early fossilization of *naturalistic* GSL acquirers. In fact, however, Higgs & Clifford (1982) have suggested something very similar when speculating on possible causes of what they call the "terminal 2" phenomenon. This concerns motivated SL learners who seem unable to progress beyond a certain (roughly "intermediate") level of proficiency, even with the aid of intensive language instruction. Many (although not all) of these learners turn out to have experienced either sudden early immersion in a SL environment, with concomitantly high output demands, and/or "communicatively"-oriented language instruction at elementary proficiency levels, with little or no emphasis placed upon accuracy. What might be called Higgs and Clifford's "output hypothesis" proposes that early interlanguage production which satisfies communicative needs can be counter-productive in the long run, leading to early fossilization (stabilization?) of a system which is later difficult or impossible to change when the learners' needs become greater.

A similar case is reported by Schmidt (1981), who describes the limited acquisition of ESL by "Wes", a commercially successful, middle-class Japanese painter, an adult immigrant to the USA. Wes's development after five years has been limited, despite plenty of informal exposure to English with accompanying practice opportunities. Note that "Wes" and Higgs & Clifford's subjects have close to optimal social-psychological profiles in Pienemann's terms, being educated, motivated, upwardly mobile military or foreign service personnel, in the latter case, studying at the Defense Language Institute in Monterey, California. These individuals, in other words, are problematic *not only* for advocates of a pure diet of "natural" exposure/teaching.

The point is, however, that even *if* the risk of early fossilization turned out to be endemic to "natural" approaches to language teaching — and this has yet to be shown — it would not alone constitute a reason to abandon such teaching, and still less an argument for a structural syllabus. For either of these claims to be justified, it would have to be shown that the kind of syllabus Pienemann proposes prevents such fossilization, or that it does better than "natural sequencing". Lastly in this context, Pienemann's likening the case of SLA through "natural" language teaching to pidginogenesis is unwarranted, for the latter is characterized not only by the immediate use of simplified SL systems to satisfy basic communicative needs, but also by restricted (and often deviant) input.

In summary, Krashen's arguments against the structural syllabus do not seem to me to be invalidated by Pienemann's rebuttal. This does not mean, of course, that Krashen and Terrell's Natural Approach is the inevitable, or even *a* logical consequence of Krashen's position, or that I accept all aspects of the position itself. For example, Monitor Theory does not seem able to explain results of those studies which show an effect for instruction (with a focus on form) on the rate of SL development in both children and adults on both discrete point and integrative tests. Pienemann (1984) is an example of such a study. I have reviewed several others elsewhere (Long 1983f). Yet another is reported by Gass (1982).

Gass taught one group of adult ESL students relativization on the object of a preposition (OPREP) for three days' classes. OPREP is the fourth lowest in Keenan & Comrie's (1977) proposed universal hierarchy of relative clause formation. A control group received the same amount of instruction in relativization, starting from the highest (subject and object) positions in the hierarchy. Subjects' knowledge of any kind of relativization was minimal, as shown by pretests consisting of both grammaticality judgement and sentence-combining measures. Post-tests using the same measures produced two main findings of interest here: (i) overall scores (all relativization positions) of the experimental group had improved significantly on the grammaticality task, and (ii) on the sentence-combining task, both groups' post-test scores were significantly improved, the experimental group's scores being better not just on OPREP relatives, but also for relatives in all the higher positions in the accessibility hierarchy, i.e. those on which they had *not* received instruction, but which would be *implied* as known by subjects who now knew OPREP relativization. As in the Pienemann (1984) study, in other words, here is more evidence not only of the effect of instruction on rate of acquisition, but also of the generalizability of the effect to *other* constructions, at least where these are the implied terms in a markedness relationship.

As mentioned earlier in this chapter, the Natural Approach also shares a common problem with Pienemann's proposal in that it, too, attempts to resolve all programme design issues by dealing with just one of them (this time, methodology), ignoring others (this time, content). I would now like to outline a proposal which I think may go some way to breaking the circle. It is an approach I call "task-based" language teaching. For limitations of space, I can only offer the briefest sketch here. I hope, however, that this will suffice to illustrate the potential of a psycholinguistically based, integrated solution to both syllabus and methodological issues in SL teaching.

Task-based language teaching

The central idea in "task-based" language teaching is simple, but not, I hope, simplistic. It is that *task* is a meaningful and viable unit of analysis in all four of what I take to be the major issues in programme design:

  (i) identifying learners' needs,
  (ii) defining syllabus content,
  (iii) organizing language acquisition opportunities,
  (iv) measuring student achievement.

If "task" will serve in all these capacities, it should provide the basis for naturally compatible decisions at all stages in programme design and implementation.

In the present context, "task" has no more or less than its everyday meaning. I define it as a piece of work undertaken for oneself or for others, freely or for some reward. Thus, examples of tasks include painting a fence, dressing a child, filling out a form, buying a pair of shoes, making an airline reservation, borrowing a library book, taking a driving test, typing a letter, weighing a patient, sorting letters, taking a hotel reservation, writing a cheque, finding a street destination and helping someone across a road. In other words, by "task" is meant the hundred and one things people *do* in everyday life, at work, at play, and in between. "Tasks" are the things people will tell you they do if you ask them and they are not applied linguists. (The latter tend to see the world as a series of grammatical patterns or, more recently, notions and functions.)

Tasks in learner needs identification

As indicated above, for the purposes of learner needs identification, tasks have an initial advantage over linguistic units of analysis in that they are meaningful for participants. That is, tasks are the way non-linguists conceive what they do. People talk about the kind of day they have had that way, children play that way ("Let's go get some ice-cream"), job descriptions are written that way.

Ready-made job descriptions in task format abound. The Dictionary of Occupational Titles (U.S. Department of Labor, 1977), for example, includes several thousand. This is potentially invaluable to needs analysts, who are often required to investigate occupations which are completely foreign to them. Even when, as occasionally happens, the applied linguist also has professional training and/or experience in the field concerned, introspective analyses of its *linguistic* make-up turn out to be unreliable (Lamotte, 1981).

The applied linguistics literature is full of imaginative but time-consuming solutions to the analyst's problem of being an outsider. They include participant and non-participant observation (e.g. Jupp & Hodlin, 1975), interviews and questionnaires (e.g. Mackay, 1978), and the use of specialist informants to validate discourse analyses of scientific prose (Selinker, 1979). Even after employing procedures like these, however, materials writers usually feel the need to seek specialists' judgements as to the authenticity of the finished product, often only to be told that it is lacking.

In sum, needs identification is a notorious bottle-neck in the design of specific purpose language programmes. It is not only costly, in both time and money, but frequently ineffective. The basic problem is the applied linguist's (understandable) lack of expertise in the range of specialized occupational, academic and vocational domains s/he is confronted by. This situation is compounded by the typical procedure of attempting to carry out the analysis in linguistic terms, which are not the way participants think of what they do.

By way of contrast, analyses of the same fields in terms of the *tasks* involved has several advantages. Most obviously, it can sometimes circumvent the necessity (for applied linguists) to conduct needs analyses altogether, since adequate descriptions of many occupations already exist in task format. Where they do not, the fact that tasks have psychological reality for the people who are experts in the fields being analysed means that their specialist knowledge can be accessed directly and reliably.

Applied linguists can, of course, be expected to provide better *linguistic* analyses of the same fields. But this is only relevant if linguistic analyses are relevant. In language teaching circles, it is widely assumed that they are — presumably for the same reasons that it is widely assumed that language (or bits of language per lesson) should be the overt focus of language instruction. It is not a necessary assumption, however, and one that has yet to be justified either theoretically or empirically by those who routinely make it. (Showing that performance on isolated SL or interlingual structures can be accelerated by linguistically focused instruction is not, of course, such a justification, as discussed on pp.82–89.)

Towards a task syllabus

The purpose of a needs identification is to obtain information which will determine the content of a language teaching programme, i.e. to provide input for syllabus design. Inventories of tasks that result from the type of analysis described above are necessary for this purpose, but insufficient. They are only the raw data, and must be manipulated in various ways before they are transformed into a syllabus usable in classroom teaching. The steps in this procedure are as follows:

1. Conduct a needs analysis to obtain an inventory of *target tasks*.
2. Classify the target tasks into *task types*.
3. From the task types, derive *pedagogical tasks*.
4. Select and sequence the pedagogical tasks to form a *task syllabus*.

Let us call *target tasks* those tasks identified as required in order for an individual to function adequately in a particular target domain, be it occupational, vocational or academic. Inspection of lists of target tasks reveals that there is often considerable overlap among those required in different domains. Consider, for example, the following excerpts from two entries in the *Dictionary of Occupational Titles* (p.187):

222.387.038 *Parcel-Post Clerk* (clerical)
Wraps, inspects, weighs and affixes postage to parcel-post packages and records c.o.d. and insurance information. Wraps packages or inspects wrapping for conformance to company standards and postal regulations. Weighs packages and determines postage, using scale and parcel-post zone book ... May compute cost of merchandise, shipping fees, and other charges and bill customer. May sort parcels for shipment, according to destination or other classifications ... May fill orders from stock ...

222.387.050 *Shipping and Receiving Clerk* (clerical)
Verifies and keeps records on incoming and outgoing shipments and prepares items for shipment. Compares identifying information, and counts, weighs or measures items ... to verify against bills of lading, invoices, orders, or other records. Determines methods of shipment, utilizing knowledge of shipping procedures, routes and rates. Assembles wooden and cardboard containers ... Posts weights, shipping charges and affixes postage ...

The above are only excerpts from longer descriptions, and concern only two occupations, one traditionally in the public sector, one usually in the private sector. Yet even in rather different jobs like these, both inventories of target tasks include weighing items, determining the best or correct delivery route, calculating the cost of mailing/shipping, and affixing postage. For several reasons (see below), we will wish to classify target tasks into *task types*, superordinate categories, whose members share common characteristics, although differing in detail. Thus, the target tasks: "weigh a parcel" and "weigh a container" are obviously both examples of a task type: "weigh (an item)". Similarly, a railway ticket clerk "selling a train ticket" and a travel agent "selling an airline ticket" are both, at the level of task type, "selling tickets". And within a single occupation, a flight attendant who "serves breakfast", "serves lunch" and "serves dinner" (three target tasks), is performing one task type: "serving meal". (Note that target tasks are generally specified by verb plus NP, and task types by verb alone, or by verb plus generic NP.)

There are several reasons for classifying target tasks into task types. First, it is more cost-effective to teach a more general task type if it will transfer to several target tasks. Second, when faced with a class of occupationally somewhat heterogeneous learners, it will often be possible to work on a task type which is useful to all students, even though their target tasks may differ in some way(s). Working on one or more target tasks for a subset of the learners could be demotivating for others in the class.

A third reason for classifying target tasks into task types is to allow for the subsequent principled selection of *pedagogical tasks*, i.e. the tasks teachers and students will actually work on in the classroom, at least initially, until they are capable of tackling the full version of the target task. Note that, while necessary for various reasons given above, classification of target tasks into task types involves abstracting away from the level at which pieces of work are recognizable parts of real world activities. A railway ticket clerk, for example, does not "sell tickets" (task type); s/he "sells *train* tickets" (target task). Thus, constructing pedagogic activities around task types themselves would mean engaging students in opaque, decontextualized events whose internal structure and language requirements would no longer be verifiable. *Pedagogical tasks* handle this potential problem by providing a number of simplified, but transparent, concrete exponents of task types for classroom use. An example should serve to clarify the procedure.

Suppose it has been established that part of a railway ticket clerk's duties involve the service encounter in which the clerk sells train tickets to passengers (*target task*). Suppose it has also been established that other target tasks for these individuals (who will work at small, rural stations, where they are the sole staff member) include selling newspapers, cigarettes and candy to passengers, too. One *task type* of importance for this occupation is clearly "selling (items)". Assume that the learners are of only elementary SL proficiency. It would clearly be unreasonable for the materials designer (through the teacher) to set the students the task, perhaps through role-play, of "selling something". Without knowing who is selling what to whom, where, in what circumstances, there is no way for either students or teacher to know how the task can be accomplished. In an obvious way, for example, lexical items will be unpredictable. But more important than this, such factors as the existence of choice in the purchase (one train only to a single destination or several trains with differently priced seats, one brand of cigarettes or many, and so on) will determine such features of the conversation as who initiates, who controls topic choice and shift, how much need there is for precision, and whether clarifications and confirmations will be required. Where the encounter takes place (at the front of a line of commuters during rush-hour at a busy terminus, in the supermarket check-out line, or at the corner store on a quiet afternoon) will determine such things as the length and speed of the conversation, and its ease in terms of surrounding noise level, etc.

Pedagogical tasks, therefore, are necessary elements in the design of a *task syllabus*. The latter is simply the final sequence in which selected *pedagogical tasks* are presented to the classroom language learner. *Selection* of tasks is handled through ensuring that task types are adequately represented by the pedagogical tasks chosen. *Grading* is determined by the degree of difficulty of the pedagogical tasks themselves (from simple to complex), as well as such normal considerations as variety, pace and duration. "Difficulty", here, however, does not mean difficulty in terms of the linguistic demands of the full version of a given target task which indirectly motivated selection of a particular pedagogic task. Rather, it refers to the difficulty of pedagogical tasks in such aspects as the number of steps involved in their execution, the number of parties involved, the assumptions they make about presupposed knowledge, the intellectual challenge they pose, their location (or not) in displaced space and time, and so on. Thus, of two pedagogic tasks involving one person selling another an airline ticket, the version in which the ticket was the last available would be ordered, all other things being equal, before a situation in which several options were open, e.g. between aisle and window seats, and in smoking and non-smoking sections.

To summarize, the content of task-based language teaching is determined by a needs analysis of the tasks someone must be able to perform satisfactorily in order to function in a particular field. These *target tasks* are classified, at a more general and abstract level, into *task types*. From these are derived *pedagogical tasks*, which form the basis of classroom activities for teachers and students. Selection and grading of pedagogical tasks results in a *task syllabus*, which is the final specification of the "what" of a task-based language teaching programme.

Methodological issues: Language acquisition tasks

Like Krashen (1982 and elsewhere), I see the primary function of the SL classroom as being the provision of opportunities for natural SLA. These are difficult for learners to obtain elsewhere, not only in foreign language environments, where they are almost never available, but in second language situations, too. As Krashen has detailed, there is a limitless amount of SL input on the American street, but it is of little (probably no) use to the beginner for the simple reason that it is incomprehensible. (For literature supporting this position, I refer the reader to Krashen's work, and to references cited in pp.84–86 of this Chapter.)

Krashen and others have also documented the features of conversation which promote comprehensible input (see, e.g. Hatch, 1978; Krashen, 1982; Long, 1983c). Most important among these, as with caretaker speech, is that the parties be focused not on the language itself, but on communication. Krashen & Terrell have gone on to implement these insights, as they see them, in the Natural Approach.

As should by now be obvious, a course taught using the Natural Approach will differ from task-based language teaching in terms of its content. In the Natural Approach, the content of instruction will be defined by whatever teacher and students happen to talk about, and so runs the risk, incidentally, of being the same for all types of learner. In task-based language teaching, on the other hand, the content will be defined by a syllabus, which, as described earlier, will differ for different groups of learners, and do so in a principled fashion.

Where methodology is concerned, the Natural Approach and task-based language teaching share several features in common. Both approaches focus on communication, not form, and both attribute a central role to the provision, through communication, of large amounts of comprehensible input. Consequently, both approaches eschew error correction, and both accept interlingual forms from learners, (as would Pienemann, this volume).

Given the differences in content, however, there are one or two inevitable differences in the methodological domain, too. Primary among these is the question of sources of input. While the teacher is the basic source of target language data in the Natural Approach, the fact that often quite specialized learner needs are being addressed in task-based language teaching means that alternate sources must be provided, and may even predominate. Thus, utilizing traditional teacher resources, such as taped dialogues, original documents and simplified versions thereof, models of language use accompanying performance of target tasks will be provided to learners. There is nothing new in this, of course. Unlike traditional SL teaching, however, the purpose of such models is not to induce accurate replication by the learner. Rather, the models are to serve as a target towards which learners approximate, over time, as the pedagogic tasks the models accompany gradually increase in complexity until they attain full target difficulty. The focus throughout is resolution of the problems posed by the *pedagogic tasks* themselves, and learner success on these is judged by task accomplishment, not target-like linguistic production while achieving this.

Measuring learner achievement

Again due to space limitations, treatment of this topic must inevitably be superficial. Suffice to say that developments in criterion-referenced testing in the last decade hold great promise for language teaching in general, and for task-based language teaching in particular. The natural focus of such tests is whether or not students can perform some task to criterion, as established by experts in the field. The driving test is an example of a criterion-referenced test. Testees have to show they can manage a vehicle in traffic at a level of proficiency and safety accepted as necessary for the protection of other motorists and pedestrians. The testee is competing against an externally imposed criterion in this regard and passes or fails the examination regardless of how well other testees perform. It is simple to see how SL proficiency could be measured in the same way, namely by measuring the learner's ability to perform target tasks determined by specialists as appropriate for performance in a given domain.

Conclusion

A problem for applied linguists working on SL programme design is the tendency for developments in syllabus design and teaching methodology to occur independently of one another, and both independently of psycholinguistic research. The sketch of task-based language teaching is not offered as the solution to this problem. Instead, as stated earlier, it is provided as an example of what an integrated, psycholinguistically based solution might look like.

The description itself has, of necessity, been extremely brief and superficial. Any reader familiar with issues in syllabus design, for example, will have noticed that I have assiduously avoided discussion of several potential problems. These include the criteria to be applied in classifying *target tasks* into *task types*, and the related question of just how abstract task types can be before they become unusable in designing a syllabus. "Selling a ticket", for instance, is clearly an example of "selling something". At a higher level, we could also say it is an example of "selling". But if so, one can easily think of cases of "selling" which would look very different from the original target task ("selling a ticket"), both in the interactional and linguistic structure of the encounter (e.g. "selling an insurance policy"). Similar concerns arise over the need for a heuristic for deriving *pedagogic tasks* from *task types*. Also, how many criteria (other than those listed) are relevant in sequencing *pedagogic tasks*, and which (if any) preempt application of which others?

I do not yet have answers to all these questions, and so am not yet ready to advocate task-based language teaching as the, or even *a* solution to our professional needs. Working with several groups of students during the past three years, however, I have conducted some small-scale studies of some of them — principally studies involving native and non-native speaker dyads working on pedagogic tasks — and am reasonably confident that most are solvable. With other students, I have also recently worked on designing prototype task-based teaching materials (for children of limited English proficiency in Hawaii's public schools). This work, together with a far more explicit and detailed description of task-based language teaching, will appear in another paper (Long, in preparation).

Meanwhile, I think it wise to close on a note of caution. Like many others working in SLA research, I am excited by the progress made in such a short time (little more than 15 years). I am also confident that many, although by no means all of the issues in SL teaching can eventually be resolved by this work. I do not think, however, that anything like enough empirical studies have been done on (especially instructed) SLA — or in such areas as sociolinguistics and classroom processes — to support many of the implications and applications currently espoused in the literature. Further, I am anxious that hasty conclusions *not* be drawn, lest they turn out to be wrong, and lead teachers to become as sceptical about SLA research as they have (understandably) become about much writing on teaching methodology. When genuine solutions *are* available, it will be a pity if no one listens.

References

Andersen, R.W. 1983, The one to one principle of interlanguage construction. Paper presented at the 17th annual TESOL Convention, March 15–20, Toronto, Canada.

Bever, T.G. 1981, Normal acquisition processes explain the critical period for language learning. In K.C. Diller (ed.), *Individual Differences and Universals in Language Learning Aptitude*. Rowley, Mass.: Newbury House, 176–98.

Chaudron, C. 1983, Simplification of input: topic reinstatements and their effects on L2 learners' comprehension. *TESOL Quarterly* 17, 3, September, 437–58.

Clahsen, H. 1984, The acquisition of German word order: a test case for cognitive approaches to second language acquisition. In R.W. Andersen (ed.), *Second Languages*. Rowley, Mass. 219–42.

Felix, S.W. 1981, The effect of formal instruction on second language acquisition. *Language Learning* 31, 1, 87–112.

Forster, K.I. 1979, Levels of processing and the structure of the language processor. In W. Cooper & E. Walker (eds), *Sentence Processing: Psycholinguistic studies presented to Merril Garrett*. New York: Halsted.

Gaies, S.J. 1977, The nature of linguistic input in formal second language learning: linguistic and communicative strategies in teachers' classroom language. In H.D. Brown, C.A. Yorio & R.H. Crymes (eds), *On TESOL '77*. Washington, D.C.: TESOL, 204–12.

—— 1983, The investigation of language classroom processes. *TESOL Quarterly* 17, 2, June, 205–17.

Gass, S. 1982, From theory to practice. In M. Hines & W. Rutherford (eds), *On TESOL '81*. Washington, D.C.: TESOL, 129–39.

—— 1983, Interlanguage syntax state of the art: language transfer and language universals. Paper presented at the 17th annual TESOL Convention, March 15–20, Toronto, Canada.

Hatch, E.M. 1978, Discourse analysis and second language acquisition. In E.M. Hatch (ed.), *Second Language Acquisition: a book of readings*. Rowley, Mass.: Newbury House, 402–35.

Jupp, T. & Hodlin, S. 1975, *Industrial English: an example of theory and practice in functional language teaching*. London: Heinemann.

Higgs, T.V. & Clifford, R. 1982, The push toward communication. In T.V. Higgs (ed.), *Curriculum, Competence, and the Foreign Language Teacher*. Skokie, Illinois: National textbook Co., 57–79.

Keenan, E. & Comrie, B. 1977, Noun phrase accessibility and universal grammar. *Linguistic Inquiry*, 8, 63–100.

Krashen, S.D. 1977, Some issues relating to the monitor model. In H.D. Brown, C.A. Yorio & R.L. Crymes (eds), *On TESOL '77*. Washington, D.C.: TESOL, 144–58.

—— 1982, *Principles and Practice in Second Language Acquisition*, New York: Pergamon.

Lamotte, J. 1981, English for specific purposes: consulting the experts. Term paper, Ed. 570, University of Pennsylvania.

Lamotte, J., Pearson-Joseph, D. & Zupko, K. 1982, A cross-linguistic study of the relationships between negation stages and the acquisition of noun phrase morphology. Term paper, Ed. 676, University of Pennsylvania.

Long, M.H. 1981, Input, interaction, and second language acquisition. In H. Winitz (ed.), *Native Language and Foreign Language Acquisition. Annals of the New York Academy of Sciences* 379, 259–78.

—— 1982, Adaption an den Lerner. *Zeitschrift für Literaturwissenschaft und Linguistik* 45, 100–19.

—— 1983a, Native speaker/non-native speaker conversation in the second language classroom. In M.A. Clarke & J. Handscombe (eds), *On TESOL '82.* Washington, D.C.: TESOL, 207–25.

—— 1983b, Input and second language acquisition theory. Paper presented at the 10th annual Michigan Conference on Applied Linguistics, October 28–30, Ann Arbor, Michigan.

—— 1983c, Native speaker/non-native speaker conversation and the negotiation of comprehensible input. *Applied Linguistics* 4, 2, Summer, 126–41.

—— 1983d, Linguistic and conversational adjustments to non-native speakers. *Studies in Second Language Acquisition* 5, 2. 177–93.

—— 1983e, The effect of speech adjustments on non-native speaker comprehension of a lecturette. Ms. University of Hawaii at Manoa.

—— 1983f, Does second language instruction make a difference? A review of research. *TESOL Quarterly* 17, 3, September, 359–82.

—— In preparation, Task-based language teaching. Ms. University of Hawaii at Manoa.

Long, M.H. & Sato, C.J. 1983, Classroom foreigner talk discourse: forms and functions of teachers' questions. In H.W. Seliger & M.H. Long (eds), *Classroom-Oriented Research on Second Language Acquisition.* Rowley, Mass.: Newbury House, 1983, 268–286.

Mackay, R. 1978, Identifying the nature of the learner's needs. In R. Mackay & A. Mountford (eds), *English for Specific Purposes.* London: Longman, 21–42.

McLaughlin, B. 1978, The Monitor Model: some methodological considerations. *Language Learning* 28, 2, 309–32.

Meisel, J. 1982, Reference to past events and actions in the development of natural second language acquisition. Paper presented at the 2nd European-North American Cross-Linguistic Second Language Acquisition Workshop, Göhrde, West Germany.

Meisel, J., Clahsen, H. & Pienemann, M. 1981, On determining developmental stages in natural second language acquisition. *Studies in Second Language Acquisition*, 3, 2, 109–35.

Nicholas, H. & Meisel, J. 1983, Second language acquisition: the state of the art. In H. Wode & S. Felix (eds), *Language Development at the Crossroads.* Tübingen: Gunter Narr, 63–89.

Pica, T. 1983, Adult acquisition of English as a second language in different language contexts. *Language Learning* 33, 4, 465–97.

Pienemann, M. 1984, Psychological constraints on the teachability of languages. *Studies in Second Language Acquisition*, 6, 186–214.

Schmidt, R.W. 1981, Interaction, acculturation and the acquisition of communicative competence: a case study. University of Hawaii *Working Papers in Linguistics*, 13, 3, September–December, 297–77.

Schumann, J.H. 1978, *The Pidginization Process. A Model for Second Language Acquisition.* Rowley, Mass.: Newbury House.

Selinker, L. 1979, On the use of informants in discourse analysis and "Language for specialized purposes". *International review of Applied Linguistics* 17, 2, 189–215.

Stauble, A.M. 1981, A comparative study of Spanish-English and Japanese-English continuum: verb phrase morphology. Unpublished Ph.D. dissertation in applied linguistics. Los Angeles: University of California.

Swaffer, J., Arens, K. & Morgan, M. 1982, Teacher classroom practices: redefining method as task hierarchy. *Modern Language Journal* 66, 1, 24–33.

Wilkins, D.A. 1976, *Notional Syllabuses. A taxonomy and its relevance to foreign language curriculum development.* Oxford: Oxford University Press.

Wode, H. 1981, *Learning a Second Language. Vol. 1. An Integrated View of Language Acquisition.* Tübingen: Gunter Narr.

4 Can language acquisition be altered by instruction?

PATSY M. LIGHTBOWN

Concordia University, Montreal, Canada

Researchers in both first and second language acquisition have claimed for several years that one cannot teach a learner what he is not ready to learn (e.g. Braine, 1971; Corder, 1967; Krashen, 1982). And, as Pienemann (this volume, Chapter 2) has pointed out, the recommendations for language teaching based on this claim have ranged from proposals which establish teaching sequences on the basis of observed "natural sequences" in acquisition (early papers by Krashen) to proposals which renounce entirely a language-based (i.e. grammar- or structure-based) curriculum in favour of one which is "content-based" and which leaves the acquisition of linguistic form and structure to take care of itself (see Newmark, 1966, for an early recommendation).

Pienemann has proposed pedagogical recommendations which appear to avoid these extremes. On the basis of his research and that of others, he concludes that some aspects of language are variable in their patterns of emergence and mastery while others follow apparently "universal" developmental patterns in a given L2. According to Pienemann, those aspects of language which exhibit variable patterns may be taught at any point in the developmental cycle. Presumably the usual pedagogical principles of careful introduction, practice, and review would apply. On the other hand, aspects of language which appear to have universal patterns of development can be *taught* most successfully if they are presented in a sequence which respects the "natural sequences" observed in the L2 acquisition of learners who do not receive formal instruction. At the same time Pienemann does not suggest that the learner's input be

101

restricted to the forms he is "ready" for, but only that one should provide instructional focus on linguistic structures in the order in which they have been observed to be acquired.

Pienemann's proposals for syllabus construction are intriguing and important, and I applaud his attempt to bring to bear on language teaching the knowledge we have gained in the last fifteen years of language acquisition research. However, I have some questions regarding details of his proposals, based on some reservations or perhaps on differences of interpretation, some of which will be discussed below. Even if I had no questions about these details of Pienemann's proposal, I would still wish to emphasize the need for caution in attempting to apply directly to teaching the knowledge we currently have of L2 acquisition. I believe we should be careful not to promise another "scientific approach" to language teaching. The danger lies in the possibility that practitioners will adopt again — not a renewed openness to the learners' needs, but a new rigidity which would run counter to the expressed intention: teaching L2 learners what they are ready to learn.

Significantly, in his 1984 paper, Pienemann himself has argued against such rigidity, and I do not mean to suggest that he has now taken such a stand. Rather, it is the history of language teaching, with its frequent shifts to new "bandwagons", which makes me pessimistic about getting practitioners to adopt the *spirit* rather than the *letter* of proposals such as Pienemann's.

Before I proceed, I should quickly state that I agree with Pienemann that we should not "abandon teaching". The title chosen for this paper may not make that clear. And it is true that when I first chose the title "Can language acquisition be altered by instruction?" I intended it to reflect the conclusion, drawn from my own research, that much language teaching is ineffective or even counter-productive — actually frustrating the process of language acquisition rather than serving it. In this research, we observed adolescent learners whose principal exposure to L2 was in the classrooms where they were taught English as a second language for 30 to 60 minutes per day. In these classes, the learners heard and practised certain language forms — correct grammatical forms, of course — dozens or even hundreds of times. In class and, for a period of time, outside of class, they appeared to "know" these forms in the sense that they used them correctly in appropriate contexts. Later however, some of these "correct" forms disappeared from the learners' language and were replaced by simpler or developmentally "earlier" forms. For example, learners who had correctly inflected verbs with the progressive *-ing* began producing verbs with no inflections (Lightbown 1982, 1983a,b). After a period, the correct use of *-ing* increased slowly, eventually coming close to the earlier levels of accuracy.[1] We hypothesized that, had these learners been exposed to English in an environment where there was a wider variety of language forms in the input and where there was less pressure to practise correct forms, the learners would have used the base forms — the uninflected verbs — in their earliest utterances, adding the grammatical inflections at a later developmental stage. In this sense, it could be argued that their development had been slowed down by the too-early insistence on correct production of certain language forms which would be expected to come later in a "natural sequence".

The tentative recommendation with which we concluded our reports on the research described above was that the insistence on practice of correct forms be replaced by a greater emphasis on providing learners with a variety of language in meaningful and motivating contexts. This recommendation deals, in Pienemann's terms, with "teaching methods" rather than "grading", and there were several reasons for making this recommendation rather than one which would derive more specifically from what we know about acquisition sequences.

First, the emphasis on meaningful and motivating contexts is based on the observation that there was an urgent need to (re)capture the students' attention and to challenge them to make some effort to become more involved in their own language acquisition. They had come to expect a degree of "spoon-feeding" and short-term correction which removed the motivation to be truly engaged in the language learning process.

Second, I believe we are still at too early a stage in our understanding of how natural acquisition sequences can or should be related to teaching sequences to make specific recommendations for "grading" or sequencing — even if we accept the claim that considerably more progress has been made for German than for English as a second language (see Lightbown, 1985).

A third reason for not having made recommendations on "grading", brings me to one of the specific points on which I question Pienemann's proposals. It has not been demonstrated that it is to the learner's advantage to have language material presented in the order in which we have observed these structures are acquired outside classroom-settings. Indeed, there are at least two kinds of evidence to suggest that this may not be the case: (1) We know that learners in "natural environments" are exposed to a rich and varied linguistic input containing many forms and structures which they will not acquire for many months or years. Furthermore, no two learners can be said to receive the same input in natural settings. And yet, acquisition sequences are quite similar across learners.[2] (2) Recent research carried out from the perspective of linguistic markedness has suggested that, while learners exposed (in an instructional setting) to unmarked forms may learn these forms, they will not be able to generalize to the marked forms within the same linguistic structure. On the other hand, learners who are taught marked forms appear to be able to generalize to the unmarked forms. (Gass, 1982; Zobl, 1983, 1985). In these studies, markedness was defined at least partly in terms of natural acquisition sequences where the acquisition or correct use of marked forms implied the prior acquisition and use of the unmarked forms (see also Hyltenstam, 1982).[3]

The findings on markedness appear to differ from those of Piene-mann (1984 and this volume) who concludes that learners cannot success-fully be taught structures which are more than one stage removed from their own developmental stage. The research in this domain is far from conclusive, of course, and the studies are all quite "short-term" in evaluating effects of instruction. And it is important to point out that these experimental studies provided intensive short-term input to learners with considerable exposure to the language — not to learners whose only exposure was a systematic classroom presentation of these structures. Nevertheless, such research draws attention to the tentativeness of our knowledge of what kind of input learners can use in the development of their own linguistic systems.

Another question I have regarding Pienemann's proposals is one which he anticipated: Even if we accept that it is appropriate to organize teaching in terms of natural sequences, do we know enough about acquisition sequences to permit us to plan such teaching programmes? I would certainly answer in the negative for English and for French; Pienemann answers in the affirmative for German. Even for German, however, there is a great deal of information missing. For example, the influence of L1 is still under-researched. By far the greatest amount of information available comes from learners whose L1 was a romance language. (see Pienemann's Table from Nicholas & Meisel, 1983). It may indeed prove to be the case that learners from other L1 backgrounds will fall neatly into place. But this is an empirical question which must be addressed if teaching programmes are intended to be usable in other settings.

An example of how apparently universal sequences may be affected by L1 is reported in a paper by Mace-Matluck (1979). Every previously (and subsequently) published English morpheme acquisition study has reported that the plural *s* is acquired before the possessive *s*. But in Mace-Matluck's study of a very large number of learners of English L2, aged 5–10, only the Spanish L1 group conformed to the predicted plural-before-possessive order. Learners from the three remaining L1 groups in her study (Ilokano, Tagalog, Cantonese), acquired the possessive first and maintained higher performance on the possessive through all the proficiency and age levels. In her discussion, Mace-Matluck suggests how the structure of the learners' first language could have predisposed them to seek or at least to recognize a possessive inflection on nouns in English. To further complicate the picture, there is considerable evidence that different L1 structures may affect the L2 at different developmental points and with different degrees of persistence — according to similarities and differences in L1 and L2. (See for example, Zobl, 1980 a,b; Gass, 1984; Schachter, 1974; Andersen, 1983; Wode, 1977, 1981).

Furthermore, even if every currently described sequence were completely and universally correct, we would still be left with a syllabus sufficient to cover — at most — the first few months of language teaching. Where to go from there? Do we assume that the learner would now be ready to "sink or swim"? If not, and there is no evidence that Pienemann's proposals are meant to be relevant for only the earliest phases of language instruction, what would be the next teaching phase? Current L1 and L2 acquisition research which is conducted from the perspective of linguistic theory always impresses us not only with the complexity of the learner's task but with the researcher's task as well. In many cases we have not even had a very good idea of what to look for because our own knowledge of the structure of both the L2 and the learners' L1 is itself so restricted (see Felix, 1982 and White, 1983 for discussion).

A further practical question arises with regard to the proposal that language structures be presented and taught following natural sequences: How do we teach a whole class? Pienemann's suggestion (p.48) that learners be "grouped according to stages of acquisition" appears to be naïve both pedagogically and psycholinguistically. The pedagogical problem of grouping learners is in fact well known to Pienemann who, in his own research (Pienemann, 1984), found the task of sampling and analysing learners' language for subsequent selection of subject groups a formidable one. From the psycholinguistic point of view, the question which comes immediately to mind is "how long would the groups remain homogeneous?"[4] For, as sure as we are that some natural sequences exist, we are equally sure that there can be dramatic differences in rate of acquisition. Thus, a class which is homogeneous in October will be heterogeneous in December (see also Nicholas, this volume, Chapter 8).

As I said earlier in this Chapter, I do not propose that we "abandon teaching". Language teaching can affect language acquisition. I am convinced of that, but I must acknowledge that my conviction is based largely on intuition — and a certain educational conservatism. In his recent review of research on the effect of second language instruction, Long (1983) pointed out the paradox in the fact that, as language teachers, we seek to "improve" language teaching methodology, thus assuming that what we teach determines or at least strongly influences what is learned. The paradox lies in the fact that there has been little research to support — and some evidence to refute — the underlying assumption that instruction has any effect on the path and rate of L2 acquisition for learners who also have informal exposure to the language. For learners without informal exposure, the effect of instruction could lie simply — or mainly — in the opportunity to hear the target language used in contexts which make it meaningful and comprehensible rather than in the systematic instruction in the language itself (Krashen, 1982, Chapter 4).

Long's review of the effect-of-instruction research led him to conclude that, in general, instruction *does* have a positive effect. That is, in studies where learners' out-of-class exposure to the language was comparable, those who received (more) instruction were more proficient in the language.[5] However, as Long has been careful to show, the advantages of instruction have been documented principally through the use of tests. And even though both so-called "discrete point" and "integrative" tests seem to point to the same conclusions, most language acquisition researchers would be reluctant to equate test results with all aspects of language knowledge and use. No doubt, part of the advantage of instruction lies in making learners better test-takers — for all kinds of tests. Long did not address, in his review, the question of whether one *kind* of instruction is more effective than another, a question which could not have been answered on the basis of the research he reviewed. Nor could Long's review address specific questions of *how* instruction increased proficiency or whether all individuals benefited equally from instruction relative to exposure. We are still, in fact, quite far from having sufficient empirical evidence to answer such questions. Long ends his review with a list of fundamental questions which have by no means received satisfactory answers:

1. Does (second language) instruction make a difference?

2. Does type of instruction make a difference?

3. Does type of learner make a difference?

4. Does type of instruction interact with type of learner? (Long, 1983: 380).

Thus, even though many second language acquisition researchers agree (on the basis of research evidence or their own introspection) that language teaching does — at least in some cases — positively affect acquisition, we do now know *how*.

One explanation for the positive effectiveness of instruction is no doubt the one suggested by Pienemann's paper: Sometimes the instructional material matches that (those) element(s) of language which would come next on the learner's developmental agenda.[6] Perhaps, by happy accident, or intuition developed through experience, teachers manage to hit this target with some frequency.

Another way in which teaching may be helpful is in terms of Krashen's comprehensible input hypothesis. Krashen (1982) has suggested that the classroom may be the only place where the learner, particularly at the beginning stages, can find someone to talk to him in language that he can understand (because of the linguistic or non-linguistic context) and which contains what Krashen calls "i + 1", linguistic forms which are at a level one step beyond the learner's current developmental stage (Krashen, 1982, Chapter 4). The difference between Krashen and Pienemann appears *not* to be in their views of *what* the learner needs in order to progress but in *how* it should be provided. Both agree, it seems, that what Krashen calls i + 1 is what is required, but while Pienemann wishes to see something equivalent to i + 1 operationally defined and its content explicitly incorporated into teaching programmes, Krashen recommends that the instructional setting provide meaningful, comprehensible input which will, in his view, automatically include appropriate (i + 1) input.

Another crucial element of Krashen's hypothesis is that of the "affective filter" (a notion for which he always gives credit to H. Dulay & M. Burt). According to the "affective filter" hypothesis, learners will not be able to "use" comprehensible input at i + 1 if they are for some reason not receptive to the language learning opportunity (Krashen, 1982). Boredom in a classroom would surely tend to "raise" the filter. In this case, the most carefully worked out programme of language teaching based on developmental sequences could be sabotaged. This suggests further reason to be cautious in proposing a teaching programme based on the *what* ("grading", in Pienemann's terms) of second language acquisition without carefully considering the *how* (what Pienemann calls "teaching methods").

Another proposal for how instruction may aid acquisition is that it provides learners opportunities to focus on particular elements of language, recognize and tag them, even practise using them in a deliberate (controlled) manner (see, e.g. Bialystok, 1978, 1981; McLaughlin, 1978). Although Krashen sees the role of such formal instruction as minimal, this proposal may, in fact, be compatible with Krashen's view in that formal, controlled practice makes it possible for learners later to recognize (and thus *understand*) these elements in the L2 input they encounter. That is, even if we accept that developmental sequences of acquisition generally override the sequences imposed by formal instruction in terms of what the learner actually incorporates and in what sequence, formal instruction may provide "hooks", points of access for the learner. That is, a certain amount of information *about* the language together with contextual cues — may make it possible for the learner to understand the L2 samples he is exposed to, making the input comprehensible, thus available for language acquisition processing.

For learners who are literate, of course, instruction tends also to offer increased access to comprehensible input which includes elements of Krashen's i + 1 through reading. Certainly literate learners without instruction may also choose to read in the L2, but instructional materials have the potential for providing input which is ready at the convenience of the learner and is at a more appropriate level than input the learner might happen upon outside a classroom. The value of reading as communicative comprehensible input has long been emphasized — albeit from different theoretical perspectives (see, for example, West, 1941, Widdowson, 1978, as well as Krashen, 1982).

Again, for learners who are literate and accustomed to formal instruction, formal instruction may be useful by alerting learners to the regularities of patterning in the language. From Krashen's point of view (in terms of his Monitor Theory) such instruction — aimed at least in part at developing metalinguistic awareness— would not help the learner very much except under discrete point test conditions, and then only if the learner "knows the rule" (Krashen, 1981). However, there is evidence to suggest that learners have multiple levels of metalinguistic awareness and that even learners who are illiterate may be able to shift to more formal — or more native like — usage when they are thinking about the language, focussing on correctness, even if they cannot articulate the rule(s) they are varying (Trévise & Noyau, 1984).

For learners who are not literate, the classroom can provide both modified input (language which is at least approximately appropriate to the learner's level) and modified interaction, (opportunities for the negotiation of meaning) which may be difficult for certain learners — for reasons of social isolation or discrimination — to find outside of classroom.[7]

Following what may appear to be lengthy challenge to Pienemann's proposal, I should emphasize there is considerable agreement between us. In reading his summary of the guidelines he proposes (p.63), I find no disagreement on two of the three guidelines: (2) ... do not introduce deviant forms; (3) the general input may contain structures ... not introduced for production. It is in the *interpretation* of his first general guideline. (Do not demand a learning process which is impossible at a given stage, i.e. order of teaching objectives (should) be in line with stages of acquisition), that I foresee the difficulties I have discussed above. If the guideline were re-worded to say "Do not expect or require that learners perform accurately on linguistic structures which are beyond their current developmental stage (for example, we know that learners will not master 'INVERSION rules in German before they have acquired rules for ADVERB PREPOSING ...')", then I think we would be completely in agreement. As I understand it, however, my proposed rewording is not simply a rewording but represents a fundamental difference between my view and Pienemann's view of how our present knowledge gained from language acquisition research can be applied to classroom teaching. While I see the application of our current knowledge principally in terms of being able to tell teachers, testers, and programme planners what to *expect* learners to do in certain situations, Pienemann is ready to make some more explicit recommendations about what practitioners should *do*. For all the reasons discussed above, I fear that this could lead to frustration and then to a too-early rejection of the valuable contribution language acquisition research can make to L2 teaching.

I see Pienemann's proposal for grading as a proposal for future research rather than as a proposal for pedagogical action. The kind of research which needs to be done includes that which Pienemann himself has already begun, namely, investigating the effect of teaching specific aspects of language to learners at different development stages (Pienemann, 1984). In addition, related research should be carried out, in which the same linguistic content is taught to learners judged to be at the same developmental stage but using different teaching methods.

The list of areas where research needs to be done and the various research designs appropriate to disambiguating the results would be long indeed. Nevertheless, we must continue to carry out well-designed research — both "pure" and "applied" — in language acquisition if we are to be truly helpful to language teachers and learners.

Notes to Chapter 4

1. A similar phenomenon, referred to as "u-shaped development", that is, early accuracy followed by an increase in error and subsequent improvement to the earlier level, is observed in natural language acquisition as well (see Kellerman, 1985, for L2; Bowerman, 1982, for L1). In the classroom environment which restricts the learner's input to certain forms in isolation, early accuracy on a limited number of forms does not prevent subsequent errors based on more knowledge.
2. I am aware of suggestions in the literature that acquisition sequences are positively correlated with frequency in the input (Larsen-Freeman, 1976), and I have observed in my own research that items with extremely low frequency in the input appear to be late- or never- acquired (Lightbown, 1980, 1982). However, there is considerable evidence that input frequency cannot satisfactorily predict acquisition sequences in L1 (Brown, 1973) and for L2, we are all aware of high frequency items in the input which are for a long time not incorporated in interlanguage systems (Harley, 1982; Lightbown, 1983b).
3. Markedness need not be thus defined, of course, and for some structures, the presence of so-called marked forms may not imply the presence of the related unmarked forms.
4. Long (this volume, Chapter 3) points out a related problem — that we have very little evidence to suggest that learners who are at the same "stage" in one structural area can be assumed to be at the same "stage" in others. Pienemann has done considerable work in this area, but much remains to be done (see Pienemann, this volume, Chapter 2).
5. Here I have collapsed several categories which Long treated separately.
6. I leave aside for this part of the discussion the question of how "variable" elements of language would be affected by instruction and refer only to those Pienemann would consider developmental, and thus "universal" in terms of acquisition sequences.
7. See Long (1981) for discussion of the possible roles of modified input and modified interaction in second language acquisition and Long (1985) for an experimental study of the effect modified interaction on comprehension in a classroom setting.

References

Andersen, R. 1983, Transfer to somewhere. In S. Gass & L. Selinker (eds), *Language transfer in language learning*. Rowley, Mass: Newbury House.
Bialystok, E. 1978, A theoretical model of second language learning. *Language Learning*, 28, 60–83.
—— 1981, Some evidence for the integrity and interaction of two knowledge sources. In R. Andersen (ed.), *New dimensions in second language acquisition research*. Rowley, Mass.: Newbury House.
Bowerman, M. 1982, Starting to talk worse. Clues to language acquisition from children's late speech errors. In S. Strauss (ed.), *U-shaped behavioral growth*. New York: Academic Press.
Braine, M. 1971, On two types of models of the internalization of grammars. In

D.I. Slobin (ed.), *The ontogenesis of grammar: some facts and several theories*. New York: Academic Press.

Brown, R. 1973, *A first language*. Cambridge, Mass.: Harvard University Press.

Corder, S.P. 1967, The significance of learners' errors. *IRAL*, 5, 161–70.

Felix, S.W. 1982, What you always wanted to know about cognition and language development. Paper presented at the Second European-North American Workshop on Cross-Linguistic Second Language Research. Göhrde, West Germany.

Gass, S. 1982, From theory to practice. In M. Hines & W. Rutherford (eds), *On TESOL '81*, Washington, D.C.: TESOL.

—— 1984, Language transfer and language universals. *Language Learning*, 34, 115–32.

Harley, B. 1982, Age-related differences in the acquisition of the French verb system by anglophone students in French immersion programmes. Ph.D. thesis, University of Toronto.

Hyltenstam, K. 1982, Markedness, language universals, language typology and second language acquisition. Paper presented at the Second European-North American Workshop on Cross-Linguistic Second Language Research. Göhrde, West Germany. August.

Kellerman, E. 1985, U-shaped behaviour in advanced Dutch EFL learners. In S. Gass & C. Madden (eds), *Input in second language acquisition*. Rowley, Mass.: Newbury House.

Krashen, S.D. 1981, *Second language acquisition and second language learning*. Oxford: Pergamon Press.

—— 1982, *Principles and practice in second language acquisition*. Oxford: Pergamon Press.

Larsen-Freeman, D.E. 1976, An explanation for the morpheme acquisition order of second language learners. *Language Learning*, 26, 125–34.

Lightbown, P.M. 1980, The acquisition and use of questions by French L2 learners. In S. Felix (ed.) *Second language development: trends and issues*. Tübingen: Gunter Narr Verlag.

—— 1982, Classroom language as input to second language acquisition. Paper presented at the Second European-North American Workshop on Second Language Acquisition Research. Göhrde, West Germany. August.

—— 1983a, Exploring relationships between developmental and instructional sequences in L2 acquisition. In H. Seliger & M. Long (eds), *Classroom oriented research in second language acquisition*. Rowley, Mass.: Newbury House.

—— 1983b, Acquiring English L2 in Quebec classrooms. In S. Felix & H. Wode (eds), *Language development at the crossroads*. Tübingen: Gunter Narr Verlag.

—— 1985, Great expectations: second language acquisition research and classroom teaching. *Applied Linguistics*, 6, 2, 74–90.

Long, M. 1981, Variation in linguistic input for second language acquisition. Paper presented at the European-North American Workshop on Cross-Linguistic Second Language Acquisition Research, Lake Arrowhead, California.

—— 1983, Does second language instruction make a difference? A review of research. *TESOL Quarterly*, 17, 359–82.

—— 1985, Input and second language acquisition theory. In S. Gass & C. Madden (eds), *Input in second language acquisition*. Rowley, Mass.: Newbury House.

McLaughlin, B. 1978, The monitor model: some methodological considerations. *Language Learning*, 28, 309–32.

Mace-Matluck, B.J. 1979, The order of acquisition of English structures by

Spanish-speaking children: some possible determinants. In R. Andersen (ed.), *The acquisition and use of Spanish and English as first and second languages.* Washington: TESOL.

Newmark, L. 1966, How not to interfere with language learning. *International Journal of Applied Linguistics*, 32, 77–83.

Nicholas, H. & Meisel, J. 1983, Second language acquisition: the state of the art. In S. Felix & H. Wode (eds), *Language development at the crossroads.* Tübingen: Gunter Narr Verlag.

Pienemann, M. 1984, Psychological constraints on the teachability of languages. *Studies in Second Language Acquisition*, 6, 186–214.

Schachter, J. 1974, An error in error analysis. *Language Learning*, 24, 205–14.

Trévise, A. & Noyau, C. 1984. Adult Spanish speakers and the acquisition of French negation forms: Individual variation and linguistic awareness. In R. W. Andersen (ed.), *Second language acquisition: a cross-linguistic perspective.* Rowley, Mass.: Newbury House.

West, M. 1941, *Learning to read in a foreign language.* London: Longman.

White, L. 1983, Markedness and parameter setting: some implications for a theory of adult second language acquisition. Paper presented at the 12th Annual University of Wisconsin-Milwaukee Linguistic Symposium. March.

Widdowson, H.G. 1978, *Teaching language as communication.* Oxford: Oxford University Press.

Wode, H. 1977, On the systematicity of L1 transfer in L2 acquisition. In C. Henning (ed.), *Proceedings of the Los Angeles Second Language Research Forum.*

—— 1981, *Learning a second language: an integrated view of language acquisition.* Tübingen: Gunter Narr Verlag.

Zobl, H. 1980a, Developmental and transfer errors: their common bases and (possibly) differential effects on subsequent learning. *TESOL Quarterly*, 14, 469–79.

—— 1980b, The formal and developmental selectivity of L1 influence on L2 acquisition. *Language Learning*, 30, 43–57.

—— 1983, Primary data and learners' rule projections. Paper presented at the Seventeenth Annual TESOL Convention, Toronto, March.

—— 1985, Grammars in search of input and intake.

5 L2 learners' variable output and language teaching

KENNETH HYLTENSTAM

University of Stockholm, Sweden

Introduction

Researchers in the area of second language acquisition are often asked how their findings are applicable to second or foreign language teaching. This is, of course, a very natural and relevant question. Knowledge from the area of acquisition, it seems, must have a bearing on the practice of teaching. The problem is however, that the researchers are not always able to tell exactly in what ways the results of particular studies should be applied to teaching. One can wonder why this is so, and why researchers must so frequently disappoint teachers and others by not giving them answers that seem concrete and detailed.

I can think of several reasons for this, two of which are the following: Firstly, the question assumes that research into second language acquisition or foreign language learning is, in fact, the same thing as research into second or foreign language teaching. Although it may seem so, if one considers the common situation where the language learner gets instruction in a classroom, this is of course by no means the case. Given the results from second language acquisition research, the researcher and the layman or teacher alike are confronted with the same question: What are the implications of these results for teaching? And in most cases, the answer of this question cannot just be given straight away, but must be found in teaching practice, in controlled teaching experiments, and in methodological research within the area of second language teaching in general.

A second reason why the researcher might not be so concrete in his answers is that he may not have considered in detail how the results of a particular study are applicable to teaching. And this may be quite legitimate, for second language acquisition research does not have as its only aim to be directly applicable to second language teaching, i.e. the questions that are asked are not always derived from the teaching problems. If this were the case, the second language researcher's often open-ended answers would seem remarkable, indeed. The central aim of second language acquisition research is to gain as many insights into the phenomenon of second language acquisition as possible. As such, the area is self contained and parallel to other areas of research, where researchers try to enlarge our knowledge in order to understand various phenomena in the world around us. In this respect, the results are applicable at a very general level, in that such understanding should be the basis for *each individual's creative acting*, rather than the basis for detailed prescriptions for action in specified situations. Thus, knowledge about second language acquisition at a general level — along with various other types of knowledge — should open up a number of alternatives for acting, for example in the language classroom, that may be hidden without such knowledge.

Besides this central aim of understanding second language acquisition as such, there is also the broader aim of understanding the principles governing human language and human linguistic functioning in general. During the last ten years, second language acquisition research has gained wider importance in the investigation of these questions (cf. Wode, 1981).

Application of second language acquisition research at two levels

In this perspective, the direct applicability to second language teaching of second language acquisition research is one of a number of aims in the area. I think the applicability issue can be looked upon at two levels. At a very *specific* and narrow level, we would like to be able to say: "Given fact x about the phenomenon of acquisition, do y in teaching." For example, we would like to be able to state in what cases and to what extent acquisitional sequences that have been established in second language acquisition research should be followed in the teacher's presentation of the language or in the grading of textbooks. Or, to take another example, we would like to be able to give detailed and exact advice for a line of action to a teacher who is confronted with a learner who has fossilized in a certain area. Such exact procedures — if they are at all possible to arrive at — need to be worked out empirically in second language teaching research. So far, this has not been done.

At another, more *general* level, second language acquisition results may be applied to teaching immediately in time — that is: now — but with a certain indirectness. Here I am thinking of the level where the teacher's general knowledge about the phenomenon of second language acquisition influences his daily practice in the classroom in various ways. Numerous examples of how a teacher having insights into second language acquisition research results would differ from one who lacks such insights can be imagined. For instance:

A teacher who has knowledge about second language acquisition would probably not insist that everything that is uttered in the classroom should be correct according to the target norm at all phases of acquisition and in all situations; from all what is known about acquisition, it is impossible to develop a language with total correctness from the beginning. It seems that the learners must have the opportunity to try out their own versions of the target language and rely as much — or even principally — on their own ability to build up a grammar for the target language, as on the help they can get from the teacher.

Another example: A teacher possessing knowledge about second language acquisition would not claim straight away that certain concepts are lacking in the learner's language if these are not expressed in a targetlike manner. Rather, he would ask himself: How does this learner express concept x, if at all? It is a well established fact in second language acquisition research that learners find their own ways of expressing the concepts they need in conversation, ways that in many cases are not in accord with the target language norms, but which nevertheless may be quite systematic.

A third example: A teacher who has knowledge about second language acquisition would not tell a learner the following: "Since you make this error on word order again, you have not mastered the word order rules. Look here, word order rules of your L2 look like this..." + explanation of the phenomenon of word order. Instead, he would listen and try to discover whether this learner *always* gets a certain word order phenomenon wrong, or if there are some cases where the learner gets it right. The teacher may even be able to find out what these right cases are — since they may systematically belong to a certain category. What he would say to the learner would rather be something like: "Look here, you master word order quite well now, but there are still some cases where your rule does not work. This is what you do when you are right ... so try to do the same also in these cases." This teacher, it may be noted, will not tell a learner who is in fact well on his way with a certain phenomenon that he has not mastered the phenomenon at all.[1] Further background to the reasoning in these examples will be given throughout this article.

At this level, then, all types of second language acquisition results may be of importance for the teacher, even those gained in research not aimed at direct application to teaching; for here it is the teacher himself who acts on the basis of his own accumulated knowledge.

Specific and general applications

Manfred Pienemann, in his position paper in this volume, has chosen to consider one aspect of application of second language acquisition research to teaching, viz. application in the area of syllabus construction. In terms of the two levels of application that were distinguished above, specific and general, Pienemann's suggestion as to how grading of text-books could be based on second language acquisition results belongs to the specific one. This is also true for Clahsen's suggestion (this volume, p.283) about how an assessment instrument, giving a qualitative profile of a particular learner's interlanguage at a certain point in time, could in principle be developed. These two approaches are illustrative examples of how results from second language acquisition research can be made the basis for *hypotheses* about instructional issues. Both suggestions also illustrate the necessity of testing such hypotheses empirically, and both authors certainly give some hints at how this can be done (cf. especially Pienemann's teaching experiment with the rule of inversion in German (Pienemann, 1984)).

In addition, both discussions demonstrate the acute difficulties one is confronted with when one works with applications at this specific level. It is true that Pienemann bases his discussion on empirical results from a teaching experiment — and these results are important, since it is the first time we have supporting, more controlled empirical data on what interlanguage researchers have believed for a long time, i.e. that it is useless to teach items to a learner who does not have these items on his "list" of what ought to come next (Corder, 1967; Platt, 1976; Wode, 1981) — but we must bear in mind that the generalizability of the results is, to say the least, unknown. Replications and other corresponding experiments on different linguistic phenomena with different groups of learners are strongly needed, and should be undertaken.

Similarly in Clahsen's case, the next step to take with his assessment test is to validate it through experiments with larger numbers of learners. Here again, the step Clahsen has taken in developing a principled instrument for assessing learner profiles is an extremely important one, since it presents us with something concrete to modify and develop further.

Because of these present difficulties in applying second language acquisition results, I feel a little sceptical about one passage in Pienemann's discussion (pp. 54ff.): Having argued in favour of the necessity for structural grading, i.e. a fixed progression, in teaching materials or in the presentation of target language units generally, Pienemann rightly claims that decisions concerning the order in which items of the L2 are introduced in the classroom have up until now been based on intuition rather than on facts about when items are learnable. He also claims that there is enough knowledge from second language acquisition research about acquisitional orderings to replace intuition by such knowledge. On the other hand, as regards *teaching methods*, where the basic question according to Pienemann is "how the respective items (of L2, KH) are optimally learnable", he agrees with those who mean that our knowledge of L2 development is too fragmentary to be applicable to teaching practice.

Firstly, Pienemann may be right that there is a great deal of knowledge about second language acquisition sequences, especially if one thinks of target languages like German and English. But I would hesitate to grant that even this knowledge is sufficient, and I would emphasize that the situation is worse for all other languages that are taught as second and foreign languages.[2]

Secondly, there is a problem with the notion of teaching method. Some of the existing approaches to language teaching have been promoted to the status of method more by arbitrary labelling than by rational reasoning about what constitutes a method. Existing "methods" seem either to have no basis in learning theory, or they are based on very limited aspects of our knowledge about learning. Future teaching methods should of course be based on a theoretical framework that also considers existing knowledge about second language acquisition.

Thirdly, Pienemann's discussion gives the impression that we have on the one hand the syllabus and on the other teaching methods, and that these are unrelated units. To me it seems that these entities are closely intertwined and are dependent on one another.

In conclusion, then, contrary to Pienemann's position, I think that second language acquisition research results are still too fragmentary to allow for their *detailed* application in syllabus construction, test design etc. This does not mean that I think second language acquisition results should be ignored, which I hope is obvious from the discussion above. On the contrary, the results we have must be taken into account, and I agree with Pienemann that we can never go back and work with intuition only, for example when syllabuses are laid down. In a similar manner, I think that future developments in teaching methods must take those facts about second language acquisition that are available into account. Furthermore, while we are waiting for a more detailed basis for syllabus construction and a well-founded teaching method, I think second language acquisition research, together with other kinds of knowledge, can have great bearing on daily teaching practice, in that a greater knowledge about the learner and the learner's obstacles in approaching his L2 would make it easier for the teacher to adjust his instruction to the learner's needs.

Exemplifying general level applications

My position, then, is that we should not only think of specific level applications of our research, and say that those research results that are not directly applicable at this level are of no use to the language teacher. To do this would be to underestimate the impact that broad knowledge may have on altering attitudes and behaviour. What I wish to discuss here is just *how* attitudes and behaviour may be altered with the help of such knowledge.

I would like to approach this question in the light of second language acquisition research results from one area that seems central to me, viz. variation in the learner's output. Anyone who has listened carefully to the form of an L2 learner's utterances has noticed that there is usually a number of instances of variation between two or more equivalent forms (see Bickerton, 1971: 458 for this notion). What may be easiest to observe are cases where one form is correct and another incorrect according to the target language norm; for example in the variation between forms like *I know where you are going/I know where are you going*. This kind of variation occurs at different linguistic levels, in phonology, grammar, and lexicon. And, parenthetically, it is not restricted to the language of L2 learners, but occurs also, albeit not always in the same linguistic areas, among L1 speakers. The difference, if any, between L1 and L2 speakers seems to be chiefly a quantitative matter, variable phenomena being an outstanding characteristic of L2 speakers.

For a long period of time, the phenomenon of variation was disregarded both in language description generally, and in the description of interlanguage. This neglect was certainly a consequence of contemporary assumptions about how language was represented in the brain, and also of insufficiencies in linguistic theories to deal with variable phenomena (cf. discussion in Hyltenstam, 1981). In the early seventies, when it had been firmly established in sociolinguistic studies that it was possible to gain

insights into ongoing language change by studying variable speech phenomena in a speech community (cf. Weinreich *et al.*, 1968), variation in the
L2 learner's interlanguage started to be a phenomenon of research
interest. If ongoing changes in a language or in a language variety could be
studied through variation in a speech community, then the changes that
occur at a given point in time in an individual's linguistic system should also
be reflected in this person's output variation. More concretely, if a learner
at a certain point in time (T I) can be observed to make categorical use of
rule x and at a later point (T II) has substituted the categorical use of rule
x+1 for rule x, we can expect that his output reflects a variation between x
and x+ 1 in the period of time between T I and T II:

$$\overline{\text{T I} \qquad \text{T II}} \longrightarrow$$
$$x \quad x/x+1 \quad x+1$$

The study of the variation between x and x+1, then, is assumed to
give detailed insights about *how* the learner takes the step of substituting
one rule for another. This type of knowledge is extremely valuable for the
teacher, who can consequently strive to create conditions as favourable as
possible for a learner to make substitutions of target language rules for
non-target-like interlanguage ones.

At this point, a note on terminology is appropriate. As may already
be clear to the reader, the terms *variable* and *variation* are used in different
senses in this volume. Pienemann, Nicholas and Clahsen talk about
variable — or *variational* — features, as opposed to *developmental* features
(see e.g. page 37) (Clahsen *et al.*, 1983). The distinction between variable
and developmental is based on the observation that second language
development in some linguistic areas is invariable in the sense that all
learners seem to go through the same developmental sequences in those
areas. The linguistic features that are involved in this development are
labelled *developmental*. The features of those linguistic areas where such
uniform — or invariable — development can not be observed are called
variable. Within this framework, the term variable thus has a quite specific
meaning. Naturally, the concept of *individual variation* plays an important
role here. This aspect is treated extensively in the article by Nicholas (this
volume, Chapter 8, p. 177). As indicated above, my own use of the term
variable is in line with the general usage in sociolinguistic, historical,
dialectal, and creole studies of linguistic variation.

I hope the following discussion will show how knowledge about
variable phenomena in the learner's output can help the teacher change

some of the daily practices in the classroom in a more rewarding direction. I think a change of focus of attention on the teacher's part from the "wrong-cases" to the "sometimes-wrong-sometimes-right-cases", would mean that the teacher could give more adequate comments to the learner on the nature of his learning problems.

As was implicitly assumed above, there are a number of different backgrounds for the variation in the learner's output. All variation is probably not a reflection of an ongoing rule substitution. Therefore, it would be valuable if the teacher could make a good guess as to the nature of a particular instance of variation. In the following, I would like to relate the discussion about some types of variable phenomena to basic knowledge about second language development. The following fairly well established facts seem to be of particular relevance for this purpose. The first two points are most clearly the background for discussing ongoing rule substitutions of the kind noted above, while the other points constitute the background for some other types of variation:

1. Second language acquisition involves *development of a less complex to a more complex language system* (cf., for example, the discussion in Corder, 1978). Also, it involves *other changes* in the learner's interlanguage system, where the states before and after the change can not be claimed to differ in degree of complexity.
2. This development of the system is not random, but rather follows *specific acquisitional sequences* (cf Pienemann, this volume, for example). *Some* of the structural patternings seem to be *parallel to language universal patternings* (Hyltenstam, 1984; Hyltenstam & Magnusson, 1981; cf. also discussion in Eckman, 1977 and Hyltenstam, 1982).
3. Like first language acquisition, second language acquisition involves *both rule generalization and holophrase incorporation* (Hakuta, 1976; Wong-Fillmore, 1979), i.e. acquisition of units, the inner structure of which is not analysed by the learner.
4. Unlike non-pathological first language acquisition, second language acquisition may come to a halt, *fossilize*, at various points before nativelike command is reached (Selinker, 1972). Social and psychological factors, including motivation, are claimed to play an important role as determinants of whether fossilization will occur or not (Schumann, 1978a; Klein & Dittmar, 1979; Clahsen *et al.*, 1983), but there seem to be any number of different factors involved (Schumann, 1978b). *Some changes in the learner's system – or rather in some learners' systems – seem to occur very slowly*. It

may therefore be hard, due to observational difficulties, to determine whether fossilization has taken place or not.

5. The learner's underlying linguistic system is reflected differently in
   different situations. The output may, for example, be more target-
   like in more formal contexts, or when more attention is directed
   towards form (Dickerson, 1975).

Systematic variation and second language development

To illustrate how output variation is related to the facts stated in
points 1 and 2, I will use an example from Cazden *et al.* (1975), which
simultaneously points to the *progressing complexification* that takes place
in the learners' interlanguage and defines a particular *developmental
sequence* for the acquisition of wh-questions. Cazden *et al.* (1975:38)
arrived at the following developmental pattern for this syntactic area in
their ten-month longitudinal study of the untutored acquisition of English
by six native speakers of Spanish:

Stage I – Undifferentiation: Learner did not distinguish between
simple and embedded *wh-questions*.

a. uninverted: Both simple and embedded *wh-questions* were uninverted.

   simple: *What you study?*

   embedded: *That's what I do with my pillow.*

b. variable inversion: Simple *wh-questions* were sometimes
   inverted, sometimes not.

   inverted: *How can you say it?*

   uninverted: *Where you get that?*

c. generalization: Increasing inversion in *wh-questions* with
   inversion being extended to embedded questions.

   simple: *How can I kiss her if I don't even know her name?*

   embedded: *I know where are you going.*

Stage II – Differentiation: Learner distinguished between simple and embedded *wh-questions*.

simple: *Where do you live?*

embedded: *I don't know what he said.*

To see how this example illustrates ongoing complexification of the learners' system, it is necessary to briefly discuss the notion of "complex". What is linguistically simple and complex is by no means an uncomplicated issue (cf. Meisel, 1980). The notions cannot be adequately discussed without taking particular theoretical frameworks into account, but, roughly, when the notion of linguistic complexity is used in second language acquisition research, there seem to be two major senses which are referred to. The obvious and straightforward sense would be the equating of complexification with enlargement of the interlanguage system at various points, for example, enlarging NP's with (more) determiners, enlarging the number of phrase structure alternatives for sentences, or, in the area of lexicon, enlarging the number of units employed to express a semantic field. The second sense of the notion is less straight forward in that it relates the notion of complex to a particular psycholinguistic theory and its assumptions about psycholinguistic functioning. In this sense, inversion, to take one example discussed in Pienemann's position article, can be claimed to be more complex than SV-order in a language such as German; inversion is then assumed to involve an operation on underlying SV-order.

The example above from Cazden *et al.* (1975) illustrates how the system of the learner becomes more complex in both these senses. Firstly, the learner starts out with uninverted wh-questions, which psycholinguistically are assumed to be less complex than inverted ones. Secondly, the step from the undifferentiated stage, i.e. Stage I, to the stage where the learners distinguish between simple and embedded wh-questions involves an enlargement of the system; more rules are required for the generation of utterances at Stage II than at Stage I. The two senses of complex do not exclude each other. Many of the changes that can be claimed to be complexifications in the psycholinguistic sense also involve enlargements of the system and vice versa.

The Cazden *et al.* example was chosen because it explicitly mentions the period of variable use of the rule of inversion as a phase of the development from uninverted wh-questions to inverted ones. Such phases are usually implicitly assumed in most studies of developmental sequences, and this is also the case in the Cazden *et al.* example at another point in the development, i.e. the development from Stage I to Stage II. It is, of course, not to be assumed that this differentiation occurs abruptly.

Even if the phase of variation is explicitly mentioned in the Cazden *et al.* study, no investigation was undertaken regarding possible systematicity in this variation. Therefore, the only thing we know is that wh-questions were sometimes inverted and sometimes not. We do not know if certain contexts were more favourable for inversion than others. In a study of adult second language acquisition of Swedish (Hyltenstam, 1978), the variation between inverted and non-inverted sentences was studied in more detail.

In Swedish, inversion occurs

- in simple yes/no-questions (*Kommer Kalle imorgon?*, literally: *Comes Charlie tomorrow?*)

- in simple wh-questions (*När kommer Kalle?* literally: *When comes Charlie?*)
  if the interrogative word is not the subject (*Vem sitter här?* literally: *Who sits here?*)
  or contained in the subject as a determiner (*Vilken dörr går till källaren?* literally: *Which door leads to the cellar?*)

and

- in declaratives after sentence-initial non-subjects (*Imorgon kommer Kalle*, literally: *Tomorrow comes Charlie*).

Parenthetically, the inversion rule in wh-questions and in declaratives can be considered to be one rule, since the conditions for application are exactly the same: when a sentence starts by a constituent that is not the subject, the subject is placed immediately after the finite verb. In wh-questions this constituent happens to consist of or contain the interrogative word.

The result of this study pointed to auxiliary verb contexts as favourable contexts for inversion in yes/no questions, i.e. in sentences where the finite verb was *kan, ska, vill* etc, inversion occurred more often, and it was therefore hypothesized that inversion developed earlier in this context. In interrogative word questions and in declaratives no such pattern could be found. This result does not, of course, guarantee that there are not particular contexts that are more favourable in these cases, only that no such patterning could be detected on the basis of the study.

Variation and the parallel between language universal and second language patterning

In order to further illustrate the systematicity that can be detected in variable output, I will briefly mention two studies from other linguistic areas. In the field of interlanguage phonology, 16 Finnish speaking learners of Swedish[3] were studied in a cross-sectional study for their variable manifestation of stops in Swedish (Hyltenstam & Magnusson, 1981). Ten of the subjects were adults and 6 were children between 4 and 6 years of age. The subjects were chosen on the criterion that they exhibited variable manifestation of Swedish voiced stops. Swedish has both the voiceless (/p/, /t/, /k/) and the voiced series (/b/, /d/, /g/), while Finnish has only the voiceless series, except marginally /d/. Our hypothesis on contextual differences in the manifestation of voiced stops, i.e. on what context factors would be more and less favourable, was based on language universal patternings (Jakobson, 1941; Dinnsen & Eckman, 1975) according to which voiced stops are generally more marked than voiceless stops, and, as regards phonotactic conditions, it is more marked to make the voice distinction word finally than word medially, where the distinction in turn is more marked than word initially. Our hypothesis then was that it is easiest for the second language learner to make a distinction between voiced and voiceless stops in word initial position followed by word medial and word final position.

The result is displayed in Table 1. As can be seen, a higher percentage of acceptable manifestations of voiced stops was obtained in typologically less marked contexts, which gives support for our hypothesis, although the difference between medial and final position is very small in some cases, notably for /d/.

In another study, Finnish, Spanish, Greek and Persian learners of Swedish were studied for their use of pronominal copies in Swedish relative

TABLE 1 *Proportions of acceptably produced voiced stops in word-initial, -medial, and -final position*

		#'_V	V_V	V_#
/b/	children	44	40	10
	adults	68	38	33
/d/	children	92	56	55
	adults	89	87	86
/g/	children	64	60	30
	adults	59	56	45

clauses (Hyltenstam, 1984). There were 12 subjects in each group except in the Finnish one, which contained only 9. The study was undertaken with the goal of illuminating the relative importance of language universal patterning and patterning in the learner's mother tongue as determinants for L2 development patterning. Typologically, there are languages which do not use pronominal copies in relative clauses at all, such as English, Finnish, and Swedish, and languages that use such elements to various degrees, such as Greek and Persian. In Spanish, the use of pronominal copies seems to be confined to non-standard varieties. In these languages, a pronoun that is coreferent with the head noun of the relative clause is a constituent of the relative clause. The following examples, which are taken from Schachter (1974), and which are unacceptable in English, illustrate how relative clauses with pronominal copies in the position of different constituents are structured:

Subj: the boy that *he* came

Dir. Obj: the boy that John hit *him*

Indir. Obj: the boy that I sent a letter to *him*

Obj. Prep: the boy that I sat near *him*

Poss NP: the boy that *his* father died

Obj. Comp. Part: the boy that John is taller than *him*

Typological studies show that there is a hierarchy from Subj. to Obj. Comp. which is reflected, among other things, in the use of pronominal copies. Lower down in the hierarchy pronominal copies are supplied more frequently (Keenan & Comrie, 1977). Now it can be claimed that the insertion of pronominal copies is psycholinguistically less complex than deletion, since relative clauses with pronominal copies more clearly reflect the underlying structure on the surface. This means that the development of an interlanguage system from one with pronominal copies in relative clauses to one without would involve a complexification of the system.

The result of the study under review was clearly that learners from all native groups variably employed pronominal copies in their Swedish relative clauses, i.e. even the Finnish group to a small extent, despite the fact that Finnish does not contain such elements. Interestingly, the variation in insertion/deletion of pronominal copies was not random, but generally followed language typological patterning, as can be seen from Tables 2–5. One can conclude that the learners vary systematically in their use of pronominal copies in relative clauses according to contexts which

TABLES 2–5 *Retention (+) and deletion (−) of pronominal copies for four groups of learners of Swedish. Implicational scaling according to the NP Assessibility Hierarchy (Keenan & Comrie, 1977). Deviations from the implicational pattern are circled. From Hyltenstam (1984).*

TABLE 2 *Speakers of Persians. Scalability 93.1*

Subj nr	SU*	DO	IO	OBL	GEN	OCOMP
21	−	−	−	−	−	−
32	−	−	−	−	+	+
17	−	⊕	⊕	−	+	①
18	−	⊕	⊕	−	+	+
7	−	−	+	+	+	+
16	−	−	+	+	+	+
6	−	−	+	+	+	+
34	−	+	+	+	+	+
30	−	+	+	+	+	+
28	−	+	+	+	+	+
29	−	+	+	+	+	+
15	−	+	+	+	+	+

TABLE 3 *Speakers of Greek. Scalability 97.1 (if 0 = −), 98.7 (if 0 = +)*

Subj nr	SU	DO	IO	OBL	GEN	OCOMP
20	−	−	−	−	−	−
41	−	−	−	−	+	①
14	−	−	−	−	+	0
43	−	−	−	−	+	+
12	−	−	−	−	+	+
13	−	−	+	+	+	+
40	−	−	+	+	+	+
27	−	+	+	+	+	+
42	−	+	+	+	+	+
22	−	+	+	+	+	+
11	−	+	+	+	+	+
10	−	+	+	+	+	+

TABLE 4 *Speakers of Spanish. Scalability 90.3*

Subj nr	SU	DO	IO	OBL	GEN	OCOMP
2	−	−	−	−	−	−
31	−	−	−	−	⊕	−
37	−	−	−	−	⊕	−
33	−	−	−	−	⊕	−
3	−	−	−	−	−	+
8	−	−	−	−	+	+
5	−	−	⊕	−	+	①
4	−	−	⊕	−	+	+
9	−	−	⊕	−	+	+
19	−	−	+	+	+	+
24	−	+	+	+	+	+
35	−	+	+	+	+	+

TABLE 5 *Speakers of Finnish. Scalability 85.2–92.6. depending on whether 0 = + or −.*

Subj nr	SU	DO	IO	OBL	GEN	OCOMP
48	−	−	−	−	0	−
52	−	−	−	−	0	−
44	−	−	−	−	⊕	−
47	−	−	−	−	⊕	−
51	−	−	−	−	⊕	−
45	−	−	−	0	⊕	−
50	−	−	−	−	0	+
46	−	−	−	−	+	+
49	−	−	−	−	+	+

*SU = subject, DO = direct object, IO = indirect object, OBL = oblique object; in English – and Swedish – object of preposition, GEN = genitive, OCOMP = object of comparison.

can be specified as favourable and unfavourable for pronominal copy deletion, even in terms of language universals.

Now, what does the discussion in the last two sections imply for teaching? First of all, since we are discussing general level applications, it would be unrealistic for teaching to wait for research to specify what contexts, if any, are favourable for the acquisition of every target language rule of all target languages. And, certainly, this would neither be necessary nor desirable. What is important in teaching, I think, is that areas of variation in each learner's output are observed in the classroom, because if certain linguistic contexts are more favourable, for whatever reason, for the application of new rules or items, it seems essential to have this in mind both during the presentation of new material (so that favourable contexts can be chosen for the display of the new phenomenon[4]), in the diagnosis of learner problems, and in correction, where a praxis could be to relate a learner's "wrong-cases" to the same learner's "right-cases". In order to find out what contexts are more or less favourable, it would be helpful to be able to make good guesses from the outset. Orientation in the field of language typology might be the best basis for such guesses.

Furthermore, if it is the case that variation is a necessary concomitant of development, then variation is the symptom the teacher should look for to see what areas of the learner's interlanguage are developing. The fact that a new item or rule is applied even to a low degree can, as Pienemann states in his position paper (p.38), be seen as an indication that this new structure is processable by the learner. This means that it is precisely in those areas where the learner exhibits variation that instruction should help the most.

After this rather long discussion of points 1 and 2 on p.120, we will go back and look at point 3.

Variation as an effect of holophrase incorporation

This point concerned rule generalization and holophrase incorporation. During the process of acquisition, the learner identifies phrases or words from the target input which he then uses without having (implicitly) analysed their internal structure; they are holophrases. For example, when learners of Swedish in early phases of acquisition use the phrases *Ja, det är det* (literally: *Yes, that is it* = *Yes, it is*) and *Nej, det är det inte* (*No, that is it not* = *No, it isn't*) – and they are encouraged or forced to do so, if they go to Swedish language classes – at such a phase, there is no way for the learner to grasp the inner structure of the phrase and relate it to the linguistic system he has developed so far. These phrases are usually used very early in classroom conversation, for example in the following types of dialogues:

Är det här en bil?	Ja, det är det.
Is this a car?	Yes, that is it. = Yes, it is.
Är det här ett hus?	Nej, det är det inte.
Is this a house?	No, that is it not. = No, it isn't.
Är han hemma?	Ja, det är han.
Is he at home?	Yes, that is he. = Yes, he is.
Är han sjuk?	Nej, det är han inte.
Is he ill?	No, that is he not. = No, he isn't.

As is evident in the second pair of sentences, the phrase *det är han* contains an instance of inversion, *är han*, and the initial *det* is an anaphoric pronoun referring to the content of the preceding VP. Similarly, in *det är det*, it is the second *det* which is the subject. This means that the small and frequent phrase, *det är det*, meaning *it is*, contains a number of difficulties that are dealt with much later in the formal instruction: inversion between subject and finite verb, a dummy verb viz. the copula (many languages do not use a copula in this case), and an obligatory anaphoric pronoun as verb complement or predicative.[5] What the learner has to do is to use these phrases as holophrases, a fact that the teacher should realize. So, when, for example, inversion occurs in the learners output in stereotype utterances and not in creatively generated utterances, it is not a case of true variation from the learners point of view; it is only the observer who sees this as variation.

I would like to discuss the question of identifying instances of true variation in contradistinction to this kind of "observer variation" in the light of an empirical example taken from Kotsinas (1982 and 1984). Kotsinas studied the Swedish vocabulary in the spontaneous speech of six adult untutored second language learners, five of which had Greek as their L1 and one Polish. In the semantic field of Verbal Communication, for example, the six learners made use of different numbers of lexical units to express the basic subfields that are indicated in Table 6.

What is interesting to see here is the extension of the form *fråga* = "ask" to all the subfields of verbal communication that are represented in the vocabulary of one of the Greek subjects (Di). In the vocabulary of another Greek subject (Ta), the same form has a somewhat more narrow extension, but it is still overextended in relation to the Swedish norm to cover also the subfield UPPMANA, = "TELL TO DO". It should be noted that these learners know no other languages than their mother

TABLE 6 *Verbs of verbal communication in the speech of six L2 learners of Swedish (from Kotsinas, 1984).* (*Numbers within brackets refer to tokens*)

Semantic subfield	SÄGA, 'SAY'	UPPMANA, 'TELL TO DO'	SAMTALA, 'TALK'	FÖRKLARA, 'EXPLAIN'	FRÅGA, 'ASK'	SVARA, 'ANSWER'
Basic target language vocabulary	*säga, 'say' berätta, 'tell'*	*säga till, 'tell' 'order'*	*tala, 'talk', 'speak' prata 'chat'*	*förklara, 'explain'*	*fråga, 'ask'*	*svara 'answer'*
Learner						
Ge	sägla (9)	–	diskutera (1)	–	fråga (3)	–
Di	fråga (1)	fråga (1)	tala (1) fråga (13)	–	fråga (4)	–
Ta	säga (9) berätta (2)	fråga (4)	tala (1) prata (1)	förklara (5)	fråga (3)	svara (5)
Ka	–	–	–	–	–	–
Ni	–	–	–	–	–	–
Ma	säga (16)	–	prata (2)	förklara (1)	fråga (3)	svara (2)

tongue and Swedish. The example is just one of many on semantic overextension, and it is typical in the way a lexical form is extended to systematically cover closely related meanings, i.e. lexical forms which do not accord to the target norm are not used arbitrarily to mean just anything.

If we look at the vocabulary of Di for expressing verbal communication, we note that one verb, *fråga*, is used, except for one instance of *tala*, = "speak", "talk". In Table 6, only cases which seem to be creative vocabulary use are displayed, but in Kotsinas' data, there are 5 other instances of *tala* (Kotsinas, 1982:74). These instances, however, all occur immediately after the word *tala* has been used by the native speaker interlocutor. This fact may be interpreted such that Di is well aware of the existence of the verb *tala*, he understands it and can use it in his own production, but only when it has been actualized in the conversation. This might indicate that he is in the very initial phase of acquiring this form. The fact that he uses *tala* creatively once (see Table 6) is also compatible with this interpretation.

Di also uses *prata*, = "talk", 23 times (Kotsinas 1982). The reason these cases are not included in Table 6 is that *prata* is always used in connection with languages, for example *prata svenska* = "talk Swedish", *prata grekiska* = "talk Greek" etc., which, incidentally, is correct Swedish. He never uses *tala* in these cases, which would also be correct in Swedish. The use of *prata* can therefore be characterized as stereotypic and the phrase *prata x* a holophrase. We see here, then, that the variation between *fråga* and *prata* for target *prata* is not a sign of ongoing change in the same way as the variation between *fråga* and *tala* above. The verb *prata* has been restricted to a small part of its normal use in Swedish, while *tala* seems to be on its way to be sorted out to cover its more specific part of the semantic field of Verbal communication.

Variation and fossilization

As regards fossilization, our 4th point on p.120, it is unknown if there are certain points in the development of a particular rule or area, which are more sensitive to fossilization than others. Therefore, it is difficult to know whether an ongoing change can come to a halt at any point. If it can, we may expect variable output of a certain rule to be permanent. Another unknown fact about fossilization is whether a fossilized area can be brought to develop at a later point in time. It is a veritable challenge for language teaching research to work with these questions, but much remains to be discovered also about the nature of fossilization as a phenomenon in second language development. For one thing, if some changes in a linguistic system are so slow that development is hard to observe, then it may be hard to distinguish really fossilized areas from areas of slow development.

Variation and the situational context

Finally, as pointed out in point 5 on p.121, variation that is attributable to the situational factors of the conversation may be found in the learner's output. As all teachers know, a learner may well use the target language correctly in some situations, but "forget" the correct usage in others. Actually, this does not seem too surprising if we acknowledge that development takes place successively. Situational factors, including the possibilities the learner in a communicative situation has to pay attention to form, seem to naturally influence the extent to which an innovation in the learner's system may be utilized. Empirical data supporting this observation can be found in, for example, Dickerson (1975), where it was found that Japanese second language learners' pronunciation of English was closer to the norm in more formal types of data.

During the period of acquisition, it may thus be quite normal that a learner is able to produce more targetlike utterances in some situations than in others. A teacher who realizes this possibility does not need to give up when confronted with learners who seem to forget all they have learnt as soon as they leave the classroom.

Conclusion

In this paper, I have argued that we may consider applications of second language acquisition research at two levels. At a specific level, the focus is on a detailed application of individual facts about acquisition. At a general level, second language acquisition is applied through the teacher in his daily creative acting in the classroom. I have used one area of second language acquisition results to illustrate such a general level application, viz. structural variation in the learner's L2 output.

Both levels of application have been claimed to be valuable and necessary. In most cases, knowledge about specific level applications must be gained through teaching experiments and detailed methodological research. The general level application in the sense of this discussion is immediately at hand, since it involves a direct diffusion into the classroom of the developing body of second language acquisition research.

And the fact that it is a developing body, which causes some of yesterday's facts to disperse in today's light, should not distress anyone. This is how knowledge develops in all areas of human interest; there is no reason to expect higher standards in second language acquisition research. And no one, I believe, would claim, for example, that it is of no use for a medical doctor to learn about healthy and pathological corporal functioning, since what we think we know today will not be true tomorrow.

After this article's uninhibited praise of the direct relevance of second language acquisition research for language teaching, a word of moderation would not be out of place: I do not believe second language acquisition research is the key to all the language teacher's problems. Indeed, whenever possible, I have tried to intersperse an *along-with-other-kinds-of-knowledge* proviso in the text. I believe that knowledge from the field of second language acquisition is necessary for good language teaching, but that it must be supplemented by knowledge of what political, socio-psychological and pedagogical factors determine the possibilities to back up language acquisition in the classroom.

I also believe, in spite of what I have said above about the usefulness of all kinds of second language acquisition results, that there is a great deal of work in the area that is not worth taking seriously. But the only guarantee, actually, for a teacher not to take the bad work seriously, is to be able to distinguish the bad from the good. And this in turn presupposes a broad orientation in the field.

Let me finish by underscoring the central idea around which this chapter has been built: In my view, the most useful application of second language research at present is its implementation by individual language teachers who, on the basis of what they hold to be true within as broad an area of knowledge as possible, can act creatively and freely, not hampered by particular textbooks or other regulations. Within the total amount of relevant knowledge, knowledge about second language research is but one part. The individual teachers' internalized knowledge should make it possible for them not only to better understand and diagnose learner problems, and to find ways to help the learners overcome such problems, but also to evaluate new information regarding the content of their profession.

Notes to Chapter 5

1. My reasoning in this last example is based on the assumption that metalinguistic reasoning, i.e. explicit focus on form and/or content and their relations,

contributes to language learning and acquisition, an assumption which is made explicit in Pienemann's article in this volume, but one which is not held by all scholars. I think this view should not be given up too easily in favour of some of the more or less well-founded argumentations currently in fashion. For one thing, *very many* learners seem to be able to make good use of metalinguistic information. For another, *nothing* seems to contradict the contention that learners can make use of *both* "naturally tuned" or "comprehensible" input and metalinguistic information, although, as it seems, to different, individually determined, degrees. If this is true, teaching should provide both kinds of input in order to satisfy different learners.

2. In Pienemann's section *Final remarks*, p.68, a more cautious view, similar to the one proposed here, is expressed.

3. This group of second language learners of Swedish was compared to both normally developing and language disordered first language learners of Swedish. The results were parallel in all groups, except for a minor deviance in the language disordered group.

4. An alternative, which has been shown to be viable in some studies would be to present a new item in a less favourable context and obtain learner generalizations to all more favourable contexts. See the experiment by Gass (1982) on relativization and the study by af Trampe (1982) on the leasing of the Cyrillic alphabet and word identification in Russian by Swedes.

5. For a description of these facts of Swedish and a discussion of their weight in an L2 acquisition context, see Hammarberg & Viberg (1977).

References

Bickerton, D. 1971, Inherent variability and variable rules. *Foundations of Language*, 7, 457–92.

Cazden, C.B., Cancino, H., Roansky, E. & Schumann, J.H. 1975, Second language acquisition sequences in children, adolescents, and adults. U.S. Department of Health, Education and Welfare National Institute of Education Office of Research Grants, Final Report Project No. 7 307 44 Grant No. NE–6–00–3–0014.

Clahsen, H., Meisel, J.M. & Pienemann, M. 1983, *Deutsch als Zweitsprache. Der Spracherwerb ausländischer Arbeiter*. Tübingen: Gunter Narr.

Corder, S.P. 1967, The significance of learners' errors. *IRAL*, 5, 161–70.

—— 1978, Language-learner language. In J.C. Richards (ed.), *Understanding Second and Foreign Language Learning*. Rowley, Mass.: Newbury House.

Dickerson, L.J. 1975, The learner's interlanguage as a system of variable rules. *TESOL Quarterly*, 9, 401–407.

Dinnsen, D.A. & Eckman, F.R. 1975, A functional explanation of some phonological typologies. In R. Grossman, J. San and T. Vance (eds), *Functionalism*. Chicago: Chicago Linguistic Society, 126–34.

Eckman, E.R. 1977, Markedness and the contrastive analysis hypothesis, *Language Learning*, 27, 315–30.

Gass, S. 1982, From theory to practice. In M. Hines & W. Rutherford (eds), *On TESOL '81*. Washington D.C.: TESOL, 129–39.

Hakuta, K. 1976, A case study of a Japanese child learning English as a second language. *Language learning*, 26, 321–51.

Hammarberg, B. & Viberg, Å. 1977, The place-holder constraint, language typology, and the teaching of Swedish to immigrants. *Studia Linguistica*, 31, 106–63.

Hyltenstam, K. 1978, Variation in interlanguage syntax. *Working Papers*, 18. Department of General Linguistics, Lund University.

—— 1981, Dynamic change in the acquisition of a second language as exemplified by negation and interrogation. In J.-G. Savard & L. Laforge (eds), *Actes du 5e congrès de l'Association Internationale de Linguistique Appliquée*. Québec: Les Presses de l'Université Laval, 179–94.

—— 1982, Markedness, language universals, language typology, and second language acquisition. Paper presented at the 2nd European North American Workshop in Cross-Linguistic Second Language Acquisition Research, Jagdschloss Göhrde, West Germany, August 22–29, 1982. In C. Pfaff (ed.), *Cross Linguistic Studies of Language Acquisition Processes*. Rowley, Mass.: Newbury House.

—— 1984, The use of typological markedness as predictor in second language acquisition: the case of pronominal copies in relative clauses. Paper presented at the European North American Workshop on Cross-Linguistic Second Language Acquisition Research, Lake Arrowhead, Los Angeles, September 7–14, 1981. In R.W. Andersen (ed.), *Second Languages*. Rowley, Mass.: Newbury House.

Hyltenstam, K. & Magnusson, E. 1981, Typological markedness, contextual variation, and the acquisition of the voice contrast in stops by first and second language learners of Swedish Papers presented at the 6th International Congress of Applied Linguistics, Lund, August 9–14, 1981. In T.K. Bhatia & W.C. Ritchie, (eds), Progression in Second Language Acquisition – Part I. *Special Issue of Indian Journal of Applied Linguistics*.

Jakobson, R. 1941, Kindersprache. *Aphasie und allgemeine Lautgesetze*. Uppsala: Almqvist & Wiksell.

Keenan, E.L. & Comrie, B. 1977, Noun phrase accessibility and universal grammar. *Linguistic Inquiry*, 8. 63–99.

Klein, W. & Dittmar, N. 1979, Developing Grammars. *The Acquisition of German Syntax by Foreign Workers*. Berlin: Springer.

Kotsinas, U.-B. 1982, Svenska svårt. Några invandrares svenska talspråk Ordförrådet Meddelanden från Institutionen för nordiska språk vid Stockholms universitet (MINS) 10.

—— 1984, "Ask maybe ten hours". Semantic over-extension and lexical over-use. In *Scandinavian Working Papers on Bilingualism 2*. Inst. of Linguistics Stockholm University. 23–42.

Meisel, J.M. 1980, Linguistic simplification. A study of immigrant workers' speech and foreigner talk. In S.W. Felix (ed.), *Second Language Development. Trends and Issues*. Tübingen: Gunter Narr, 13–40.

Pienemann, M. 1984, Psychological constraints on the teachability of languages. *Studies in Second Language Acquisition*, 6, 186–214.

Platt, J.T. 1976, Implicational scaling and its pedagogical implications. *Working Papers in Language and Linguistics*, 4. Monash University, 46–60.

Schachter, J. 1974, An error in error analysis *Language Learning*, 24, 205–14.

Schumann, J.H. 1978a, *Second Language Acquisition: The Pidginization Hypothesis*. Rowley, Mass.: Newbury House.

—— 1978b, Social and psychological factors in second language acquisition. In J.C. Richards (ed.), *Understanding Second and Foreign Language Learning*. Row-

ley, Mass.: Newbury House, 163–78.
Selinker, L. 1972, Interlanguage. *IRAL*, 10, 209–31.
af Trampe, P. 1982, *Two Experimental Studies in Foreign Language Learning/ Teaching*. Department of General Linguistics, University of Stockholm.
Weinreich, U., Labov, W. & Herzog, M.I. 1968, Empirical foundations for a theory of language change. In W.P. Lehmann & Y. Malkiel (eds), *Directions for Historical Linguistics*. Austin: University of Texas Press, 95–195.
Wode, H. 1981, Learning a Second Language. Vol.1. *An Integrated View of Language Acquisition*. Tübingen: Gunter Narr.
Wong-Fillmore, L. 1979, Individual differences in second language acquisition. In C.J. Fillmore, D. Kempler, and W.S.-Y. Wang (eds), *Individual Differences in Language Ability and Language Behavior*, New York: Academic Press.

6 Linguistic simplicity and learnability: Implications for language syllabus design

TERESA PICA

University of Pennsylvania, Philadelphia, U.S.A.

Judging from the diverse assortment of syllabi which have formed the basis for second language instruction in recent years, it is evident that syllabus design is one of the most fluctuating and controversial areas of second language pedagogy. Decisions regarding syllabus content have been made from a variety of perspectives on the organization of language — its grammatical structures, its notional or functional categories, the situations in which it is employed, or the topics which form the context of its use. The selection, sequencing, and grading of this content have been based on numerous criteria, including social usefulness, frequency and range of occurrence, and degree of difficulty for the learner. However, as Pienemann emphasizes in his critical review (this volume, Chapter 2), the various syllabi available, in spite of their differences in content and theoretical grounding, do share a common, underlying theme: Their construction has centred around their author's theoretical perspectives on the structure and organization of language. Syllabus design has thus been based on the assumption that languages are learned in the ways that linguists describe them, and has been disappointingly lacking in empirical evidence as to whether these are the ways in which adults and children actually learn a second language.

Issues and questions

Particularly representative of this underlying theme has been the long-standing practice of basing syllabus specifications on gradations of syntactic complexity in the "target language" to be learned. The assumption here is that there is an inverse relationship between the linguistic complexity of a structure and its "learnability"; therefore, it is argued, a syllabus should present target items to the learner in an order of increasing linguistic difficulty. Thus, simple structures are selected for initial presentation and more complex structures are introduced at later points. Decisions as to what is simple vs. complex in the target language are based on linguistic analyses of the target grammar. Structures which require few transformational operations for their realization and grammatical forms which serve only one or two functions are presented earlier than those which are transformationally more complex or whose form-function relationship is less transparent. Thus, simple, declarative sentences are introduced prior to question forms, and yes-no questions are presented earlier than wh-questions. Regular plural is taught before articles *a* and *the*.

Such organization of material in the instructional syllabus from simple to complex is intuitively appealing. However, it has lacked empirical support demonstrating its impact on second language acquisition. With regard to English grammatical morphemes, for example, research has shown that the factor most critical to their order of appearance in the learner's developing interlanguage is not their degree of relative linguistic simplicity, but, rather, their frequency of occurrence in the input available to the learner (Larsen-Freeman, 1975, 1976a, b).

Crucial to the relevance of this finding for syllabus design is the fact that the data for determining morpheme production order were collected primarily from subjects learning English in *both* the naturalistic community *and* the second language classroom. All subjects, therefore, had access to naturalistic input, which may have served as their primary resource for second language acquisition. This is not an unlikely possibility as, in contrast to findings from Larsen-Freeman (1976b), a recent study of teachers' speech during English language lessons (Long & Sato, 1983) found no significant correlation between morpheme frequency order in the teachers' input and the morpheme accuracy order of second language acquirers who had access to the wider community. Unless comparisons are made between subjects acquiring English in naturalistic settings and those who are learning English through formal instruction exclusively, there is no way of knowing whether classroom input, in which grammatical forms and functions are isolated for presentation, then organized according to gradations in linguistic complexity, can alter the natural course of second language acquisition, i.e. inhibit the sequences and processes through which a second language is acquired in the classroom.

Linguistic complexity and second language acquisition: Previous research on plural -s, articles, and progressive -ing

Although not focused on classroom second language learning, a number of researchers in second language acquisition have examined the relationship between linguistic complexity of certain English grammatical morphemes and the ease with which they are acquired. Krashen, for example (Krashen, 1977, 1978, 1981) has claimed that some morphemes are easier to "learn" than others. According to Krashen's definition of the term, "learning" as the conscious internalization of target language rules, the forms and functions of morphemes such as plural -s can be brought to the learner's attention because they are easy to identify and few in number. For plural -s, three allomorphs — /s/, /z/, and /ə z/ — each phonologically conditioned, are used to express more than one countable item in a straightforward and transparent form-function relationship. Articles, on the other hand, are "hard to learn". Rules for their use often depend on a variety of linguistic and extra-linguistic factors pertaining to their associated noun referent. Such factors include the referent's first or second mention in the discourse and its degree of representativeness, visibility, or familiarity to speaker and listener. These factors are not fixed, but rather, subject to setting, topic, and interlocutor relationships, and hence, are difficult to isolate for the learner. According to Krashen, articles cannot be learned through isolated presentation and practice, but must be acquired through negotiated interaction with speakers of the target language.

Wagner-Gough (1978) and those who have drawn from her research (Wagner-Gough & Hatch, 1975; Larsen-Freeman, 1980), have written extensively about the complex relationships between the grammatical morpheme progressive -ing and the numerous functions it serves in expressing verb aspect. Additional complications are posed because the form, -ing, can function not only in aspectual constructions, but in nominal subjects and objects, as well as participial modifiers.

Linguistic complexity and learnability: In classroom second language acquisition

The study to be reported in this chapter (based in part on research from Pica, 1982, 1983), which investigated the sequences and processes of second language development among adult acquirers of English L2 Spanish L1, has also provided information relevant to the learnability of plural -s, articles, and progressive -ing. Pica compared the acquisition of English grammatical morphology among 18 subjects, each representing one of the three following conditions of target language exposure: (1) formal classroom instruction; (2) naturalistic input; and (3) a combination of instruction and naturalistic input. She found the following results with regard to the developmental sequences and processes involved in second language acquisition:

1. All three groups bore striking resemblance to each other in their acquisition of article *a*. They followed a developmental sequence in which initial accuracy was achieved in chunk-like expressions (e.g. *a little, a lot*), then analysed into noun object constructions (such as *have a friend, went to a movie*). This pattern appeared to be unaffected by the way in which article *a* had been presented in classroom instruction.

2. Subjects who had experienced exclusive exposure to classroom input (condition 1) achieved a higher rank order accuracy for plural *-s* than subjects from the other two conditions, but a lower rank order accuracy for progressive *-ing*. In addition, similar processes of oversuppliance and omission of target morphology (e.g. *one books, many friend*) were used by all subjects. However, these proportions differed according to target language exposure condition.

The results of Pica's research (to be discussed more fully below) suggest that classroom instruction can accelerate natural sequences and processes of second language acquisition for linguistically simple morphology such as plural *-s*, but can also retard these sequences and processes for the more linguistically complex progressive *-ing*. For highly complex grammatical items such as article *a*, instruction appears to have little impact, as learners follow naturalistic processes and sequences which appear to be unrelated to the ways in which articles are taught in their classrooms or presented in their textbooks.

Pienemann argues (this volume) that in order for syllabus design to be effective, it must be based on principles of natural second language acquisition. It will be proposed in this chapter that principles of classroom second language acquisition, related to linguistic features of target morphology, should also be taken into account in syllabus design. Claims will be made that: (1) When English grammatical morphology is presented in the classroom through isolation of forms and practice of functions, factors of linguistic complexity of individual morphemes can affect learners' natural psycholinguistic processing tendencies; and (2) These factors should have a bearing on not only which English grammatical morphemes should be selected for incorporation into the teaching syllabus (e.g. plural *-s*), but which can or should be excluded as well (e.g. article *a* or progressive-*ing*).

The present study: Research design

Subjects for the study consisted of 18 adult native Spanish speakers, ages 18–50, representing the three different conditions of target language exposure cited above. There were six Instruction Only, six Naturalistic, and six Mixed subjects. Subjects were selected according to the following criteria:

Instruction Only: Subjects came from one or two large English language schools in Mexico City. With the exception of minimal input from films, television, music, newspapers, and magazines, their only exposure to and conversation with English speakers came through classroom and textbook instruction. Classroom lessons included both explicit grammar instruction and communicative practice activities, and provided students with opportunities for teacher feedback on their production of English. These subjects never resided in a setting in which English was spoken primarily or even frequently.

Naturalistic: Subjects' exposure to and conversation with English speakers came from residence in Standard English speaking communities in the United States. Although English grammars and textbooks and native speaker informants were available within their communities, subjects did not use these resources in their English acquisition. Only two subjects had ever attended an English language class, and in both cases, attendance was restricted to a few introductory lessons at most.

Mixed: Subjects' exposure to and conversation with English speakers came from both classroom and textbook instruction and the wider community. Subjects from this condition were attending an intensive English programme at a university in the United States, where classes focused on both grammatical forms and communicative functions of English. Opportunities were available for teacher feedback on production. All subjects resided on campus, or in nearby communities. Each had either a regular conversation partner or an American roommate.

It was important to control for proficiency level of the subjects in the three exposure conditions in order to provide a comparable cross-section of each group and to insure that any differences identified among the groups were not due to differences in overall level of second language proficiency. Therefore, in the Instruction Only and Mixed conditions, two subjects each were chosen from the Beginner, Intermediate, and Advanced Intermediate divisions of their respective schools. Placement in these sections was determined by standardized test scores and teacher assessment.

Since this selection procedure could not be followed for the Naturalistic subjects, and additional procedure was used as a control for proficiency level. This involved choosing subjects in each condition who were at different stages along a continuum of negation development identified by Stauble (1981). Each group therefore represented a cross-section of negation development, ranging from early through intermediate and advanced stages.[1] Negation stage was chosen as a control for proficiency level because Stauble's findings showed that it was a gross indicator of acquisition for verb phrase morphology and suggested that it might have similar sensitivity to other areas of morphological development. Thus, there were two independent measures of proficiency for subjects in the Instruction Only and Mixed conditions — school placement and negation stage, and one measure for the Naturalistic subjects — negation stage.

Data for the study consisted of hour-long audiotaped conversations between each subject and a researcher, based on a variety of topics selected between them. All of the data from the conversations were transcribed according to standard orthography and the following analyses were conducted on each subjects' interlanguage production:

1. Percentage of target-like use (TLU) for English grammatical morphology. This analysis was conducted according to guidelines from Lightbown et al. (1980) and Stauble (1981). Morphemes were first scored for correct use in obligatory contexts. This score then became the numerator of a ratio which included in its denominator the sum of both the number of obligatory contexts for suppliance of the morpheme and the number of non-obligatory contexts in which the morpheme was supplied inappropriately. The formula for Target-Like Use Analysis is presented in Figure 1.

$$TLU = \frac{n \text{ correct suppliance in obligatory contexts}}{(n \text{ obligatory contexts} + n \text{ suppliance in non-obligatory contexts})} \times 100$$

FIGURE 1   *Formula for Target-Like Use Analysis of Morphemes*

2. Rank orders of morphemes based on TLU percentage scores, for each group of subjects. The group rank orders were then compared using Spearman rank order correlation coefficients for their strength of association with each other ($\alpha = 0.05$). It was hypothesized that the rank order for the Instruction Only group would be different from that of the other groups.

3. Individual subjects' TLU scores for production of article *a* in each of the following linguistic environments:
(a) Chunk-like units produced either in isolation, or in predicate structures such as *(have) a little, (like) a lot, (visit) once a month*
(b) Noun complements and direct objects in predicate constructions such as *is a friend, have a son, read a book.*
(c) Noun objects of prepositions, e.g. *in a minute, with an accent.*
4. Dominant error types used by subjects in their interlanguage production of plural *-s* and progressive *-ing*. It was believed that identification of error type would give insight into the subjects' processing of the target language and their formation of hypotheses about English grammatical morphology. Among the error types examined were:
(a) Over-application of *-s* and *-ing* to linguistic environments where its use was not required, e.g. *I have two* childrens, *I read one* books, *I like to* studying *English.*
(b) Omission of *-s* or *-ing* in required linguistic environments: *I have two* child, *I read three* book, *I was* study *languages all last year.*

Findings: Acquisitional sequences and production rank orders

Spearman rank orders for TLU percentages on all grammatical morphemes produced by the three subject groups are indicated in Table 1,

TABLE 1   *Correlations between TLU Rank Orders of Each Group of Subjects*

Morpheme	Instruction Only		Naturalistic		Mixed	
	TLU %	rank	TLU %	rank	TLU %	rank
progressive -*ing*	69	5	87	2	74	3
plural -*s*	85	2	72	4.5	71	4
singular copula	89	1	88	1	94	1
progressive auxiliary	59	7	71	6	52	7
the	81	3	80	3	75	2
a	80	4	72	4.5	68	5
past irregular	66	6	65	7	64	6
past regular	47	9	58	8	44	8
third person singular	52	8	22	9	19	9

Rank over correlations with instruction only order:	Naturalistic:	$r_S = 0.87$, p <0.002
	Mixed:	$r_S = 0.90$, p <0.001
Rank order correlation with naturalistic order:	Mixed:	$r_S = 0.96$, p<0.000

together with correlation coefficients computed among them. Correlation among the groups was found to be statistically significant, indicating that all groups, across language exposure conditions, exhibited a highly similar overall rank order of morpheme target-like use. This finding suggested that formal teaching did not alter the natural course of second language development among the instructed subjects. Such claims have been made by Felix (1981) and Wode (1981), whose research has revealed similar sequences in negation and question development among learners in formal and naturalistic settings.

Of particular relevance for the present chapter, however, is the finding that, although overall rank order correlations were statistically significant, individual group ranks for certain morphemes differed considerably. As shown in Table 1, similar ranks were found for article *a* (at 4 for the Instruction Only group, 4.5 for Naturalistic, and 5 for Mixed); however, such comparable rankings were not shown in other areas. The Mixed and Naturalistic groups scored two and 2.5 ranks below the Instruction Only group for plural -*s*, but were two and three ranks *above* them for progressive -*ing*. Closer investigation of individual morpheme ranks for plural -*s* and progressive -*ing* thus indicated that exclusive exposure to classroom instruction had altered their relative order in the natural acquisitional sequence, assisting the acquisition of plural -*s*, but retarding that of progressive -*ing*. Such alterations in morpheme rank order were not found for most other morphemes such as article *a*. In fact, further inspection of production scores for *a* revealed that not only did classroom learners produce this morpheme in a rank order comparable to the Naturalistic group, but their acquisitional processes were similar as well.

Acquisition of article a

For individual subjects, across language exposure conditions, production accuracy for *a* was highly related to the linguistic environments in which this morpheme was required. According to an implicational series constructed to display the data, all subjects' production accuracy for *a* showed the following pattern: greater target-like use of *a* first in isolated units, then in noun complements and direct objects, and finally in noun objects of prepositions. Table 2 displays these data.[2] A coefficient of reproducibility (see Nie *et al.*, 1975) computed for this implicational series was $C_r = 0.926$, indicated that it was a valid scale for displaying the acquisitional pattern for article *a* for all subjects.

Individual subjects with total or partial access to classroom instruction in article *a* thus showed a sequence of development which was

TABLE 2   *An implicational table of TLU scores for article a in three sucessive linguistic environments for individual subjects*

Subject	Language exposure condition*	TLU a	Linguistic environment		
			(V)-Isol	V-$\dfrac{Obj}{Comp}$	Prep-Obj
Guillermo	N	96	100	96	95
Carmen	I	87	92	85	89
Carlos	M	84	96	78	100
Jorge	M	86	100	91	50
Samuel	I	80	100	88	44
Froylan	I	80	(100)	100	(0)
Hjalmar	M	77	100	81	40
Ignatio	I	69	(100)	86	(25)
Francisco	I	79	97	72	67
Josephine	N	58	100	58	33
Edgard	N	53	(100)	50	–
Luis	N	39	100	38	13
Jenny	M	21	(100)	40	0
Jose	M	17	86	0	0
Ophelia	I	25	(50)	(0)	(0)
Eugenia	N	33	–	40	(0)
Milagro	M	20	–	50	(0)
Josef	N	9	(0)	13	(0)

C_{rep} = 0.926
*N: Naturalistic
  I: Instruction only
  M: Mixed

statistically similar to those subjects acquiring English naturalistically. The overall pattern identified — that *a* became more target-like in isolated units before verb or prepositional phrase environments — gave strong indication that all subjects in the study first learned to use *a* in synthetic, chunk-like utterances, later broke down these units into separate morphological components, and then incorporated individual morphemes such as *a* into other structures. This tendency for an initially synthetic approach to language acquisition on the part of the learner has been identified under other naturalistic language learning conditions by Peters (1977) in her study of a child's first language development, and by Wong-Fillmore (1979) in her research on child L_2 acquisition.

The fact that English teaching textbooks and grammars (see, for example, Danielson & Hayden, 1973; Krohn, 1971; Praninskas, 1975; and Thomson & Martinet, 1980) do not teach article *a* in the ways that learners appear to acquire it, but instead through presentation and practice of rules for non-specificity and first mention, makes this finding particularly striking. In spite of the fact that classroom learners are given rules for processing and producing article *a*, they appear to follow natural processes identified in untutored first and second language acquisition. Instruction on complex morphology such as articles appears to have little consequence for the way in which article *a* is acquired.

In terms of syllabus design, this suggests that the forms and functions of complex morphology may be excluded from specific rule presentation to the learner. The fact that articles have been identified as a frequently occurring feature of both naturalistic input (Larsen-Freeman, 1975, 1976a) and teacher speech to students of English as a second language (Larsen-Freeman, 1976b; Long & Sato, 1983), suggests that they may be omitted from explicit presentation in the teaching syllabus and left to their inevitable inclusion in the teacher's communication to the learner.

Acquisition of plural -s: The role of formal instruction

As shown in Table 1, the rank order accuracy for plural *-s* was considerably higher for the Instruction Only group as compared with the Naturalistic and Mixed. In addition, a production pattern distinctive to the Naturalistic subjects was only mildly apparent in the two other groups. This was the tendency to express plural by using a free-form quantifier such as *a few*, *many*, *several* or a numeral, while omitting the *-s* inflection, a kind of production strategy which has been identified among a number of pidgin languages (Todd, 1974). Thus productions such as *three book*, *a few month*, and *many friend* were significantly more common among the Naturalistic subjects than among subjects who received classroom instruction.

Table 3 shows the raw frequencies of omission of plural *-s* in the presence of a premodifying quantifier (e.g. *I read three book*) and omission of plural *-s* without premodifying quantifier (e.g. *I read the book*) in obligatory context for plural. Proportionately more omission of plural *-s* in the presence of a premodifying quantifier was found among the Naturalistic group compared with the Instruction Only and Mixed groups. These differences were statistically significant ($\chi^2 = 17.02$, df = 1, p <0.001 and $\chi^2 - 12.26$, df = 1, p <0.001, respectively). There was no statistically significant difference in proportions of plural -s omission with premodifying quantifier and plural -s omission without quantifier between the Instruction Only and Mixed groups ($\chi^2 = 1.402$, df = 1, p <1.32, n.s.).

Based on these findings, it appeared that classroom instruction enhanced the acquisition of plural -s. Greater production accuracy was achieved much earlier in the overall order of morpheme development for subjects who had exclusive exposure to classroom input. In addition, the use of non-target-like production processes found in pidginized languages was greatly reduced among *all* subjects who had been exposed to classroom instruction, i.e. subjects from groups (1) and (3). The apparent ease with which plural -s was acquired by classroom learners may have been related to its linguistic simplicity. Its phonologically conditioned allomorphs and straightforward form-function relationship make it easy for the learner to recognize in classroom presentation and practice.

In naturalistic input, identification of the plural -s inflection may not be as obvious, as it is a bound morpheme, always attached to the lexical item it quantifies. For naturalistic acquirers, plural -s may thus be quite imperceptible in the stream of conversational speech, and when it occurs in redundant linguistic environments, in which plural nouns are preceded by free-form quantifiers (e.g. many books, three months), plural -s may be simply overlooked by the learner. The fact that plural -s is easy to recognize in isolation, but can go unnoticed in conversational speech may

TABLE 3 *Numbers and proportions of Plural -s omission with premodifying quantifier and without premodifying quantifier in obligatory context for each group of subjects*

	-s Omission with quantifier		-s Omission without quantifier		Total	
	n	*%*	*n*	*%*	*n*	*%*
Instruction Only	16	42	22	58	38	100
Naturalistic	90	76	28	24	118	100
Mixed	45	52	42	48	87	100

χ^2 Instruction only × Naturalistic[1]	17.02, p < 0.001
χ^2 Instruction only × Mixed[1]	1.402, n.s.
χ^2 Naturalistic × Mixed[1]	12.26, p < 0.001

1. df = 1, p < 0.05

have been a powerful factor in its accelerated rate of acquisition for the Instruction Only learners. The findings regarding classroom acquisition of plural -*s* thus offer support for inclusion of the plural -*s* morpheme as an isolated form and function in the language teaching syllabus.

The case of progressive -ing

Of additional relevance to the consideration of target structure learnability in selecting items for the second language syllabus is the grammatical morpheme, progressive -*ing*. The form, -*ing*, suffixed to a base verb, serves quite disparate functions in English. It is used not only (1) to indicate progressive aspect, but also as (2) a pre- and post-modifier and (3) a nominal subject or object:

1. He's smoking two packs of cigarettes a day.
   While he was smoking a cigarette, he began to cough.
2. He picked up the smoking cigarette from the ashtray.
   The man smoking the cigarette is my uncle.
3. Smoking can be dangerous for your health.
   He quit smoking last year.

Presenting and ordering rules for progressive -*ing* can thus be a complicated task for the syllabus designer since the form -*ing* serves more functions than the indication of verb aspect.

As shown above, in Table 1, the rank order accuracy for progressive -*ing* was much lower for the Instruction Only group as compared with the Naturalistic or Mixed groups. In addition, the dominant error pattern for all instructed subjects (groups (1) and (3)) was to overuse the -*ing* form, suffixing it to base verbs where its use was not required. However, this tendency was particularly strong among subjects from the Instruction Only group. Productions such as the following were significantly more frequently in the interlanguage of the instructed subjects, compared with that of the naturalistic:

1. I don't *understanding* these people
2. You don't *smoking* anymore?
3. (When I first got married), I don't *working*
4. I *thinking* in this holiday I don't start to work
5. (Every day) in the afternoon, I'm *returning* to my house and I have something to eat
6. I would like to *continuing* with these areas
7. Since that time, I started to *liking* English
8. It's so hard because I have to *remembering* all the rules

It appears from these findings that explicit instruction in the progressive -*ing* morpheme may not be beneficial to the promotion of its target-like use. Instructed learners, perhaps confused by the many possibilities for using -*ing* in English, added it to verbs where it was not required: Naturalistic acquirers, left to make their own hypotheses about the rules for progressive -*ing* based on available input, were more successful in restricting its use to those verb environments in which progressive aspect was required. The finding that progressive -*ing*, as articles, occurs frequently in teachers' speech to students of English (Larsen-Freeman, 1976b), suggests that this morpheme may be acquired more efficiently if excluded from formal presentation in the teaching syllabus and made available through less formal interaction between teacher and learners.

Overview and outlook

In designing an effective syllabus for the classroom language learner, it must be taken into account that isolation of grammatical forms and structures, provision of teacher and textbook explanation, and teacher feedback on production, all characteristic features of the classroom setting, can have an impact on the natural sequences and processes of second language development. There is empirical evidence, however, that this impact is not uniform, but depends on the complexity of individual grammatical structures in the target language. Classroom instruction appears to accelerate the acquisition of the linguistically simple plural -*s*, retard the acquisition of the more complex progressive -*ing*, but have no effect on the developmental course for the highly complex article *a*. These three findings suggest that research on classroom second language acquisition can provide criteria for the selection as well as exclusion of target structures for direct presentation in the language syllabus. Such exclusion of complex items from direct classroom presentation and practice necessitates that other ways be found for assisting their acquisition in the classroom. Hopefully, further study of classroom second language acquisition will provide information on the ways in which complex grammatical structures can be learned efficiently in classroom settings.

There is the possibility, however, that teachers and curriculum developers, who often have different perspectives from researchers regarding the language learner's task, may find little to abstract from second language acquisition research which is relevant to their concerns for language syllabus design. This is because a principal goal of most language instruction is to help the learner to use grammatical utterances in order to interact successfully in various academic, professional, or social situations.

However, studies of second language acquisition, including the one described in this chapter, have focused on how learners acquire the grammatical system of the second language, rather than how they develop the ability to use this system for communicative purposes. This kind of research can inform the teaching of target grammatical constructions, but not necessarily their appropriate use in target discourse.

By encorporating into a communicative syllabus, principles for structured grading which have been derived from second language acquisition research, Pienemann's plan shows promise in this area..Further work is needed, however, in specifying the variations which occur in the structural devices used to fulfil target language functions, depending on setting, topic, participant roles, and other sociolinguistic factors. This will require more empirical data than are available at present regarding ways in which native speakers use the grammar of their language in social interaction.

Information regarding effective syllabus design must come therefore, from an integrated perspective drawing from research in a number of areas, including both naturalistic and classroom second language acquisition, psycholinguistic and sociolinguistic dimensions of interlanguage development, discourse analysis of native speaker interaction. The enormity of this task will call for contributions from not only the second language researcher, but the linguist and classroom teacher as well.

Notes to Chapter 6

1. Stauble has labelled these negation stages as basilang, mesolang, and acrolang, based on analogy with basilect, mesolect, and acrolect from pidgin studies.
2. Italicized production scores indicate deviations from the implicational pattern. Scores based on fewer than five obligatory contexts are shown in parentheses. Dashes indicate an absence of obligatory context for *a* in a linguistic environment.

References

Danielson, D. & Hayden, R. 1973, *Using English*. Englewood Cliffs: Prentice-Hall, Inc.

Felix, S. 1981, The effect of formal instruction on second language acquisition. *Language Learning*, 31, 87–112.

Krashen, S.D. 1977, Some issues relating to the monitor model. In H.D. Brown, C. Yorio & R. Crymes (eds), *On TESOL '77*. Washington, D.C.: TESOL.

—— 1978, Individual variation in the use of the monitor. In W. Ritchie (ed.), *Second Language Acquisition Research*. New York: Academic Press.

—— 1981, *Second Language Acquisition and Second Language Learning*. Oxford: Pergamon Press.

Krohn, R. 1971, *English Sentence Structure*. Ann Arbor: The University of Michigan Press.

Larsen-Freeman, D. 1975, The acquisition of grammatical morphemes by adult ESL learners. *TESOL Quarterly*, 9:4, 409–19.

—— 1976a, An explanation for the morpheme accuracy order of learners of English as a second language. *Language Learning*, 26:1; 125–35.

—— 1976b, ESL teacher speech as input to the ESL learner. *UCLA Workpapers in Teaching English as a Second Language*, 10: 45–49.

—— 1980, *Discourse Analysis in Second Language Acquisition Research*. Rowley, Mass.: Newbury House.

Lightbown, P., Spada, N. & Wallace, R. 1980, Some effects of instruction on child and adolescent ESL learners. In S. Krashen & R. Scarcella (eds), *Research in Second Language Acquisition: Selected Papers of the Los Angeles Second Language Acquisition Research Forum*. Rowley, Mass.: Newbury House.

Long, M. & Sato, C. 1983, Classroom foreigner talk discourse: forms and functions of teachers' questions. In H. Seliger & M. Long (eds), *Classroom Language Acquisition and Use: New Perspectives*. Rowley, Mass.: Newbury House.

Nie, N., Hull, H., Jenkins, K., Steinbrenner, K. & Bent, D. 1975, *Statistical Package for the Social Sciences*. New York: McGraw-Hill.

Peters, A. 1977, Language learning strategies: Does the whole equal the sum of the parts? *Language*, 53, 560–73.

Pica, T. 1982, Second language acquisition in different language contexts. Ph.D. dissertation, University of Pennsylvania.

—— 1983, Adult acquisition of English as a second language under different conditions of exposure. *Language Learning*, 33,4.

Praninskas, J. 1975, *Rapid Review of English Grammar*. Englewood Cliffs: Prentice-Hall, Inc.

Stauble, A.M. 1981, A comparison of a Spanish–English and Japanese–English second language continuum: verb phrase morphology. Paper presented at the first Europe–North American workshop on cross-linguistic second language acquisition research. Lake Arrowhead, CA.

Thomson, A.J. & Martinet, A.V. 1980, *A Practical English Grammar. New Edition*. London: Oxford University Press.

Todd, L. 1974, *Pidgins and Creoles*. Boston: Routledge and Kegan Paul.

Wagner-Gough, J. 1978, Excerpts from comparative studies in second language learning. In E. Hatch (ed.), *Second Language Acquisition. A Book of Readings*. Rowley, Mass.: Newbury House.

Wagner-Gough, J. & Hatch, E. 1975, The importance of input data in second language acquisition studies. *Language Learning*, 25, 297–308.

Wode, H. 1981, *Learning a Second Language I. An Integrated View of Language Acquisition*. Tübingen: Gunter Narr.

Wong-Fillmore, L. 1979, Individual differences in second language acquisition. In C. Fillmore, D. Kempler & W. Wong (eds), *Individual Differences in Language Ability and Language Behavior*. New York: Academic Press.

7 Learnability and learner strategies in second language syntax and phonology

BJÖRN HAMMARBERG

University of Stockholm, Sweden

In his paper "Learnability and syllabus construction" in this volume, Manfred Pienemann discusses a type of learning barrier in second-language syntax which he relates to constraints on the learner's capacity of processing sentence structure. Drawing on the findings of the ZISA research group (cf. Meisel *et al.*, 1981; Clahsen *et al.*, 1983; Clahsen, 1984; Pienemann, 1984), he deals with the so-called developmental features of the learner's interlanguage, i.e. features that have been found to be acquired in an invariable sequence by learners in an untutored L2 acquisition setting. In the ZISA investigations, a number of word order rules have been particularly identified as developmental interlanguage features. Pienemann's current examples are the German rules "adverb-preposing", "verb separation" and "inversion" as acquired by Italian and Spanish migrants to West Germany. The criterion of developmental features is that they appear in the acquisitional sequence in a fixed implicational order of priority, common to different learners, whereas other features, such as the rule of using a copula, do not pattern in this regular way (Meisel *et al.*, 1981:123). The fixed acquisition sequence is explained by the ZISA group (Clahsen, 1984) in terms of a set of learner's strategies for processing sentence structure. These function as constraints on complex structures and can, according to Pienemann, only be overcome step by step in the course of interlanguage development. Thus the cited word order rules represent acquisitional stages which are "interrelated in such a way that at each stage the processing prerequisites for the following stages are developed" (Pienemann, this volume, Chapter 2, p. 37).

This hypothesis is attractive because, if it holds true, the ordering of developmental features furnishes useful criteria for determining learner's developmental stages and finding a suitable order of progression in teaching and in syllabus grading. On the other hand, however, the hypothesis also implies a pedagogical constraint in that the rigid ordering conditions of developmental features impose restrictions on teachability. From an experiment in teaching German word order to Italian migrant children, Pienemann (1984) draws the conclusion that insurmountable learning barriers will arise if the proper order of acquisition is violated in the syllabus, or if any step in the sequence is left out.

In the present chapter I shall point to some other aspects of learnability in second language acquisition, also taking phonology into account. I shall not be primarily concerned with chains of acquisitional stages, but rather consider some types of learnability conditions which affect learners' solutions in interlanguage. Hence, unlike Pienemann in his present paper, I shall not limit the discussion to those features of interlanguage which pattern in uniform acquisitional sequences. But it seems to me that the problem of learning barriers which Pienemann brings up in his chapter forms an interesting point of departure for a discussion.

Processibility constraints and communicative relevance: Evidence from word order acquisition

We may concentrate for a moment on the word order rules and take a closer look at one point where I feel hesitant about Pienemann's conclusions.

The point I have in mind is the problem of how to treat *inversion* in a graded syllabus. Inversion, i.e. the element order Finite Verb – Subject, is used in German
   (a) in main clause *statements* in which an element other than the
        subject is placed first in the sentence;
   (b) in direct *wh-questions* in which the wh word or a phrase containing
        the wh word is not the subject;
   (c) in direct *yes/no-questions*; here the finite verb occurs initially.

Pienemann maintains that it is necessary to postpone the systematic teaching of inversion until the earlier rules in the natural sequence have been acquired; when there is need to use questions at the beginner's stage one should resort to simplified syntactic patterns (even though these have a stylistically somewhat special status in the target language) rather than use the normal question patterns with inversion. The reason for this is that the acquisition of inversion is assumed to require the structure-processing capacity that is developed at the earlier stages. More precisely, Clahsen (1984) postulates a "canonical order strategy" (i.e. a strategy of keeping to a uniform word order in sentences at early stages of L2 acquisition), and an "initialization/finalization strategy" (which would successively replace the former and would allow the movement of constituents to the beginning or end of sentences only, but not to internal positions). Inversion, then, is assumed to require the abandonment of both these strategies.

An informal observation made by teachers of Swedish as a second language is that inversion in yes/no-questions is relatively easy to learn whereas inversion in statements with a preposed element is a more persistent problem. Comparing German and Swedish as L2 is not out of place here, for the relevant parts of the word order systems are rather similar in the two languages. There are some conspicuous word order differences between German and Swedish, to be sure — notably the different placement of negation, non-finite verb forms and verb particles, and the finite verbs of sub-clauses — but they do not seem to interfere significantly with the issue of inversion which concerns us here. Inversion works alike in the two languages. In other words, the rules (a), (b) and (c) as stated above are equally valid for both German and Swedish. The following simple standard-language examples will illustrate this; the cases of inversion are italicized:

MAIN CLAUSE STATEMENT:
1. Peter kommt heute./Peter kommer idag.   'Peter will come today.'

2. Heute *kommt Peter.*/Idag *kommer Peter.*   'Today Peter will come'.

3. Peter kennt ihn./Peter känner honom.   'Peter knows him'.

4. Ihn *kennt Peter.*/Honom *känner Peter.*   'Him Peter knows.'

5. Er kommt, wenn er fertig ist./   'He will come when
   Han kommer, när han är färdig.   he is finished.'

6. Wenn er fertig ist, *kommt er.*/   'When he is finished,
   När han är färdig, *kommer han.*   he will come.'

DIRECT WH-QUESTION:
7. Wer kommt heute?/Vem kommer idag?   'Who will come today?'

8. Wann *kommt Peter?*/När *kommer Peter?*   'When will Peter come?'

9. Wann *ist er* fertig?/När *är han* färdig?   'When will he be
                                                   finished?'

DIRECT YES/NO-QUESTION:
10. *Kommt Peter* heute?/*Kommer Peter* idag?   'Will Peter come today?'

11. *Kennt Peter* ihn?/*Känner Peter* honom?   'Does Peter know him?'

12. *Kommt er*, wenn er fertig ist?/   'Will he come when
    Kommer han, när han är färdig?   he is finished?'

Sentences 1 to 9 conform to the "verb-second" principle, i.e. the finite verb always forms the second constituent of the (surface) sentence, regardless of whether the subject or another element is placed first. Inversion applies in the latter case, as in 2, 4, 6, 8 and 9. The difference between statement and wh question structure lies in the fact that the wh word is obligatorily placed initially in the questions, whereas the choice of initial constituent in statements is allowed to alternate according to considerations of text structure. In wh-questions, then, inversion applies when the wh-word does not function as subject, as in 8 and 9, as opposed to 7. Yes/no-questions, on the other hand, do not adhere to the verb-second principle, but require initial placement of the finite verb; cf. 10 vs. 1 & 2, 11 vs. 3 & 4, and 12 vs. 5 & 6. Hence, inversion applies throughout in yes/no-questions.

In the ZISA studies as well as in Pienemann's teaching experiment, the acquisition of inversion is treated as a single task, the differentiation of sentence types being regarded as a matter of the distribution of the rule over different syntactic contexts.

However, a closer inspection of what inversion is used for in the language shows that it serves different functions in different syntactic contexts. (The workings of inversion and other word order rules in Swedish and related languages is dealt with extensively in Hammarberg & Viberg, 1977 where, in particular, the functions of word order in expressing syntactic role, sentence type and sentence hierarchy are discussed.) In yes/no-questions, inversion serves as a question marker, distinguishing direct questions from statements. This stands out especially clearly in Swedish where intonation often does not differ in any essential way in yes/no-questions and the corresponding statements. Thus, here inversion is connected in a straightforward way with a very central and easy-to-grasp communicative function.

The role of inversion after a preposed non-subject is less obvious and far less likely to make sense at the beginner's stage. Being a main clause phenomenon, inversion is part of a larger syntactic machinery for signalling sentence hierarchy (main vs. subordinate clause). But mostly, inversion is not the only cue present in the sentence to show this distinction, nor is it always applicable; cf. Hammarberg & Viberg (1977) for details. Also, the communicative functions connected with subordination (which have to do, e.g. with the information structure of the utterance, or with reported vs. direct speech) are surely more subtle than the question/statement distinction.

In studies of L2 Swedish, there are some indications that learners acquire inversion in questions earlier than in statements, even if this issue has so far not been investigated very intensely.

Thus, in a little study by a group of immigrant teachers (Edström *et al.*, 1983), based on written composition data from adult learners with a wide range of L1 backgrounds, learners were compared with respect to length of course participation and mastery of inversion in questions and statements. Learners with long-time residence in Sweden before course participation formed a separate group. Table 1 is adapted from that study. it shows that acquisition of inversion in questions was in general markedly ahead of acquisition of inversion in statements. The difference was especially drastic at the lower stages and in the group of learners who had picked up Swedish on their own for a long time before coming to courses.

A similar tendency is apparent in Hyltenstam's (1978) data which are based on an elicitation test with adult learners with various L1's. Hyltenstam displays the use of inversion in various contexts in a number of

TABLE 1

Group of subjects	Weeks of instruction	% correct inversion	
		Questions	Statements
I	< 9	92	40
II	9–16	85	46
III	17–24	87	65
IV	25–32	100	80
V	33–40	100	86
VI	> 40	100	100
VII	Mixed; 1–3½ years' stay in Sweden before course	92	49

diagrams which make it possible to extract comparative information on inversion in statements, yes/no-questions and wh-questions, as well as in direct vs. indirect questions. Many of the test subjects show low values for the use of *inversion in statements*. Yet, at the same time variation along the scale of mastery is great, and several subjects show high values, too. According to Hyltenstam's interpretation, this shows that "... the rule is difficult to get going. However, once the initial inertia for this structure is overcome, learning rapidly gains momentum and development to target behaviour is rapid" (p. 36). For *inversion in direct questions*, high values dominate which indicates that the rule is mastered more easily in this context. Another point which is also illustrated in the data is that inversion is used to a large extent (erroneously) in embedded questions, too. This confirms the expectation that the main-clause marking function of inversion should be harder to grasp than the question-signalling function, and it fits well with the result that inversion in statements is difficult. Finally, *direct yes/no-questions* and *direct wh-questions* can be compared. With the reservation that the amount of data is slight on this particular point, we may note that inversion in both types of questions appears to be about equally easy to acquire.

Summarizing and drawing conclusions from these various findings, we may first note that inversion seems to be acquired earlier and more easily in yes/no-questions than in statements with a preposed non-subject. This can be explained along two separate lines. In terms of structure-processing load, the two cases of inversion are actually not on a par. According to Clahsen and Pienemann, inversion is difficult because it violates two processing strategies at the same time, the one that favours a canonical order and the one that favours movement of elements to initial or final position only. But whereas this is true of sentence-internal inversion, inversion in yes/no-questions is actually in harmony with the second strategy since it amounts to initialization of the finite verb. It should therefore, from this point of view, be expected to be easier. The other line of explanation is of course the communicative relevance of the question function. Inversion in yes/no-questions is likely to make more sense to the learner at early stages than inversion in statements because it expresses a pragmatic function that is useful and needed early.

But what about inversion in wh-questions? It is sentence-internal, and hence should be assumed to require great processing capacity. Moreover, it is not a question marker in the target language, but an effect of the initial placement of a non-subject wh word, i.e. a manifestation of the same "verb-second" principle that also applies to statements. Why then should inversion in wh-questions be easy to acquire, as Hyltenstam's data suggest? The following explanation may be proposed. Even though inversion in wh-questions is not a valid question marker *for the speakers of the target language*, it is possible that *the learner* at some stage of his interlanguage development interprets inversion in this context as a question-marking device by generalization from yes/no-questions where it clearly has this role — given the fact that wh-questions, too, are questions and given that other functions of inversion are hard to discover. This would then favour his use of inversion in wh-questions, but not in statements. This would mean, however, that the learner in this case is guided more by direct communicative relevance than by structure-processing strategies. Yet it does *not* imply that structure-processing strategies are generally unimportant in L2 acquisition.

Admittedly, the cited comparative data for inversion in yes/no-questions and wh-questions are rather scanty and must be seen as preliminary evidence. We may gather some parallel information from research on the acquisiton of question structure in English (as L1 and as L2). Zobl (1980), in discussing some such studies, points out that some of them show that inversion is acquired earlier in yes/no-questions than in wh-questions — i.e. that yes/no-questions have an "innovative role" in the acquisition of inversion. Other studies show no time difference between the two question types. Thus yes/no-question inversion appears to be either earlier in the acquisition sequence than wh-question inversion, or simultaneous. No studies show them to be acquired in the reversed order. In explaining these findings, neither the structure-processing factor nor the communicative relevance factor can be ruled out.

Structure-processing strategies of the kind proposed by Clahsen for word order are strategies of simplification. Slobin (1973), who proposed a set of "operating principles" for L1 acquisition from which he derived a set of "universals of grammatical development" much similar to Clahsen's strategies for L2, speaks of these principles as heuristics which "guide the child in developing strategies for the production and interpretation of speech and for the construction of rule systems" (1973:194). It is not difficult to think of the L2 processing strategies as useful for the learner, in that they help him cope with the unfamiliar language, making it manageable for him at his current stage of proficiency and offering him an orderly approach to sorting out its structure. A crucial question then is what makes the learner abandon the processing strategies in the course of his second-language development. One very general answer would be that as the learner's language grows and is used for a richer variety of communicative tasks, it will be inadequate to adhere to strategies such as canonical order or initialization/finalization, because that would prevent the necessary structural diversification from developing. In other words, the processing strategies impose strong limitations at the early stages, but give way successively as the size of the learner's language grows. This is in effect a dynamic model of language acquisition in which the learner's progress is conditioned by competing forces, or competing requirements. On one side are the coping strategies, on the other the various needs, more or less urgent or ambitious, of expressing or comprehending diverse messages in the language. Here, however, I think the inversion example has shown that the latter is not only a matter of the functional expansion of the learner's language in general, but that we must also consider the relative importance of specific communicative needs which may stand out as relevant to the learner and cause him to suppress a processing strategy which he would otherwise have adhered to. Expressing questions may be such a communicative need at an early stage, and this may facilitate coping with inversion in questions (without necessarily having much effect on inversion in statements). The learner is likely to identify different communicative needs as having different degrees of importance at a given point of interlanguage development, and under given external conditions.

The idea that learners are sensitive to a factor of communicative relevance is of course not new. After all, "notional" or "communicative" approaches to language teaching are based on the assumption that the teacher can successfully arouse the learner's interest in particular notions or communicative needs, and then teach the pertinent means of expressing them. What I think Pienemann's chapter and the present discussion indicate is that *the interplay of structure-processing strategies and the communicative relevance factor* in L2 acquisition should be worthwhile exploring further.

A phonological perspective

Let us now turn our attention to aspects of learnability in phonology. In particular, let us address the question whether structural processibility and communicative relevance are factors that may influence learnability in phonology, too. After our discussion of syntactic matters, there are a couple of remarks that need to be made at the outset.

First, the basis for communicative relevance is somewhat different in phonology than in morpho-syntax, due to the fact that phonological structure is more indirectly related to semantic notions. The most direct relationships can be found in the area of suprasegmental phonology, where e.g. sentence intonation in some languages can perform the same function as inversion or question morphemes in others to signal question, or where we may identify traits of intonation and stress as meaningful in various ways in the discourse. Otherwise, the function of phonological structure is rather to build up the higher levels of structure in language. Thus, we may relate traits of word prosody in Germanic languages (stress placement, tonal accents, quantity patterns) to the morphological structure of words. The function of segmental phonological structure — which I will concentrate on here — can be seen as primarily lexical: to build up an adequate variety of pronounceable words that can form the lexical stock of the language, and to make it possible to discriminate between these forms. Also, some phonological rules serve the execution of speech; in particular, a speech-economizing function is apparent in assimilation and reduction rules. Consequently, the communicative function that concerns us here is not immediately connected with traits of phonological structure, but with the meaningful elements which they build up and express. A word form in the lexicon or an inflectional form may be felt by learners as being more or less communicatively interesting because there is a certain content attached to it, and correspondingly it may be interesting for a learner to grasp its exact phonological form. But it is not the phonological structure itself that produces degrees of communicative relevance.

Second, it is a frequently made observation that the role of transfer from L1 in L2 acquisition appears to be more prominent in phonology than in morphology or syntax. Even researchers who have deliberately searched for non-transfer phenomena have tended to stress the abundance of transfer in phonology; cf., e.g. Garnica & Herbert (1979). Both transfer solutions and simplification solutions have been noted as major factors shaping the phonological form of interlanguages; for a research survey see Tarone (1978). A discussion of learnability in phonology in terms of structural manageability can therefore hardly overlook the transfer factor.

Convergence of simplification and transfer: the case of vowel substitutions

The last-mentioned point becomes more interesting, however, with the observation that there are systematic connections between transfer and simplification solutions. The two are often indistinguishable in actual practice. This can be explored in a typological or universalist context. I will give an example from the field of vowel system typology to illustrate this tendency.

A common observation in multi-language comparisons is that different languages display structuring solutions of varying complexity on a given point in the language, and that there is a tendency to favour simplicity in the design of languages so that the relatively simple solutions tend to occur in a larger number of languages than the complex ones.

Thus, in the case of vowel phoneme systems, a simple five-vowel system, /i, e, a, o, u/, is found in many languages throughout the world. Furthermore, the shape of vowel systems has been shown to be predictable from the number of vowel phonemes that are distinguished in the language. This works with fairly good accuracy especially with the smaller systems; cf. Liljencrants & Lindblom, 1972; Crothers, 1978; Lindblom, forthcoming. The explanation for this is that the need for maximal perceptual contrast between the vowel phonemes in the paradigm causes the vowels to fill out the available acoustic vowel space in an optimal way. This also leads to implicational relationships in the buildup of the world's vowel systems to the effect that the smaller systems tend to form subsets of the larger ones, with minor phonetic adjustments, in a hierarchical order. The hierarchy shown in Figure 1 has been proposed by Crothers (1978) on the basis of observed types of vowel systems. (This is to be understood as a hierarchy for *typological tendencies*, which are not borne out faithfully in every particular language.)

If we choose to look at Swedish as a target language for L2 acquisition, we are faced with a rather complex vowel system of a less common kind, displaying, for one thing, the extremely unusual property of

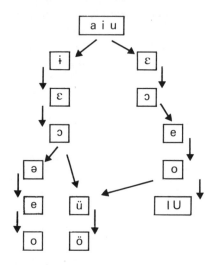

FIGURE 1   *Implicational relationships in the structure of vowel systems in languages. From Crothers (1978).*

distinguishing two kinds of rounded vowels, the "out-rounded" [y] type and the "in-rounded" [ʉ] type, beside the unrounded type. The acoustic relationships of the Swedish vowels are shown in an Fl-F2 diagram in Figure 2. According to some phonologists, Swedish has a nine-vowel system, plus a length distinction which causes the vowels to occur with a centralized-short and a noncentralized-long (or in some cases diphthongal) variant. According to others, there is an 18-vowel system with length as a distinctive feature in the vowels. [æ] and [œ̞] are positional variants occurring before /r/.

Bannert (1980) has made an extensive inventory of pronunciation errors in L2 Swedish, based on recorded interviews with adult learners representing 25 different L1 backgrounds: American English, Arabic, British English, Chinese, Czech/Slovak, Dutch, Finnish, French, German, Greek, Hindi, Hungarian, Icelandic, Japanese, Persian, Polish, Portuguese, Punjabi, Russian, Serbo-Croatian, Spanish, Swahili, Tamil, Thai,

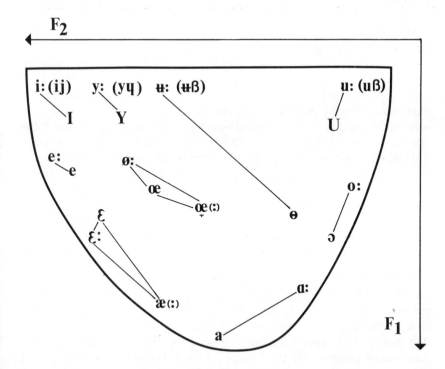

Figure 2 *Swedish vowels in the acoustic vowel space. The corresponding long (or diphthongal) and short vowels and some major positional allophones are connected with lines.*

and Turkish. The inventory has the form of a chart for each of the 25 L1 backgrounds, where the occurring deviations from the target language pronunciation have been noted. Bannert's data for vowels in stressed syllables will concern us here. It is interesting to study some overall tendencies that they exhibit.

Even with the necessary reservation that this particular sample of L1's is not an ideal typological representation of the world's languages — a fact that we cannot blame the author for since his intentions with the material were different — there is still enough typological differentiation for the material to serve as an illustrative example in the present discussion.

Two things soon become apparent at a closer study. First, checking with descriptions of the 25 first languages (as given in Ruhlen, 1975) shows that deviations from the target pronunciation usually go in the direction toward L1 counterparts, i.e. they are either L1-like or form phonetically logical compromises between an L1 and an L2 sound. It is clear that deviations are regularly made to meet the constraints imposed on the speakers by their L1 phonological competence. Second, the types of deviations occurring in learners with different L1's tend to converge. Figure 3 shows this second tendency. Here I have counted the L1's for which a particular type of sound substitution has been noted. This number thus constitutes the *cross-L1 range* (within the given sample of L1's) of the substitution in question. (Substitutions with a range number below 4 have been left out of the figure.) This makes a characteristic pattern of substitution emerge. We can see that for some sound types substitution goes more often *from* the sound in question than *towards* it. That is, these sound types tend to be *under-used* which is an indication that they are difficult. (Vowels in circles in the figure.) With other sound types the reverse is true: substitution more often goes towards them than from them. In other words, they tend to be *over-used* which indicates that they are easier alternatives. (Vowels in squares in the figure.)

Now, if we look at the over-used sounds, [ɪ ɛ æ a ɔ ʊ], we see that they form a set that is well spread over the vowel space and would actually not be too unnatural for a six-vowel system in a real language. (It comes close to the Persian vowel system, for example.) This is a piled-up result that can also be traced for the various L1's. We could go through the substitution patterns for the separate L1's in Bannert's material and see that they each show a tendency in this direction, at the same time as the actual set of substitute vowels in each case varies to approach the size and shape of the respective L1 vowel system.

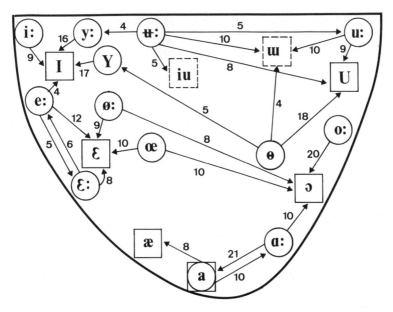

FIGURE 3   *Cross-L1 range of vowel substitutions in L2 Swedish, based on Bannert's (1980) data (with certain revisions of phonetic symbols).*
Legend:
→   = *Substitution direction. The number indicates the number of L1's (out of 25) for which the substitution in question has been noted (= range figure).*
◯   = *The vowel is under-used by learners.*
▢   = *The vowel is over-used by learners.*
⌐⌐   = *The vowel does not occur in the target language.*

In summary, the set of vowel sounds we arrive at when looking for substitute vowels in learners' L2 performance (a) tends to meet the demands of the L1 in categorizing the vowel space, (b) tends to conform to a typological hierarchy for vowel systems, and (c) tends to comply with the acoustic-perceptual requirements for a phonetically optimal simpler version of the L2 paradigm. What we see is a natural coincidence of transfer from L1 and simplification of the L2 paradigm.

Some possible frameworks

There are various conceivable ways in which we may attempt to relate these observations to a theory. One approach is in terms of "typological markedness" (Greenberg, 1966). Those vowels that are more basic in the vowel hierarchy are less marked. Our vowel example can be said to illustrate a "natural selection" of the typologically less marked features of language structure in learner's interlanguages. To the extent that markedness relationships can be identified on independent grounds, markedness may therefore be useful as a predictor of difficulty in L2 acquisition.

An attempt to formulate a principle for such predictions is the "Markedness Differential Hypothesis" proposed by Eckman (1977:321). It states that those areas of the target language which differ from the native language and are more marked than the native language will be difficult, the relative degree of difficulty then corresponding to the relative degree of markedness, whereas those areas which are different but not more marked than the native language will not be difficult.

Eckman's favourite example in phonology has been word-final voiced obstruents in English, a phenomenon that can be shown to be highly marked and where learners are seen to come up with less marked solutions, such as devoicing the obstruent or adding a word-final vowel (Eckman, 1981 a,b). Notice that, unlike our example with the vowel paradigm, the concept of markedness is applied here to a context-sensitive, or syntagmatic regularity in phonology.

There have been a number of studies in recent years dealing with the acquisition of L2 syntax and phonology in a markedness framework, and therefore I will not pursue this topic further here. Compare Hyltenstam (forthcoming) for a research survey and a discussion of some issues.

In phonological theory, the notions of "naturalness" and "psychological reality" have bearing on what is easy or difficult in L2 acquisition. Judging from what has been demonstrated so far, it seems that the phonological regularities or limitations of L1 that tend to effectively govern the learner are those that are phonetically motivated in one way or another, whereas regularities that lack such motivation, such as morphologically conditioned rules or the more "abstract" rules proposed in generative descriptions, seem to have no influence on the learner.

In the theory of "natural phonology" put forward by Stampe (cf. Stampe, 1969, 1979; Donegan & Stampe, 1979), this dichotomy is expressed in the distinction between (phonetically motivated) *natural processes* and (phonetically unmotivated, merely conventional) *rules*. Typical examples of "processes" are the devoicing of obstruents, and especially devoicing in final position, as in German *Tag* [ta:k] "day" vs. *Tage* [ta:gə] "days" and *los* [lo:s] "loose" vs. *lösen* [lø:zən] "loosen". A typical "rule" is English Velar Softening which accounts for such alternations as *electri*[k] – *electri*[s]*ity*.

In Stampe's view, the full set of natural processes is inborn in the child, and the learning of the first language involves the gradual suppression of more and more of the processes until only those processes that limit the mature L1 system are operative; in addition, the learner will acquire a set of non-natural rules required by the L1 system. In acquiring an L2, then, it is the natural processes, and not the non-natural L1 rules, that may raise barriers. Some, but not all, of the previously unfamiliar phonological patterns of L2 are likely to demand further suppression of processes beyond what has been achieved in acquiring L1. Thus, in those cases where the acquisition of an L2 phonological pattern runs against an unsuppressed natural process, there will be a resistance to learning. The similarity between this hypothesis and Eckman's Markedness Differential Hypothesis is obvious.

A related, but somewhat different approach is taken by Linell (1979) in an attempt at a functional typology of phonological rules. Here, Morphophonological Rules Proper (MRP) and Phonotactic Rules (PhtR) are characterized as having the cognitive function of *governing the structure of "phonetic plans"*, whereas Perceptual Redundancy Rules (PRR) and Articulatory Reduction Rules (ARR) serve to *govern the execution of "phonetic plans"*. The rule types form a continuous scale, from less to more phonetically motivated: MRP – PhtR – PRR & ARR. Correspondingly, there is a scale of productivity, involving also the propensity for being transferred from L1 into an interlanguage. MRPs are usually not transferred, PRRs and ARRs usually are, and PhtRs seem to form a mixed category in this respect. It should be pointed out that the boundaries between the rule types are assumed to be fuzzy. This allows rules to change status in the course of language history (particularly to lose their synchronic phonetic motivation and to become improductive). It also matches the fact that individual rules are often found, synchronically, to have an intermediate or complicated status.

Towards formulation of processing strategies for L2 phonology

Summing up, it appears that the structural factors that shape learner solutions in L2 phonology are of basically two kinds: (1) a "simplifying" tendency, describable with concepts like phonetic motivation, naturalness, unmarkedness, and linked with properties such as productivity and insuspensibility; and (2) a tendency to rely on familiarity, especially on patterns established in the L1 (the transfer tendency). And further, it appears that these two factors often occur together, interacting with and supporting each other.

We may now venture to suggest, in very broad terms, some strategies that learners seem to apply in order to cope with L2 phonological structure, especially at early stages of L2 acquisition. I will draw examples from an investigation of adult Germans' performance in Swedish in a largely untutored L2 acquisition setting. The data are presented and discussed at greater length in Hammarberg (forthcoming).

A. *Identify easy-to-grasp categories.* This principle favours reliance on L1, i.e. identification with familiar segments, feature configurations etc. in L1.

For example, Swedish has a series of retroflex consonant sounds, [ʈ ɖ ɳ ɭ ʂ], which are derived by assimilation from /rt rd rn rl rs/. Typically, Germans render the first three of these either as dentals [t d n] or as sequences of /r/ + dental. I will exclude [ɭ] from the discussion because my interlanguage data are insufficient on this point. [ʂ], however, is more often rendered in a very target-like fashion by a sound whose source is obviously German [ʃ]. Whereas Sw. [ʂ] and Ge. [ʃ] overlap each other largely in acoustic quality and are thus good phonetic counterparts, there are no German equivalents for the other retroflex sounds. Thus, both for [ʂ] and for [ʈ ɖ ɳ] it seems that the learners seek the most plausible identification available with familiar sound categories in L1.

Among the Swedish vowels, short [ɵ] is the one that causes the greatest confusion which is shown by the fact that it gives rise to a larger number of different substitute variants in an identification test than any other vowel in the system. It is certainly a highly marked vowel and may hence be expected to be difficult. But at the same time, long [ʉ:] and [y:] which are also highly marked, are readily identified (both of them) with German [ü:]. This is indeed a clear deviation from the L2 target values, but it also shows that the learners have an easier choice with these two L2 vowels than with [ɵ] which lacks a plausible counterpart in L1.

B. *Follow productive/natural phonological rules.* There is ample evidence that L2 learners tend to adhere to those rules of L1 that have natural phonetic motivation and disregard rules that do not. To pick just one illustrative example out of the German-Swedish interlanguage study, consider the different effect of the following two neutralization rules which are operative in German:

(1) Final Devoicing
    "Obstruents in syllable-final position are voiceless"

(2) Initial z
"A word-initial dental fricative immediately followed by a vowel is voiced"

(1) rules out final voiced obstruents (b d g v j), and (2) rules out sequence of initial [s] + vowel, both of which occur in Swedish. Rule (1) proves difficult for the learners to abandon, whereas (2) does not. Parallel evidence can be drawn from the assimilation of loanwords in German where (1) is a perfectly productive rule which applies without exceptions (as in *Snob*, *Moped* with [-p], [-t]) whereas (2) may be ignored (as in *Sir* with [s-]). This difference in productivity corresponds well to the fact that (1) is phonetically better motivated than (2). In short, there are two things that speak for the phonetic naturalness of (1): due to the obstructive effect that strong constriction of the vocal tract has on voicing, voicelessness tends generally to be favoured in obstruents; and the end of words or syllables is a favoured position for the neutralization of phonological oppositions. For similar reasons, the phonetic motivation for [z] in (2) appears rather weak. Although the voiced quality can be explained as a result of assimilation to the following vowel, the preferred voicelessness of obstruents, together with the fact that the consonant paradigm tends generally to be relatively well differentiated in initial/prevocalic position, makes the neutralization to [z] here seem less natural.

C. *Reduce unmanageable structural complexity* by eliminating less essential elements, simplifying syllable structure, changing phonetically complicated sound types into less demanding variants, etc. For example, the Swedish word-final cluster /-rj/ (*färg* "colour", *korg* "basket" etc.) is hard to master for the German learners. The following substitute types have been noted:

Reduction to [r] or [j]
Syllabization: [ri]
Epenthetic vowel: [rjə]
Final devoicing: [rç]

All of these are solutions which not only meet the demands of German syllable structure, but also simplify the target structure in various ways. The variants [r] and [j] are the most reductive ones; [ri], [rjə] and [rç] are more elaborated in that they incorporate more of the phonetic "ingredients" of the target structure.

D. *Reduce alternation of linguistic form.* Of course, the second strategy above, that of applying natural rules, may introduce cases of phonological alternation into the interlanguage which are not in line with the target norm. This is certainly the case with Final Devoicing, and it is true in many other cases, too, e.g. when a rule of /r/ Vocalization is applied, so that /r/ gets a vocalized allophone [ɐ] in post-vocalic position, contrary to the target norm. But creating alternation in form provides no advantage in itself. Rather, as an opposite or complementary tendency we can observe a principle of dispensing with unmotivated form alternation in the interlanguage. A case in point is the Swedish rule (actually a part of a wider rule) stating that /ɛ:/ is lowered to [æ:] before /r/. This appears to be a rather unnatural rule (cf. Hellberg, 1978). It is frequently ignored by the German learners of Swedish who instead produce a non-lowered quality throughout — a clearly simplifying solution. To phrase this observation in terms of natural phonology, we may say that whereas the natural processes that are in conflict with L2 (such as Final Devoicing or /r/ Vocalization) must be suppressed by effort, the non-natural alternation rules of L2 (such as /ɛ:/ Lowering) must be acquired by effort.

The communicative relevance factor in phonology

Let us now return to our original problem: is learnability co-determined in phonology too by a factor of communicative relevance?

Recall that we have used the expression "communicative relevance" with reference to specific notions conveyed by meaningful elements in the utterances. If we looked at such phonological phenomena as sentence stress and intonation patterns, it seems likely that it could be shown that solutions in interlanguage are guided by the learner's hypotheses about what constitutes communicatively meaningful prosodic patterns. However, I will not elaborate on this, but instead discuss an example from segmental phonology where the connection to semantics is usually regarded as more remote. Again, this case is presented in greater detail in Hammarberg (forthcoming).

In the discussion above, I already touched briefly on the assimilation rule known as Retroflexion. It is one of the more salient typological characteristics in the phonology of Central Swedish. What it amounts to, basically, is that an /r/ and a following dental consonant /t d n l s/ are fused and form a retroflex segment [ʈ ɖ ʂ ɳ ɭ], as in the following examples:

> karta /kɑːrta/ [kɑːʈa] "map"
> bord /buːrd/ [buːɖ] "table"
> barn /bɑːrn/ [bɑːɳ] "child"
> pärla /pɛːrla/ [pæːɭa] "pearl"
> fors /fors/ [fɔʂ] "rapid (in river)"

The assimilation also operates across morpheme and word boundaries which creates abundant morphophonemic alternation; cf. hör [hœːr] "hear", supine *hört* [hœːt], past participle *hörd* [hœːd], present passive *hörs* [hœːs̺], and *hör ni* [hœːɳiː] "hear you (= do you hear?)". The orthography renders /r/ + dental, as the examples show. The assimilation may occasionally be suspended in slow, explicit speech, especially across word boundaries, but also sometimes in names and other words that need particular clarification. Retroflexion is largely confined to the dialect area of Central and Northern Sweden. Finland Swedish mostly has unassimilated /r/ + dental, and Southern Swedish has uvular /R/ + dental. These various facts indicate that there are a number of clues for the learner of Swedish to discover that a rule of retroflexion is operative in the language: spelling, morphophonemic alternations, explicit-making forms, and cross-dialect evidence.

In the investigation referred to earlier, German beginners and early interlanguage speakers were tested on Swedish Retroflexion. An attempt was made to explore separately how the speakers reacted when they had to concentrate on the phonetic sound quality, and when they produced meaningful, intentional speech. Repetition tests with nonsense words represented the first approach, and picture-naming and free conversation the second. In terms of information processing, the first approach was intended to accentuate the "bottom-up" or "data-driven" processes in speech perception and constrain the possibilities of "top-down" or "conceptually driven" processing (cf. Lindsay & Norman, 1977). In other words, the repetition tests were meant to favour purely phonetically based learner solutions in interpreting and rendering the retroflex sounds. The second approach did not impose this limitation on speech processing, but would leave room for the learner's experience with morphophonemic structure, orthographic form etc. to play a part in the process.

In the repetition tests, /rt rd rn/ were with very few exceptions rendered as dentals, and /rs/ as a retroflex or [ʃ]-type segment. Thus all the four units were treated as monosegmental. In picture-naming and conversation, however, bisegmental sequences of /r/ + dental were the predominant solution for /rt rd rn/. For /rs/, the monosegmental retroflex or [ʃ] was still the most frequent solution, occurring about half the time. But the bisegmental variants /r/ + dental and /r/ + retroflex also occurred. Since bisegmental variants were practically non-existent in the repetition tests, the monosegmental variants seem to be the preferred phonetically based solutions, and bisegmental solutions may be regarded as based on the learner's concepts of linguistic structuring in one way or another.

Now there is one additional conceptual factor that turned out to be worth looking at. Since German and Swedish are related languages, and also since the Swedish vocabulary has been strongly influenced by German, there are many cognate words. It seemed that bisegmental solutions were especially frequent in such words. I therefore hypothesized that German learners would tend to go for bisegmental solutions right from the beginning and sacrifice phonetic approximation if the Swedish word was transparent enough to be identified with a cognate lexical item in L1; and if the form was not transparent, learners would be more inclined to choose monosegmental solutions. To test this, an experiment in two parts was carried out.

The first part consisted of an experiment which was presented as a word-learning task. Five German newcomers to Sweden were shown, in individual sessions, a number of picture-cards and were told for each picture the Swedish word that was illustrated. No written stimuli were presented. After 12 to 15 cards had been presented, the bunch was run through again, and the subject was required to say the illustrated words. If he failed to answer or gave a radically deviant answer (not only due to foreign pronunciation), the word was given once again. The bunch was run through a few times, until all or almost all test words were mastered. The test was recorded on tape. Those words for which there were three to five answers were included in the further analysis. The procedure was repeated on two later occasions, one and three months later.

It turned out that for retroflex consonants there was variation between bi- and monosegmental solutions. Scoring two points for only bisegmental solutions for a given test word on one test occasion, one point for bi- and monosegmental solutions in alternation, and no point for only monosegmental solutions, an "index of bisegmentality" was established, ranging from 30 (all answers bisegmental) to 0 (all answers monosegmental).

The second part was designed to elicit expert judgements on cross-lingual lexical transparency. The informants were ten linguists and phil-ologists at the University of Stockholm who had good command of both languages and were not aware of the first part of the experiment. The following six test words were selected:

> *tårta* [toːʈa] "cake", Ge. *Torte*
> *karta* [kɑːʈa] "map", Ge. *Karte*
> *svart* [svaʈ] "black", Ge. *schwarz*
> *fjorton* [fjuːʈɔn] "fourteen", Ge. *vierzehn*
> *bord* [buːɖ] "table", Ge. *Tisch* (cf. *Bord* "shelf", "board")
> *barn* [bɑːɳ] "child", Ge. *Kind*

The informants were first introduced to the notion of cross-lingual trans-parency with the help of some dummy examples. They were then asked to go through a list where the six test words had been paired in all possible combinations, and underline the member of each pair that they considered to be the more transparent member. The scoring of one point per underlining produced an "index of transparency".

The result is summarized in Table 2 which shows a near-perfect correlation of the bisegmentality and transparency scales. This supports the hypothesis and thus confirms that the choice of phonological solution is guided by the degree of cross-lingual lexical transparency.

Interpreting this result, we may conclude that the learner primarily tries to grasp the new word as a lexical concept. If he finds that he can associate it with a counterpart in L1 which is similar enough in form, this will give him hints about its phonemic representation, i.e. cause him to interpret the word as containing a phoneme sequence /r/ + dental, and there will be routines from L1 available for him to convert phonemes into sound. Thus he will in this case tend to derive pronunciation in the interlanguage on conceptual grounds, by way of lexical identification and a given phonological automatism. If there is no plausible cognate form, the learner will have to rely more on the exact phonetic input, i.e. the way the target language speaker pronounces the word, in order to establish the form of the new lexical item in his interlanguage. The conceptual way appears to be given precedence where there is a choice. Apparently the learner in this case goes for communicative relevance and chooses the interpretation of the L2 word that makes most sense to him.

TABLE 2

Test word	Transparency		Bisegmentality	
	Index	Rank	Index	Rank
tårta	85	1	29	2
karta	84	2	30	1
svart	67	3	21	3
fjorton	39	4	18	4
bord	22	5	17	5
barn	0	6	14	6

Conclusion

In this chapter I have taken the standpoint that learnability is a relative matter, and that it can be explored in relation to the various factors that influence the shape of learner solutions in (untutored) L2 acquisition. I have concentrated on language-internal factors, leaving open the discussion of factors of instruction and extra-linguistic socio-psychological factors which may influence the learner's motivation in a wide sense of the woŕd. I have tried to demonstrate with examples from both syntax and segmental phonology that factors of structural manageability and communicative relevance interact in an intricate way to favour or disfavour particular learner solutions, and consequently to facilitate or obstruct solutions that approximate the target language norm. In this sense, the relative learnability of a particular solution on a given point in a learner's interlanguage seems to be determined, in part, by the interplay of structural and communicative factors. The teacher, then, may find it useful to be able to play the game with these various factors in arranging what is to be taught and in working with the learner.

Acknowledgements

Part of the work underlying this paper has been made possible by a grant from the Swedish Research Council for the Humanities and Social Sciences, grant no. F 510/80.

References

Bannert, R. 1980, Svårigheter med svenskt uttal: inventering och prioritering, *Praktisk Lingvistik*, 5, University of Lund, Dept. of Linguistics.
Clahsen, H. 1984, The acquisition of German word order: a test case for cognitive approaches to L2 development. In R. W. Andersen (ed.), *Second Languages*, Rowley, Mass.: Newbury House.
Clahsen, H., Meisel, J. & Pienemann, M. 1983, *Deutsch als Zweitsprache. Der Spracherwerb ausländischer Arbeiter*. Tübingen: Gunter Narr.
Crothers, J. 1978, Typology and universals of vowel systems. In J.H. Greenberg *et al.* (eds), *Universals of human language. Vol. 2. Phonology*. Stanford: Stanford UP, 93–152.
Donegan, P.J. & Stampe, D. 1979, The study of natural phonology. In D.A. Dinnsen (ed.), *Current approaches to phonological theory*. Bloomington & London: Indiana UP. 126–73.
Eckman, F.R. 1977, Markedness and the contrastive analysis hypothesis. *Language Learning*, 27, 315–30.
—— 1981a, On the naturalness of interlanguage phonological rules *Language Learning* 31, 195–216.
—— 1981b, On predicting phonological difficulty in second language acquisition. *Studies in Second Language Acquisition*, 4, 18–30.
Edström, M., Kilpeläinen, K., Rosén-Blomqvist, K., Törnqvist, M. & Zetterlund, C. 1983, *Inversion. ett kommunikativt problem?* Course project report in Teaching Swedish as a Second Language, Univ. of Stockholm, Depts. of Scandinavian Languages & Linguistics. Ms.

Garnica, O.K. & Herbert, R.K. 1979, Some phonological errors in second language learning: interference doesn't tell it all. *International Journal of Psycholinguistics*, 6–2, 5–19.

Greenberg, J.H. 1966, *Language universals*. The Hague & Paris: Mouton.

Hammarberg, B. forthcoming, *Studien zur Phonologie des Zweitsprachenerwerbs*.

Hammarberg, B. & Viberg, A. 1977, The place-holder constraint, language typology, and the teaching of Swedish to immigrants. *Studia linguistica*, 31, 106–63.

Hellberg, S. 1978, Unnatural phonology. *Journal of Linguistics*, 14, 157–77.

Hyltenstam, K. 1978, Variation in interlanguage syntax, *Working Papers* 18, Lund University, Phonetics Laboratory & Dept. of General Linguistics.

Hyltenstam, K. forthcoming, Markedness, language universals, language typology and second language acquisition. Paper presented at the 2nd European–North American Workshop on Cross-Linguistic Second Language Acquisition Research, Jagdschloss Göhrde, West Germany, Aug. 22–29, 1982. To be published in C. Pfaff (ed.), *Cross Linguistic Studies in Language Acquisition Processes*. Rowley, Mass.: Newbury House.

Liljencrants, J. & Lindblom, B. 1972, Numerical simulation of vowel quality systems: the role of perceptual contrast. *Language* 48, 839–62.

Lindblom, B. forthcoming, Phonetic universals in vowel systems. Ms., Dept. of Linguistics, Univ. of Stockholm. To appear in J. Ohala (ed.), *Experimental phonology*. New York: Academic Press.

Lindsay, P.H. & Norman, D.A. 1977, *Human information processing. An introduction to psychology*. 2nd ed. New York etc.: Academic Press.

Linell, P. 1979, *Psychological reality in phonology*. Cambridge etc.: Cambridge University Press.

Meisel, J.M., Clahsen, H. & Pienemann, M. 1981, On determining developmental stages in natural second language acquisition. *Studies in Second Language Acquisition*, 3, 109–35.

Pienemann, M. 1984, Psychological constraints on the teachability of languages. *Studies in Second Language Acquisition* 6, 186–214.

Ruhlen, M. 1975, *A guide to the languages of the world*. Language universals project, Stanford Univ.

Slobin, D.I. 1973, Cognitive prerequisites for the development of grammar. In Ch. A. Ferguson, & D.I. Slobin (eds), *Studies of child language development*. New York: Holt, Rinehart & Winston, 175–208.

Stampe, D. 1969, The acquisition of phonetic representation. *Papers from the Fifth Regional Meeting of the Chicago Linguistic Society*, Dept. of Linguistics, Univ. of Chicago, 443–54. Also reprinted in Stampe (1979).

Stampe, D. 1979, *A dissertation on natural phonology*. New York & London: Garland.

Tarone, E.E. 1978, The phonology of interlanguage. In J.C. Richards (ed.), *Understanding second & foreign language learning: issues & approaches*. Rowley, Mass.: Newbury House. 15–33.

Zobl, H. 1980, The formal and developmental selectivity of L1 influence on L2 acquisition. *Language Learning*, 30, 43–57.

8 Learner variation and the teachability hypothesis

HOWARD NICHOLAS

La Trobe University, Bundoora, Australia

The teachability hypothesis is dependent on the idea that an interlanguage user (someone in the process of either acquiring or learning a second language) can only *learn* what s/he is "ready" to *acquire*. Defining "readiness" is thus of critical importance. While this is easier to do when it is possible to sequence the features to be learnt, it is less easy to do for those features which cannot be so readily sequenced. This distinction is made by Pienemann (this volume) when he differentiates between *developmental* and *variable* features. However, the exact effect of teaching on variable features is subject to multiple interpretations as Pienemann himself points out:

> "For *variable features* (as opposed to developmental) — like the insertion of the copula —there is evidence that instruction has a drastic influence on L2 speech production." (p.37)

but

> "... we may expect that such learning success is not resistant to the dynamics implied in the influence of external factors on the individual's use of L2 strategies." (p.38)

Developmental features are those features of the language which can only develop in a certain sequence. They are characterized by progressively more complex language processing requirements: If an interlanguage

177

user is able to use features from a later stage of language development, then s/he must also be able to use features from the preceding stages. It is not possible to describe such sequences for variable features since variable features cannot be related to each other according to their degrees of processing complexity.

Features are not the same as rules. A rule such as "inversion" can contain both developmental and variable features. This rule requires that the subject and the inflected verbal element are inverted (i.e. verb and subject change places) if, for example, an adverbial such as "yesterday" is at the beginning of the sentence. The *developmental feature* is that the inverted word order structure can only develop after other (less complex) word order rules (e.g. adverb preposing, verb separation) have developed (cf. Pienemann, this volume, p.35). The *variable feature* is the frequency of appearance/omission of the subject in such constructions. Even when the processing prerequisites for "inversion" have developed, certain interlanguage users will consistently omit the subject in inversion contexts. (For a more detailed discussion see Pienemann, 1981; Meisel *et al.*, 1981). Whether the interlanguage user includes or omits the subject depends on his/her *orientation* to the language development process and on the *language use strategies* which s/he has as a result of that particular orientation.

It should be noted that it is, therefore, significantly more difficult to determine the *location* of variable features in a syllabus than it is to locate developmental features — precisely because of the relationship between learner orientations and factors external to language processing. It is also more difficult to determine the *status* of such features within the syllabus. If we assume that the use of such features will reflect the orientation to the language development process that the learner brings into the classroom from "outside", we are forced to recognize that our teaching objectives for different individuals will vary — even for learners on the same stage of the developmental features. This is going to involve us in a significantly more complex evaluation and teaching process than if we only consider developmental features. This aspect also becomes apparent in Pienemann's chapter when he reports that "the accuracy of copula insertion decreased again some days after the instruction" (p.38).

This chapter will, therefore, investigate variation between interlanguage users. The suggestion will be made that both acquirers and learners of second languages display differences in their orientations to the second language development process. The existence of different orientations to, particularly, variable features of the second language suggests that "readiness" with regard to these features will need to be defined differently to the way in which it is defined for developmental features.

Whereas the sequencing of developmental features implies the acquisition of new processing strategies which build on and/or replace earlier strategies, there is no such implication with regard to variable features. However, even within developmental features there is no absolute requirement that one set of production/use strategies replace another when new processing prerequisites are present. Meisel (1980) uses precisely this fact to distinguish between different learner types. He distinguishes between those who simplify in order to learn (and thus later become more complex in their language productions) and those who simplify in order to use (and thus do not produce increasingly complex utterances). This aspect of learner orientation also needs consideration in syllabus construction. Meisel (1980) convincingly demonstrates that the distinction between learner types is based on different choices of strategies rather than on differences in language processing abilities. If this sort of distinction is relevant within a single developmental feature, then it is even more relevant with regard to those variable features where the different items can perform separate functions in the interlanguage. Thus, if a particular utterance type is not suited to the specific needs of a particular learner (or group of learners) there will be greatly varying degrees of willingness/readiness to learn that item.

The interlanguage user's needs reflect his/her orientation to the language development process and thus determine his/her language use strategies. Problems arise for the teacher when these needs are not consistent with the ultimate objectives of the syllabus. Some of the ways in which "immediate needs" of the learners might differ from "ultimate needs" as defined in the syllabus are outlined below (cf. pp. 189). These differences are based on the assumption that the *ultimate* objectives of the syllabus include equipping the learner with fairly complete and accurate abilities in the areas of second language structure and function. This sort of *ultimate/long term* objective is necessary to ensure that the learners do not develop varieties of the second language which will mark them as "social outcasts" (cf. Pienemann, this volume, p.44, p.49). However, such a "unified" ultimate objective can be in conflict with the need on the part of second language learners to "creatively construct" in the course of language learning. It can also conflict with the fact that different learners will focus their attention on different aspects of the language being taught; some will concentrate more on meaning than form, others will concentrate more on producing accurate/correct utterances. Certain learners will be content to extensively practise what they have been taught, others will want to continually move on to new areas. Not all of these approaches are equally compatible with the production of complete, well-formed, meaningful utterances. This conflict has to be recognized from the beginning.

We must, therefore, recognize that there is no unique "best" path to ultimate communicative competence in the second language. Different learners are best served by being allowed to follow different paths. Syllabuses need to be so constructed that *their* short term objectives do not conflict with the range of immediate learner needs. They also need, however, to ensure that this adaptation to immediate needs does not exclude development towards their ultimate objectives — even where the ultimate objectives of the syllabus are incompatible with the short term strategies of particular learners (cf. also Pienemann, this volume, pp.42–49).

Syllabus planning must, therefore, have two simultaneous goals:

1. to ensure that there is progression along the axis of the developmental features,

2. to ensure that the learners develop a language variety which is not stigmatized.

It must be recognized that learners may develop language systems which are compatible with only *one* of these goals, i.e. learners can have abilities in one of these areas independent of their abilities in the other.

The orientation of a particular learner to the process of language development will influence not so much *whether* s/he progresses along the developmental axis, but *how* s/he progresses. The question of how these two axes are related to each other within the syllabus will probably have to be answered differently for different groups of learners. These different groups are defined by their orientations to the language development process.

One of the aspects of language use that is susceptible to influence from "external" factors is the degree of "correctness" (cf. Nicholas, in press a; Pienemann, 1981; Clahsen *et al.*, 1983). It therefore seems extremely unlikely that "mastery" of a particular form will be an adequate measure of whether the learner has *in principle* developed the particular strategies required to produce that form. (cf. Pienemann, this volume, p.38, but for emphasis it should be restated: If a learner uses a form with 100% accuracy, we can assume that s/he has mastered that form *UNLESS* that form is a prefabricated pattern. However, infrequent but regular use of a given form also demonstrates that the learner is in principle capable of applying the necessary rules.) *Nevertheless*, the degree of accuracy is what is usually regarded as the feature to be tested to determine whether the next phase of instruction should be commenced. We will, therefore, have to distinguish between "readiness to learn" and "readiness to use", particularly with regard to variable features. Evidence for different orientations to the second language development process will be found in four areas:

1. the choice of strategies for interaction in the L2; some interlanguage users will seek to develop the ability to control the flow of the interaction in the L2, whereas others will be content to restrict themselves to reacting to the initiatives of others;

2. the way in which structures, for which the processing prerequisites have already been developed, are realized; some interlanguage users will try to apply newly developed language use strategies to as many contexts as possible, whereas others will be content to apply such strategies only in particular contexts for which they have direct evidence of appropriateness;

3. the accuracy/correctness with which utterances are produced; some interlanguage users will be concerned to ensure that all of their utterances are correct according to the rules of the L2, for others this will be far less important;

4. the extent to which the interlanguage users attempt to exploit the structural or the functional potential of the L2; some interlanguage users will attempt to express a wide range of communicative functions without worrying about the structures which are used to express these functions, others will devote more of their efforts to the exploration of the structures of the L2 with less attention being paid to the functional variation; yet others will attempt both aspects simultaneously while some will avoid exploration in both areas.

A more detailed elaboration of many of these areas can be found in Clahsen *et al.*, 1983 and Clahsen *et al.*, (in prep.).

All of these areas have implications for our assessment of the teachability hypothesis. None of them suggest that the hypothesis itself is invalid. They all suggest, however, that for many learners the path towards a target-like version of the L2 will look significantly different to that suggested by a simplistic application of the teachability hypothesis.

I will concentrate on the sequence claimed by Pienemann for his "speech act of asking" and suggest that

1. there is, in fact, evidence for two separate language functions, which implies that *for some learners* the forms which are described by Pienemann might not be sequenced in his order,

2. the learners' "readiness" to acquire features in the area of interrogation might be more dependent on the individual learner's perceived "linguistic" needs than on language processing prerequisites, and

3. that the distinction in (2) implies that at least some aspects of the L2 might be significantly less susceptible to teaching than is the case for the developmental features described by Pienemann.

In Pienemann's chapter attention is concentrated on sequenced items from the target language. The claim is made that the various word order rules of German, which constitute the developmental features of the acquisition process, can only be learnt in a particular sequence because the structures from any given stage constitute the processing prerequisites for the structures of the next stage. If a learner has not acquired the processing strategies needed to produce the structures belonging to stage x + 1 s/he cannot develop the processing strategies needed to produce the structures from stage x + 2. This reflects the fact that the processing strategies required for each subsequent stage are more complex than those required for the preceding stage(s).

Pienemann concludes, on the basis of extensive research, that the use of variable features depends on non-linguistic factors. He (in line with the findings of Clahsen *et al.*, 1983) bases this claim on the observation that variable features cannot be sequenced since they do not reflect differences in processing complexity. Unlike the word order rules which do not appear in the interlanguage until the prerequisite processing strategies have been developed, variable features such as the rate of supply of the copula can be observed at any time in the second language development process. The claim is thus made that this feature is "already acquired when (it) is applied with a higher probability than zero, *since then it can, in principle, be processed. Only for reasons of simplification or/and effectiveness the learners' strategies may lead to a low accuracy of a later stage.*" (p.38). The learners' desires for simplification or effectiveness constitute part of their orientation to the second language development process. It is this orientation which determines how "accurately" the interlanguage user applies the second language system to his/her own productions. Thus, second language teaching with regard to variable features will be attempting to influence not so much the L2 learner's language processing ability as his/her orientation to the language learning process and this will involve modification of learners' views of simplicity and effectiveness. There are two issues at stake:

1. do all second language *learners* have the same (or similar) orientations to the second language learning process?
2. is it possible to alter second language learners' orientation to the second language learning process?

I will suggest that second language learners have a wide range of orientations to the second language learning process. In line with findings from second language acquisition studies, I will claim that it should be possible to define groups of learners who vary systematically in their orientation to the task of second language development. The classroom will impose more uniform external conditions on language learners than are imposed on L2 acquirers. However, I will provide evidence that there is sufficient scope for systematic variation between (groups of) individuals in their orientation to the second language *learning* process. This will support the existence of a number of alternative paths towards ultimate competence in the second language.

With regard to the second issue, I will suggest that we need to move with considerably more caution. The results from various studies of features, which would appear to be variable rather than developmental, are contradictory (cf. Pienemann, this volume, pp.38–41). While there appears to be mounting evidence for the teachability of developmental features, the contradictions with regard to variable features indicate that our understanding of the factors which are critical in this area is significantly less advanced. However, some of the studies demonstrate that it is possible to "teach" some aspects of variable features with some degree of success. This indicates either that there are some learners whose orientation to the second language development process is compatible with the objectives of teachers, or that it is possible to alter orientations which are not compatible with teachers' objectives to such an extent that the two become compatible.

There is a growing number of studies which suggest that different second language acquiring children follow different paths during their acquisition of a second language. Studies by Fillmore (1976), Lightbown (1977), Nemoianu (1980) have all provided evidence of differences between children acquiring second languages, although some of the differences described are merely differences in the *speed* of acquisition as against differences between the *paths* followed by the different acquirers. Various reports by Nicholas (in press a, in press b, 1984) have suggested that the variation between child second language acquirers is not only in terms of speed, but also in terms of the way in which they go about the task of analysing and producing target language items. There is also evidence for this sort of variation between second language learners in structured environments. Seliger (1977) suggested that interaction patterns in the classroom influence the speed with which a second language is learnt. Fillmore (1982) concludes from her study of children in differently structured classrooms that the way in which individual second language learners go about interacting with their specific linguistic environment will influence their learning of a second language. Harley (1982) also seems to provide evidence of the development of different second language learner varieties within the Canadian immersion programmes, although she does not report this aspect in detail. Various of the studies carried out by Krashen (e.g. as reported in Krashen 1981) would also seem to provide evidence for variation in second language learning, although cast within a very specific theoretical framework.

An empirical example of the sorts of distinctions which are being discussed can be found in the performance of grade 5 (aged 10–11 years) children on a picture-based story telling task in a second language. These English-speaking children attending an Australian primary school are participating in a second language instruction programme in which they are taught for up to five hours a week in German. The subjects covered range from science to physical education. The children referred to here are in their third year in the programme. They were presented with a series of pictures showing everyday, family activities and were required to describe what they saw. Of the twelve children interviewed, nine asked no questions about unknown items. They preferred to transfer English lexical items into their German language utterances if they did not know the appropriate word. One child made statements about unknown words in English as well as asking for the appropriate German item in English, e.g.

> MY: Heidi ist getting der newspaper.
> If that's how you say it!
> MY: How do you say X?

A second child mixed German and English in statements and questions, e.g.

> SW: I've forgotten what dress is in English (*sic*).
> SW: Ich weiß nicht, was das ist.
> SW: Was ist *burnt* in Deutsch?
> SW: What is *teeth* in Deutsch?

The remaining child consistently requested the German word with a German question:

JN: Was is das?
JN: Ich weiß nicht, was das ist.

Thus we can see that different learners have used different strategies for solving the one communication problem. The majority of the children conformed to the pattern which had developed during the early phases of their contact with the second language. At that time they had been permitted to respond to German questions in English and to address their "German" teacher in English. After more than two years of the programme — and despite the fact that all of them are capable of asking fairly complex questions in German — only three children had opted for direct questioning strategies when dealing with new material. Significantly, all of the children are masters of the sort of elliptical questions described by Pienemann in his paper in this volume and they all frequently use the sorts of structures which are referred to as "prefabricated sentences". All of the children referred to here are capable of producing questions from at least Pienemann's stage 4. Some even make use (accurately) of the indirect questions, e.g. SW and JN. However, only one child has a strategy which permits him to cope with unknown material entirely in German — at least, only one child makes use of this strategy. Here, then, we find more evidence for variation in second language *learners'* orientations to the second language development process.

We, therefore, have to conclude that not all second language learners have the same orientation to the second language learning process. Thus, within our syllabuses we are going to have to make allowances for different learners reacting differently to the structures which are provided as input. This not only refers to the question of whether they will be "ready" to learn features which they are not already producing, but also the question of what use they are going to make of the material to which they are exposed. I will suggest in reaction to Pienemann's statement (p.27) that "it is the syllabus designer who has to assess the learner's actual needs and the instruments necessary to satisfy them" that we need to be cautious in our interpretation of this role. The very brief examination of some children's reactions to situations in which they are required to cope with new language material is still sufficient to suggest that both the learner's needs and the appropriate instruments are likely to vary significantly between learners.

Pienemann suggests a five stage sequence for the development of interrogation. Quite rightly he draws attention to the fact that we too often

ignore instruments for the expression of interrogation such as elliptical
questions and prefabricated sentences. His sequence progresses from

(a) *elliptical questions*

    e.g. da ist der spielplatz

    wo?

to (b) *Prefabricated sentences*
    e.g. was/wer ist N?
to (c) *rising intonation questions*
    e.g. ich schreibe da
    or warum du nicht deutsche sprechen?
to (d) *inversion questions*
    e.g. warum hast du auch eine nase?
    or gehst du noch in der schule?
to (e) *indirect questions*
    in which the interrogative is realized in a subordinate clause which,
    in German, requires that the finite verb be in final position.

As Pienemann points out, the sequencing of the last three stages is fairly
well documented since the majority of studies have concentrated on
"sentence type questions". I do not wish to attempt to dispute the validity
of the sequencing of stages 3, 4 and 5. However, I think there is room for
debate about the sequencing of stages 1, 2 and 3.

In carefully pointing out that the teachability hypothesis has only
been demonstrated for children, Pienemann avoids one potential trap with
regard to the sequencing of question structures since it would seem that
adults are not necessarily bound to produce copula structures similar to the
"prefabricated" sentences before they produce rising intonation questions
(cf. Clahsen *et al.*, 1983). Children, it seems are much more likely to
concentrate their initial second language productions on such copulaic
structures and are thus more likely to produce "prefabricated sentence"
questions before they produce rising intonation questions. The earlier
appearance of copula questions than of full verb rising intonation questions
occurs in the language of very young children. It is reported by both
Nemoianu (1980) and Nicholas (1984). However, what both of these
authors point out is that these sorts of prefabricated sentence questions
have a very specific function which makes it difficult to group them in the
same speech act of "asking" as the later full verb rising intonation
questions. The prefabricated sentence questions used by the second

language acquirers in the studies carried out by Nemoianu and Nicholas were used to focus attention on a topic of conversation. As such they were not asking so much for information, as for the person, with whom the child was talking, to say something about whatever interested the child. As Nemoianu (1980: 34–5) states

"... there were instances when they (the children in her study) sincerely requested information, not only about the English equivalent, but also about the identity of the object itself. In such instances, the utterance took a variety of forms, none of them correct (e.g. 'What a dis?', 'What dis?', 'What is?')."

Thus, it would seem to be the case that the prefabricated structures belong to a different functional group to the utterances which are used to express the speech act of "asking". If this is the case, then the universality of the development sequence for interrogative must be questioned. If we take another look at prefabricated structures, we find that not only do relatively simple structures, such as the copula structures, appear in a prefabricated form, but that much more complex structures also appear in this way. Hakuta (1974:293) in his discussion of prefabricated patterns claims that

"From the very first sample, *do you* appeared in questions such as the following:
How do you do it?
Do you have coffee?
Do you want this one?"

This sort of structure incorporates processes from stages which will only occur much later in non-rote speech. Inversion is already present in a *prefabricated form* in the language of Hakuta's informant. This does not mean that the processing prerequisites for this structure have been acquired and so it does not invalidate the claim about the relative sequencing of non-inverted and inverted utterances, but it does indicate that maybe we need to re-examine the role of prefabricated sentence structures in the interlanguages of second language acquirers. We have so far examined two pieces of evidence which suggest that prefabricated patterns cannot be lightly listed in a "sequence" of developing interrogative forms. There is no denying that prefabricated patterns are present in interlanguages, nor do I wish to deny that these patterns appear early. Perhaps we need to re-examine the functions of the various interrogative types and their different roles in the interaction between interlanguage users and native speakers.

I wish to suggest that both prefabricated patterns and elliptical questions have very specific functions in the interlanguage of second language acquirers. Further, I wish to suggest that interlanguage users with different orientations to the second language development process will make different use of these different interrogative types precisely *because* they have these different functions The implication of this sort of consideration is that the developmental sequence for these early interrogative types will not be identical in all interlanguage users.

Let us consider first the general case of prefabricated patterns or as Fillmore (1976) refers to them "formulaic units". Fillmore points out that child second language acquirers depend on formulae to differing extents. While all of the second language acquirers studied by Fillmore were initially reliant on formulae, there were significant differences between the extent of the initial reliance by the various children on such formulae and the extents to which they remained reliant on formulaic speech in the course of their second language acquisition. Those who were least reliant overall were also those who most quickly acquired an independent command of the second language. Fillmore attributes these differing extents of reliance to differing personality structures and approaches to the interaction situation. This is part of what I have been referring to as the orientation of the interlanguage user.

There is another aspect of prefabricated patterns which needs to be considered and that is their role in enabling the interlanguage user to participate in verbal activities. If a child wishes to play an active *initiating* role in a particular verbal activity, s/he is going to need to be able to engage the attention of those with whom s/he is playing. There are various means by which this can be done, but one of the more linguistically sophisticated of them is the use of a number of rote-learnt items, i.e. prefabricated patterns. The use of this sort of structure means that the interlanguage user is not dependent on the utterances of the person with whom s/he is talking. If an interlanguage user has no means of initiating verbal interaction then s/he is forced to wait for questions or statements from the person with whom s/he is talking. This means that the interlanguage user must continually provide answers (to questions which s/he has perhaps not understood) or restrict him/herself to confirming the content of the question or statement just made by the other person. It is this sort of confirming/checking function which is fulfilled by Pienemann's stage one elliptical questions. I will return to them later.

The copula type prefabricated pattern is an ideal means of enabling the second language acquirer to initiate verbal interaction. If a learner or an acquirer is the type who likes to feel in control of the situation, then this sort of structure enables him or her to participate and control *from the beginning of second language development*. Since the use of such items is not dependent on any level of structural knowledge because the utterances are not processed in the same manner as independently produced utterances, any number of such formulae can be used from the beginning of second language development. The question is then not so much "when are such patterns used?" as "who uses this sort of pattern and for what purpose?". This is a question which is equally applicable to second language learning and second language acquisition contexts since the different "early" interrogative types fulfil specific functions which differentially satisfy the varying needs of interlanguage users. However, whereas Pienemann regards the copulaic questions as formulae, there is some evidence that they may not be so. Nicolas (1984) discusses this question in some detail, but in brief it must be pointed out that both Felix (1978) and Huang (1971) provide evidence that some second language acquirers pass through a stage early in their second language acquisition in which the copula is not present even in these apparently formulaic utterances. Both authors show that this cannot be related to interference from the first language, so again it would seem to be the case that learner orientations are influencing the sort of language development which is taking place. This view is also supported by the evidence presented in Pienemann (1981). Thus, it is even questionable whether copula questions with the topic focussing function (e.g. as described by Nicholas (1984) and Nemoianu (1980) can be regarded as formulaic/prefabricated patterns (for all interlanguage users). If we allow that one of the factors influencing the way in which second language learners approach the language learning task is the degree to which the particular learner likes to initiate conversational interaction, i.e. to *control* what is happening, then we must recognize that learners will vary *independently of the syllabus* in the extent to which they are content to learn/use elements from the target language which do not allow them to control what is happening. Thus, readiness has a radically different meaning in the context of some variable features to its meaning in the context of developmental features.

If we contrast the elliptical questions and the prefabricated patterns we find, somewhat simplistically, a contrast between a form which prevents control of conversation because it is reactive and a form which permits control because it allows the user to initiate interaction. We thus find a three way distinction between elliptical questions, prefabricated patterns, and sentence-type questions. The use of sentence-type questions (regardless of the stage of their syntactic development) implies a fairly free participation in conversation. Both elliptical questions and prefabricated patterns can imply a restricted style of conversational interaction. The extensive use of elliptical questions implies a very reactive style of interaction suggesting that the learner is not producing a great deal of "complex" language. The extensive use of prefabricated patterns also implies that the learner is not processing a large amount of syntactically complex productions, but this type of learner is distinguished from the one who uses elliptical questions by the fact that s/he is participating more in decisions about what is being discussed and is thus better able to devote attention to the way in which the utterances are formed. Participation in the decision about what is being discussed means that the learner is able to reduce the number of unknowns involved in any given conversation. If s/he has nominated the topic of conversation then s/he is aware of at least some of the things that might be said about that topic. S/he is thus in a better position to understand what is being said by the interlocutor. If the learner needs to devote less effort to understanding the relevant utterance, s/he will be able to devote more attention to the means used to convey that message. If the interlanguage user can devote more attention to the way in which the utterance is constructed, s/he has a better chance of systematizing that knowledge, i.e. of making it a part of his/her own interlanguage system.

It is, however, precisely at this point that "readiness" with regard to variable features becomes so hard to define. As was pointed out above, certain aspects of formulaic language usage permit increased contact with the second language in a way which is advantageous to the second language acquirer. However, it is questionable

1. whether the same advantages can be derived from such interlanguage use in the classroom and
2. whether all aspects of formulaic language use are of benefit to the interlanguage user.

To deal with the second point first, Fillmore (1976:715) points out that overuse or extended use of formulae appears to correlate with lack of development in the second language.

> "... the fact that Jesus did not analyze his expressions quickly and play with them cannot be taken as evidence that he was unable to do so. He eventually did analyze some of his expressions and was able to use the structures productively. It was not that he could not see the structural possibilities of the expressions in his repertory; he just was not looking for them."

Thus it seems to be not so much the generalized use of formulae which is critical in determining orientations, but rather the specific functions which the formulae have in the interlanguage user's linguistic system. I would suggest that specific formulae are better adapted to assisting second language development than are others. Thus, it would seem to be the case that those learners who make more use of *specific* formulae will experience more "success" in the second language learning process. On the other hand, at least some of the factors which contribute towards a tendency to use formulae of the beneficial variety will also be such as to encourage the use of formulae in general and thus inhibit general second language development.

One example of this kind of factor would seem to be the classroom since this environment (at least traditionally) emphasizes the value of accuracy and being "right". It would seem that these sorts of values encourage the use of formulae, since formulae enable the second language learner to function adequately in the traditional classroom environment. At the same time, it would seem to be the case that an emphasis on values such as "accuracy" or "correctness" (either on the part of the learner or of the teacher) would seem to inhibit other language using strategies which the child would seem to need in order to analyse the second language so that s/he can try various production strategies. Again we return to the dual functions of formulae. Those formulae which can be used to fulfil an initiating function would seem to encourage and support language development, whereas those formulae which express reactive functions (non-initiating language, i.e. language which does not encourage the interlocutor to produce additional expansive language) would seem to reduce the rate of language development.

One example of non-expansive language is teacher evaluation, whereby an interlanguage user's utterance is classified as "right" or "wrong" instead of being regarded as something to be built upon by the teacher. Here it can be clearly seen that "readiness" is crucially dependent on the attitudes of the participants in the particular language situation. The forces operating in the classroom situation require a certain type of interaction and, thus, put pressure on the interactants to produce a certain type of language. To the extent that this type of language inhibits the development of the second language (cf. Hahn 1982), progress in that language is dependent on the learner having the desire to "break the pattern" and establish a different type of interaction between him/herself and the teacher. How, when and why a particular learner will be prepared to try to establish a new type of interaction pattern are little-understood phenomena, but they certainly do not appear to be dependent on the learner's *ability* to apply a given type of language processing strategy to his/her own productions.

We are, however, aware that not all learners will have an identical approach to the second language learning process. Thus, we cannot assume that all learners will be producing the same sort of language, i.e. assuming that the classroom requires a more formulaic type of language, we cannot assume that all learners will have responded in the same way to this pressure. Thus, we can expect that some learners will produce significantly more formulaic language than others. Also, there will be significant differences between the learners with regard to their willingness to surrender formulae as their chief means of communication. Thus, while it is not unreasonable to suppose that formulae will appear early in the development of the question function, it is extremely uncertain whether we can actually consistently sequence the development from formulae to sentence questions. Even more uncertain is the sequence "elliptical question" before formulaic question, since this area would seem to be very much influenced by individual learner orientations and, thus, the functions which the particular learner wishes to express.

We can now return to the second of the issues mentioned earlier: Is it possible to alter second language learners' orientations to the second language learning process? There is some evidence that this is *not* possible. Schumann (1978) discusses a case where he was able to obtain very accurate performance from a "fossilized" second language acquirer in a formal language teaching context, but where the same "learner" reverted to his original language variety once he was no longer in the formal testing situation. Similarly, Fillmore (1982) provides evidence that regardless of the teaching situation, different learners will perform in different ways, i.e. the learner orientation is more significant than the language learning environment. Hahn (1982) and Felix (1981) also discuss the way in which the learners' "natural" approaches to the language learning process seem to be impervious to attempts by the teacher to have the learners do something else. As Lightbown (1983:116) concludes as a result of her study of traditional language teaching classrooms:

> "What is more striking in the results, given the teachers' zeal in correcting errors in precisely these forms (that have been investigated), is that there was relatively little improvement over time in the accuracy of learners' use of the grammatical morphemes investigated ..."

Lightbown, however, also points out that it would be premature to regard other language teaching methods as automatically better since there is no research to prove the case one way or the other.

On the other hand, as Fillmore (1976) points out, it does not automatically follow that deviation from a path taken by a very rapid or accurate language acquirer should be equated with eventual/final lack of success in second language development. There is certainly mounting evidence from first language acquisition research that variation in paths does not have to mean variation in the final destination (in terms of linguistic ability). This point has also been made with regard to adult second language acquirers by Meisel et al. (1981) and also in Pienemann's 1981 study. There is therefore some evidence for the argument that learner orientations should be "left alone" since the learner will choose the path which best suits him/her in the course of language development. There are also, however, serious weaknesses in this approach which have already been indicated by Pienemann.

The clue lies perhaps in our search for a universal solution to such questions. If we recognize that learner orientations vary, then we must also recognize that this implies that different learners react to the same set of factors *in different ways*. Research has not yet provided enough evidence to describe accurately the different developmental paths, nor to accurately pinpoint the factors to which the learners react (although there are many hypotheses). To the extent that we know that it is possible to successfully intervene in the language learning process, we know that it is possible to influence individual learners' approaches to the target language and the target society. Certainly, research with contrastive models of language teaching such as Clyne (1983), which shows that children in certain types of instruction programme appear to "perform" significantly better than do children in other types of instruction, seems to indicate that certain aspects of language teaching procedures can be changed to facilitate second language development[1] (cf. also Swain & Lapkin, 1982). However, as the research by Harley appears to show, even within this seemingly "universal" improvement, there is significant variation between learners. As Fillmore (1982:295) points out

> "A critical difference between situations that promote language learning and ones that do not lies not only in the amount of exposure to the new language, but also in how the language is used."

Learner orientations result from a combination of individual reactions to different combinations of external circumstances and factors. While it would seem, at least theoretically, possible to change these influences, the attempt to alter them and their linguistic consequences can be neither universally applied nor exclusively restricted to linguistic features.

Note to Chapter 8

1. It should be pointed out that despite the "average" improvement obtained by moving from one method to another, there were significant differences within both types of programmes according to the age, sex, and learner type of the children. Certain programmes seem to better suit certain learners at certain times.

References

Clahsen, H., Meisel, J.M. & Pienemann, M. 1983, *Deutsch als Zweitsprache: Der Spracherwerb ausländischer Arbeiter*. Tübingen: Narr.

Clahsen, H., Köpcke, K.-M., Meisel, J. M., Nicholas, H.R. & Vincent, M. in prep., *Sprachentwicklung in der zweiten Sprache*.

Clyne, M. 1983, Bilingual education as a model for community languages in primary schools. *Journal of Intercultural Studies*, 4/2, 23–36.

Felix, S.W. 1978, *Linguistische Untersuchungen zum natürlichen Zweitsprachenerwerb*. München, Fink.

—— 1981, The effect of formal instruction on second language acquisition. *Language Learning*, 31, 87–112.

Fillmore, L.W. 1976, *The second time around: cognitive and social strategies in second language acquisition*. Ph.D. Thesis. Stanford University.

—— 1982, Instructional language as linguistic input: second language learning in classrooms. In L.C. Wilkinson (ed.), *Communicating in the classroom. Language, thought, and culture: advances in the study of cognition*. New York: Academic Press.

Hahn, A. 1982 *Fremdsprachenunterricht und Spracherwerb. Linguistische Untersuchungen zum gesteuerten Zweitsprachenerwerb*. Ph.D. Thesis. Universität Passau.

Hakuta, K. 1974, Prefabricated patterns and the emergence of structure in second language acquisition. *Language Learning*, 24, 2. 287–97.

Harley, B. 1982, *Age-related differences in the acquisition of the French verb system by Anglophone students in French immersion programs*. Ph.D. Thesis, University of Toronto.

Huang, J.S.P. 1971, *A Chinese child's acquisition of English syntax*. M.A. Thesis, University of California, Los Angeles.

Krashen, S. 1981, *Second language acquisition and second language learning*. Oxford: Pergamon Press.

Lightbown, P. 1977, *Consistency and variation in the acquisition of French: A study of first and second language development*. Ph.D. Thesis, Columbia University.

—— 1983 Acquiring English L2 in Quebec classrooms. In S.W. Felix & H. Wode (eds), *Language development at the crossroads*. Tübingen: Narr.

Meisel, J.M. 1980, Strategies of second language acquisition: More than one kind of simplification. *Wuppertaler Arbeitspapiere zur Sprachwissenschaft*, 3.

Meisel, J.M., Clahsen, H. & Pienemann, M. 1981, On determining developmental stages in second language acquisition. In *Studies in Second Language Acquisition*, 3. 109–35.

Nemoianu, A.M. 1980, *The boat's gonna leave: A study of children learning a second language from conversations with other children.* Amsterdam: John Benjamins B.U.

Nicholas, H.R. 1984, To be or not to be; is that really the question? Developmental sequences and the role of the copula in the acquisition of German as a second language. In R. W. Andersen (ed.), *Second Languages*, Rowley, Mass.: Newbury House.

—— in press a, Contextually defined queries: Evidence for variation in orientations to second language acquisition processes? Paper presented at the second European–North American Workshop on Cross-Linguistic Second Language Acquisition Research, 1982.

—— in press b, "dann wenn ich bin gut kann ich – kanne schule gehen": Variation, second language acquisition and learning. Paper presented at the Seventh Annual Congress of the Applied Linguistics Association of Australia, 1982.

Pienemann, M. 1981, *Der Zweitspracherwerb ausländischer Arbeiterkinder.* Bonn: Bouvier.

Schumann, J. 1978, *The pidginization process: a model for second language acquisition.* Rowley, Mass.: Newbury House.

Seliger, H.W. 1977, Does practice make perfect? A study of interaction patterns and L2 competence. *Language Learning*, 27, 263–78.

Swain, M. & Lapkin, S. 1982, *Evaluating Bilingual Education: A Canadian Case Study.* Clevedon: Multilingual Matters Ltd.

9 Medium or object – different contexts of (school-based) second language acquisition[1]

MICHAEL G. CLYNE

Monash University, Clayton, Australia

Introductory remarks

This paper will attempt to discuss the importance of the sociolinguistic context in the classroom development of a second language, partly in relation to some questions raised by Pienemann (this volume, Chapter 2) and Long (this volume, Chapter 3). While the situation I am describing is a specific one — in Melbourne, Australia — it could easily be transferred to many other countries. One point that needs to be made, however, is the position of "community languages other than English" (i.e. ethnic/immigrant) languages in Australia. Almost three quarters of a century of assimilationist, anglo-conformist attitudes has been followed by a decade of commitment to the concept of multiculturalism and, within that, to multilingualism. There is no dominant minority language comparable to Spanish in the U.S. Among community languages other than English, German rates third throughout Australia, well below Italian and Greek. In Melbourne, the number of German speakers (46,000 regular users in 1976) also falls below that of Serbo-Croatian speakers. The German-speaking communities are very dispersed throughout the metropolitan area (Clyne, 1982).

I would contend that psycholinguistic and sociolinguistic considerations of second language acquisition issues should be seen as complementary. For reasons which I shall outline in the course of my paper, I would not question taking account, in a syllabus, of the natural order of the

197

acquisition of structures discussed by Pienemann. But the functions for which the language can be used, together with variation in the learning context, I believe, play an even more important role in the L2 acquisition process.

The desirability of an integrated approach is well argued by Long, who has convincingly answered most of Pienemann's criticisms of Krashen's Natural Approach. One problem with Long's own alternative, Task Based Language Teaching, is its limited applicability to young children learning an L2. Do you assess the future needs of the child as an adult or consider only the child's present L2 needs? What if these are very restricted or even non-existent? How can you predict his/her future needs? It is recognized that tasks will take quite different forms depending on whether the target language is a foreign language, the national language or a community language other than the national language.

Among the more successful examples of what Pienemann terms the "Abandon teaching" philosophy — i.e. the one based on letting the learner acquire L2 through use by means of a comprehensible input — have been the immersion programmes which have become an important feature of Canadian education systems over the past 1½ decades. They still function within the classroom situation. Children receive all or a significant part of their instruction across the curriculum through the medium of L2 (usually French) in programmes generally commencing at the kindergarten level (age 5) but sometimes delayed until Grade 3 or even Grade 7. Evaluations have shown repeatedly that children in immersion programmes perform better in all skills in L2 than do children in traditional primary school second language programmes. However, there is evidence of the development of pidginized forms, which may be stigmatized, as Pienemann points out (p.43). The host of research publications and reports outlining the encouraging results of the programmes are discussed by Swain & Lapkin (1982) and Genesee (1983).

The programmes

I would like, within the context of the discussion in this volume, to deal with aspects of two primary school language programmes — one in which German is acquired as a medium of instruction, the other in which it is the object of instruction. Initially I shall confine myself to the first two years of the programmes.

School A is in a predominantly upper working class suburb on the outskirts of Melbourne, in which German speakers form the largest non-British ethnic group, and there are a number of German "institutions" (shops, community hall, three churches, two part-time ethnic schools, two old people's homes, and a nursing home). However, because of the age distribution, there are few children from German-speaking families in the programme, and the examples in this paper are from pupils from English-speaking homes. The children entered the programme in Grades 1 and 3 (aged 6 and 8) respectively. The teacher speaks German only, in the classroom, on the playground and on excursions, and the programme is based on the one person, one language principle well-known from bilingual language acquisition (see e.g. Ronjat, 1913; Leopold, 1939–1949; Saunders, 1982).

Owing to the sociopolitical situation in Australia being different to that in Canada, we have to experiment with a view to developing models that achieve goals reasonably at the minimum cost. Consequently the programmes are very modest compared to their Canadian counterparts. In the first two years of the programmes, School A taught five subjects in German for one hour each (language arts was added in the second year for the older pupils and in the third year for the younger group — see below). While the Canadian French immersion programmes are intended basically for children from non-French backgrounds, School A offers its programme to children from both non-German- and German-speaking families. We are testing the acquisition of L2 by beginners from different age groups (6, 7, 8, 9) as well as in different model programmes, so we have not settled for particular entry ages.

School B is situated in a middle class Melbourne suburb with relatively few non-English speakers (but still a sizeable German-speaking minority). The children in the parallel classes commenced at the same time as those in School A and have received two half hours per week of German — based on functional rather than grammatical syllabuses, but with structured language lessons and very much more emphasis on grammar, for the language is the object (and largely the content) of the lessons. One teacher was shared between the two schools in 1981–2, but she used English at times as a "short cut" in School B.

At School A, each of the subjects taught in German has contributed in a different way to the children's L2 acquisition, providing the pupils with both linguistically and cognitively comprehensible input as well as a multitude of specific tasks. (Cf. Long, this volume.) The three subjects taught entirely in German – Science, Physical Education and Art – are all "doing subjects" with a strong non-verbal component. Physical Education promotes listening skills as well as the development of notions and functions relating to human activities. Science is a "discovery" and "classificatory" subject furthering a close relationship between linguistic and cognitive development and frequent teacher-pupil interaction. Art, while in general a linguistically more passive subject, does provide opportunities for more personal interaction between teacher and individual pupils. Because of their large cultural content, Music and Social Studies are taught partly in English and partly in German by two teachers, using different syllabuses. The English-medium segments are Australian oriented and the German-medium ones are European oriented. In addition to its role in the language-culture link, Social Studies promotes both speaking and listening, and introduces concepts from the home, work and institutional domains. The language arts periods (half hour per week for some children in the second year of the programme, 1 hour per week in the third year) are used to supplement the development of literacy and grammatical awareness. However, formal grammar is not taught. While the traditional style of correction, which can greatly inhibit motivation (cf. Krashen, 1982) is not followed, the teacher will praise a reply with correct information but an ungrammatical form, and then repeat it correctly. This is in accordance with the idea of acquiring L2 while using it to learn other subjects.

For some of the children in School A, the classroom is the only contact with German; others employ it to German-speaking friends, neighbours or shopkeepers, or to siblings also in the German programme, and many listen to German "ethnic radio" broadcasts or watch German children's films on TV. On the whole, the pupils at School B see German more as the language of foreign countries than as a community language in Australia.

Evaluation

Regular testing is enabling us to compare models in relation to children commencing German at different ages. In keeping with the aural-oral emphasis in the earlier phases of the programmes (cf. Donoghue & Kunkle, 1979), most of the tests over the first two years were aural or oral — listening comprehension, sound discrimination, conversation, telling and retelling of stories, elicited sentence imitation (indicating language processing), and grammatical development (genders, transformation of singular to plural and of verbal forms, partly using words unfamiliar to the pupils, tested with pictures). Cloze tests and one test each of dictation, reading and verbal translation were also employed. In some cases, the entire class was tested; in others, children were selected, matched between classes and schools for background, sex, and pre-programme scores in the Peabody Picture Vocabulary Test. Some of the children were followed through longitudinally. In the first two years, we collected 28 comparative test measures, apart from tests of functions, notions and skills relating to work done in subject areas, which were administered at School A only. Specific data on teacher-pupil interaction and phonological development are also being gathered by observation and with the aid of a radio microphone worn periodically by the teacher.

The test results (Table 1) indicate the following comparisons:[2]

(i) Programme A children performed better in sound discrimination. This difference is significant only for the younger group.

(ii) Programme A children performed significantly better in listening-comprehension tests than Programme B. (This applies to both age groups.) In Programme B only, those who began in Grade 3 obtained significantly better results than the younger group.

(iii) Both grades in Programme A scored significantly better at speaking than their counterparts in Programme B even though the emphasis in Programme A had been less directly on active skills than at the other school. As we shall illustrate below, the pupils in Programme A are far more creative in their use of German.

(iv) Both classes in Programme A performed very significantly better than the pupils in Programme B in the Cloze tests.

(v) Both classes in Programme A did better at dictation than their counterparts in Programme B, but this difference is significant only for the younger group.

(vi) Though the degree of grammatical accuracy is not very high at either school, the results were very significantly better in Programme A than in Programme B, even though the latter programme placed more emphasis on correctness. It is by no means children in School A that produce the most pidginized forms (cf. Pienemann, this volume).

(vii) The difference between the high and low scores in any class in all skills tested is greater in Programme B (Table 2).

Thus, in terms of numerical results, children in Programme A performed better in every test, and significantly better overall in practically every skill, than the comparable class in School B. The difference can, in my opinion, be attributed to the stress, in the bilingual programme, on communicative need and the communicative function of L2, also essentials of naturalistic L2 acquisition. The accent on communicative function is strengthened by the functional specialization (Fishman, 1980) between the languages and the "one person, one language" model.

The older children have performed better than the younger ones at School B (though this difference is significant only in comprehension).

TABLE 1 Test results (x^2 with 2 degrees of freedom)

Sound discrimination (3 tests)

	Good	Comparatively average	Poor	
A	20	4	4	A > B. not sign.
B	18	7	9	a > b. sign. 2.5%
a	21	5	7	A > a. not sign.
b	7	6	13	B > b. not sign.

Comprehension (5 tests)

	Good	Comparatively average	Poor	
A	20	9	1	A > B. sign. 0.5%
B	7	13	12	a > b. sign. 0.5%
a	22	9	3	A > a. not sign.
b	7	6	13	B > b. sign. 5%

Orals (6 + 4 tests)

	Good		Average		Poor		
	Comp	Prod	Comp	Prod	Comp	Prod	
A	10	8	3	8	4	1	A > B. Prod. sign. 5%
B	5	3	3	6	7	6	a > b. Prod. sign. 5%
a	7	5	6	7	4	5	A > a. not sign.
b	1	–	4	3	7	9	B > b. not sign.
							Comp. not sign.

		Good	Average	Poor	
Cloze Test (2 tests)	A	15	8	–	A > B, very sign. 1%
	B	3	12	10	a > b, very sign. 1%
	a	18	8	3	A > a, not sign.
	b	2	13	6	B > b, not sign.
Grammar (4 tests)	A	6	3	–	A > B, very sign. 0.05%
	B	–	1	8	A > a, not sign.
	a	6	3	2	Others: too many empty cells
	b	–	–	9	
Dictation (1 test)	A	12	5	6	A > B, sign. 1.5%
	B	4	14	9	a > b, not sign.
	a	11	9	7	A > a, not sign.
	b	8	16	6	B > b, not sign.

A = Grade 3, Programme A
a = Grade 1, Programme A
B = Grade 3, Programme B
b = Grade 1, Programme B

COMP = Comprehension
PROD = Production

TABLE 2   *Coefficient of Variability*

	Sound Discr.	Comphren-sion	Orals Comp.	Prod.	Cloze	Grammar
A	0.11	0.10	0.24	0.12	0.15	0.20
B	0.15	0.17	0.34	0.24	0.33	0.33
a	0.11	0.12	0.15	0.18	0.25	0.40
b	0.20	0.20	0.40	0.38	0.29	0.62

This can be explained by the greater awareness of L1 in the older children (cf. Cummins's (1979) interdependence hypothesis; also Skutnabb-Kangas (1981)). However, this factor does not seem to affect the results in Programme A very much, if at all.

Features of pupils' language

There are a number of issues that are obscured in numerical scores. I would like to focus on three of these:

(i)   Are there differences between the children in the two pro-grammes as regards interlanguage, code-switching, transfer-ence patterns and L2 creativity?

(ii)   The importance of the classroom situation – notably of teacher-pupil interaction – on the grammatical development of children in the two programmes.

(iii) The importance of the classroom situation – notably of teacher-pupil interaction – on the discourse development of children in the two programmes.

(i) One of the major features of Programme A, on which visitors have generally commented, is the pupils' readiness to communicate in the classroom situation whether they have the means in German or not. Where necessary, the children will code-switch, transfer from English or create analogical formations. The code-switching and integration patterns are common to them and to German-speaking immigrants in Australia, some of the integration patterns being an indication of an internalized L2 grammar (See Clyne, 1967). Programme A children possess a strong metalinguistic awareness. For instance, one class roared with laughter when one of their number momentarily confused German *Ei* and English *eye*. Some examples of the above phenomena:

Grammatically integrated lexical transfers
ich runne, er pullt, sie climbt, readen, gewalkt

Phonologically integrated lexical transfers
[ʃnoːman] "snowman", [ʃliːp] "sleep", Kupf "cup"
Semantic transfers
Mädchenfreund "girl friend", Papier "(news)paper", still "still",
Trink "drink" (noun)
Mixed idioms
Ist das right? Was sprichst du about?
Neologisms
Händewascher (face-washer, wash-cloth, flannel), Hampelfrau (in:
"Du bist eine Hampelfrau") < Hampelmann (jumping jack)
Code-switching anticipating a trigger word (Clyne, 1967:Ch. 5)
Vater steht bei dem Fleisch und drinkt <u>beer</u> (Bier).
Großvater liegt <u>on the grass</u> (Gras) and schläft.
(————— indicates trigger-word.)
Instances of analogical formations are:
Meine Katze *habt* "hat"; er *bint* "ist" (in early stage of programme)

The children in Programme B, on the other hand, are far less creative. They have learned some expressions from memory, e.g. "Ich heiße...", "Ich bin...Jahre alt" but, when confronted with a problem, they tended to remain silent. One and two word sentences in German were more prevalent in Programme B, as were purely English responses. Mixed sentences were far less common than in Programme A, and the children were generally unable to integrate English material into their German.

(ii) Canadian scholars (e.g. Harley & Swain, 1978) have commented on the fossilization of pidginized forms among immersion children. This is attributed to the ability of the children to communicate in L2, leaving them without a strong incentive to adopt native speaker norms (Harley & Swain, 1978:76) and has its parallels among some of the pupils in our two programmes. But the importance of teacher-pupil interaction on the development of grammatical forms should not be underestimated. In fact, some features of the interlanguage of our subjects have, to my knowledge, not been observed in other studies of L2 acquisition.

Towards the end of the first year of Programme A, most of the children over-generalized the 2nd person singular possessive pronoun *dein(e)* to cover the meaning of not only other possessive pronouns (notably *sein(e)* and *ihr(e)*, but also the definite article, which appears to be used less in the teacher's discourse in the classroom. (N.B. also the phonological similarity betwen *dein* and the masculine accusative definite article *den*.) By the third year of the programme, at least half the pupils still employed *dein* instead of *sein* and *ihr*, many in variation with these, but very few of them used it instead of the definite article:

Heidi geht off dem Bett und zu die Toilette und putzen *deine* (= ihre) teeth.
Heidi ist essen mit *deine* (= ihren) Finger.
Heidis doll hast *dein* (= das) Papier. (All different speakers.)

The reason for the overgeneralization is most likely the prevalence of teacher questions.

Teacher questions are probably also responsible for the predominance of *-st* (2nd person singular) forms of the verb among children in the second year of the programme, and after the generalization of *-en* forms in the first year (cf. the overgeneralization of the *-en* or Ø form in other contexts, such as Guest Worker German (see e.g. Orlović-Schwarzwald, 1978; Meisel, 1977; Clyne, 1968):

Pinkel spring*st*.
Vater ha*st* dein Breakfast (Vater ißt sein Frühstück.)

By the middle of the third year of the programme, the *-t* form has taken over as the most common, the verbal system is generally falling into place, and some of the pupils make few or no errors while others still experience unsystematic variation between *-en*, *-st* and *-t* forms. (Transferred verbs ending in *-t* are not inflected by most children in the 3rd person singular, *er get*, *er* put). *-en* for *-e* (e.g. *ich gehen*) is to be found especially in children's written work. The *-st* overgeneralization was rare in Programme B, where verbs were used mainly formulaically. Otherwise the endings were characterized by unsystematic variation.

(iii) Another possible effect of classroom language in Programme A is a retardation in the development of the children's discourse, something that cannot be separated from their grammatical development. Most of the children's utterances are necessarily answers to the teacher's questions or elucidations of her statements. She provides the linguistic context (*scaffolding*, as Slobin (1981) terms it) for the children's German speech. In this co-operative situation (cf. Grice, 1975), the children's German utterances have comprised principally nouns, uninflected adjectives, noun phrases, infinitives or past participles of verbs, or interjections. Many of the children will switch to English (usually with some German lexical transfers) as soon as they have to produce a continuous narrative comprising several sentences, especially to express causal or temporal relationships, e.g.

Heute we I went down to the milk bar all by myself riding mein Fahrrad.
(Ganz allein bist du gefahren? Sehr gut) and when I rode down, I rode real fast (schnell oder langsam?) Schnell, and I nearly ran into a Fenster. (Temporal)

Mein Großvater and meine Großmutter have come to stay at our place because meine Mutter is in the Krankenhaus and she's had a baby.
(Causal)
Some of the children, notably a number of Grade 5 boys who have developed some in-group resistance to developing their own German discourse, have continued to rely on the "scaffolding". Code-switching has become habitual to them, and this is inhibiting their grammatical development.

The demands of the classroom situation have also given rise to the major type of syntactic transference. While the children are exposed daily to German present tense in narrative contexts where the English equivalent would be a progressive (present continuous), some of the children, when faced with developing their own German narratives, will generalize a home-made German progressive (e.g. *ist trinken*) or switch for the participle (e.g. *ist drinking*):

Der Mann ist still reading die Newspaper.
Heidi ist trinken Milch and ist essen.
Heidi ist laufen auf dem Bett. Die Mutter ist schlafen.

(Telling of story based on picture sequence. All different speakers.)
Quite a number of Programme A children do this, but near-generalization of the construction (i.e. for all but common verbs) is limited to some Grade 5 boys.

All this seems to suggest the need for more grammatical intervention (according to a grammatical syllabus) as the programme develops. This would have to take natural acquisition order into account. However, the interaction situation in the classroom does appear to have prompted grammatical phenomena that are outside the "natural sequence".

Learner's orientation

In his chapter, Nicholas (this volume) stresses the importance of differences in the learner's orientation — reflecting the ZISA Project's distinction between structural and functional orientations (Meisel, 1981), a dichotomy which is being found useful for the evaluation of the programmes under discussion. The more functionally-oriented learners operate on the assumption that, whatever language a German speaker in Australia may address them in, he (she) will be able to understand an English or mixed utterance. These pupils' comprehension skills are well developed, as are their communication strategies. The more structurally oriented learners have a genuine interest not only in how the language works but also in keeping the systems (at least outwardly) "apart". A major manifestation of the functional-structural difference in orientation is therefore one between code-switching (especially unsystematic code-switching) and the use of integrated lexical transfers. Another is the greater amount of correction in structurally-oriented learners. Some examples:

(a) Heidi macht das Vater helfen, das Vater helf Heidi. *Then Heidi gets the paper* und Vater macht breakfast/*the doll* setzen *on the table*. Das Vater reit [bereit?] *their breakfast. Then the* Vater *reads the* Papier und Heidi essen *the breakfast and the* Vater *still read the* Papier.
(Grade 3 boy, more functionally oriented. *NOTE* code-switching.)

(b) Heidi helf den Vater zu'z'an den/helf den Vater *put* den Bademantel an. Heidis Vater *help put* Heidis Bademantel an. Da Heidi ist neben den Schuhe und sie hat den/sie hat die Zeitung. Da Heidis Vater ist *getting* der Food/ *is getting* der Frühstück. Heidis Puppe hat den Brief und der/ich weiß nicht, was das ist.
(Grade 3 boy, more structurally oriented. *NOTE* correction; relatively little code-switching.)

(c) Heidis Mutter ist *pouring her tea*. Heidis Mutter muß es trinken. Heidi ist *getting* unter das Bett.
(Grade 5 boy, more functionally oriented.)

(d) Heidi bringt das Essen zu Mutti. Heidi find' die Mutter. Die Mutter ist im Bett. Heidi macht ein *Trink vor* (for) die Mutter. Heidi ist auf die Toilette. Heidi zieht das Pyjama *auf* (= off). Heidi macht das *dressing-gown* auf.
(Grade 5 girl, more structurally oriented. *NOTE* transference rather than code-switching.)
(Excerpts from story-telling based on picture sequence – Programme A)

I have mentioned, under 2, the greater difference between the highest and lowest scores in Programme B. This could perhaps be attributed to the relatively poor performance of the more functionally oriented learners of Programme B (especially in conversation and grammar tests). Perhaps structurally oriented learners, especially those who are 8 when they enter the programme, are more suited for a more "grammatical" approach than those with a more functional orientation and those who begin L2 at the age of 6. The different quality and quantity of input could enable children in Programme A to capitalize more on the "silent period" (Krashen, 1982).

We can summarize the differences between the second language and "bilingual" primary school programmes as in Table 3.

TABLE 3   *Differences between "bilingual" and second language programmes*

	A.–"Bilingual"	B.–Second language programme
1. Grammatical development	Codetermined by interactional requirements of classroom situation (e.g. *dein*; *-st*; progressive).	Incidental or determined by grammatical content of syllabus.
2. Qualitative results in L2 (comprehension and production)	Better because of emphasis on functions and functional specialization and due to greater exposure (because L2 is acquired via subjects which would otherwise need to be taught in L1).	Inferior; more limited exposure (L2 occupies special slots on "competive" time table).
3. Functional/ structural orientation	Programme suitable for both structurally and functionally oriented learners.	Programme would seem to benefit structurally rather than functionally oriented learners.
4. Content	Different subjects are used for the acquisition of different functions and notions and emphasize different language skills.	Content for L2 classes needs to be explicitly developed and/or sought.
5. Language-culture link	Naturally developed through the teaching of parts of Social Studies and Music in L2 (i.e. culture *in* as well as *through* L2).	Needs to be explicitly developed; is aided by incorporating "culture" content taught in L2; otherwise culture *through* L2.
5. Discourse development	Problems outlined under 3. *Features of pupils' language* above; however, children are creative in L2.	Children have not yet reached the stage of formulating their own long stretches of discourse. In the first two years, silences 1- or 2-word responses, and formulaic replies.

Further developments

School A's nearest neighbour (C), introduced, at the beginning of 1983, a programme based on a "compromise model" between A and B. Those subjects taught in German for 2 hours per week (1 hour Science, half hour Social Studies, half hour Music and Movement) are complemented, right from the beginning, with an hour of language arts in German (half hour in Grades 1 and 2), where the emphasis falls on discourse through role play and drama. Thus there is a combination of input and instruction as from the beginning. A parallel programme is offered in Italian.

School A has introduced a bilingual stream of beginners in Grades 2 and 4 this year. This is facilitating further comparisons between two models (A,C) for four different entry ages at the primary level (6, 7, 8, 9). Testing and data analysis are in progress. So far, the preliminary results are far from clear cut (see Table 4).

The Grade 1 and 3 results are based on testing in 1981. At this early stage of the programme in C 1–4 and A 2 and 4, it should be taken into account that the younger children are less familiar with any testing situation and tend to be less socially competent at communicating with strangers. It must also be mentioned that Programmes A and C are taught by different teachers. It is too early to compare the interlanguage and communication strategies of the pupils in School C with those of School A.

In this chapter I have attempted to demonstrate the effects of different classroom learning contexts on second language development

TABLE 4 *Preliminary comparison between "bilingual" (A) and "compromise" (C)*

Sound Discrimination

Programme A (%)		Programme C (%)	
Gd. 4	86.67	Gd. 4	82.41
3	89.66	3	77.78
2	98.39	2	78.0
1	92.97	1	84.48

Listening-comprehension

Programme A (%)		Programme C (%)	
Gd. 4	94.83	Gd. 4	91.61
3	90.92	3	84.75
2	97.34	2	77.39
1	93.48	1	79.73

Oral Tests

	Progamme A (%)		Programme C (%)	
	Comp.	Prod.	Comp.	Prod.
Gd. 4	73.15	96.3	58.3	92.59
3	97.78	96.3	90.74	90.78
2	68.75	79.2	92.59	92.59
1	82.22	92.67	75.0	92.59

rather than to suggest the actual contents of a syllabus. In the process I have discussed the validity of a "natural" approach; certain shortcomings of such an approach and the need for limited grammatical intervention; the extent of pidginization and the fact that this is not restricted to the more "natural" approach; the prevalence of variation; the role of the pupils' linguistic creativity and the suitability of more or less structured approaches for particular kinds of learners.

Notes to Chapter 9

1. Sections of this contribution have evolved out of a paper read at the annual conference of Applied Linguistics Association of Australia, November 1982, of which Clyne (1983) is a revised version.
2. Tests were set in such a way and based on such material that would not disadvantage children in School B.

References

Clyne, M.G. 1967, *Transference and Triggering*. The Hague: Nijhoff.
—— 1968, Zum Pidgin-Deutsch der Gastarbeiter. *Zeitschrift für Mundartforschung*, 35, 130–39.
—— 1982, *Multilingual Australia*. Melbourne: River Seine.
—— 1983, Bilingual Education as a Model for Community Languages in Primary Schools. *Journal of Intercultural Studies*, 4, 2, 23–36.
Cummins, J.P. 1979, Linguistic interdependence and the educational development of bilingual children. *Review of Education Research*, 49, 2, 222–51.
Donoghue, M.R. & Kunkle, J.F. 1979, *Second Language in Primary Education*. Rowley, Mass: Newbury House.
Fishman, J.A. 1980, Bilingualism and biculturalism as individual and as societal phenomena. *Journal of Multilingual and Multicultural Development*, 1. 1, 3–15.
Genesee, F. 1983, Bilingual Education of Majority Language Children: The Immersion Experiments in Review. *Applied Psycholinguistics*.
Grice, H.P. 1975, Logic and Conversation. In P. Cole & J.L. Morgan (eds), *Syntax and Semantics. 3: Speech Acts*. New York: Academic Press. 41–59.
Harley, B. & Swain, M. 1978, An analysis of the Verb System used by Young Learners of French. *Interlanguage Bulletin*, 3, 1, 35–79.
Krashen, S.D. 1982, *Principles and Practice of Second Language Acquisition*. Oxford: Pergamon.
Leopold, W.F. 1939–49, *Speech Development of a Bilingual Child*. (4 vols.) Evanston, Ill: Northwestern University Press.
Meisel, J. 1977, Linguistic Simplification. A Study of Immigrant Workers' Speech and Foreigner Talk. In S.P. Corder & E. Roulet (eds), *The Notions of Simplification, Interlanguages and Pidgin and their Relation to Second Language Pedagogy*. Geneva: Librairie Droz. 88–113.
—— 1981, Natural Second Language Acquisition/Processing. (Mimeo.)
Orlović-Schwarzwald, M. 1978, *Zum Gastarbeiterdeutsch jugoslawischer Arbeiter im Rhein-Main Gebiet*. Wiesbaden: Franz Steiner.

Ronjat, J. 1913, *Le développement du langage chez un enfant bilingue*. Paris: Librairie Ancienne H. Champion.
Saunders, G.W. 1982, *Bilingual Children: Guidance for the Family*. Clevedon, Avon: Multilingual Matters Ltd.
Skutnabb-Kangas, T. 1981, *Tvåspråkighet*. Lund: Liberläromedel.
Slobin, D.I. 1981, Reference to the Not-here and Not-now. (Mimeo)
Swain, M. & Lapkin, S. 1982, *Evaluating Bilingual Education: A Canadian Case Study*. Clevedon, Avon: Multilingual Matters Ltd.

PART II

10 Assessing proficiency: An overview on some aspects of testing

D.E. INGRAM

Darwin Institute of Technology, Casuarina, Australia

Introduction

It is doubtful whether any field of applied linguistics is, at the same time, so conservative and so radical or so arcane and yet so popularly practised, as second language testing. On the one hand, many Public Examination systems, at least in Britain and Australia, have departed little from tests based on grammatical knowledge, translation, and pseudo-literary appreciation. On the other hand, testing specialists, teachers and even some education systems have been experimenting with many different approaches varying from those focussing analytically on components of language knowledge and behaviour using minimal context and "integrative" methods to approaches focussing on total language behaviour itself as a communicative activity. Again, on the one hand, testing experts are seeking precision by analysing and testing different types of control over the language or by introducing complex statistical procedures to validate or elucidate the precise nature of their tests, whereas, on the other hand, almost every teacher however well- or ill-trained produces and administers tests many of which may, eventually, have a profound impact on the lives of their students. This chapter seeks to provide a brief overview of the field but focussing almost exclusively on the assessment of proficiency in a "second" or "foreign" language. In fact, in this chapter, the term "test" refers to any activity in evaluating or measuring some part or all of a learner's language proficiency. As the chapter proceeds, reference will be

215

made to test types and published tests, to their development, strengths and weaknesses, and to their actual and defensible uses.

Historically changes in language testing (at least in the research and development aspects if not in educational practice) have accompanied changes in our understanding of the nature of language, of how it is learned, and of how it is most desirably taught (cf. Alderson's introduction to Alderson & Hughes, 1981: 6; see also Spolsky, 1978; Brière, 1972: 322–5; Farhady, 1979: 347–9; Burner, 1980). When language learning was seen as a process of learning grammatical rules and vocabulary and then "rewriting" from one language into another, tests could be based on grammatical knowledge and translation: in Spolsky's terms (1978), this was the "pre-scientific" period in language testing. When behaviourist language learning theories and structuralist linguistic theories were in vogue and language was seen as a multitude of discrete patterns learned by stimulus-response habit formation, tests focussed on individual patterns or "discrete points" from the language and were designed to provide a stimulus to which the learner provided (or completed) an appropriate response. Thus, test items took forms such as this:

Instruction:	*Tick the answer that best fills the gap.*
Question:	"How old is Joe?"
	"He's two years younger ＿＿ his brother, Bill."
Answer:	that ☐
	as ☐
	than ☐
	of ☐

This type of item was also defensible when, later, under the influence of generative linguistics, language was seen as a system of internalized patterns or "rules" whose learning involved, in Carroll's words,

> " ...a process of acquiring conscious control of the phonological, grammatical and lexical patterns of a second language, largely through study and analysis of these patterns as a body of knowledge." (Carroll, 1966:102)

Whether the explanation of such "discrete point" tests was behaviourist or cognitivist, this approach measured language proficiency by testing the learner's knowledge of the many discrete items of grammar or vocabulary and the many discrete aspects of skills (e.g. vowel discrimination, sound-symbol correspondence, articulation of consonant clusters, etc.) that were seen as adding up to make language proficiency. This view of language and its testing fitted well into the psychometric methods of other behavioural sciences which were, then, applied to and came to dominate language testing during the "psychometric-structuralist" period (Spolsky, 1978).

As the complex, integrated, and inherently redundant nature of language was realized and as more value came to be attached to the close interrelationship and interdependence of the component parts of the language and of each part or "discrete point" with its linguistic, non-linguistic and purposive context, so testers sought to utilize the principle of redundancy as a means of assessing proficiency and to integrate their test items into a total language event. Thus "integrative" and, later, "communicative" tests became popularized in what Spolsky (1978) terms the "integrative-sociolinguistic" phase of language testing. A further phase that may be distinguished focusses on the total outcome of language learning and lays most stress on the learner's total communicative skills. In other words, it focusses on what learners can do with the language, on the tasks they can carry out and how they carry them out, or, in other words, on their total language behaviour and its productive capacity. This approach to language testing has emerged with growing importance at the same time as functional views of language, function-based descriptions of language learning, and functional–notional or communicative approaches to language teaching. It is a "behavioural" (but not "behaviourist") and "authentic" approach to testing in the sense that it focusses directly on total language behaviour rather than on its component parts; it assesses that behaviour by observing it in real or, at least, realistic language-use situations which are as "authentic" as possible. It is examplified in testing based on the use of rating scales such as the Australian Second Language Proficiency Ratings (ASLPR) (Ingram & Wylie 1979, 1982a, 1982b, 1982c) or the scale of the United States Foreign Service Institute School of Language Studies (the FSI Scale).

The preceding historical description provides one way of classifying language tests and shows something of the diversity of approaches tests cover. Many other ways of classifying tests and approaches to testing are possible with each "cut" through the field highlighting different contrasts: developmental and non-developmental; discrete point, integrative and behavioural; norm-referenced and criterion-referenced, psychometric and edumetric; or indirect, semi-direct and direct. Some of these will be referred to in the course of this chapter but it will be evident that the different "cuts" and the classifications within them are rarely discrete either in their theoretical bases, in their test formats, or in their historical development. To a large extent, the different types of tests presuppose different concepts of what is meant by "proficiency" and we will now consider briefly some of the issues and contrasting views that underlie the tacit or overt definitions of language proficiency that have influenced the path that language testing has taken at different times. At the same time, though, it is necessary to consider whether the tests proposed to measure whatever is intended by "proficiency" are successful in doing so, i.e. one can ask whether the tests proposed are valid (i.e. do they set out to measure proficiency and do they in fact do so?), reliable (i.e. do they consistently assess the same level of proficiency as being at the same level?), and useful (i.e. do they state the learner's proficiency in a way that is comprehensible and unambiguous whether or not the people using them are experts in testing?).

The central problem: Proficiency

A construct

At one end of the continuum of views on the nature of proficiency that emerges in the literature on testing is the view that "proficiency", like the psychological concept "intelligence", is an artificial or "formal" construct measured and defined by language proficiency tests. Vollmer (1981:152) introduced his discussion of general language proficiency in this way:

> "I should like to start out by saying that language proficiency is what language proficiency tests measure. This circular statement is about all one can firmly say when asked to define the concept of proficiency to date."

Such definitions are common enough, implicitly, if not explicitly, in psychometric approaches to psychological measurement. If proficiency is considered a formal construct, then one is essentially saying that the actual nature of "proficiency" and the form of the test are less important than that the results should separate the more proficient learners from the less proficient. In fact, this approach merely moves the problem from defining "proficiency" to defining "more" or "less" "proficient", a task which, psychometrically, can be achieved by comparing the learners' results with their performances on other things such as a language course or in some subsequent activity such as academic study or the work-place. This implies, however, that "proficiency" is a definite, if intuitively held, concept and not just a formal construct.

Proficiency as knowledge

Traditionally, as we observed earlier, "knowing" or "having proficiency in" a language was seen as a matter of knowing grammatical rules and vocabulary and could be measured by measuring the learner's grammatical and lexical knowledge. Thus, one component (a third by weighting) of CELT (Harris & Palmer, 1970) tests syntax and another component (also a third by weighting) aims at vocabulary. However, *knowledge* and *proficiency* are not the same: one can have much knowledge about a language and even be able to recall and consciously apply many grammatical rules and yet not be proficient in the sense of being able to utilize that knowledge readily for practical communication purposes. Seliger (1979) found no significant relationship between what the learners gave as rules and their actual language performance. Similarly, in a study of the EFL proficiency of students in a foreign languages institute in China in December 1980, the present writer found the students scoring relatively high on the CELT Structure Test (mean for the Third Year group 81.67%, in the 73 percentile of the most relevant criterion group in the CELT Manual) but relatively low on the ASLPR (around 1+, Survival Proficiency, in all macroskills) (Ingram, 1980, 1982a, 1982b). On the other hand, Madsen & Jones (1981: 20) cite cases where learners with relatively inferior grammatical knowledge as reflected in discrete-point tests, nevertheless produced superior performance in oral (particularly conversation) tests.

In fact, the level of correlation between tests of formal knowledge and tests of practical proficiency seems to depend on the nature of the course or the environment in which the language has been learned. Where it has been learned in an "acquisition-rich", especially *second* language learning situation, a closer match could be expected between knowledge of rules and practical proficiency, between formal and informal learning, between what has been learned and what has been acquired, regularly mobilized, and is available for spontaneous use (see Krashen, 1976, 1980, 1981a, 1981b for the acquisition-learning, informal-formal distinction). Where the language has been learned in a "learning-rich" but "acquisition-poor", especially *foreign* language learning situation, one would expect the match to be less. Palmer (1979) cites a number of studies to support his distinction between "compartmentalized" and "integrated" control, the former developing where focus is on formal learning of specific components of the language and the latter developing where teaching focusses around more communicative activities: results on discrete-point tests of grammatical knowledge correlate more highly with communication test scores where teaching aims at integrated control. In other studies, a much lower and less stable correlation has been found between direct and indirect tests amongst *foreign* compared with *second* language learners (direct tests emphasizing practical proficiency and indirect tests placing more emphasis on formal knowledge). Mullen (1978b), for instance, reported correlations between TOEFL (indirect test) results and a modified FSI-type interview (direct test) little above zero when the learners had learned English as a foreign language in traditional, largely passive, (hence, learning-rich) courses though, when the same learners were re-tested after a period in an English-speaking (hence, acquisition-rich) environment, overall correlations were a little above 0.4. Correlations between the ASLPR and CELT also seemed to depend on the learning situation: with ESL learners in Australia, correlations were high (r or rho ranging between 0.87 and 0.96 for the various macroskills and CELT Totals) while, with EFL learners in China, correlations were much lower and unstable ranging between 0.3 and 0.64 for one group and 0.002 and 0.58 for another (see Ingram, 1982a:44–47, Tables 3–5 and especially pp.13–17 where other direct-indirect test correlations are also referred to).

To sum up, knowledge and proficiency in a language are not the same thing, the latter entailing not just knowledge but the ability to mobilize that knowledge in carrying out particular communication tasks in particular contexts or situations. Tests of grammatical knowledge can be used to indicate proficiency levels only if one considers the nature (learned or acquired) of the grammatical knowledge being elicited, the macroskill and context of use for which proficiency is to be measured, the learning situation, and the teaching/learning activities previously encountered. For this reason, attempts to define "proficiency" more adequately for test construction purposes have sought to take account of tasks and context.

Proficiency defined through tasks

The task-oriented approach to describing proficiency essentially adopts the view that the components (such as knowledge) that make up language are important only insofar as they can be mobilized, integrated and used in carrying out communication tasks. Subsumed in the ASLPR, for example, is the view that proficiency is best described in terms of the sorts of tasks a learner can carry out and how they are carried out (Ingram, 1979b, 1980b, 1982c). This seems to accord with the intuitive view that what is meant when we say that someone is proficient in a language is that that person can do certain things in that language. Such an approach accords well with the trend to competency-based assessment in general education (implemented in Queensland Secondary Schools, for example, from 1982) and with functional–notional and communicative approaches to syllabus design and methodology in second and foreign language teaching. In the latter, proficiency is definable in terms of the functions that can be carried out and the notions that can be expressed but also, since language necessarily occurs in situations which, to a greater or lesser degree, influence the forms that occur, in terms of the situations in which the learner can perform. In a "graded objectives" approach to syllabus design, the situations, functions and notions in which learners will be able to use the language are specified and, in turn, testing in such an approach aims to assess the learners' ability to carry out the specified functions and express the specified notions in the specified situations (perhaps using specified syntax and lexis).

However, the concept of proficiency in a language seems, at least intuitively, to relate not only to a person's ability to carry out communication tasks but also to how he carries them out, i.e. to the linguistic forms through which those tasks are realized. One might, for example, communicate successfully in a shop (i.e. carry out a communication task) by pointing to the desired object and allowing the situation to suggest the meaning "I want..." or "I want to buy..." but this would not mean one had proficiency in the language. Thus proficiency needs to be defined in terms of not only the tasks that can be carried out but how they are carried out. This notion takes the definition of language proficiency beyond a task-oriented to a behavioural definition.

Proficiency defined behaviourally

Proficiency rating scales such as the ASLPR or the FSI Scale seek to define proficiency levels by describing the language behaviour observable at different stages as learners develop from zero proficiency to native-like. These descriptions generally refer both to tasks and how they are carried out and include reference to such features as range of situations in which the learner can operate, syntax, lexis, discourse, pronunciation, register sensitivity and flexibility, and cultural factors. Learners are "tested" by being encouraged to demonstrate their maximum language behaviour in activities chosen for the purpose. Most frequently, this behavioural approach to defining and measuring proficiency has been seen to be relevant to oral skills or, as in the FSI Scale, to "speaking" (which includes listening) and "reading". The ASLPR, however, applies it to all four macroskills since there seems no valid reason why the concept of proficiency defined as the sorts of tasks learners can carry out and how they are carried out should be more or less applicable to any of the four macroskills (see Ingram, 1982c, 1980e).

The behavioural and, to some extent, the task-oriented approaches to defining and measuring language proficiency raise a number of difficult issues inherent in the nature of language proficiency and with important implications for how it is measured. Though, for convenience, these issues are discussed now in the context of behavioural definitions of proficiency, they are equally relevant to any general discussion of proficiency and its measurement.

Proficiency and the complexity of language and language development. First, if one defines proficiency in terms of total language behaviour (rather than in terms of single components such as syntax, lexis, articulation or functions) then one has to allow for the possibility of different rates of development within different components of the behaviour. More or less development within one component may be counter-balanced by less or more development in some other and result in the same effective level of proficiency. So, for example, a Vietnamese learning English may seem to develop the phonological and syntactic components at rates different from those of a Scandinavian; during trials of the ASLPR, a Chinese business-woman showed exceptional ability to comprehend sums of money even though her listening skills, overall, were at a very low level (viz. L:O+) (see Ingram, 1979b). To allow for such phenomena, behavioural approaches to defining and measuring proficiency aim to provide a global picture of the behaviour observable at each level rather than a checklist of features mandatorily to be observed before a rating at that level can be assigned. This approach may seem to make the assessment process more subjective because the rater has, essentially, to use judgement in balancing different aspects of development against each other in order to arrive at an overall, global judgement of the scale level description that best matches the learner's observed behaviour. However, that subjectivity is necessitated by the sheer complexity and redundancy of language and its development and, though subjective, the approach is not impressionistic since it requires the deliberate matching of observing behaviour with the global descriptions of language behaviour provided.

Proficiency: Underlying versus particular. Second, it is necessary to distinguish the underlying general proficiency from its realization in a particular task in a particular situation: therefore the words "sorts of tasks" were used above rather than "actual tasks". Someone who has never used public transport, for instance, may not know what to do and so fail to carry out the necessary tasks readily or appropriately if he has to buy a bus or train ticket or use a timetable to find out bus numbers, routes and times even though he has mastered such "functions" as seeking information. A foreign language learner in a country without door-to-door milkmen may be unable to write an appropriate note in order to change a daily order even though in some other situation (e.g. a note to a teacher to explain an absence) he is able to perceive a relationship and the information to be conveyed and to select from his language repertoire the minimum language forms needed to carry out the note-writing task. In other words, one can distinguish the underlying general proficiency a learner has in a particular macroskill from that learner's ability to carry out an absolutely specified task in a specified situation. This distinction makes for an important difference between the "graded objectives" concept of proficiency and its measurement and what has been called here the behavioural approach to the definition and measurement of general proficiency. It leads to important issues in test development.

Standardized tests necessarily require that the language be used in a fixed set of tasks and so leave one uncertain whether the learner lacks the underlying proficiency or is unfamiliar with the particular situations and tasks chosen by the test writer: clearly, sampling becomes of critical importance, but no test could be so long in time or variety of items as to treat all learners equally validly and reliably. For this reason, behavioural instruments such as the FSI Scale and ASLPR are not accompanied by an immutable set of test activities but consist of general descriptions of observable behaviour together with, in the case of the ASLPR, "Examples of Specific Tasks" that exemplify the sorts of behaviour observable. In order to rate a learner's proficiency, the interviewer is advised to vary the situations in which the learner is asked to demonstrate his behaviour so as to provide a picture of the learner's underlying proficiency and to ensure, at one extreme, that the learner is not just performing from rote memory and, at the other extreme, that his inability to cope is not just the result of unfamiliarity with a particular situation (cf. Ingram, 1979b, 1980b, 1982c and, for the FSI Scale, Lowe, 1981).

General versus situational or special purpose proficiency. Third, the fact that language necessarily occurs in situations that, to a greater or lesser degree, determine the forms that occur raises particular problems both for the concept of proficiency and for testing. For example, since language occurs only in situations and varies from situation to situation according to who is using it, to whom, about what, where, the speaker's mood, the speaker's role, and so on, any language use and, therefore, any test could be considered situation-specific. On the other hand, most tests tacitly or, as with the ASLPR, overtly claim to measure general proficiency[1], i.e. not just the ability to operate only in special areas of the language but a more widely applicable ability, the ability to operate in what James & Rouve (1973) term the "non-specialist register". Whether this is linguistically or even logically defensible warrants consideration.

The situation-dependency of language would suggest that one cannot speak of "general proficiency" but only proficiency in a language in this situation or that, in this register or that. There is no doubt that register flexibility, the ability to operate in different situations, in different registers, is part of language proficiency. Cohen & Olshtain (1981) seek to measure one aspect of it when they test "sociocultural competence" or a learner's ability to select the forms of apology appropriate in different situations. Yet to restrict the concept of proficiency to just ability to operate in specific registers in specified situations at least seems to be counter-intuitive. If we say that X speaks Chinese or Y speaks French, we do not mean that X can only give a lecture on engineering in Chinese or Y can talk only about neurosurgery. Rather, we mean that X and Y can speak the language in the everyday situations that people commonly encounter and general proficiency refers to the ability to use language in such situations. In addition, even though registers differ, they are not entirely discrete or they would not be recognized as part of the language. General proficiency would seem to entail the ability to use the commonly occurring features (e.g. of phonology, syntax, lexis, discourse, functions, etc.) and would seem to underlie the learner's register flexibility or his ability to cope with new situations and to select within his language repertoire to modulate his language according to situational need. This concept of general proficiency seems necessarily to be assumed in any test claiming to measure general proficiency (e.g. CELT, TOEFL, FSI Scale, ASLPR, etc.).

Proficiency: Unitary or macroskill-specific

The term "general proficiency" in the preceding discussion was used to refer to a learner's ability in the "non-specialist register" in each macroskill. That use must be distinguished from how "general proficiency" is used (e.g. Vollmer, 1981) in the debate, especially vigorous through the 1970's, over the unitary or macroskill-specific nature of language proficiency. Drawing on studies showing a high level of correlation between different tests (e.g. Oller, 1973a, 1973b, 1974, 1976, 1980; Oller & Streiff, 1975; Oller & Khan, 1980; Yorozuya & Oller, 1980), Oller in particular has argued that underlying ability in any macroskill is a general or unitary proficiency, an "attained level of mastery within a given language" (Vollmer, 1981: 152), that is manifested through each macroskill and is independent of test modality or method (cf. Vollmer, 1981: 152). To Oller, this common underlying proficiency is based on the learner's "expectancy grammar" (Oller, 1973a, 1973b, 1976; Oller & Streiff, 1975) which, in Vollmer's view, is related to the Chomskyan notion of "linguistic competence" (Vollmer, 1981; cf. Spolsky, 1973: 173).

Nevertheless, it is significant that most of the evidence for the unitary theory seems to come from studies involving foreign students in the United States, i.e. well-educated subjects who have learned to learn through reading and writing and who would more readily generalize what was learned through one macroskill to the others. This could not always be expected in other learner populations. The experience of teachers working in adult immigrant education programmes (e.g. the Adult Migrant Education Program of the Australian Department of Immigration and Ethnic Affairs) seems to be that the educational backgrounds and first language of the learners as well as such individual factors as aural acuity or kinaesthetic sense differentially influence the rate of development of proficiency in each macroskill. In studies involving the ASLPR with 16 moderately to well educated ESL learners in Australia, high correlations were found between all four macroskills, but, considered individually, only 4 of the learners were rated at the same level on all four macroskills and any individual's macroskills differed by up to 3 steps on the 12-step ASLPR. Anecdotal evidence from the Australian Adult Migrant Education Program and more extensive data collected during its formal evaluation (Ingram, 1980e) indicate that, where learners cover a wider educational span, the differences may be still greater. Furthermore, Bachman & Palmer cite a number of recent studies which demonstrate that "the unitary trait hypothesis is not supported empirically" (Bachman & Palmer, 1982: 451) and others (e.g. Vollmer, 1981; Davies, 1981 and Alderson, 1981a) have suggested that evidence for or against the unitary hypothesis may be the product of the statistical methods used. More satisfactory than the unitary model of proficiency is one including "a general trait and one or more specific traits" (Bachman & Palmer, 1982: 451; cf. 1981: 84–85). Oller himself is now reported as supporting such a view (Bachman & Palmer, 1982: 45) and, in fact, in a 1979 publication, he stated:

"It is possible that there is a basic grammatical system underlying all uses of language, but that there remain certain components which are not part of the central core that account for what are frequently referred to as differences in productive and receptive repertoires." (Oller, 1979: 6)

The implications are important for language testing: any test (e.g. CELT, TOEFL or most others) that provides only a single measure of language proficiency is giving at best a partial indication of actual practical proficiency since, in practice, language proficiency is realized through a macroskill whose own distinctive features together with the learner's learning style affect its development and the practical proficiency demonstrable (cf. also Vollmer, 1981: 159; Spolsky, 1973: 173; Spolsky in Jones & Spolsky, 1975: 69). For these reasons, the ASLPR states a learner's proficiency in a profile rating each macroskill separately, e.g. S: 1, L: 1+, R: 1, W:1-.

Proficiency as communicative competence

The notion of communicative competence evolved in order to account for the fact we have already observed that linguistic competence does not adequately account for how a language is used or the forms that occur in actual use. (Cf. Hymes, 1972). Other writers (e.g. Kelly, 1981: 169) distinguish "communicative competence" from "communicative performance" but this distinction seems often not to be maintained especially in general discussion so that "communicative competence" is used in many different ways (cf.Madsen & Jones, 1981: 21) and, in particular, is often equated with the ability to communicate (e.g. Frink, 1982: 281). Both the looser and more rigorous definitions have implications for testing.

Undoubtedly it is a learner's ability to communicate that is of ultimate interest to most "consumers" of language tests and their results (cf. Kelly, 1981: 169; Ingram, 1980a: 124). However, the ability to communicate entails much more than both linguistic competence and communicative competence and includes personality factors such as introversion and extroversion, intelligence, experience, education, and the willingness of an interlocutor to accommodate a learner's non-native forms, and even social norms (cf. Edmondson, 1980: 276-77).

In fact, it is unlikely that a valid and reliable test of "communicative competence" in the looser sense of the ability to communicate is ever likely to be devised and, in that many things beyond language itself are entailed, it is probably not appropriate for the language tester to seek to measure it (cf. Alderson, 1981b: 62). Rather, his concern is with the learner's ability to mobilize language in carrying out communication tasks, i.e. with language proficiency. The essential problem entailed in this distinction between language proficiency and the ability to communicate is highlighted by Sollenberger (1978:8):

"The person's so-called language proficiency, while it may have been quite accurate in technical skill terms, did not mean effectiveness in *communication*. In some cases, it may have enabled the person to misrepresent or foul up more effectively... I'm sure we all know people who talk nonsense fluently.

"On the other hand I know people who butcher the language, whose accents are atrocious and whose vocabularies are limited. For these reasons we give them a low proficiency rating. Yet, for some reason, some of them are effective communicators."

In the more rigorous sense of communicative competence, considerable problems also remain for testing, not least because of the sheer complexity of the factors involved and the need to distinguish the complex knowledge of how language is used from its application in use. These have at least three effects for testing. First, as in the direct testing of proficiency, it is probable that only subjectively could one bring and balance together all the factors that contribute to communicative competence and allow for compensatory development in them. No such widely accepted instrument of this sort has yet been published.

Second, the complexity of "communicative competence" and the features that comprise it have led to attempts to measure it by focussing on one or two of its constituent features. Cohen & Olshtain (1981) seek to measure "sociocultural competence" by focussing on just one speech act (apologizing) and comparing the learners' responses, in eight different situations with native speaker responses and rating them against a rating scale. Citing Farhady's work, they also suggest (1981: 126) that a multiple-choice test could be designed requiring learners to choose the most culturally and stylistically appropriate response in a given situation. In fact, such approaches, like more traditional tests of linguistic competence, are analytic in the sense of testing just one limited aspect of communicative competence in a significantly de-contextualized situation; they entail similar problems to other discrete-point tests, viz., they focus more on knowledge than behaviour and one is left unaware of whether the learners can mobilize their sociocultural knowledge together with their other language knowledge in real-life situations.

Third, part of the difficulty with communicative competence as a criterion in testing is to know exactly what it entails and current research seems more aimed at assessing the nature and construct validity of "communicative competence" and the definitions that exist rather than devising tests (e.g. Canale & Swain, 1979, 1980, 1981; Palmer & Groot, 1981; Bachman & Palmer, 1982).

Varieties and registers

Part of language proficiency entails the ability to operate in different registers, Hymes's notion of communicative competence as well as other subsequent definitions (Hymes, 1972; Canale & Swain, 1979, 1980, 1981; Palmer & Groot, 1981; Bachman & Palmer, 1982; Kelly, 1981) entail knowing how the language varies according to different situational require-ments, and Cohen & Olshtain (1981) and Farhady (1980) suggest some ways to measure this "sociocultural competence". As the learner's lan-guage base increases, so he can choose more deliberately from his language repertoire to modify his language to match different situations and to extrapolate meaning for new items and he becomes more aware of the denotative and connotative meanings associated with choice of words, syntax and other linguistic features. In other words, he develops register flexibility and register sensitivity. Consequently, proficiency tests at this level (3 or 4 on the ASLPR and FSI Scale) should include attention to the learner's ability to cope with different registers.

The existence of "varieties" also poses important issues for language testing. First, there is the question of which variety to test and, second, the question of learners' ability to cope with varieties other than that they are themselves learning, e.g. British or Australian English or, within a variety, the dialect such as Broad, General, or Educated Australian. The first question is important, first, because tests sample language and so the variety from which the sample is taken must be selected and, second, because instruments such as rating scales essentially take the span from zero to native-like proficiency and cut it up into intervals. Clearly, the native-like variety seen as the uppermost level affects the nature of all levels within the span; yet, if scales are to be widely applicable, the broad stages and parameters of change through which learners pass must be seen as identical. In addition there is no reason why a second language learner whose sociocultural milieu leads him to identify with and learn some sub-cultural dialect other than the standard educated one should not also be seen as developing towards and perhaps ultimately attaining native-like proficiency. The ASPLR contrasts with the FSI scale in that the former tries to accommodate any dialect whereas the latter sees the ultimate goal as "educated native-like".

The second question raised is an outcome of learners' growing proficiency and their consequent ability to utilize more and more of the language to facilitate comprehension. As their resources develop and as, phonologically, they experience a greater variety of matrices into which to slot speakers' sounds, so they become able to cope with varieties that differ from their own. In the ASLPR, for example, the ability to cope with different varieties or dialects becomes a significant parameter of change at levels 4 to 5 (native-like).

Analytic versus synthetic

In this discussion, two contrasting approaches to describing and assessing proficiency have emerged: analytic and synthetic. Analytic approaches, sometimes called "atomistic" (Morrow, 1981: 10), seek to describe the components that make up the concept "proficiency" and measure it by measuring one, some or all of the identified components. Cooper's "language testing framework" (1972) represents such a model of proficiency and its measurement. The "framework" is represented by a cube in which phonology, syntax, semantic and "total" form one side, the four macroskills another, and varieties a third. The total cube represents proficiency while each cell represents a particular aspect of knowledge as it occurs in a particular macroskill in a particular variety (Cooper, 1972: 336–38). Each "cell" might appear in a test and proficiency is measured as the sum of all the cells. The problem, however, is that language is not just the sum of its parts but the parts have to be mobilized and integrated together to carry out particular tasks in particular situations.

Synthetic approaches seek to bring the components of language together as they describe or assess proficiency. They include integrative tests (briefly described in pp.215–18 and 239–56) and, especially, more global tests such as rating scales that consider proficiency in terms of the total language behaviour demonstrated by the learner or its outcome. In fact, of course, it is a question of what one wants from the test that determines which approach and what test should be used. Although analytic methods give a more detailed picture of the components that make up language proficiency (cf. Knibbler, 1980), "global" or synthetic methods balance in a natural manner the components of proficiency within the total language behaviour and seem, therefore, likely to give a more accurate and more readily interpretable picture of practical language proficiency. In the conclusion to their paper, Oller & Khan (1980: 28–29) state:

> "Using phonology without syntax is a little like using a carburettor without an engine, or a set of wheels without an automobile. It makes little practical sense ... it does mean that tests focussed exclusively on isolated phonological elements, or isolated vocabulary or isolated syntactic rules, or notions/ functions, or whatever make less practical sense than discourse-oriented testing procedures that integrate many of the fore-going hypothesized components."

Solutions to the problem of proficiency measurement

In the preceding section, we have considered different perspectives on the concept of proficiency and the implications of those perspectives for testing. In this section, we shall look at some of the ways in which the problem of how to measure proficiency has been resolved, i.e. we shall consider different types of tests, how they are developed, scored and interpreted, and their strengths and weaknesses (including aspects of their validity and reliability).

Proficiency tests may be categorized in a number of different ways (cf. Madsen & Jones, 1981) but, here, we shall first consider those tests that relate their selection of content, methods and scoring procedures to the way in which language develops and those that do not (hence, developmentally versus non-developmentally based tests). We shall also consider tests according to the "directness" with which they measure proficiency (hence, indirect, semi-direct and direct tests), and, in passing, the basis of their validation (hence edumetric and psychometric tests). These categories are not entirely mutually exclusive (cf. Cziko, 1981) but they provide a convenient way to organize the discussion.

Non-developmental versus developmental basis for test development

In writing a test, one has to select content to be included, means by which to have the learner demonstrate facility in that content, and means by which to score the responses. Proficiency may be viewed more or less statically as facility in handling certain language content (a synchronic, linguistic perspective) or it may be viewed developmentally (a diachronic, psycholinguistic perspective) so that, for example, the learner is seen as progressing from zero to native-like proficiency and the tester's task is to identify at what point along that developmental path he is located.

Non-Developmental. Non-developmental tests may select the content of the test in a seemingly *ad hoc* manner, on a linguistic basis, or on a behavioural basis. They are principally justified either by the way in which they sample the language or behaviour to be assessed (content and construct validities), by their correlation with existing, accepted tests (concurrent or immediate pragmatic validity), or by the extent to which they predict some other desired behaviour (predictive or ultimate pragmatic validity). The contribution to them from psycholinguistics is minimal except where learning theory is involved in their justification (as in contrastive tests) or in the analysis of language behaviour (as may occur, but not necessarily, in behaviourally-based tests).

Ad hoc tests use items and techniques chosen simply on the intuition and "experience" of the examiner and whether or not they "work". Often the examiner's intuition is assisted by "tradition" though the forms endorsed by "tradition" are ultimately often equally ad hoc and intuitive. Whether ad hoc tests work or not is often an equally intuitive judgement but their justification may also be based on statistical analysis showing the difficulty level and discriminating power of each item. The test developed may be further validated by being correlated with other tests or some other related performance (e.g. success in an education programme or in the workplace). Many Public Examinations, at least in the present writer's experience in Australia and Britain (see, for example, Ingram, 1978: Chapter 3), and probably most regular teacher-prepared tests traditionally fall into this ad hoc category but so do other apparently more expertly designed and statistically controlled tests. In describing the test development procedures they adopted with CELT, Harris & Palmer (1970:1) say:

> "The CELT materials were prepared by experienced test writers in the field of English as a second language, and all items were pretested on large samples of students of diverse language backgrounds enrolled in intensive, college-level programmes of ESL. Both the results of item analysis and the comments of classroom teachers were utilized in the assembly of the final forms of the three tests..."

Palmer (1972) provides another example of essentially non-developmental, ad hoc tests with his oral communication tests in which learners obtain information from or communicate it to an examiner. From the high correlations (0.517 to 0.795) claimed between these and other established tests, Palmer concludes that his tests measure "oral communication proficiency" (1972: 40,43). However, except to the extent that efficiency in communication tasks would seem likely to increase with increased proficiency, there is no obvious developmental justification for the selection of the test content, activity, or scoring method. Rather these seem to be selected intuitively and justified by concurrent validity.

Non-developmental proficiency tests prepared on a linguistic basis set out from a concept of the nature of language or the relevant domain of the language, which they seek to sample by either reflecting it or assessing the learner's ability to operate within it (cf. Alderson, 1981b: 56). Such tests may be based, for example, on frequency counts of lexical and structural items or on some other observation of the language behaviour that occurs. Cloze tests can be considered to fall into this category since, provided they are suitably long (e.g. 40 to 50 deletions in a 400 to 500 word passage) and provided that the deletions occur at regular intervals (e.g. every 9th word), then the total language is said to be randomly sampled and, for this reason, cloze gives a good measure of general proficiency. However, we shall see later that studies have shown that the random sampling of the language is not assured, results differ not only according to the deletion-frequency but also according to where one starts counting in order to insert the deletions. In other words, the reality is that cloze tests make claim to a linguistic basis of construction but they are, in fact, partially "ad hoc" since their validity and reliability seem to depend at least partially on the test writer's intuition in selecting the passage, in adopting a deletion rate, and in choosing the starting point for the nth word count.

Contrastive linguistics and error analysis have also provided a linguistic basis for test construction. Contrastive linguistics was especially important in audiolingual days when more emphasis fell on the view that learning a second language entailed habitualizing new language patterns and eradicating the inappropriate (or "interfering") patterns transferred from the first language. Proficiency assessment was then seen partially at least as a process of assessing to what extent learners had overcome inappropriate habits and learned new ones. Such tests often tended to concentrate on the "difficulties" (i.e. sources of interference) and there-fore sampled the second language in an unbalanced way giving an unbalanced perspective of the learner's proficiency. Error analysis contri-butes similarly to contrastive analysis in test construction by identifying errors or sources of difficulty in learning the language and, though it avoids the psycholinguistically contentious issue of the role of language transfer in second language learning (cf. Felix, 1977), it has similar problems.

Behaviourally-based tests are those that identify a particular lan-guage behaviour or aspect of language behaviour as a criterion against which proficiency is to be assessed. For example, the behaviour may be defined in terms of the language skills needed for success in an academic course or some other activity and testing may aim to establish whether or not these skills can be carried out. Some "graded objectives" tests fall into this category in that, irrespective of possible developmental schedules or the learners' on-going development of linguistic creativity, the test aims to assess the learner's ability to carry out specified language tasks in specified situations.

Developmental. Because language development (whether first or second language) is systematic and not random, it would seem likely that developmental psycholinguistics could provide firm criteria against which to develop tests of language proficiency. Developmental approaches to measuring language proficiency seek to relate statements of language proficiency to the learner's overall schedule of development in the language. Not least, in direct testing, they seek to relate test development to the evolving language or language behaviour of second language learners (cf. Oller, 1979: 415; Brindley & Singh, 1982). The ASLPR and the FSI Scale, for example, try to identify how a second language learner's language behaviour develops from zero to native-like proficiency in each macroskill. Learners are rated, i.e. their proficiency is measured, as the point at which their proficiency level lies is identified along that developmental path. Clearly developmental psycholinguistics would seem, potentially, to have much to contribute to this approach to language proficiency assessment. Nevertheless, certain limitations to its applicability need to be considered.

First, although there seems to be general agreement among psycholinguists that learners acquire language in much the same way following at least broadly the same developmental schedule, there seems to be less agreement on the detail of that schedule. In other words, it is probably premature for language testers to rely very heavily on the findings of developmental psycholinguistics to the extent, for instance, of using a specified sequence of syntactic structures as the basis for estimating the learners' proficiency levels. To do this would assume that there is a universal syntactic schedule which correlates for all learners with a universal schedule of development in their observable language behaviour or practical proficiency to the extent that ability to produce structure X indicates a proficiency level Y. Nevertheless, this has been attempted with some success in the AMES Scale by Brindley and others (e.g. Brindley & Singh, 1982) who use dictation focussing on specific syntactic items to assess syntactic mastery and these results are then correlated with the AMES Scale, a "subjective" speaking proficiency rating scale. However, Brindley and his colleagues are careful to limit their claims of applicability to streaming in the particular adult migrant education programme with which they are involved in New South Wales, Australia.

Second, Krashen has adduced the distinction between learning and acquisition, formal and informal learning, in order to account for different schedules emerging in different studies (e.g. Krashen, 1976, 1980, 1981a). If the Krashen distinction is accepted, then it is clearly necessary for proficiency tests to distinguish knowledge ("formal learning") from its mobilization in use (where acquired language becomes more prominent). Hence, to measure practical proficiency, tests should be planned to encourage natural language use and, except perhaps in writing, to minimize monitoring.

Third, developmental psycholinguistics has, up to the present, tended to focus on discrete components of the language such as syntax, functions, lexis or discourse but the ultimate users of language proficiency tests are not so much interested in the development of such components as in what the learner can use the language for, i.e. in what his overall task-oriented language behaviour might be. Hence, developmental psycholinguistics will be of most interest to proficiency assessment when it provides a comprehensive picture of the development of language behaviour as a whole and its practical effectiveness.

Fourth, the applicability of findings about discrete components in language development is limited by the fact already observed that language is not just the sum of its parts and, in any case, those parts may progress at different rates. Thus, even if fully agreed, universal, developmental schedules in the various components of a language (e.g. syntax) were available, proficiency assessments that were related too closely to them may not give a true picture of practical proficiency and, for this reason, a proficiency rating scale such as the ASLPR allows, as we saw earlier, for some flexibility by focussing on the global behaviour at any proficiency level while recognizing that, at any level, different components may have developed to different but compensating degrees.

The implications thus far drawn from developmental psycholinguistics have related especially to direct tests, but psycholinguistics may also have particular input to make to other types of testing. Indirect tests might be structured to establish what point in the developmental schedule the learner has reached. For this to be possible, however, a common developmental schedule has to be identified and sufficiently clearly delineated to make test construction feasible. In addition, the learning-acquisition distinction and the concept of monitoring mean that the interpretation of results on indirect tests must take into account the time allowed (cf. also Carroll, 1972: 318). Madsen (1979) concluded, for example, that, for a listening test done in writing to be substituted for a direct listening test, time (hence monitoring) had to be constrained. For this reason, cloze or dictation utilized to identify ability to use specific structures in a manner similar to the proposal by Brindley & Singh (1982) may more nearly reflect acquisition and practical facility in the structures. Furthermore, developmental psycholinguistics may, even at this stage, assist in decisions of ordering. If the test's aim is to assess where the learner falls in the developmental schedule, then the items should be progressively more "difficult" in the sense of reflecting more and more advanced proficiency levels. In fact, Dieterich *et al.* (1979:545) have shown that some tests do not make use of the linguistic and psycholinguistic insights available with the result that they seem to be invalidated. They say:

"... Rather than testing for structures in terms of their increasing difficulty or lateness of acquisition, they test more difficult items first, and sometimes never get to the easier ones...

"... If a test is going to test for discrete structures, they should at least occur in some recognized sequence of complexity or acquisition."

Clearly, one can conclude that, at the present stage of development, psycholinguistics has contributions to make to the writing and evaluation of proficiency tests but, on the other hand, there remain contentious issues and many unanswered questions and much of the established wisdom of the last decade (e.g. the universality of the developmental schedule) is now being modified or, at least, being interpreted less simplistically. Despite this, broad trends are emerging and psycholinguistics is at least contributing to the dissolution of some unjustifiable practices. In that the developmental approach takes fuller account of the psychological and psycholinguistic processes that underlie language learning and use and provides a criterion (the natural developmental schedule) which, however tentative it might be, can inform tests and provide a means to evaluate the test content, it is contributing significantly to more rational principles and practices in proficiency assessment. Whatever the insights provided, however, they are futile until realized in actual tests and the next two sections will consider briefly some major test types.

Discrete point and other indirect tests

Discrete point tests, which were briefly described in pp.215–18, essentially analyse the language into its smallest units (e.g. a grammatical rule or a phonemic distinction) and assess the learner's knowledge of or ability in these. Probably the archetype of the approach is found in the work of Lado (e.g. Lado, 1961). Though commonly one associates discrete point tests with tests of syntax, lexis, or phonology, they can be used with any aspect of language including aspects of skills, discourse and functions (cf. Cziko, 1981: 33). As a test of proficiency, the approach is "analytic" or "atomistic" (cf. Morrow, 1981: 10) in that it assumes that proficiency is the result of the additive proficiency of all the component items, skills and sub-skills in the language (see Carroll, 1972: 317–18 for one analysis) and that it may be measured by testing each of the discrete items that make up the language and adding together the results. Thus, it is a basic principle of discrete point testing that one thing is tested at a time (cf. Farhady, 1979: 348). In this way, interference from other factors (e.g. another macroskill) is eliminated as much as possible, the tester can be sure exactly what the learner does or does not know, and, for that reason, the approach retains value for diagnostic purposes. However, language by its very nature generally seems to involve at least two macroskills operating together and complete isolation of the macroskills or of discrete points is hard to achieve and often unrealistic in terms of language functioning when it is.

Because discrete point tests essentially see proficiency as proficiency in the multitude of discrete items that compose the language, for proficiency to be validly and reliably measured, it is important that the items included adequately sample all aspects of the language or the target domain being tested (or, more commonly, its grammar, vocabulary and phonology). Because each item is usually short and rapidly answered, a large number of items may be used in order to sample more comprehensively. However, as already observed, knowledge is not the same as ability to use language and the correlations reported between discrete point tests and tests of practical proficiency are not always very high.

The justification for the approach lies, linguistically, especially, in structuralist linguistics with its view of language as a set of more or less discrete patterns; the psychological and psycholinguistic justification lies in behaviourist psychology so that ideally the pattern being tested is contained in a stimulus-response exchange. Linguistically this minimal contextualization is important because it brings the approach a little closer to real language use and partly accounts for the correlations that are found between such minimally contextualized discrete point tests and integrative tests (cf. Krashen, 1981a; Farhady, 1979). Nevertheless, a fundamental criticism of discrete point tests remains that they involve an unnatural, largely decontextualized and mechanical use of language use where meaning is much subordinated to form (cf. Oller, 1973a; 1973b; 1972a: 352–53); they differ fundamentally from more "direct" tests because their focus is still on the piece of knowledge or skill being tested and their aim is to discriminate amongst the learners rather than specifically to assess their proficiency.

The principal strengths of the discrete point approach lie in its objectivity, its ease of marking, the quantifiable nature of its scores (cf Morrow, 1981: 11) and, consequently, its suitability for psychometric purposes. It is objective in that each item in the test generally has a single right answer and tests may be constructed for entirely mechanical, even machine, marking, especially where a multiple-choice format is used (see, for example, Harris & Palmer, 1970). However, in multiple choice formats, guessing affects scores and, though statistical procedures are available to correct for it, they necessarily apply indiscriminately whether or not a learner actually has guessed. In addition, the objectivity claimed for discrete point testing (frequently called "objective testing") is not as great as, at first, it seems. Objectivity exists more at the scoring stage where there is generally only one right answer to be selected from a group of alternatives. In the test development stages, ideally sampling would be objectively random across the language or related to the developmental schedule but, in practice, it is more often the result of the examiner's judgement (cf. Farhady, 1982: 56) and sometimes the test may even focus principally on the points of difficulty, especially those where the grammars of the first and target languages contrast. Further judgement enters as the examiner chooses the technique to be used to test an item and the presentation and ordering of the test. The fact that discrete point tests are not entirely objective is an important issue to be remembered as we consider later the subjectivity of direct tests.

Discrete point tests characteristically fall into the category of indirect tests. They are indirect in a double sense. First, they measure one thing (e.g. knowledge or speed of communicating cf. Palmer, 1972) in order to say something about something else (e.g. proficiency or communication ability). They are indirect also in their interpretation, i.e though they are used as measures of proficiency, their actual role is to discriminate amongst and rank-order learners and the learner's proficiency level is measured in relation to the performance of other learners, i.e. all one can directly say about the results of such tests is that on Test X Learner A was better or worse than Learner B or than n% of the other learners who took the test. Harris & Palmer, for example, provide percentile ranks of CELT scores for five criterion groups so that any learner's results might be compared with those of the group whose personal characteristics most closely resemble his own (Harris & Palmer, 1970: 10–13). Thus, indirect tests are best seen as psychometric, norm-referenced tests whose aim is to distribute learners along a curve from worst to best; the items are chosen in order "to maximize total score variance" (Cziko, 1981: 35) and are statistically assessed by seeing to what extent the better (more proficient) learners tend to get them right and the weaker ones to get them wrong.

In practice, it is difficult to find ways of confidently translating discrete point or indirect test results into measures of proficiency. One way is to try to relate test scores to ability to use the language in practical lanaguage tasks, e.g. in the workplace. Madsen & Jones (1981) illustrate the problem when they cite two students who had lived in Germany, topped their group in the oral examination, but performed at or below B level in the "standardized multiple choice exam" (cf. also Brindley & Singh, 1982). In fact, few if any adequate studies exist relating indirect tests to real life or workplace use of the language (i.e. predictive or ultimate pragmatic validity), e.g. though TOEFL and CELT are used to assess foreign students' suitability for tertiary studies, the minimum score requirements are somewhat arbitrary and no adequate study of their predictive validities for university study is available. This deficiency is not altogether surprising since such studies are difficult to structure because many non-language factors intrude in determining academic success. Another way to translate discrete point or indirect test scores into proficiency measures is to correlate their results with results on direct tests such as the ASLPR or FSI Scale. Though this has been done often enough (e.g. Ingram, 1982a; Mullen, 1978a; Carroll, 1967), the results show that indirect test scores cannot be readily or automatically related to practical proficiency: correlations vary widely depending on whether second or foreign language learning has occurred, personality factors, nature of the course, and anything else that contributes to learners' ability to mobilize their knowledge in carrying out language tasks (Ingram, 1982a; Mullen, 1978a). Hence we come back to the point that the only defensible way to interpret scores on discrete point or indirect tests is to compare one learner's results with others' and such tests are best seen as norm-referenced tests. Consequently, most reputable tests show in their manual how differing groups of learners have performed (cf. Harris & Palmer, 1970).

It was observed earlier that discrete point tests yield readily quantifiable data very suitable for psychometric analysis and this may be considered an advantage for them over, for example, rating scales. However, if discrete point tests are considered to be tests of language proficiency, a difficult statistical problem intervenes. Suppose, for example, one learner scores 40 on a 100 item test and another learner 80. While the scores are in a ratio of 1:2, it is false or, at best, meaningless, to consider the second learner to be twice as proficient as the first. Yet many studies involving proficiency measurements seem to use statistical procedures based on standard deviation, not just to examine distribution of scores but with the clear implication that proficiencies are being statistically compared. The literature of applied linguistics abounds with studies using, for example, Pearson's Product-Moment correlation to compare scores yet this necessarily assumes that the proficiency scale subsumed in the scores is as parametric as the numerical scores. In brief, whereas at first sight it seems as though discrete point tests are more suitable for statistical procedures than direct tests, this is not so and care is needed with the use and interpretation of such procedures.

The validity of discrete point tests would seem to depend largely on the adequacy with which they sample the target language or domain. At least, this will determine the face validity or the test's acceptance by its users. However, in practice, the extent to which such tests reflect the language or domain is less important than that the final results as statements of proficiency should seem to accord with the learner's subsequent performance. Yet we have already noted that rigorous studies of the predictive validity of such tests are rare and difficult to construct and, therefore, it is easier to assess a test through its concurrent or immediate pragmatic validity by comparing the test's results with those of other proficiency tests. So Harris & Palmer (1970:9) provide data on the correlations between CELT and the Michigan Achievement Series A, the Michigan Test of English Language Proficiency, TOEFL, and student class location. The evaluation of the ASLPR included a study of the correlations between ASLPR ratings, CELT scores, and MLA French and Italian tests (Ingram, 1982a, 1980d, forthcoming). However, this last example highlights a serious problem: if tests are assessing exactly the same thing, the new test is redundant; if they are assessing different things, there is little interest for validation purposes in whatever correlations emerge. Nevertheless, concurrent validity has generally provided one of the firmest bases on which to estimate the validity of discrete point tests but the better they sample the target language or domain and reflect the construct (e.g. "proficiency") being measured, the more likely they would seem to have other forms of validity and the more readily could their results be interpreted.

Undoubtedly the principal weakness of discrete point tests is that the language use they entail lacks authenticity (cf. Oller, 1973a: 189; Whiteson, 1981: 348). In seeking this, researchers have gone beyond discrete point testing to consider approaches that more closely reflect real language use. For this reason, there has been increasing interest in integrative tests, both semi-direct and direct.

Integrative tests

One of the problems we have seen with discrete point testing is that it isolates the language components whereas, when language is being used in real life, it is in a linguistic and situational context where all the components are together, supporting each other in meaning and dependent on each other structurally; part of the skill of using language involves being able to put all the components together and to comprehend them when they are received together. Integrative approaches to testing seek to integrate the language components into a total language event of some sort and to assess the learner's performance on that event. Carroll (1972: 318–19) considers that they more broadly sample the language, are less likely to be course specific, and are more readily interpreted. Some types (e.g. cloze, especially selective cloze, and some communicative tests) allow one to focus on specific items and they can thus become contextualized tests of knowledge of specific items or aspects of skills (e.g. phoneme discrimination) and communicative performance (e.g. particular functions). They differ from discrete point tests largely in their contextualization in a total language event (e.g. listening to and comprehending a speech or conversation, reading a story). Translation and guided composition may be used as integrative tests though often the context of each item may be largely disregarded by both learner and marker and, when this occurs, such tests more closely resemble discrete point tests. With some types (including cloze, dictation, white noise and, again depending on how it is set and marked, possibly translation), interest is on the learners' overall performances which are ranked according to total scores gained and proficiency ratings, or other grades are then assigned. With other types (e.g. oral interviews and other direct tests), the learner's overall performance is rated in some way, desirably using specified performance criteria. In particular, one can distinguish two types of integrative tests: semi-direct and direct tests.

Semi-direct Tests. The commonest semi-direct tests are cloze and dictation but others include the "white noise" and interlinear tests. Undoubtedly it is John Oller, Jr., who, more than anyone else in the last two decades, has stimulated interest in semi-direct tests, especially cloze and dictation, which he classifies as "pragmatic tests" (e.g. Oller, 1979: Chapter 3). "Semi-direct" tests are so called because they partly resemble direct tests and partly indirect. They are indirect in the sense that they are used to rank-order learners and proficiency grades are assigned by the tester who allocates cut-off points for them in the range of possible scores; however, they are nearer to direct tests in that they demand more natural, contextualized language behaviour than do discrete point tests. Semi-direct tests are norm-referenced and psychometric in the way that grades are assigned and interpreted but, as Cziko observes (1981: 34), they are more like edumetric tests in their claim to randomly or representatively sample the language or that particular domain of it (e.g. a "special purpose" register) whose proficiency is being measured.

Semi-direct tests are based especially on the redundancy principle. Because language is redundant, any specific item, such as a discrete point test may focus on, is not necessarily essential to a speaker's successful functioning in the language since the deficiency may be compensated for by guessing based on the rest of the syntactic, discourse or semantic context (cf. Brière, 1972: 325). As learners develop proficiency in the language, so they master more of the systems that make up language (i.e. the higher the level of redundancy in the language) and the more they are able to predict the language that will occur or to compensate for items in the written or aural signal that are deleted or obscured. Oller (e.g. 1973a, 1973b, 1974) speaks of the learner's "expectancy grammar" and so a learner's proficiency is measurable by the extent to which his expectancy grammar is developed and he is able to compensate for gaps or intrusions in the language signal. Thus, with cloze, words are deleted at regular intervals (hence, it is claimed, randomly across the language) and proficiency is indicated by the extent to which the learner is able to fill in the gaps. If general proficiency is at issue, then clearly the passage must be long enough to enable the language to be comprehensively sampled: 40 or 50 deletions are generally considered the minimum desirable for general proficiency measurement and a deletion rate of approximately every ninth word (though deletion rates may differ between five and twelve or more words). "White noise" tests work similarly but, instead of gaps, the aural signal is obscured by random "white noise" (e.g. Gaies et al., 1977; Leventhal, 1980). When dictation is given appropriately (see Oller, 1979: 267–82), each dictated "chunk" is long enough to exceed the learner's capacity to retain the words in immediate memory and so the forgotten items have to be filled in from the context and the learner's knowledge of the language, a process Oller calls "analysis-by-synthesis" (Oller, 1972a: 352). Interlinear tests insert additional inappropriate words in the text and these have to be deleted again by the learner drawing on his "expectancy grammar" (cf. Bowen, 1978; Davies, 1975).

Semi-direct tests may be random or selective. In a selective cloze, for example, instead of deleting every nth word, the tester deletes those he wishes to test (e.g. the articles, auxiliaries or other syntactic forms that are critical in the learner's stage of development) or he might make an intuitive choice according to the particular passage or according to the particular grammatical or other forms taught in a course. With dictation, we have already seen how Brindley & Singh (1982) select the content to reflect key items in the learner's developmental schedule, the assumption being that the learner will be able to comprehend, recall, and write down only syntactic forms that are already in his interlanguage. The selective approach is especially useful for diagnostic purposes and, if Brindley & Singh (1982) are correct, to relate the learner to a point on the developmental schedule. However, selection implies judgement by the tester, increases the subjectivity of the test, and destroys the "random sampling" principle that is held to be one of the strengths of semi-direct tests.

Whether or not selection decreases or increases the validity and reliability of semi-direct tests is somewhat disputed in the literature. Traditionally, for example, the random and objective nature of cloze deletion has been seen as one of its strengths. Yet there is evidence that the actual items deleted affect the validity and reliability of cloze tests (e.g. Bachman, 1981; Porter, 1978; Alderson, 1979). Alderson (1979) and Bachman (1981) suggest that selective deletion may actually enhance the performance of cloze tests, Bachman arguing (1981: 66) that random deletion is more subject to change and, therefore, yields inconsistent results. In addition, in contrast to Oller's (1975) evidence that random cloze is sensitive to discourse constraints extending well beyond the immediate words surrounding the deletion, Bachman argues that more clause-bound words are likely to be deleted, thus focussing measurement on lower-order skills whereas rational deletion may focus on cohesive features and so yield measures of higher order, discourse skills. Selective cloze is especially suitable for diagnostic purposes, allowing one to randomly or selectively sample the language and then, by analysis of the errors and correct responses, to identify the language behaviour going on and the likely causes of the responses (e.g. knowledge of syntax or lexis, discourse mastery, or functional skills) (e.g. Ingram, 1980d).

Semi-direct tests have become popular not least because they are often considered easy to construct, objective in their marking, and having close correlation with other tests of general proficiency. All three claims have been disputed. At first sight, their construction seems to be simply a matter of choosing a passage at random and, for example, giving it as a dictation or deleting every nth word to turn it into a cloze. Yet, in practice, passages are rarely chosen at random, i.e. a tester's judgement enters into the selection, and it has been shown that different difficulty levels lead to different levels of correlation with general proficiency and discrete-point tests. In studies comparing cloze and dictation, on the one hand, and the ASLPR and CELT, on the other, the cloze correlations were found to differ by up to 0.3 from easy to difficult passages and dictation up to 0.2 (see Ingram, 1982a: 43 and 45). Alderson (1979) shows that different passages and, especially, different deletion rates can have significant effects on the correlations achieved between cloze and indirect tests (specifically, ELBA (Elizabeth Ingram, 1964). Hughes (1981) found significant differences arising in the correlations between cloze and general proficiency as measured by ELBA (Elizabeth Ingram, 1964) according to the mode, style and subject-matter of the text, a cloze based on a transcribed conversation providing the highest correlation with oral proficiency results. Porter (1978) showed that, with cloze, the nature of the passage and where one started deleting and hence the nth- word count significantly altered the results and he concludes that one cannot assume that any two cloze will yield the same results. Alderson (1979:226) concludes that, as with other testing techniques,

> "(Cloze) is in fact merely a technique for producing tests...and is not an automatically valid procedure. Each test produced...needs to be validated in its own right and modified accordingly."

One of the problems in "validating" and "modifying" integrative tests is, as Cziko notes (1981: 37–40), that, though their results seem psychometrically processable, "they are not constructed according to the psychometric principles of test construction" (1981: 38) and they do not contain individually assessable and variable items as do discrete-point tests. This is clearly the case with dictation and, with cloze, once gaps are moved from the regular nth word, the principle of randomness is lost (though the earlier comments on some possible advantages of selective cloze should be noted). Nevertheless, the construction problems of semi-direct tests are no more severe than in other tests and, in fact, Cziko suggests (1981: 39) that one of the reasons for their good psychometric qualities is that, unlike multiple choice tests, they do not contain "gifts" (even cloze where guessing is likely to be successful only if it is "based on an adequate knowledge of the language" (1981: 39) nor do they contain "gyps" or "cleverly disguised distractors" except to the extent that the exact-word method of scoring cloze seems to reject acceptable insertions, which accounts for the closer correlation with other proficiency measurements of cloze marked by the "acceptable word" method (Cziko, 1981: 39). With interlinear tests, in contrast to cloze, deliberate decisions have to be made concerning what distractors are to be inserted and, moreover, Bowen (1978) argues that random insertions are of little value unless they damage "the grammatical and lexical integrity" of the passage. In other words, Cziko's "gifts" and "gyps" are more prone to occur in interlinear tests, and they are more difficult to construct than are other integrative tests.

In all, as with all tests, the better the tester understands the nature of semi-direct tests, their procedures, variables and effects, the more likely he is to construct them validly and reliably. Their apparent ease of construction comes from the automatic nature of some stages of construction (e.g. deletion rates) but this does not mean that all aspects of their development, presentation, scoring or, least of all, interpretation are automatic or free from sources of error.

Second, objectivity in marking also varies from type to type in semi-direct tests. Interlinear tests would seem most automatic since one can assume that the inserted distractors are, in fact, wrong unless errors have occurred in the test construction phase. Oller's rules for scoring dictation (1979: 276) seem to make for reliable, objective marking yet, in practice, it is often a matter of judgement whether, for example, an error is merely spelling (to be disregarded) or phonological or grammatical. With cloze, we have already noted that the exact word method (the most objective) seems to have a lower level of concurrent validity than the acceptable word method where, however, the tester's judgement enters and where, even with native speaking testers, acceptability is sometimes a matter for dispute (cf. also Porter, 1978; Shohamy, 1982b; Goodrich, 1978; Oller, 1972a; Brown, 1980). In other words, semi-direct tests are not always objective in their marking stage and, with cloze, it is arguable that validity is higher when the marking's less objective.

Third, the concurrent validity of semi-direct tests, i.e. the extent to which their results correlate with results on other tests of general proficiency has received much attention (especially correlations with discrete point tests). There are many studies that suggest moderate to high correlation levels between cloze and other tests especially in Oller's many studies and the others he cites (e.g. Oller, 1979: Chapter 3, Oller, 1972a, 1973a, 1973b, also Alderson, 1979: 220; Shohamy, 1981; Streiff, 1978, Irvine et al., 1974). Irvine et al. (1974) go so far as to say that the total score on TOEFL provides little interpretable information not provided by cloze or dictation (Irvine et al., 1974: 251). As in this study, comparisons of dictation with the ESL Placement Examination at UCLA showed dictation correlating more highly with each section of the test and the total than the sections did with each other (Oller, 1972a; cf. Oller, 1979) and Oller concludes (1972a: 348) that the dictation is the best measure of the total skills measured by the ESL Placement Test. (Nevertheless, it is significant that Oller was testing well educated foreign students and one might not expect similarly high correlations with less literate learners (see also Spolsky et al., 1972: 222)). In other studies, Cziko (e.g. 1981) showed that cloze consistently discriminated amongst four different groups of children, three of non-native French learners at different proficiency levels and one of native French speakers (1981: 38): in other words, cloze seems to be sensitive to differences in general proficiency. Shohamy (1982b), testing foreign university students, found correlations better than 0.8 between cloze and oral interview ratings.

On the other hand, Vollmer (1981: 167) cites studies in which the correlation between cloze and speaking proficiency as measured by an FSI-type interview was no more than 0.6 and he concludes that cloze cannot replace "more complicated and more costly" tests without significant loss of information. Furthermore, since cloze is not usually so time-constrained as natural language use, it would seem likely that some monitoring may intrude, that short-term memory constraints are less likely to intrude (cloze being written) (see Oller, 1973a: 114–16), and that, consequently, cloze would weigh slightly more to learning than to acquisition, and so contribute to the moderate level of correlation between cloze and direct tests. This possibly accounts for the generally slightly higher correlation the present writer found between cloze and CELT than cloze and the ASLPR and for the slightly lower correlations between cloze and the ASLPR speaking and listening ratings compared with cloze and reading and writing where more monitoring is possible (Ingram, 1982a: 43,45). In addition, it was noted earlier (see pp.219–20) that the extent of the correlation between direct and other tests differs between second and foreign language learners.

Correlations between dictations and tests of general proficiency are comparable to those between cloze and general proficiency. The present writer found correlations generally above 0.8 between dictation and the ASLPR and generally above 0.9 between dictation and CELT for second language learners but around 0.5 for dictation-ASLPR correlations for foreign language learners (cf. Ingram, 1982a: 43 and 45). Stansfield (1981), after citing correlations around 0.8 between dictation and discrete-point tests in French and English, reports significantly lower correlations for Spanish at about 0.6. He hypothesizes that the phonetically more regular Spanish orthography enables the learner to transcribe without being so dependent on his expectancy grammar (Stansfield, 1981: especially, 348–50). Oller (1972a) reports a correlation of 0.88 between a dictation and the ESL Placement Examination at UCLA and he concludes that dictation is a valuable test of language proficiency (1972a: 353).

Interpretation of results on semi-direct tests remains a problem. However well cloze, for example, might have discriminated between the different groups in Cziko's study of French immersion programmes (reported in Cziko, 1981: 38), one is nevertheless left not knowing exactly what the results mean in terms of what the learners can do in the language and, in general, it is difficult to relate their results to actual performance criteria (though, in Cziko's view, it would be relatively simple to transform them into "tests with excellent edumetric (hence, criterion-referenced) characteristics" (1981: 40)). Their performance implications may be made clearer by relating their results to those on other direct or indirect tests but we have seen that the correlations are moderate rather than high and differ in different circumstances. In addition, it should be noted that even quite high correlations do not mean that any individual has performed similarly on both tests and one must conclude that their most suitable use (other than for diagnostic purposes) would seem to be where one wants a quick group measure of proficiency rather than a precise individual measurement.

Semi-direct tests have, in fact, been used for many different purposes. The earliest use of cloze was especially to measure readability (cf. Oller, 1973a: 106); as noted earlier, cloze (and, similarly, interlinear tests) have some diagnostic value (cf. Henning, 1978) especially for vocabulary usage (cf. Oller, 1973a: 106) and discourse (e.g. in Ingram, 1982b) and, if deletions (or insertions) are selective, the focus can be quite specifically on the aspects of the language one wishes to assess. Undoubtedly selective cloze could be structured to elicit the learner's stage in the developmental schedule in much the same way as Brindley & Singh (1982) propose for dictation. There is also some indication that cloze can be used to measure proficiency across languages, e.g. in bilinguals (e.g. Okoh, 1981). White noise tests seem less appropriate for specific diagnostic purposes and more suitable for general proficiency measurement especially, though probably not only, in listening. However, less attention has been given to white noise (and interlinear) tests than to cloze or dictation and, especially in view of the resemblance of the white noise test situation to real-life listening situations where extraneous noise continually intrudes, its potential as a measure of proficiency has probably not been fully exploited. Dictation can serve diagnostic purposes in phonological, syntactic, lexical and graphological aspects of the language as well as in terms of locating the learner in the developmental schedule (cf. Brindley & Singh, 1982). In addition, as has been seen, it can provide an approximate, desirably group, indication of proficiency level though Oller values it much more highly than this for proficiency measurement (e.g. Oller, 1972a: 353; Oller & Streiff, 1975; Oller, 1979: Chapters 3 and 10). In all, semi-direct tests provide a useful approach to testing not least because of their relative (if deceptive) ease of construction and administration and their correlation with other tests of general proficiency. However, like indirect tests, their interpretation remains a problem because of the difficulties of relating their scores to performance criteria and so increasing interest has been shown in approaches to proficiency testing that focus directly on actual language behaviour.

Direct Tests. Earlier in this chapter (see pp.215–18 and 221–24) direct tests were described as belonging to the "behavioural" approach to testing. In contrast to semi-direct and indirect tests, which, we have seen, rank order learners or measure one thing (especially knowledge) and try to make a statement about something else (e.g. language proficiency), *direct* tests focus directly on the learner's proficiency as demonstrated in the way he carries out actual communication tasks and proficiency statements are made in terms of the learner's actual language behaviour. Learners are rated by being matched against the level on a scale consisting of a series of proficiency descriptions that best describes their language behaviour. In other words, direct tests are criterion-referenced or edumetric tests.

Compared with indirect and semi-direct tests, relatively few direct instruments in the form of rating scales have been developed. Most frequently when direct testing is referred to in the literature, it is in connection with speaking proficiency or with speaking and listening combined in some sort of conversational measure (see, for example, Madsen & Jones, 1981). However, as argued earlier (pp.221–24), there is no obvious reason why the principle of direct testing should apply any more or less to one macroskill than another: the ASLPR, in fact, contains four parallel scales for speaking, listening, reading and writing and the "Provisional Proficiency Guidelines" of the American Council on the Teaching of Foreign Languages (1982) includes a scale for each macroskill and for culture. The difference between the macroskills lies not in the applicability of the concept of direct testing but in the way that the language behaviour in each is observed. With speaking and writing, the behaviour to be observed is more overt except that, in practice, it is more economical of time to have learners do the writing tasks "en masse" and to use their scripts to deduce the writing behaviour that produced them. Listening and reading behaviours are more internal, less directly observable, and answers to questions and other learner responses have to be used to enable the rater to deduce the behaviour going on.

Undoubtedly the scale that has been in use longest and most widely is the "Absolute Language Proficiency Ratings" of the United States Foreign Service Institute School of Language Studies, commonly known as the FSI Scale though recently re-named the ILR Scale (Inter-Agency Language Ratings). The FSI Scale was developed for use especially with well-educated civil, military and foreign service personnel learning a language other than English for professional purposes. Inevitably, it reflects this in its format with the clear assumption underlying the scale that the language is being used for professional purposes. In addition, it contains only two sub-scales (viz., Speaking, which includes listening, and Reading) and six defined levels from zero to native-like. Because of these constraints and the fact that it lacks discrimination at the lowest proficiency levels (where most learners in classes fall), it has limited applicability in contexts such as school foreign language learning or in large-scale immigrant language programmes (such as the Australian Migrant Education Program) where the learners also range widely in social, vocational and educational backgrounds. For these reasons, Elaine Wylie and the present writer developed the Australian Second Language Proficiency Ratings (ASLPR).

The ASLPR was initially developed and trialled for use in Australia's Adult Migrant Education Program but was further developed and trialled for use with adolescents and adults learning English and other foreign languages. Versions of the ASLPR specifically for French, Italian, Japanese and Spanish as foreign languages now exist though it may equally be applied to any other language.

The ASLPR describes language behaviour at nine proficiency levels along the developmental path from zero to native-like. An additional three intermediate levels are available for use at 2+, 3+ and 4+ though they are not described. Each macroskill is described separately so that the ASLPR actually consists of four separate but conceptually related scales and a learner's proficiency is stated in a profile indicating proficiency in each macroskill separately, e.g. S:1+, L:2, R:1, W:1. However, the numerical scores are only short-hand codes that are accompanied by short descriptive titles (e.g. S:3 is Minimum Vocational Proficiency in speaking) and that represent the behavioural descriptions. In other words, rather than the outcome of direct testing being, as in indirect or semi-direct testing, a number of no obvious behavioural or task-oriented significance, the outcome is a statement of what the learner's behaviour is in terms of the tasks he can carry out and how he carries them out. Clearly, therefore, interpretation of the score is direct so that one knows immediately what sorts of things the learner can do in the language and how his language will appear. It is undoubtedly in the clarity and directness of their scoring and interpretation where the major advantages of direct tests based on rating scales lie.

Use of the ASLPR has expanded very rapidly reflecting a long-felt need for such an instrument in Australia and possibly elsewhere. Its uses include measuring practical language proficiency (its fundamental use), streaming learners into migrant English classes to the extent that proficiency is the basis for streaming, assessing a non-native speaker's responsibility in a court of law, assessment by the Queensland Board of Teacher Education of the English proficiency of non-native English speaking applicants for teacher registration, assessing the proficiency of applicants for enrolment in a tertiary institution, sociolinguistic surveys, and many others.

In developing the ASLPR, Elaine Wylie and the present writer[2] set out to describe language behaviour at nine proficiency levels along the developmental path from zero to native-like. The emerging scale was reassessed and elaborated in face-to-face interviews with over 200 adolescent and adult learners of English as a Second Language, and of French, Italian, Japanese and Spanish as foreign languages. Early versions of the scale were first released for use in the Adult Migrant Education Program in February 1979, thus providing feedback on its adequacy as a result of its practical implementation.

Formal trials were conducted to assess the validity and reliability of the ASLPR when used with adult ESL learners, adolescent ESL learners, and adolescent and adult foreign language learners of French, Italian and Japanese. Most fundamentally, these trials aimed at assessing the extent to which native English speaking Australian teachers, non-native English speaking Chinese teachers, and native English speaking American teachers (these last being speakers of a different variety of English from the ESL learners' target variety) could interpret and apply the ASLPR in the same way as did the developers of the scale, i.e. the trials were especially concerned with inter-rater reliabilities and intra-rater reliability (since, in the latter case, the Australian teachers rated the same videotaped learners on two occasions twelve months apart). In addition, various forms of validity were examined with concurrent validity assessed by looking at the correlations achieved between the ASLPR, CELT, cloze, and dictation. The results are reported in Ingram 1982a and 1982c and are summarized in what follows.

For ESL learners in Australia, the correlations between ASLPR ratings and CELT were high, ranging from r = 0.83 (ASLPR Speaking and CELT Structure) to rho = 0.96 (ASLPR Reading and CELT Total) with significance levels throughout at or beyond the 0.001 level. In fact, these coefficients are higher than in many similar studies of the FSI Scale and other standardized tests reported in the literature (e.g. Mullen, 1978b; Clifford, 1978; Carroll, 1967; Politzer *et al.*, 1982). However, for English as a *Foreign* Language learners in China, the correlation coefficients were very different. For one group they ranged from rho = 0.01 (ASLPR Reading and CELT Vocabulary) to rho = 0.59 (ASLPR Speaking and CELT Structure) and r = 0.64 (ASLPR Writing with CELT Listening and Total) with generally moderate significance levels; for the other group, they ranged from rho = 0.002 (ASLPR Reading and CELT Total), r = −0.06 (ASLPR Speaking and CELT Listening) to rho = 0.62 (ASLPR Writing and CELT Listening) with significance levels up to 0.003 but generally very low. These ambivalent results showing different levels of correlation for different groups of learners are similar to those found in other studies of direct and indirect tests (e.g. Mullen, 1978b; Palmer, 1979) and seem not to arise from any instability inherent in the ASLPR or direct testing itself but from the phenomenon already discussed (pp.219–20) where *second* language learners were seen to be better able to mobilize their knowledge of the language in practical communication tasks than were *foreign* language learners.

Inter- and intra-rater reliability coefficients when each Australian and Chinese teacher's ratings were compared with those assigned by the developers of the scale were found to be quite high. Correlations between the ratings assigned by the developers of the scale and the Australian teachers ranged from r/rho = 0.89 to 0.99 with the means around 0.95. For the Chinese teachers, they ranged from 0.83 to 0.98 with the means around 0.94. For the Australian teachers, intra-rater reliability ranged from 0.87 to 0.99 with means around 0.96. All correlations were significant at or beyond the 0.001 level (r) or 0.000 (rho). These results suggest that most of the teachers interpreted and applied the scale in essentially the same way as did its developers and, furthermore, that even non-native speakers could use the ASLPR with reasonable accuracy.

The concepts of validity and reliability as applied to direct tests require special consideration since the psychometric notions of "validation" and "standardization" that apply to indirect tests (essentially assessing the validity and reliability of new tests and establishing norms for learner performance on them) carry over only partially and with significant modification to direct tests. Reference was made earlier to the problem of concurrent validity that arises because more traditional established tests such as CELT and TOEFL are essentially testing different things from direct tests. Furthermore, a basic aim of indirect, psychometrically designed tests is, we noted earlier, to discriminate amongst learners irrespective, almost, of the nature of the language behaviour entailed by the test item whereas direct instruments such as the ASLPR or FSI Scale seek content and construct validity in the sense of describing in their sequence of behavioural descriptions the way in which language behaviour changes from zero proficiency to native-like. As described in the process used in developing the ASLPR, the validity of such instruments is best established by assessing the extent to which the scale seems to describe cogently, consistently and comprehensively the behaviour of a series of learners distributed along the developmental path from zero to native-like. The reliabiliity of direct instruments relates to the extent to which raters are able to consistently interpret the scale (i.e. perceive through it the same picture of proficiency in its various developmental stages as the developers of the instrument had) and the extent to which the raters are able to consistently apply it to rate learners. Hence, the trials for the ASLPR involved comparing the ratings assigned by different teachers with those assigned by the developers of the scale and the ratings assigned by the same raters on different occasions.

In practice, however, other aspects of validity and reliability enter into direct instruments through the interview process. The interview is designed to elicit the language behaviour observed by the rater as he assigns proficiency ratings. Ideally, the rater would watch the learner using language in real-life, everyday situations (cf. Madsen & Jones, 1981: 21) but, first, this would be very time-consuming and, second, it could just happen that the rater never saw the learner in a situation that fully extended his language ability. The interview is, then, in practice an essential part of the use of direct instruments since it elicits the language behaviour observed in establishing the learner's proficiency and it can be so structured as to fully extend the learner. Even though, in order to rate writing proficiency, the tester has the learner carry out certain writing tasks, the same concept underlies the purpose, nature and use of this activity as in the other macroskills and, hence, with the ASLPR, the term "interview" is used to apply to all four macroskills (e.g. Ingram 1979b, 1980b, 1982c).

With the ASLPR and FSI Scale as, in general, with other direct behaviour-based instruments, the interview is so structured as to elicit language activity that is as natural as possible. For the learner, the interview should be as relaxed and informal as is appropriate to elicit his best language performance but, for the interviewer, it should be deliberately developed to explore all those features delineated in the scale that distinguish one level from another and to ensure that the full extent of the learner's language proficiency is observed and rated. Broadly, the interview has three parts: first, an *exploratory* stage in which the interviewer settles the learner down and gets an approximate idea of where the learner's proficiency falls and what topics it would be useful to pursue; second, an *analytical* stage in which the interviewer explores all the features of the learner's language behaviour, especially those described or exemplified in the scale, gives him an opportunity to use whatever language he can, and leads him on to his "linguistic breaking-point"; and, third, a *concluding* stage in which the interview is rounded off and, for a moment or two, the interviewer reverts back to activities well within the learner's ability so as not to send him away with a sense of failure after having been taken to his "linguistic breaking-point".

The interview, then, is a deliberately structured series of activities designed to elicit the learner's maximum language behaviour in whatever situations and tasks are most appropriate to him so that that behaviour can be matched against the scale descriptions. Although, as was observed earlier, this approach is subjective, it is not impressionistic and interviewers and raters are required to refer to the scale continually so as to carefully compare the learner's language behaviour with the scale descriptions. In fact, one can say that, whereas in discrete-point and other psychometric approaches to testing, validity and reliability ride on the adequacy of the standardization procedures applied to the test items worked by the learners, with direct testing, the crucial issues are the extent to which the scale provides an accurate picture of how a second language develops and the extent to which interviewers and raters can elicit maximum language behaviour and then interpret and apply the scale (hence, the quality of their training is critical).

The interviewer would seem to be a pivot around which direct testing would ride or fall. There is evidence in the literature that properly conducted interviews can yield valid and reliable results (e.g. Adams, 1981; Mullen, 1978a, 1978b). Exactly what contribution to validity and reliability the nature of the interview makes is still unclear. One would anticipate that an interviewer could, for example, fail to extend a learner or establish an intimidatory atmosphere, both of which would lead to under-rating. The ASLPR trials (Ingram, 1982a) did not set out to consider interview quality and its effect on validity and reliability but the use of two interviewers who, it turned out, contrasted in quality in the final videos provided some opportunity to consider the issue. In fact, in contrast to the decisive difference in quality of the interviews, little difference in validity and reliability emerged. It is possible that this approach to testing is more robust and less dependent on interview quality than one might expect and, provided that a reasonable opportunity to perform is given, the language behaviour that emerges enables rating to be carried out validly and reliably.

The validity and reliability figures that have been discussed here suggest that the frequent criticism that direct testing is unduly subjective is ill-founded (cf. Madsen & Jones, 1981: 16). First, the subjectivity that does exist seems necessary to accommodate the complexity of language and its development, its redundancy, the fact that different rates of development may occur at different times in any of the diverse strands that go to make up language proficiency, and the fact that greater or lesser development in one strand may be compensated for elsewhere. Second, we have already seen that subjectivity enters at some point in all testing, even indirect and semi-direct testing. The form it takes is different in different approaches but its adverse effects in one approach are not necessarily more or less than in others: essentially, it is the training, understanding and skill of the tester that is at issue in any approach rather than an excess or otherwise of subjectivity. Third, while the use of a rating scale such as the ASLPR or FSI Scale involves a judgement on the part of the rater, that process of judging is a natural activity that native speakers at least can do with a fair degree of accuracy. There is evidence, for instance, that native speakers intuitively judge the level of a non-native speaker's language and adjust their own language accordingly (e.g. Long, 1981; Corder, 1967; Hatch, 1979) and Mattran (1977) showed that native speakers can intuitively judge learners' proficiency with a high level of agreement (cf. also Spolsky et al., 1972: 229). In the ASLPR and other direct tests, it is that intuitive ability that is harnessed, constrained by being related to specific criteria (viz., developmentally related descriptions of language behaviour), and made more readily interpretable by those criteria.

Furthermore, it seems that such learner factors as fear and test anxiety may intrude less with direct tests than with others. In the exploratory stage of direct tests, the interviewer is advised to "settle the learner down" and establish an atmosphere and relationship that will facilitate maximum language behaviour. Anecdotal evidence from work with the ASLPR shows that skilful interviewing may create such an atmosphere that the learner is unaware that a test is proceeding, to the point, in fact, where, at the end of the interview, they have asked when they would "come back for the test" (Ed Burke, personal communication, 1982). Shohamy (1981) showed that students significantly favoured the oral interview over cloze. Again, Madsen (1982) found the oral interview the least anxiety-producing of six tests (including cloze, reading, writing, listening and grammar).

A stronger criticism of direct tests is that they fail to discriminate sufficiently amongst learners. To some extent this is correct. Madsen & Jones (1981: 16) report criticism that direct oral tests fail to discriminate at the higher levels while many teachers complain that they fail to discriminate sufficiently for class placement and course grades purposes at the lower levels. One reason for this deficiency is that scales consist of verbal descriptions of language behaviour and, as Elaine Wylie and the present writer have found in work on the ASLPR[3], while one can perceive, for example, a level 3+, it is a very much more difficult problem to find the words to describe it adequately in such a way that it would be clearly differentiated from 3 and 4. The problem would be still more acute if one sought to write in another level between 3 and 3+ or 0+ and 1−.

Nevertheless, some of the criticism of lack of differentiation seems to be ill-founded. First, it is common observation that many teachers, whatever scale they have (even a 0 to 100 scale), try to use additional points such as 87½ or 56¼. Furthermore, it would seem probable that, as the number of levels increased, so reliability would decrease and anything more than the existing 12 levels available on the ASLPR would seem likely to decrease reliability. Second, this criticism sometimes seems to come from a confusion over course attainment and proficiency. The former relates, especially, to the learner's formal learning of the language content presented, which undoubtedly is of interest to the teacher and may be assessed by indirect means, whereas the latter relates more to what the learner has acquired and has available for ready use in practical language tasks. Proficiency in this sense changes slowly and, in fact, if the figures published by the FSI School of Language Studies (1973) are even a rough guide, there would seem little value in assessing the proficiency of learners in classes more frequently than once in about 300 hours. Third, it is difficult to see what practical value there would be in finer discrimination than that provided by the 12-level ASLPR, especially if reliability were to suffer as a result.

Yet another criticism of direct tests is that the descriptions are, of necessity, only partial descriptions of complex language behaviour. To the extent that they fail to provide a complete picture of the behaviour observable at a level, first, they will be harder to use and their validity is reduced because the behaviour observed and that entailed in the descriptions will not match and, second, reliability will suffer. However, the longer the descriptions become, the more unmanageable they are because there are too many parts in the descriptions to be retained in memory, matched with observed behaviour, and balanced against each other. To help overcome the problem of partial descriptions and an overload of abstract characteristics, the ASLPR provides examples of what the learner can do at any level to exemplify the descriptions and this may account for the slightly higher reliability claimed for the ASLPR (see Ingram, 1982a).

Several difficult issues arise from the fact that, in rating a learner, the rater essentially has in mind a concept of language proficiency and how it develops from zero to native-like; the learner is slotted in to the point where his proficiency falls in the developmental span. First, while one can conceive of a single span from zero to native-like for adolescents and adults, it is harder to do so with younger children whose upper levels would seem to change regularly, i.e. the span from zero to native-like will be changing regularly and it is possible that for young children one could need a dozen or more scales. Nevertheless, there is no obvious reason why one should not be able to provide behavioural descriptions of young children's language and the principle of direct testing would seem applicable even though, as yet, little or no work has been done on the development of appropriate rating scales. Second, one might question whether non-native speakers whose proficiency is less than native-like are able to rate reliably learners whose proficiencies may be higher than their own. In fact, work on the ASLPR shows that they can. Undoubtedly there would be a proficiency level below which a rater would be unable to rate reliably but it was clearly demonstrated when the ASLPR trials were conducted in China that teachers whose proficiencies were around 3 in all macroskills and who had been trained to use the ASLPR could do so with reliability coefficients only slightly below those of similarly (or even more thoroughly) trained native English speaking Australian raters (see the figures cited earlier and Ingram, 1982a).

Undoubtedly the most serious criticism of direct tests is that they are time-consuming and, where large numbers of learners are involved, simply impracticable for that reason. In fact, to rate speaking, listening and reading, the ASLPR and the FSI Scale require interviews from 10 to 25 minutes in length. The actual length varies with the experience of the interviewer and the actual proficiency of the learner (i.e. if a learner falls characteristically at a level, his proficiency in speaking, listening and reading may be assessed quite rapidly, perhaps in as little as five to ten minutes but one who is less characteristic of a particular level or who seems to fall between two levels will take longer to assess). In reality, of course, the traditional "oral examination" generally took ten or more minutes and when time for doing and marking a written script is added to this, the time taken on a direct test seems less exorbitant. Nevertheless, the approach is time-consuming, and ultimately, it is a matter of what is wanted from the test: if one wants a meaningful statement about a learner's practical language skills then the extra time of a direct test may be worthwhile. In addition, it may be that a combination of instruments can be most economical in terms of valid assessment and time. So, for example, the quite high levels of correlation seen earlier between the ASLPR, CELT, and semi-direct tests for second language learners suggests that in, for example, selection for entry to an educational institution, one could use an indirect or semi-direct test to "weed out" the least and most proficient learners and then interview the middle level group to establish their precise proficiencies. Essentially, again, it is a question of why one is testing: if the aim is to establish practical proficiency levels, then a direct test (especially in a foreign language learning situation) would seem to be essential.

Tests in use: Purposes and suitability

This section will consider, each very briefly, some of the many purposes for which one uses tests and the sorts of tests that might be suitable for those purposes. It is a fundamental principle in all aspects of language teaching that one's purpose must influence one's choice of methods and techniques. In language testing, one must always ask:

1. What is the purpose of the testing?
2. What is the appropriate instrument to achieve this purpose?

In considering what is appropriate, one must consider such factors as the reason for testing, the criteria to be tested (e.g. linguistic or communicative competence, pronunciation), the validity and reliability of the instruments available, the learners' proficiency levels, ages, education and language backgrounds, and the scoring procedure desirable and feasible (cf. Madsen & Jones, 1981: 15–21). To this can be added, the situation in which the testing is taking place (e.g. whether it is a second or foreign language situation), the variety and register or registers being learned, the macroskill or macroskills in question, the number of learners involved, and the practicality and interpretability of the alternative tests in the particular circumstances. There is, of course, no single test which can serve all purposes in all circumstances and the tester's first obligation is to evaluate the whole situation and select the instrument or instruments that will best meet the needs identified (cf. Madsen & Jones, 1981: 17).

Testing in society

In multilingual societies, assessment of language proficiency are made for many purposes not only in educational institutions but out in the "real world". Some of these include estimating legal responsibility (to the extent that language is an issue) (e.g. Ingram, 1980c); vocational registration; language planning; to measure national language resources, perhaps as a preliminary to national language policy-making; in psychological, psycholinguistic and social research; in identifying language needs (e.g. the large-scale sociolinguistic surveys using the ASLPR and commissioned by the Australian Department of Immigration and Ethnic Affairs as a basis for estimating the English language levels and needs in areas of high immigrant concentration across Australia).

At the individual level, decisions as to non-native speakers' language proficiencies are made every day and the educational, vocational, legal and social opportunities that those people will have available to them, often their whole future lives, rest on the outcome of the formal or informal assessment made. Very often, these decisions are made by wholly un-trained people, sometimes, for example, by an employer interviewing applicants for a position (hence, in a stressful situation where the non-native speaker is unlikely to demonstrate his real proficiency) or, worse, by the young receptionist on the front counter of a vocational registration authority. Vollmer refers to the "distinct social function" that proficiency testing serves and recommends that testing not take place if we cannot be sure of the construct validity of "proficiency" and the validity and reliability of the tests being used (1981: 168). However, the reality is that proficiency assessments occur every day in multilingual societies and the profession has an obligation to try to ensure that they are carried out on as just and informed a basis as the present state of knowledge allows. After all, many nations outlaw discrimination on the basis of race or ethnic origin (e.g. in Australia, by the Racial Discrimination Act of 1975 and the Human Rights Commission Act of 1981) and many nations have signed international agreements equally outlawing discrimination on the basis of race (e.g. the *International Covenant on Civil and Political Rights* and the *International Convention on the Elimination of all Forms of Racial Discrimination*). Discrimination arising from impressionistic, uninformed and inaccurate assessment of another's language skills is almost as damaging and common justice demands its elimination where possible.

Because of the frequency and gravity of such decisions as those referred to in the previous paragraph and because the future lives of the individuals being tested are at stake, the Australian Federation of Modern Language Teachers Associations (1982) recommended in its submission to the Senate Standing Committee on Education and the Arts during its deliberations on a national language policy for Australia that a system of accredited language testers be set up analogous to that which operates for translators and interpreters. Colleges and universities would be encour-aged to run accredited intensive courses in all aspects of language testing and a national accreditation authority formed so that, eventually, in migrant education centres and other language teaching institutions, accre-dited testers could be found to whom recourse could be had by, for example, employers wishing advice on the level and types of language proficiency needed for a position and on the suitability of a non-native speaker's language proficiency for it. In addition, non-native speakers would have available an avenue of appeal in cases where they felt they had been discriminated against by an inaccurate decision about their language proficiency made by an employer, an educational institution (e.g. in denying them enrolment), or any other person or organization. Exactly what test or tests would be used by such accredited testers would depend on the purpose which the test was serving but, where the practical proficiency of an individual was in question, one would anticipate that a direct instrument would be used and, for reasons referred to earlier, such accredited testers would have included in their accreditation requirements thorough familiarity with the major direct instruments such as the FSI Scale and ASLPR.

To measure proficiency

It has emerged through this paper that, if one wants to measure proficiency in the sense of being able to carry out practical communication tasks, a direct instrument is the most appropriate and is less open to inconsistency as a result of learning situation than are indirect or semi-direct tests. The purposes for which measures of general proficiency are required are numerous but include end-of-course assessments, vocational registration, entry to a tertiary institution, legal responsibility, language resources in a nation, and many others.

To give a quick group measure of proficiency

Even though direct instruments may give the most valid and reliable measure of proficiency, we have already noted that they are time-consuming to use. There are times when a teacher may want just a quick, approximate idea of how the class as a whole is doing and, for this purpose, an established standardized pencil-and-paper test such as CELT (for English), one of the MLA tests in other languages, or a well constructed cloze or dictation may be most appropriate. Nevertheless, we have seen also that the usefulness of indirect and semi-direct tests in providing even group measures of practical proficiency differs between second and foreign language learning situations and, probably, between different course types using different methodologies. These differences must, therefore, be taken into account when deciding whether the greater speed of using an indirect or semi-direct test for a group measure warrants the less valid and reliable proficiency measurement provided.

To conduct large-scale proficiency measurement

As noted earlier, there are times when the sheer number of learners whose proficiency is to be assessed in a short time is too great to make a direct instrument practical. If, in such circumstances, the testing is being conducted to select students for some purpose, initial selection may be carried out using a semi-direct or indirect instrument and final selection made using a direct instrument after those most and least likely to meet requirements have been eliminated from the final tests. Clearly, however, the margin of error allowed will depend on the learning situation (e.g. second or foreign language and course type) and the purpose of testing. Such an approach seems more likely to yield satisfactory results for, for example, university selection than the sole use of established indirect tests whose predictive validity has not been firmly established or the appropriateness of the cut-off points used identified.

To measure "special purpose" proficiency

Most established tests have been developed to measure general proficiency and, while such assessment, at least using the ASLPR and FSI Scale, involves, in part, consideration of register flexibility, general proficiency even amongst native speakers does not ensure proficiency in any particular specialist register. Not all native speakers, for instance, are proficient in the language of civil engineering, neuro-surgery, or radiography. If one wants to know if a second language learner is proficient in a specialist register, then one must test in that context but, in fact, relatively few attempts have been made to develop "special purpose" tests (for some examples, see Carroll, 1981; the Associated Examining Board's Test in English for Academic Purposes (TEAP), Weir, 1982; the tests of the Australian Government's Committee on Overseas Professional Qualifications (COPQ); Low, 1982; Harvey *et al.*, 1979; Smyth *et al.*, 1980; Ewer, 1979; Tan Soon Hock, 1980, and the *Specific Test Packages* in "Business", "Science and Technology", and "Everyday International Use" published by Pergamon Press, Oxford). Unfortunately, not all the attempts to develop "special purpose" tests have been successful: the COPQ tests, for example, take no obvious cognizance of the developments in language testing through the 1970's and 1980's, least of all in direct testing even though the small numbers in any vocational area and the emphasis on practical skills would seem to make direct testing worth considering. There is, in fact, great need especially in multilingual societies for good "special purpose" tests though the test development task entailed in providing tests in all the "special purpose" areas now being taught or required in society would be enormous. It may be that a direct instrument such as the ASLPR or FSI Scale could be readily adapted for that purpose but this has not yet been attempted with either instrument. How adaptable a direct instrument would be depends in part on one's concept of "special purpose" proficiency and how it can be developed. If, for example, proficiency in a specialist register is considered to develop over the same parameters as does general proficiency, then an established direct instrument could be readily adapted: it would probably require similar "interview" strategies, the general proficiency descriptions would be similar but modified to fit the specialist register, and, in the ASLPR, the "Example" column would have to provide examples of tasks from the specialist register. However, some "special purpose" courses, especially those taught to learners with little or no general proficiency, seem to be based on the view that "special purpose" proficiency develops in quite a different way and emphasis seems to fall not on systematic development but on rote memorization. The effectiveness beyond an elementary level of such an approach is doubtful but, if it does work, then undoubtedly a different type of test instrument would be needed. Carroll (1981) provides a useful, detailed discussion of the sort of issues needing consideration if the necessary array of communication-based tests in special purpose areas is to be developed. In all, probably the only safe conclusion at this stage is that much research remains to be done though the most promising possibility would seem to involve direct testing approaches and, possibly, the adaptation of an existing proficiency scale such as the ASLPR or FSI Scale.

To measure achievement in "graded objectives" courses

The theoretical problems for testing in "graded objectives" courses are not unlike those in "special purpose" courses. A "graded objectives" course closely defines the situations, functions and language elements in which learners are to develop their skills at successive stages and it is against the criterion of those specified components that testing is carried out. To the extent that these "graded objectives" contribute to the development of general proficiency (as they do in the Lothian "graded levels of achievement" approach (Clark, 1980, 1982a)), direct instruments are appropriate to measure that overall general proficiency though more specific tests may be used at intermediate points. In fact, with the Lothian "graded levels of achievement" approach, proficiency is developed in specified situations with specified functions, syntax and lexis but these are so selected and organized as to ensure the creativity of the learners' language and the development of general proficiency. In such courses, formative assessment will be based on the specified course content as it leads through the graded achievement levels; summative assessment may also be based on that specified content but measures of general proficiency (desirably using a direct instrument) are also possible and probably desirable. Put differently, the appropriate testing approach is edumetric but with two different but compatible criteria: the first criterion is the specified content of the graded levels which is tested according to the nature of that content (e.g. some communicative tests would be needed as well as tests focussing on specific items of syntax, lexis or functions); the second criterion is general proficiency tested by instruments extraneous to the course such as a direct test.

However, the objectives chosen and the teaching approach adopted in some graded objectives courses sometimes seem more like the less creative of the "special purpose" approaches referred to earlier. In such "graded objectives" courses, attainment can be tested more specifically. In particular, rather than varying the situations and tasks in order to gain a picture of the underlying general proficiency, as one does in using the ASLPR, in such "graded objectives" courses one would test specifically those language elements and functions in those situations and tasks specified in the course. Exactly what test approaches should be used will thus differ from course to course. They may include interview techniques or practical task approaches such as used in direct tests but they might also include specific knowledge-based approaches, indirect tests and tests of rote-memorized formulae. Again, the general principle in testing applies: consider the objectives, content and methods of the course, consider the purpose of the testing, and select an instrument or test items that will achieve that purpose.

To measure attainment at the end of a course (summative assessment)

The observations made in relation to "graded objectives" courses apply equally to exit-point attainment in courses in general, i.e. "summative" testing. To the extent that the course aims at general proficiency, then a direct test is appropriate. If the course aims are different (e.g. to develop knowledge about the language or to develop translation skills) then a different approach (e.g. knowledge-based approaches or translation) may be necessary and different test types should then be selected (e.g. discrete-point items or a translation test). It may also be that, in considering course attainment, one wants to know to what extent the learner has internalized the content of the course and, if so, then tests directly related to that content may be appropriate. For example, if one wants to know whether the specified grammatical content has been mastered, then discrete point tests of the grammar taught may give the most direct information. A functional or language task checklist as used on the Lothian progress cards and Waystage Tests may be used to assess achievement in the skills aspects of the course (see Clark, 1982b). If, however, one sees general proficiency as part of the course goals, as do most Secondary School language programmes and immigrant education programmes, then attainment at least at the main exit points could appropriately be measured using a direct test such as the FSI Scale or the ASLPR. At intermediate points, it is probably not appropriate to use such instruments since general proficiency changes too slowly in the usually unintensive Secondary School programmes for valid and reliable measurements of general proficiency to show much change over a period of a few weeks or even a semester or two. In other words, a combination of approaches is desirable with direct instruments being used at the exit points and more specific tests related to course content being used in between. Again with course attainment as with other testing, the general principle remains: consider the purpose or purposes and select the test or tests accordingly.

To measure how well the learners are mastering what is being taught (formative assessment)

A particular concern of teachers is how well learners are mastering what is being taught to them. This progressive assessment through the course is sometimes called "formative", "attainment" or "achievement" testing (cf. Palmer, 1979: 169; Brière, 1972: 322; Carroll, 1972: 314). Selection of the appropriate test will depend on exactly what is being taught and what the teacher wants to find out about. If one is interested in whether or not the learner is internalizing the grammar being taught, then test items that focus specifically on the grammatical rules will be most appropriate. One could also use interview techniques such as are used in direct testing and simply mark off on a checklist whether or not those grammatical items emerge. However, this is rather haphazard since, even though a skilled interviewer may feel able to so structure a situation that a particular item must be used, in fact the redundancy of language means that there are alternative ways to state most things and so one cannot be sure whether the item failed to emerge because of the learner's ignorance or simply because he did not need to use it. A discrete point approach, a selective cloze where the deletions focus on the desired grammatical rules, or even specially structured dictation containing the items would be more efficient and appropriate. If the content includes functions, then a role play approach or even an item such as "Tell me what you would say in a post office to ask the cost of sending a letter to Sydney" might be used though, to be valid, such test items must, of course, be contextualized in realistic situations with a contextual purpose for the transaction to occur. The Lothian progress cards and Waystage Tests provide a well-structured way to check the functional and activity content of the course (see Clark, 1982b). Again in formative testing as elsewhere, the general principle remains, consider what one wants to find out, consider the purpose of the test and select the test type and instrument accordingly.

The contrast in this section and the last between formative and summative assessment raises a particularly difficult issue for educational systems which use "continuous" or "cumulative" assessment. The notion is that testing spread out over the course is more valid and less anxiety-producing than a one-off, end-of-course test. While such an approach is possibly defensible in a content-based subject, it is not so in a developmental, skill-based subject such as a language. Put differently, one can contrast a long-term goal (e.g. a particular level of proficiency) with the path followed in attaining that goal. We have already noted that an additive concept of language proficiency is inaccurate but, in addition, the redundancy of language means that most communication tasks can be carried out in a variety of ways and, where general proficiency is at issue, one cannot specify the all and only functions, syntax and lexis that a learner will demonstrate at any level. Thus, different courses may follow different paths yet aim at developing the same level of general proficiency. In addition, it is necessary, as discussed earlier, to distinguish language "learning" from language "acquisition", to distinguish what is formally taught, learned or memorized from what is able to be used in practical language tasks reflecting general proficiency. Such considerations make it essential to distinguish exit-point measures of general proficiency from continuous or cumulative assessment of the learner's mastery of the teacher's formal presentations. Formative assessment may well focus on item-by-item mastery of what the teacher presents using tests that focus on the discrete items. Summative assessment where the goal of the course is general proficiency will desirably use direct tests focussing on the learner's language behaviour as he carries out practical language tasks. Whether indirect or semi-direct tests of general proficiency will be usable at the exit-point will depend on the nature of the learners, their language experience, the learning situation, the type of course followed, and its goals.

To stream learners into courses

To the extent that different classes are formed on the basis of learners' general proficiency, it is appropriate to use a proficiency measurement as one basis on which streaming is carried out. However, in principle, other factors ought also to be taken into account since, in streaming, one is aiming to make homogeneous learning groups and factors in addition to proficiency determine how similarly learners will progress; these include course factors (e.g. goals, content, and methods) and learner factors (such as needs, age, aptitude, family situation, social and psychological distance between the learner and the native speaking community, extent of fossilization or stabilization in the learner's language, attitude to the language, attitude to language learning, motivation, preferred learning strategies, relations between the learner and the teacher or the learner and fellow class members, and personal and vocational aims and interests). In other words, while language proficiency is one factor to be considered in streaming, it is only one of many and these other factors may best be measured differently using different test types or even a personal question-naire.

In addition, general proficiency is probably not the most relevant language attainment issue to be considered in streaming. Proficiency relates especially to what Krashen calls "acquired" or informally learned language while streaming is aimed principally at facilitating the teacher's presentation of language to be formally "learned". In other words, if the aim of the streaming is to place learners in the most appropriate pre-planned courses, then streaming using knowledge-based or discrete func-tion-based tests based on the language to be formally taught might give the most accurate streaming; for this purpose, discrete-point tests or role-play types, for example, might be most appropriate. However, some language programmes, Australia's Adult Migrant Education Program, for example, are planned in relation to general proficiency levels and the dominant developmental trends at each level. In such cases, instruments that measure general proficiency on a developmental scale are appropriate but, again, only to the extent that language proficiency considerations contri-bute to decisions on streaming. Other courses, including again the Austra-lian Adult Migrant Education Program, take account in course planning of each learner's own specific needs and so, for course planning purposes, additional information is needed on the detail of the learner's language development, personal characteristics and aspirations and, for these, proficiency measurements using direct tests will need to be supplemented by other instruments. Once again, the general principle remains: for streaming purposes, the basis on which the classes are to be formed and the streaming done must be determined and then one can decide what are the most appropriate test instruments to use.

To diagnose learners' strengths and weaknesses

To choose what instrument to use for diagnostic purposes, clearly one must decide what strengths and weaknesses one wishes to examine. A direct instrument can be used to focus on the learner's practical skills and, by using a checklist to mark off the acceptable and unacceptable forms or deficiencies that occur, one can diagnose the strengths and weaknesses in the components of the learner's language. However, for the latter purpose, we have already seen that interviews are not very satisfactory and test types that isolate specific elements for testing may be preferable. Developmen-tally related tests such as the Bilingual Syntax Measure or the use of dictation proposed by Brindley & Singh (1982) may be especially useful. If one wants a comprehensive diagnosis of a learner's language, a battery of instruments is probably most suitable, e.g. a direct instrument such as the FSI Scale or the ASLPR can be used to examine practical proficiency, discrete-point and other indirect tests might be used to examine specific items of functions, syntax and vocabulary, a cloze test can be used to look at discourse, and a cloze and dictation together can be used, initially, to randomly sample specific items across the learners' language knowledge and, subsequently, to focus on specific items (cf. Brindley & Singh, 1982). This battery-approach was used by the present writer to examine the nature of the English skills of learners in a foreign language institute in China (Ingram, 1980d; see also Henning, 1978).

To evaluate a second language programme

Programme evaluation raises a large number of contentious and controversial issues. Simplistically, one could say that, since the purpose of a second language programme is to increase the learner's language proficiency, all that is necessary to evaluate a programme is to measure the change in proficiency that occurs from the learners' entry to the course until they exit from it. However, many factors intervene to make a simple measure of proficiency change unsatisfactory as a basis for programme evaluation. These include the learners' aptitudes, their attitudes to the language and its learning, their motivation, their social situation, their social and psychological distance, the professional competence and language proficiency of their teacher, and so on. In addition, there are other overt and covert goals besides language proficiency that a language programme may seek to achieve (e.g. social confidence) and these must also be taken into account when a programme is being evaluated. Because of the complexity of the language teaching process (or of education in general for that matter), programme evaluation is better attempted descriptively rather than statistically though the descriptive evaluation should be supported with whatever statistical measurements can be rationally used to inform the description, the interpretative assessments, and the value judgements (e.g. see Ingram, 1980d and e). In particular, a diagnostic examination of the learners' language (preferably pre- and post-course) may, as already discussed, provide information on the learners' language with implications for the nature of the programmes followed (e.g. see Ingram, 1980d and e).

A 1976 Schools Council publication (Tawney, 1976) called this sort of approach "illuminative evaluation", describing its aim as to describe, interpret, and explain taking into account the contexts in which educational innovation must function. After criticizing the traditional empirical, statistical or "agricultural-botany" approach (such as was implied at the beginning of this section), Parlett & Hamilton (1976) sum up the case for "illuminative evaluation" thus:

> "When an innovation ceases to be an abstract concept or plan and becomes part of the teaching and learning in a school or college, it assumes a different form altogether... it is not an instructional system as such, but its translation and enactment by the teachers and students, that is of concern to the evaluator and other interested parties. There is no play that is 'director-proof'. Equally, there is no innovation that is 'teacher-proof' or 'student-proof'.
>
> "If this is acknowledged, it becomes imperative to study an innovation through the medium of its performance and to adopt a research style and methodology that is appropriate. The evaluator concentrates on 'outcomes' derived from a specification of the instructional system. Observation, linked with discussion and background inquiry, enable him to develop an informal account of the innovation in operation."

To validate tests

It is not intended here to discuss formal test standardization and validation but briefly to consider validation as it may be of interest to the teacher interested in making sure that the test or battery of tests he or she has written or has been using is measuring what he or she wants to measure. Concurrent validity is a useful concept in such circumstances because the new test or battery of tests can be validated by correlating their results with the results on a possibly more sophisticated established test. It has become commonplace to use for this purpose tests such as TOEFL, CELT or the MLA tests, or, in order to relate the new test to practical proficiency, the FSI Scale. It is important, however, that the established test chosen should be measuring the same thing as the new test or battery of tests otherwise comparison is, of course, invalid. In addition, for reasons noted earlier, one would need to exercise caution in using TOEFL, CELT or an MLA test for correlation purposes with foreign language learners though it could well be defensible with second language learners. To consider a common example, if a teacher sees the aim of the course being taught as the development of general proficiency and if, as some education systems require, student evaluation has to be carried out by a process of continuous or cumulative assessment using regular short tests, then the teacher may want to check whether the accumulated results give a reasonably accurate picture of the students' general proficiency. The learners or, if necessary, a cross-section of them, could be interviewed and rated on the FSI Scale of ASLPR and the results from the teacher's tests and the ratings compared.

In conclusion

This chapter has sought to provide a broad overview of the field of second language testing focussing almost entirely on the measurement of proficiency. It started by trying to elucidate the nature of that complex notion, how it might be described, and, therefore, how it might be measured. We examined various approaches to measuring proficiency, some of which draw significantly on the present state of knowledge of developmental psycholinguistics, some of which are derived more from a theory of language, and some of which seemed rather arbitrary. We then considered three broad approaches to testing (discrete point and other indirect tests, semi-direct tests, and direct tests) and, finally, we looked at some of the uses to which proficiency assessment is put. If there has seemed to be undue emphasis on direct tests, it is partly because, in recent years, they have been a particular interest of the present writer but, more importantly, because they seem to provide the theoretically more satisfying (if administratively more difficult) response needed in testing to what is now known about the complex nature of language and its development.

There are many important issues which this chapter has not been able to consider or has considered only in passing. There has beeen little discussion of that vast field of testing beyond the measurement of proficiency. Not least, there has been only passing reference to validity, reliability, their measurement, and their control. We have mainly observed broad test types and little mention has been made of specific tests. Readers are invited to use the bibliography to follow up points of interest more fully, to seek out tests suitable for their purposes, and to evaluate the ideas current in the field of second language testing.

If, in presenting a broad overview of second language testing, this chapter has raised, at times, contentious issues, then the field can only benefit from any minor or major research studies that might be stimulated. There can be no doubt, in fact, that there is much research still needed. In direct testing, for example, rating scales may be improved as more information on stages of development comes from developmental psycho-linguistics, there is need to develop new instruments especially for "special purpose" testing, direct instruments are needed for use with young children, and the whole area of interviewing needs much further research.

One of the potentially most useful areas for research is in self-rating and self-assessment. Their importance derives from the value being attached to direct instruments, the growth in demand for self-directed language learning programmes and various forms of "distance learning", and the emphasis currently being placed on the "response to felt need" principle in syllabus design and programme planning (cf. Ingram, 1978: Chapters 4 and 6; 1979a). As yet, however, there have been few attempts made to develop self-rating instruments or to examine systematically the problems involved. A self-rating questionnaire based on the FSI Scale has been published (FSI, undated) and two initial attempts have been made to develop self-rating techniques for use with the ASLPR (Wylie, 1983; Smith & Baldauf, forthcoming). Early results of the ASLPR studies are promising (though they emphasize the importance of clear guidelines for the learners) and Oskarsson (1981) has also shown that adult learners can assess their speaking and listening skills in much the same way as do their teachers. Other work in this area has been conducted or reported by Anderson (1982); Shranger & Osberg (1981); Huart (1978); Henner-Stanchina & Holec (1977); Ferguson (1978); Oskarsson (1978); Holec (1981) (especially for the Council of Europe), McCafferty (for the British Council), at CRAPEL in the University of Nancy in France, and in various Australian migrant education centres with the encouragement of the Australian Department of Immigration and Ethnic Affairs.

Like Farhady (1982: 57), we can conclude that language testing is "at a critical stage of evolution". Rapid changes in our understanding of the nature of language and of how second language development occurs have led many to reconsider the purpose, nature and methods of language testing. The challenges in the field are immense to develop new instruments, to reassess and renew concepts of validity and reliability, and, not least, to take the innovations that have been taking place, make them comprehensible and practicable for classroom language teachers, and ensure that their potential is made available to the broad cross-section of society that has need of them. Though the challenges are immense, their potential in improving our understanding of the learning, teaching and use of language and in helping to ensure the rights and opportunities of non-native speakers in multilingual societies is no less so.

Notes to Chapter 10

1. The sense in which "General Proficiency" is used throughout this paper must be distinguished from the unitary concept of proficiency that became a controversial issue during the 1970's and which is discussed subsequently (see pp.224–26).

2. Throughout the development of the ASLPR invaluable assistance has been received from many colleagues including staff of the Education Branch of the Australian Department of Immigration and Ethnic Affairs and of the Language Teaching Branch of the Australian Department of Education, members of the Joint Commonwealth-States Committee on the Adult Migrant Education Program, many individual teachers, and interested colleagues such as Ed Burke, Robert Kaplan, John Mills, Gary Birch, Eila Curtis, Bill Eggington, Kerry Fairbairn, Glyn John, Edwige Coulin, Fiorella Carra, Carlos Zincone, Laura Commins, Roger White, Kyooko Timlock and Ann Beaverson. The invaluable initial input from the FSI Scale is also acknowledged.
3. The ASLPR contains, in each macroskill, 9 described levels $(0, 0+, 1-, 1, 1+, 2, 3, 4, 5)$ and 3 undescribed levels $(2+, 3+, 4+)$.

References

Adams, Marianne L. 1978, Measuring Foreign Language Speaking Proficiency: A Study of Agreement amongst Raters. Paper to the conference on The Direct Testing of Speaking Proficiency: Theory and Applications. Georgetown University Washington, March 14th–15th 1978. (Reprinted in John L.D. Clark (ed.), *Direct Testing of Speaking Proficiency: Theory and Application*. 129–49.)
—— 1981, Confirming the Use Validity of the Oral Interview. Washington, D.C.: Foreign Service Institute. Mimeographed.
Alderson, J. Charles 1979, The Cloze Procedure and Proficiency in English as a Foreign Language. *TESOL Quarterly*, Vol. 13, No. 2, 219–27.
—— 1981a, Report of the Discussion on General Language Proficiency. In J.C. Alderson & A. Hughes (eds), *Issues in Language Testing*. 187–94.
—— 1981b, Report of the Discussion on Communicative Language Testing. In J.C. Alderson & A. Hughes (eds), *Issues in Language Testing*. 55–65.
Alderson, J. Charles & Hughes, A. (eds) 1981, *Issues in Language Testing*. ELT Documents No. 111. London: The British Council.
Allen, Harold B. & Campbell, Russell, N. (eds) 1972, *Teaching English as a Second Language: A Book of Readings*. New York: McGraw Hill.
American Council on the Teaching of Foreign Languages 1982, *Provisional Proficiency Guidelines*. New York: A.C.T.F.L.
Anderson, Pamela L. 1982, Self-Esteem in the Foreign Language: A Preliminary Investigation. *Foreign Language Annals*, Vol. 15, No. 2, 109–14.
Australian Federation of Modern Language Teachers Associations 1982, Submission on Aspects of a National Language Policy. Submission to the Standing Committee on Education and the Arts of the Australian Senate, November 1982. Mimeographed.
Bachman, Lyle F. 1981, The Trait Structure of Cloze Test Scores. *TESOL Quarterly*, Vol. 16, No. 1, 61–70.
Bachman, Lyle F. & Palmer, Adrian S. 1981a, The Construct Validation of the FSI Oral Interview. *Language Learning*, Vol. 31, No. 1, 67–86.
——1981b, A Multitrait-multimethod Investigation into the Construct Validity of Six Tests of Speaking and Reading. In A.S. Palmer, P.J.M. Groot & S.A.

Trosper (eds), *The Construct Validation of Tests of Communicative Competence.* 149–65.

—— 1982, The Construct Validation of Some Components of Communicative Proficiency. *TESOL Quarterly*, Vol. 16, No. 4, 449–65.

Bowen, Donald J. 1978, The Identification of Irrelevant Lexical Distraction: An Editing Task. *TESL Reporter*, Vol. 12, No. 1, 1–3, 14–16.

Brière, Eugene J. 1972, Are we really measuring proficiency with our foreign language tests? In H.B. Allen & R.N. Campbell (eds), *Teaching English as a Second Language: A Book of Readings.* 321–30.

Brindley, Geoff & Singh, Ken 1982, The Use of Second Language Learning Research in ESL Proficiency Assessment. *Australian Review of Applied Linguistics*, Vol. 5, No. 1, 84–111.

Brown, James Dean 1980, Relative Merits of Four Methods of Scoring Cloze Tests. *The Modern Language Journal*, Vol. 64, No. 3.

Burner, Sylviane 1980, Comment évaluer la compréhension globale d'un texte oral? *Les Langues Modernes*, Vol. 74, No. 1, 107–13.

Burt, Marina K. & Dulay, Heidi C. (eds) 1975, *New Directions in Second Language Learning, Teaching and Bilingual Education.* Washington, D.C.: TESOL.

Canale, Michael & Swain, Merrill 1979, *Theoretical Bases of Communicative Approaches to Second Language Teaching and Testing.* Toronto: Ontario Institute for Studies in Education.

—— 1980, Theoretical Bases of Communicative Approaches to Second Language Teaching and Testing. *Journal of Applied Linguistics*, Vol. 1, No. 1, 1–47.

—— 1981, A Theoretical Framework for Communicative Competence. In A.S. Palmer, P.J.M. Groot & S.A. Trosper (eds), *The Construct Validation of Tests of Communicative Competence.* 31–36.

Carroll, Brendan J. 1981, Specifications for an English Language Testing Service. In J.C. Alderson & A. Hughes (eds), *Issues in Language Testing.* 66–110.

Carroll, John B. 1966, The Contributions of Psychological Theory and Educational Research to the Teaching of Foreign Languages. In A. Valdman (ed.) *Trends in Language Teaching.* 93–106.

—— 1967, Foreign Language Proficiency Levels attained by Language Majors near Graduation from College. *Foreign Language Annals*, Vol. 1, No. 2, 131–51.

—— 1972, Fundamental Considerations in Testing for English Language Proficiency of Foreign Students. In H.B. Allen & R.N. Campbell (eds), *Teaching English as a Second Language: A Book of Readings.* 313–21.

Clark, John 1980, Lothian Region's Project on Graded Levels of Achievement in Foreign-Language Learning. *Modern Languages in Scotland.* No. 19, 61–74.

Clark, John L. 1982a, Graded Levels of Achievement in Foreign Language Learning (Lothian Region's Project in Modern Languages in Schools). *Language Testing Newsletter*, No. 2, 2–4.

—— 1982b, How are we to assess language learning in schools? Paper to the Fourth National Languages Conference, Perth, 3rd–6th September. Reprinted in A. MacPherson (ed.), *The Language Curriculum in the 1980's: Affective, Effective or Defective?*

Clark, John L.D. (ed.) 1978, *Direct Testing of Speaking Proficiency: Theory and Application.* Princeton: N.J.: Educational Testing Service.

Clark, John L.D. 1972, *Foreign Language Testing: Theory and Practice.* Philadelphia, Pa: Center for Curriculum Development.

Clifford, R.T. 1978, Reliability and Validity of Language Aspects Contributing to

Oral Proficiency of Prospective Teachers of German. Paper to the conference on the Direct Testing of Speaking Proficiency: Theory and Application. Georgetown University, Washington, March 14th–15th. Reprinted in J.L.D. Clark (ed.) *Direct Testing of Speaking Proficiency: Theory and Application.* 191–209.

Cohen, Andrew D. & Olshtain, Elite 1981, Developing a Measure of Sociocultural Competence: The Case of Apology. *Language Learning*, Vol. 31, No. 1, 113–34.

Cooper, Robert L. 1972, Testing. In H.B. Allen & R.N. Campbell (eds), *Teaching English as a Second Language: A Book of Readings.* 330–46.

Corder, S.P. 1967, The Significance of Learners' Errors. *International Review of Applied Linguistics*, Vol. 5, No. 4, 161–70.

Culhane, Terry, Klein-Braley, Christine & Stevenson, Douglas K. 1982, *Practice and Problems in Language Testing.* Occasional Papers No. 26. Colchester: Department of Language and Linguistics, University of Essex.

Cziko, Gary A. 1981, Psychometric and Edumetric Approaches to Language Testing: Implications and Applications. *Applied Linguistics*, Vol. II, No. 1, 27–44.

Davies, Alan 1975, Two Tests of Speeded Reading. In R.L. Jones & B. Spolsky (eds), *Testing Language Proficiency.* 119–27.

—— 1981, Reaction to the Palmer and Bachman and the Vollmer Papers. In J.C. Alderson & A. Hughes (eds), *Issues in Language Testing.* 182–86.

Dieterich, Thomas G., Freeman, Cecilia & Crandall, Jo Ann, 1979, A Linguistics Analysis of Some English Proficiency Tests. *TESOL Quarterly*, Vol. 13, No. 4, 535–50.

Edmondson, Willis J. 1980, Some Problems Concerning the Evaluation of Foreign Language Classroom Discourse. *Applied Linguistics*, Vol. 1, No. 3, 271–87.

Ewer, J.R. 1979, Evaluation in EST Programmes. *EST/ESP Chile Newsletter*, No. 6, 12–15.

Farhady, Hossein, 1979, The Disjunctive Fallacy between Discrete-Point and Integrative Tests. *TESOL Quarterly*, Vol. 13, No. 3, 347–57.

—— 1980, Justification, Development and Validation of Functional Language Testing. Ph.D. dissertation. University of California, Los Angeles.

—— 1982, Measures of Language Proficiency from the Learner's Perspective. *TESOL Quarterly*, Vol. 16, No. 1, 43–59.

Felix, Sacha W. 1977, Interference, Interlanguage and Related Issues. In S.W. Felix (ed.), *Second Language Development: Trends and Issues.* 93–107.

—— (ed.) 1980, *Second Language Development: Trends and Issues.* Tübingen: Gunter Narr Verlag.

Ferguson, Nicholas 1978, Self-assessment of Listening Comprehension. *IRAL*, Vol. 16, No. 2, 149–56.

Foreign Service Institute School of Language Studies 1968, Absolute Language Proficiency Ratings. Washington D.C.: U.S. Department of State. Mimeograph. Reprinted in J.L.D. Clark, *Foreign Language Testing: Theory and Practice.*

Frink, Helen H. 1982, Oral Testing for First-Year Language Classes. *Foreign Language Annals*, Vol. 15, No. 4, 281–87.

Gaies, Stephen J., Gradman, Harry L. & Spolsky, Bernard 1977, Toward the Measurement of Functional Proficiency: Contextualization of the Noise Test. *TESOL Quarterly*, Vol. 11, No. 1, 51–57.

Goodrich, H.C. 1978, Cloze Difficulties in ESL. *University of Southern Florida Language Quarterly*, Vol. 16, Nos. 3 and 4, 11–14.

Harris, David P. & Palmer, Leslie A. 1970, *CELT Technical Manual: A Comprehensive English Language Test for Speakers of English as a Second Language*. New York: McGraw Hill.

Harvey, Anamaria, Nillan, Ana Maria, Horzella, Maria & Sindermann, Gerda 1979, Testing and Evaluation in a ESP Operation. *EST/ESP Chile Newsletter*, Special Issue No. 1, 36–61.

Hatch, E.M. 1979, Simplified Input and Second Language Acquisition. Paper to the LSA Conference, Los Angeles.

Henner-Stanchina, C. & Holec, H. 1977, Evaluation in an Autonomous Learning Scheme. *Melanges*, 73–84.

Henning, Grant H. 1978, A Developmental Analysis of Errors of Adult Iranian Students of English as a Foreign Language. *Language Learning*, Vol. 28, No. 2, 387–97.

Holec, Henri 1981, Plaidoyer pour l'auto-evaluation. *Le Français dans le Monde*, No. 165, 15–23.

Huart, Michelle 1978, Propositions pour une auto-evaluation. *Etudes de Linguistique Appliquée*, No. 2, 6–21.

Hughes, Arthur 1981, Conversational Cloze as a Measure of Oral Ability. *English Language Teaching Journal*, Vol. XXXV, No. 2, 161–68.

Hymes, D.H. 1972, On Communicative Competence. In J.B. Pride & J. Holmes (eds), *Sociolinguistics*. 269–93.

Ingram, D.E. 1978, *An Applied Linguistic Study of Advanced Language Learning*. Unpublished thesis for the degree of Doctor of Philosophy, University of Essex, Colchester. In ERIC Collection ED168 359.

—— 1979a, Methodology. In the Teachers Manual of the Adult Migrant Education Programme of the Australian Department of Immigration and Ethnic Affairs. Canberra: Australian Government Publishing Service.

—— 1979b, An Introduction to the Australian Second Language Proficiency Ratings. In the Teachers Manual of the Adult Migrant Education Program of the Australian Department of Immigration and Ethnic Affairs. Canberra: Australian Government Publishing Service, revised edition, 1983.

—— 1980a, A Performance-Based Approach to the Measurement of Second Language Proficiency. *Australian Review of Applied Linguistics*, Vol. 3, No. 1, 49–62.

—— 1980b, The Australian Second Language Proficiency Ratings: Their Nature, Development and Trialling. In J.A.S. Read (ed.), *Directions in Language Testing*. 108–36.

—— 1980c, Proof of Language Incompetence. *The Linguistic Reporter*. Vol. 23, No. 1, 14–15.

—— 1980d, Report on the Proficiency Assessment of Second and Third Year Students at the Guangzhou Institute of Foreign Languages, Guangzhou, China. Mimeographed report to the institute.

—— 1980e, Report of the Evaluation of the On-Arrival Section of the Adult Migrant/Education Program, report to the Australian Institute of Multicultural Affairs, Melbourne. Mimeograph.

—— 1982a, *Report on the Formal Trialling of the Australian Second Language Proficiency Ratings (ASLPR)*. Canberra: Australian Government Publishing Service, reprint 1984.

—— 1982b, English Language Proficiency in China: A Study. *MLTAQ Journal*, No. 17, 21–45.

—— 1982c, New Approaches to Language Testing. Paper to the Fourth National Language Conference of the Australian Federation of Modern Language Teachers Associations. Perth, 3rd–6th September. Reprinted in A. MacPherson (ed.), *The Language Curriculum in the 1980's: Affective, Effective or Defective?*

—— forthcoming, *Report on the Further Development of the ASLPR: Adolescent ESL, French, Italian and Japanese.*

Ingram, D.E. & Wylie, Elaine 1979, revised 1982. *Australian Second Language Proficiency Ratings.* Canberra: Australian Department of Immigration and Ethnic Affairs. (First edition published 1979, current edition November 1982.)

—— 1982a, *Australian Second Language Proficiency Ratings (Version for French as a Foreign Language).* Brisbane: Brisbane College of Advanced Education, Mount Gravatt Campus.

—— 1982b, *Australian Second Language Proficiency Ratings (Version for Italian as a Foreign Language).* Brisbane: Brisbane College of Advanced Education, Mount Gravatt Campus.

——1982c, *Australian Second Language Proficiency Ratings (Version for Japanese as a Foreign Language).* Brisbane: Brisbane College of Advanced Education, Mount Gravatt Campus.

Ingram, Elisabeth 1964, *English Language Battery (ELBA).* Edinburgh: University of Edinburgh, Department of Linguistics.

Irvine, Patricia, Atai, Parvin & Oller, John W. 1974, Cloze Dictation, and the Test of English as a Foreign Language. *Language Learning*, Vol. 24, No. 2, 245–52.

James, C.V. & Rouve, Sonia 1973, *Survey of Curricula and Performance in Modern Languages*, 1971–2. London: C.I.L.T.

Jones, Randall L. & Spolsky, Bernard (eds) 1975, *Testing Language Proficiency.* Arlington, Va.: Center for Applied Linguistics.

Kelly, Robert 1981, Aspects of Communicative Performance. *Applied Linguistics*, Vol. II, No. 2, 169–79.

Knibbler, Wil. 1980, Measurement or Global Assessment of Oral Foreign Language Proficiency. *Quantitative Linguistics*, No. 6, 127–44.

Krashen, Stephen D. 1976, Formal and Informal Linguistic Environments in Language Acquisition and Language Learning. *TESOL Quarterly*, Vol. 10, No. 2, 157–68.

—— 1980, Relating Theory and Practice in Adult Second Language Acquisitions. In S.W. Felix (ed.) *Second Language Development: Trends and Issues.* 185–204.

—— 1981a, Letter. *Language Learning*, Vol. 31, No. 1, 217–21.

—— 1981b, The 'Fundamental Pedagogical Principle' in Second-Language Teaching. *Studia Linguistica*, Vol. 35, Nos. 1 and 2, 50–70.

Lado, Robert 1961, *Language Testing.* London: Longmans.

Leventhal, C.E. 1980, Measuring Intelligibility of Non-native Speakers with White Noise. *TESOL Newsletter*, Vol. XIV, No. 1, 17, 20.

Long, Michael H. 1981, Questions in Foreigner Talk Discourse, *Language Learning*, Vol. 31, No. 1, 135–57.

Low, Graham D. 1982, The Direct Testing of Academic Writing in a Second Language. *System* Vol. 10, No. 3, 247–57.

Lowe, Pardee 1981, Structure of the Oral Interview and Content Validity. In A.S. Palmer, P.J.M. Groot & S.A. Trosper (eds), *The Construct Validation of Tests of Communicative Competence.* 71–80.

MacPherson, Anne (ed.) 1982, *The Language Curriculum in the 1980's: Affective, Effective or Defective?* Perth: MLTAWA/AFMLTA.

Madsen, Harold S. 1979, An Indirect Measure of Listening Comprehension. *The Modern Language Journal*, Vol. 63, No. 8, 429–35.

—— 1982, Determining the Debilitative Impact of Test Anxiety. *Language Learning*, Vol. 32, No. 1, 133–43.

Madsen, Harold L. & Jones, Randall, L. 1981, Classification of Oral Proficiency Test. In A.S. Palmer, P.J.M. Groot & S.A. Trosper (eds), *The Construct Validation of Tests of Communicative Competence*. 15–30.

Mattran, Kenneth J. 1977, Native Speaker Reactions to Speakers of ESL: Implications for Adult Basic Education Oral English Proficiency Testing. *TESOL Quarterly*, Vol. 11, No. 4, 407–14.

Morrow, Keith 1981, Communicative Language Testing. In J.C. Alderson & A. Hughes (eds), *Issues in Language Testing*, 9–25.

Mullen, Karen A. 1978a, Direct Evaluation of Second-Language Proficiency: The Effect of Rater and Scale in Oral Interviews. *Language Learning*, Vol. 28, No. 2, 301–308.

—— 1978b, Determining the Effect of Uncontrolled Sources of Error in a Direct Test of Oral Proficiency and the Capability of the Procedure to Detect Improvement following Classroom Instruction. In J.L.D. Clark (ed.), *Direct Testing of Speaking Proficiency: Theory and Application*. 171–89.

—— 1980, Rater Reliability and Oral Proficiency Evaluations. In J.W. Oller & K. Perkins (eds), *Research in Language Testing*. 91–101.

Okoh, Nduka 1981, Biculturality and Performance in Cloze Tests of Language Comprehension: A Cross-Cultural Study. *Journal of Multilingual and Multicultural Development*, Vol. 2, No. 3, 183–94.

Oller, J.W. 1972a, Dictation as a Test of ESL Proficiency. In H.B. Allen & R.N. Campbell (eds), *Teaching English as a Second Language: A Book of Readings*. 346–54.

—— 1972b, Scoring Methods and Difficulty Levels for Cloze Tests of ESL Proficiency. *Modern Language Journal*, Vol. 56, 151–58.

—— 1973a, Cloze Tests of Second Language Proficiency and What they Measure. *Language Learning*, Vol. 23, No. 1, 105–18.

—— 1973b, Discrete-Point Tests versus Tests of Integrative Skills. In J.W. Oller & J.C. Richards (eds), *Focus on the Learner: Pragmatic Perspectives for the Language Teacher*. 184–99.

—— 1974, Expectancy for Successive Elements: Key Ingredient to Language Use. *Foreign Language Annals*, Vol. 7, 443–52.

—— 1975, Cloze, Discourse and Approximations to English. In M.K. Burt & H.C. Dulay (eds), *New Directions in Second Language Learning, Teaching and Bilingual Education*. 345–55.

—— 1976, Evidence for a General Language Proficiency: An Expectancy Grammar. *Die Neueren Sprachen*, No. 75, 165–74.

—— 1979, *Language Tests at School: A Pragmatic Approach*. London: Longman.

—— 1980, A Language Factor Deeper than Speech: More Data and Theory for Bilingual Assessment. Georgetown University Roundtable on Languages and Linguistics, 14–30.

Oller, John W. & Khan, Farida 1980, Is there a Global Factor of Language Proficiency? In J.A.S. Read, *Directions in Language Testing*, 3–40.

Oller, John W. & Perkins, Kyle (eds) 1978, *Language in Education: Testing the Tests*. Rowley, Mass.: Newbury House.

—— (eds) 1980, *Research in Language Testing*. Rowley, Mass.: Newbury House.

Oller, John W. & Richards, Jack C. (eds) 1973, *Focus on the Learner: Pragmatic Perspectives for the Language Teacher*. Rowley, Mass.: Newbury House.

Oller, John W. & Streiff, Virginia 1975, Dictation: A Test of Grammar Based Expectancies. In R.L. Jones & B. Spolsky (eds) *Testing Language Proficiency*, 71–82.

Oskarsson, M. 1978, *Approaches to Self-Assessment in Foreign Language Learning*. Oxford: Pergamon.

Oskarsson, Mats, 1981, L'autoevaluation dans l'apprentissage des langues par les adultes: quelques resultats de recherche. *Etudes de Linguistique Appliquée*, No. 41, 102–15.

Palmer, Adrian S. 1972, Testing Communication. *IRAL*, Vol. X, No. 1, 35–45.

—— 1979, Compartmentalized and Integrated Control: An Assessment of Some Evidence for Two Kinds of Competence and Implications for the Classroom. *Language Learning* Vol. 29, No. 1, 169–80.

Palmer, Adrian S. & Groot, Peter J.M. 1981, An Introduction. In A.S. Palmer, P.J.M. Groot & S.A. Trosper (eds), *The Construct Validation of Tests of Communicative Competence*, 1–11.

Palmer, Adrian S., Groot, P.J.M. & Trosper, S.A. (eds) 1981, *The Construct Validation of Tests of Communicative Competence*. Washington, D.C.: TESOL.

Parlett, Malcolm & Hamilton, David 1976, Evaluation as Illumination. In D. Tawney (ed.) *Curriculum Evaluation Today: Trends and Implications*, 84–101.

Politzer, Robert L., Shohamy, Elana, McGroarty, Mary 1982, Validation of Linguistic and Communicative Oral Language Tests for Spanish-English Bilingual Programs. Paper to the pre-conference symposium on language testing. 1982 TESOL Convention, University of Hawaii, Honolulu, Hawaii. Mimeograph.

Porter, Don 1978, Cloze Procedure and Equivalence. *Language Learning*, Vol. 28, No. 2, December. 333–41.

Pride, J.B. & Holmes, J. 1972, *Sociolinguistics*. Harmondsworth: Penguin.

Read, John A.S. (ed.) 1981, *Directions in Language Testing*. Anthology Series 9. Singapore: SEAMEO Regional Language Centre/University of Singapore.

Seliger, Herbert W. 1979, On the Nature and Function of Language Rules in Language Teaching. *TESOL Quarterly*, Vol. 13, No. 3, September. 359–69.

Shohamy, Elana 1981, Inter-rater and Intra-rater Reliability of the Oral Interview and Concurrent Validity with Cloze Procedure. In A.S. Palmer, P.J.M. Groot & S.A. Trosper (eds), *The Construct Validation of Tests of Communicative Competence*. 94–103.

—— 1982a, Affective Considerations in Language Teaching. *Modern Language Journal*, Vol. 166, No. 1, Spring, 13–17.

—— 1982b, Predicting Speaking Proficiency from Cloze Tests: Theoretical and Practical Considerations for Tests Substitution. *Applied Linguistics*, Vol. III, No. 2, Summer, 161–71.

Shranger, J.S. & Osberg, T.M. 1981, The Relative Accuracy of Self-Prediction and Judgements by Others in Psychological Assessment. *Psychological Bulletin*, No. 90, 322–51.

Smith, Kenneth P. & Baldauf, Richard B. forthcoming, The Concurrent Validity of

Self-Rating with Interviewer Rating on the Australian Second Language Proficiency Ratings Scale. *Journal of Educational and Psychological Measurement*.

Smyth, E.A., Arnold, F. & Seaton, I. 1980, An English Language Testing Service: Subject/Language Collaboration in ESP Test Design. *ELT Documents*, No. 106, 109–17.

Sollenberger, Howard E. 1978, Development and Current Use of the FSI Oral Interview Test. In J.L.D. Clark (ed.), *Direct Testing of Speaking Proficiency: Theory and Application*, 3–12.

Spolsky, Bernard 1973, What does it Mean to Know a Language, or How do you get Someone to Perform his Competence? In J.W. Oller & J.C. Richards (eds), *Focus on the Learner: Pragmatic Perspectives for the Language Teacher*, 164–76.

—— 1978, *Advances in Language Testing*. Arlington, VA.: Center for Applied Linguistics.

Spolsky, Bernard, Murphy, Penny, Holm, Wayne & Ferrel, Allen 1972, Three Functional Tests of Oral Proficiency. *TESOL Quarterly*, Vol. 6, No. 3, September, 221–35.

Stansfield, C.W. 1981, Dictation as a Measure of Spanish Language Proficiency. *IRAL*, Vol XIX, No. 4, December, 346–51.

Stevenson, Douglas K. 1981, Beyond Faith and Face Validity: The Multitrait-Multimethod Matrix and the Convergent and Discriminant Validity of Oral Proficiency Tests. In A.S. Palmer, P.J.M. Groot & S.A. Trosper (eds), *The Construct Validation of Tests of Communicative Competence*, 37–61.

Streiff, Virginia 1978, Relationships among Oral and Written Cloze Scores and Achievement Test Scores in a Bilingual Setting. In J.W. Oller & K. Perkins (eds), *Language in Education: Testing the Tests*, 65–102.

Tan Soon Hock 1980, The Role of Testing in the University of Malaya English for Special Purposes Project. *ELT Documents*, No. 107, 104–15.

Tawney, D. 1976, *Curriculum Evaluation Today: Trends and Implications*. London: Schools Council.

Valdman, Albert (ed.) 1966, *Trends in Language Teaching*. New York: McGraw Hill.

Vollmer, Helmut J. 1981, Why are we interested in 'General Language Proficiency'? In J.C. Alderson & A. Hughes (eds), *Issues in Language Testing*, 152–75.

Weir, C.J. 1982, The Associated Examining Board's Test in English for Academic Purposes. *Language Testing Newsletter*, No. 2, Spring, 8–10.

Whiteson, Valerie 1981, Foreign Language Testing: A Current View. *English Language Teaching Journal*, Vol. XXXV, No. 3, April, 345–52.

Wylie, Elaine 1983, Learner Self-Assessment, with Particular Reference to the Adult Distance Learning Program. Paper to the ATESOL Summer School, Sydney, 1983. Reprinted in *Proceedings of the ATESOL Summer School, 1983*. Sydney: ATESOL. Forthcoming.

Yorozuya, Ryuichi & Oller, John W. 1980, Oral Proficiency Scales: Construct Validity and the Halo Effect. *Language Learning*, Vol. 30, No. 1, June, 135–53.

11 Testing second language proficiency with direct procedures. A comment on Ingram

JAN H. HULSTIJN

Free University, Amsterdam, The Netherlands

In this contribution, some comments will be made on the issue of general language proficiency testing by means of direct tests, as propounded in Ingram's position paper (this volume). The term "proficiency" will be used here in the non-theoretical sense it has in the testing field, namely as "the ability to perform pragmatically useful tasks in the language" (Clark, 1978:23). In this sense, proficiency testing is juxtaposed to diagnostic and achievement testing.

First of all, it should be obvious that syllabus writers, teachers, and testers cannot wait for full-fledged theories of language proficiency to emerge from research-laboratories. In the absence of a theory, they have to work with taxonomies which seem to make sense even if they cannot be fully supported by a theoretical explanation. Thus, in L2 teaching, many curriculum designers base their curriculum not only on a linguistic description of the target language (grammar and vocabulary) but also on taxonomies of how functions and notions are expressed in that target language (Van Ek, 1977). Similarly, in the testing field, in addition to writing rather traditional tests of grammar and vocabulary, the tester may attempt to design tests that elicit performance in everyday communicative situations. Thus, a task-oriented approach towards overall proficiency testing, as adopted in Ingram's paper, seems to be a realistic choice.

Which test to choose is above all a matter that has to be decided on the basis of the test objectives. For instance, the purposes as listed in pages 256–67 of Ingram's paper, may determine to a large extent what type of test is to be selected. (One might have wanted to see these objectives listed in a more prominent place in Ingram's paper.) Thus, if the objective is to assess adult immigrants' oral second language proficiency in common, non-professional, out-of-home situations, it would seem quite natural to develop a "direct" test.

However, in addition to a direct test of the FSI or ASLPR type, it would be preferable to administer one or several other, more objective tests as well. In our example of immigrant testing, we might want to administer also a sentence repetition test, or an aural listening comprehension test. The rationale for including several tests rather than just one is that we can vary the elicitation procedures (e.g. a more and a less structured procedure) and the scoring procedures (subjective and objective procedures) so as to prevent the effect of just one testing method from biassing the results. Particularly when the tester's evaluation can affect the testee's career — as in the case of entrance examinations for immigrants, foreign students etc. — it would be mandatory to minimize the chances of erroneous evaluations by varying the testing procedures across subtests. This view was also expressed during a recently held testing symposium. In his report of a discussion of this issue, Alderson, (1981) writes:

> "(...) we must give testees a fair chance by giving them a *variety* of language tests, simply because one might be wrong: there might be no Best Test, or it might not be the one we chose to give, or there might not be *one* general language proficiency factor, there may be several." (Alderson, 1981:190, original italics.)

At several points in his paper, Ingram gives his readers the impression that the ASLPR is a test, and a direct test at that. However, the ASLPR is rather an evaluation instrument, not itself responsible for the direct nature of the test. It is crucial to differentiate between the task itself (elicitation materials, response instructions etc.) and the evaluation of the testee's task performance. Interview and role-play tasks are typically direct procedures, regardless of whether or not they are evaluated by some objective procedure (e.g. counting errors, calculating the mean length of utterance or the type/token ratio), or by a subjective procedure (e.g. performance rating with a global rating scale like the ASLPR). Furthermore, a direct test, such as an interview or a role play procedure, is not real life itself. It remains a test in the sense that its elicitation procedure purports to approximate a sample of representative real-life situations. Thus, the test researcher must attempt to determine to what extent a particular direct test does indeed measure the trait that it purports to measure (e.g. general language proficiency in non-specific, everyday situations), and to what extent it measures method effects, caused by the artificiality of the elicitation procedure. As Stevenson (1981; see also Underhill 1983) has eloquently pointed out, this must be done not only for ordinary indirect tests, but for direct tests as well:

> "To assume that an oral proficiency test such as an interview is somehow a direct test of oral proficiency is to ignore a very important point. This point, which is strongly stressed in convergent and discriminant validation theory, is that any test is a 'trait-method unit'." (Stevenson, 1981:44)

> "In an interview, for example, a 'normal' conversational question given by the examiner is both part of the trait and part of the testing method. It could be argued that such a question would be appropriate to a definition of the construct, oral language proficiency, and therefore relevant trait rather than irrelevant method. Other cases are much more problematic. At what point, for example, do the examiner's questions become more method than trait? When do they cease to be likely to occur in 'real-life' situations? Or should we assume that because few if any adult examinees are likely to forget for a moment that an interview is a test, and not a tête-à-tête, all questions within the interview are colored by 'method'?"
> (Stevenson, 1981:53–54)

That it is possible, in principle, to assess the method effects of an interview test, has been demonstrated by Bachman & Palmer (1981) in their multitrait-multimethod study with the FSI Oral Interview. (The evidence Ingram presents concerning the contribution to validity and reliability made by the nature of the interview procedure does not seem to be sufficient.)[1] It seems to me that, for an interview procedure of the FSI and ASLPR type, it would be necessary to determine:

1. the comprehensibility of the testing materials and the instructions that are used to approximate a genuine communicative situation;
2. the effect of the affective components of the formal testing situation, especially when a particular task requires the testee to perform in a relaxed and informal way;
3. the adequacy with which the native participants in the

interaction play their roles, or the effect of the interviewer's dual function as both interlocutor and evaluator.[2]

As a last comment on the issue of direct testing, let me suggest that profile assessment (describing) and level assessment (rating) be conducted in separate steps. A serious potential drawback of using a global rating scale which identifies only a small number of proficiency levels, like the ASLPR, is that raters may very soon end up not paying attention any more to the detailed descriptions of skills and activities (in the first and second column of the ASLPR scale). They may content themselves with rating their testees on what eventually turns out to be a single n-point scale from low to high proficiency. When Ingram reports that adequate reliability figures were obtained for the ASLPR, one has to bear in mind that high reliability coefficients are more likely to occur when the scale contains relatively few rating levels. This is even more so when, in terms of L2 proficiency, a heterogeneous sample of L2 learners has been tested. Obviously, it is easier to reliably and validly rank order a group of dissimilar than a group of similar individuals.

It would be preferable, then, to keep the profile assessment procedure separate as much as possible from the rating procedure. First, by means of a direct test, a sample of activities can be elicited that each purport to approximate a representative real life situation. While rating the testee's performance on each of these activities against some criterion of appropriateness, the evaluators must try to picture the testee's profile in terms of (1) what tasks can be carried out, and (2) how they can be carried out (cf. Ingram, this volume, Chapter 10, pp.220f.). Only after this detailed information has been obtained, can a conversion procedure be applied, transforming this complex profile into a single rating on a n-point scale. If this suggested two-phase procedure could be shown to be feasible, one might succeed in preventing the scaling procedure from eroding the profile assessment procedure. This appears to be desirable since the two procedures differ in function: the scaling procedure is designed to ascertain individual differences regardless of content, whereas the profile drawing procedure focusses on content while leaving individual differences out of consideration.

Notes to Chapter 11

1. In pp. 363–65 of her contribution to this volume, Fried expresses similar concerns.
2. The same type of problems appear to occur with the elicitation procedure utilized by Clahsen (this volume) for profile analysis. Clahsen's "spontaneous" conversa-

tion procedure allows for all sorts of avoidance and play-it-safe strategies on the part of the testee. It thus does not guarantee the elicitation of a representative sample of utterances, representative in terms of the test objectives (whatever functions, notions, or grammar rules in the testee's performance one wants to measure). I therefore agree with Stölting's words of caution concerning Clahsen's instrument (Stölting, this volume, Chapter 16, pp.389–93).

References

Alderson, J.C. 1981, Report of the discussion on General Language Proficiency. In J.C. Alderson & A. Hughes (eds), *Issues in Language Testing*. London: The British Council (ELT Documents 111).

Bachman, L.F. & Palmer, A.S. 1981, The construct validation of the FSI Oral Interview. *Language Learning*, 31:67–86.

Clark, J.L.D. 1978, Psychometric considerations in language testing. In B. Spolsky (ed.), *Advances in Language Testing: Series 2, Approaches to Language Testing*. Arlington, Va.: Center for Applied Linguistics.

Stevenson, D.K. 1981, Beyond faith and face validity: The multitrait-multimethod matrix and the convergent and discriminant validity of oral proficiency tests. In A.S. Palmer, P.J.M. Groot & G.A. Trosper (eds), *The Construct Validation of Tests of Communicative Competence*. Washington, D.C.: Teachers of English to Speakers of Other Languages.

Underhill, N. 1983, Commonsense in Oral Testing: Reliability, Validity and Affective Factors. In M.A. Clarke & J. Handscombe (eds), *On TESOL '82*. Washington, D.C.: Teachers of English to Speakers of Other Languages.

Van Ek, J.A. 1977, *The Threshold Level for Modern Language Learning in Schools*. London: Longman.

12 Profiling second language development: A procedure for assessing L2 proficiency

HARALD CLAHSEN

Universität Düsseldorf, West Germany

Introduction

In this chapter, I will suggest a psycholinguistic procedure for assessing L2 proficiency. The present version of the procedure focuses on the assessment of migrant workers' acquisition of German syntax. The methodological approach to L2 assessment which I am advocating is, however, also applicable to (i) languages other than German, (ii) other groups of L2 acquirers, and (iii) other linguistic areas, such as the diagnosis of phonological, prosodic, and semantic skills.

For more than twenty years now, migrant workers have been living in West Germany. The immigrants and their families must have a certain proficiency in German if they are not to be forced into a social limbo. It is the task of the German school system and the adult education facilities to make it possible for them to attain such language proficiency. However, it is generally acknowledged that instruction in German as a foreign language does not at present do justice to the needs of those immigrants who should benefit from it.

One reason which is often mentioned by the teaching profession is the lack of a suitable language assessment test. It is argued that the teacher must have detailed information as to the learners' level of linguistic development in order to tailor instruction to the learners' requirements (cf. e.g. Ihssen, 1980:40). In view of the fact that the necessary assessment

283

procedures are not currently available, those who are involved in immigrant education have repeatedly called for the development of proficiency tests for foreign workers and their children.

It is my opinion that L2 acquisition researchers should take up this challenge. In the seventies, a number of research studies on German L2 acquisition by migrant workers received federal funding. These projects have provided quite detailed information about the way German is acquired by migrant workers. It would be unforgivable if these workers were not to benefit from the findings. In particular, efforts directed towards development of assessment procedures for migrant workers should be based on the empirical results of L2 acquisition research.

It is, however, of prime importance that great care be taken in the creation of assessment tests, since there is a very real danger that such tests could give reactionaries a spurious legitimation for singling out and thus further segregating migrant workers' children from the regular school system (cf. Ludwig, 1982; Göbel, 1978). In this connection, it is reported (cf. Stölting, this volume, chapter 16) that the school administration in Berlin was planning to assign the migrant workers' children to the various elementary schools on the basis of a language proficiency test. In accordance with a proposal of the majority (Christian Democratic) party, this plan was to become law. In order to realise this plan, the Berlin Minister of Education has requested L2 researchers to develop a language proficiency test which would assign migrant pupils a mean score of their achievement in German. It should be clear to everyone involved in working with immigrants that such tests could be used, with the backing of quasi-scientific procedures, as a basis for excluding these pupils from the regular German schools. In my opinion, it would be a fatal mistake if the results of L2 acquisition research were misused for such measures, i.e. if the isolation of the foreign families were increased even more.

We are therefore confronted with a real dilemma as regards the application of results of L2 acquisition research: on the one hand, the results of the research projects which the first-generation immigrants willingly served as subjects for should now benefit them in the form of language instruction especially suited to this target group and its needs; for this, the teachers need appropriate methods they can use to evaluate their students' German language achievement. On the other hand, we wish to preclude the misuse of such methods by those whose interest lies in segregating foreign pupils within the German school system. The method I wish to present in this paper seems to offer a solution to this dilemma: it is an informal method for the evaluation of linguistic performance within the framework of the so-called profiling approach (cf. Crystal, 1982). This methodological approach to linguistic diagnosis gives the teacher a comparatively comprehensive, accurate, and detailed linguistic description of an individual learners' interlanguage and allows an assessment of his/her linguistic development.

Although misuse of this method cannot be ruled out completely, it is relatively unlikely. In profile analyses, for example, no general mean scores of L2 proficiency are calculated which could lend some spurious legitimacy to a segregation of migrant workers. Instead, profiles require qualitative interpretation, i.e. a reconstruction of the strategies and rules the learners employ. And this can be done only by a professional, i.e. the teacher. The practicing teacher — but not, however, the educational bureaucracy — would be a potential candidate for applying the procedure suggested in the present paper. Administering and, especially, evaluating the profile analyses, require some knowledge of linguistics to enable assessment of the developmental level and the particular linguistic problems an individual learner has. This, in turn, enables the teacher to adjust the instruction to the learners' communicative needs. The primary purpose of linguistic profiles is thus to serve as an aid to gearing language instruction to the actual needs of the learners. Moreover, the performance of a profile analysis is fairly time-consuming. Someone who is merely seeking an excuse for segregating migrant workers would hardly be likely to carry out interviews with the learners, transcribe the interviews, analyse them in view of certain linguistic characteristics, and then try to reconstruct the rules and strategies those learners use in dealing with the German language. On the whole, therefore, I consider profile analyses to be a reasonable alternative to currently used language assessment tests, particularly as far as the evaluation of migrant workers' and their childrens' L2 proficiency is concerned.

In the next section, some requirements for L2 assessment tests will be discussed. In section 2, the motivation for and some of the general characteristics of the notion of profiles will be described. Section 3 summarizes some of the results of the research studies of migrant workers' L2 (German) development. These results are a necessary prerequisite for the fourth section, which contains a preliminary profile of German L2 acquisition. In the final section, the use of this procedure will be illustrated by means of an analysis of two transcripts of an Italian learner.

Evaluating L2 assesssment procedures

In what follows, the criteria I used for evaluating L2 assessment tests will be established. It should be emphasized that the criteria come from a psycholinguist who has studied the strategies of migrant workers' L2 acquisition of German, and not from a professional who is involved in teaching German as a second language. Thus, certain criteria often mentioned by the teaching profession, such as easy handling, applicability in the classroom setting and the like, are not explicitly considered in the present discussion, though it is acknowledged that such criteria are important as well.

Let me begin with a requirement which does not appear to arouse significant controversy:

A. The evaluation of *oral* L2 speech *production* should be at the core of an assessment procedure which aims at identifying the general developmental level of the learners' interlanguage.

Although reading and writing abilities are particularly relevant in the classroom setting, oral language skills are more important with regard to the learners' communicative needs (cf. Portz & Pfaff, 1981:7; Ihssen, 1980:40; Luchtenberg, 1983:34). Thus, foreign language teaching as well as L2 assessment should primarily be directed towards the learners' oral language skills. In addition, claims about the general developmental level of the learners' interlanguage should be based on oral language data and should come not only from the learners' reading and writing skills (cf. Scherzinger & Scherzinger, 1981:18f.). The second requirement directly follows from the supposed relevance of evaluating the learners' oral language:

B. The assessment should be based on a representative sample of *spontaneous* speech which is gathered in a natural communicative situation.

Apart from general objections to the use of standardized language tests (cf. Ihssen, 1978:90f.), it should be emphasized that highly pre-structured test situations in which specific linguistic responses are elicited from the learners cannot be regarded as a reliable data base for evaluating migrant workers' L2 proficiency given the fact that these learners are completely unfamiliar with such tasks. Rather, a sample of spontaneous language data more adequately represents the learners' oral proficiency in the second language (cf. Ihssen, 1980:40; Scherzinger & Scherzinger, 1981:18; Luchtenberg, 1983:34; Hegele, 1981:42; Luchtenberg et al., 1982:134f.; Portz & Pfaff, 1981:7).

It is, however, striking to see that nearly all the authors who have already developed an assessment procedure for migrant workers use picture description tasks as their major data collection technique. One of the problems of this sampling method is that it cannot seriously be used with adults or adolescents, given the fact that at least some of the foreign workers justly feel such a task to be, frankly, ridiculous. A second problem concerns the validity of the language sample. Given the fact that the possible linguistic responses are narrowly constrained within picture description tasks, it may be argued that such tasks do not provide for an adequate data base in order to evaluate the learners' interlanguage. E. Hatch (1974) has already pointed out that the results of L2 acquisition research may be strongly influenced by the set-up of the data collection techniques. To mention just one example: If a learner is constantly asked "What's this?", "Is this X?", etc., it is likely he/she will answer "This...(is)...X". Thus, one should not be surprised to find that, with this kind of data collection, specific sentence types, such as copula structures, are more frequent and used earlier than others. In consequence, we should be wary of interpreting linguistic responses to picture description tasks in terms of acquisitional stages. An alternative data collection technique might be an unstructured free conversation which gives the learner the opportunity to apply spontaneously the whole range of the already acquired L2 patterns.

C. The procedure should attempt to provide a comprehensive description of the learners' interlanguage.

The motivation for this requirement is simply that, in the present state of L2 acquisition research, there is no way of deciding in advance which aspects of the interlanguage to omit from the assessment. Standardized language proficiency tests, such as the Bilingual Syntax Measure (Burt *et al.*, 1975), do not do justice to this principle. This procedure seems to be linguistically reductive, because the interlanguage is only analysed in terms of a small set of grammatical morphemes. The danger of such a procedure is that information of possible significance for the evaluation of the interlanguage is lost. There are, however, practical reasons, such as easy handling, applicability in a reasonable amount of time, and the like, forcing us to introduce some evaluation of relevance to the different interlanguage structures used by the learners. The choice of the linguistic structures to be assessed must not be arbitrary, however; rather, it has to be justified in terms of their relevance to the process of L2 development, i.e. whether the selected linguistic structures provide for a discriminating assessment of the developmental level of the interlanguage.

D. The procedure should focus on the evaluation of syntax and morphology.

The justification for this requirement is threefold. First, syntax and morphology may be regarded as the structural frame of a language. Thus, any claims about a learner's general L2 proficiency should, at least, include the evaluation of morphosyntax (cf. Ihssen, 1980: 41; Hegele, 1981: 42). Second, according to our present level of knowledge it is primarily the area of morphosyntax which causes the language problems of migrant workers and their children (cf. Scherzinger & Scherzinger, 1981: 21). Hence, in order to identify the learners' language problems, it is necessary to assess syntactic and morphological aspects of the interlanguage. Third, as most research studies on German L2 acquisition have dealt with syntax and morphology (cf. the survey presented in Nicholas & Meisel, 1983 and this chapter, pp.294–99), we know much more about the development of morphosyntax than we know about the acquisition of semantic or pragmatic skills. One of the major findings of this research was that the development of L2 syntax and morphology can be described in terms of an approximately invariant order, i.e. migrant workers seem to pass through an ordered set of developmental stages on their way to acquiring German morphosyntax. Thus, the assessment of morphosyntax may provide for a detailed account of the developmental level of an individual interlanguage. Whether the development of pragmatic and semantic skills also follows a strictly ordered acquisitional sequence has not yet been proven, at least with regard to German L2 development. In my opinion, requirement D follows primarily from the present state of L2 acquisition research. As long as we do not know whether the assessment of pragmatics, semantics, vocabulary, etc. provides for a discriminating evaluation of the developmental level of the interlanguage, we have no other alternative but to restrict ourselves to the assessment of morphosyntax. If, however, developmental sequences of, for example, pragmatic and semantic skills could be defined, it would become necessary to revise the procedures and to include such results into a comprehensive evaluation.

E. The procedure should grade the linguistic structures used by the learners in terms of the order of acquisition in natural L2 development.

To be pedagogically relevant, an assessment procedure must not be restricted to a linguistic description of the learners' language, but it should also allow one to make specific claims about the developmental status of the interlanguage under evaluation. It is such a process of a developmental grading which makes detailed assessments possible and suggests potential teaching goals.

There are, however, several measures which might be used as grading devices. One might, for example, grade the learners' utterances in terms of their distance from the target norm. This is, in fact, what most currently available assessment procedures for migrant workers do (Scherzinger & Scherzinger, 1981:21f.; Luchtenberg et al., 1982:153ff.; Luchtenberg, 1983:36; Hegele, 1981:43ff.; Portz & Pfaff, 1981:56ff.). The data gathered from an individual learner is simply analysed with regard to its correspondence to the German standard; most procedures only distinguish between correct and incorrect utterances. The first objection to the use of such a grading device is that one cannot draw any conclusions about the developmental level of the interlanguage from the number of errors. Longitudinal studies of German L2 acquisition have shown that the frequency of certain errors may fluctuate (cf. Molony, 1977:279; Pienemann, 1981). In a longitudinal study dealing with adult L2 acquisition, the ZISA research group (cf. this chapter, pp.294–99 and Clahsen, 1981) found that there are interlanguage structures which show a high risk of error but are acquired fairly early and continue to be used "deviantly" until very late. Thus, if we restrict ourselves to measuring the distance of an interlanguage from the target norm in terms of errors, we cannot adequately assess the developmental stage reached by an individual L2 learner.

A second objection to such a grading device is that this procedure does not capture the learners' creative innovations. It is now generally acknowledged in L2 acquisition research that the learners develop a set of "approximative systems" on their way to the target variety; these systems have been called "interlanguages" (cf. Nemser, 1971; Selinker, 1972). Interlanguages get a certain structural autonomy from characteristic linguistic features and rules, some of which might be deviant in terms of the target language. From this perspective, the method of interpreting L2 learners' ungrammatical utterances simply as errors has been rejected. Rather, the researcher's task is to find out what the learners' interim hypotheses about the target language look like. Thus, the interlanguage hypothesis forces us to reconstruct the transitional rules the learners are using.

Quantitative measures, such as mean length of utterance (MLU) and the like, might be regarded as an alternative way of grading the linguistic structures used by L2 learners. In some of the currently available assessment procedures for migrant workers, the MLU is claimed to be a reliable index of language development (cf. Ihssen, 1980:40; Scherzinger & Scherzinger, 1981:20). The empirical basis for such a grading device is the relevant *L1* research, in particular R. Brown's work on the acquisition of *English* as a first language (cf. Brown, 1973). However, longitudinal studies of child as well as of adult L2 acquisition of German have shown (cf. Pienemann, 1981; Clahsen et al., in prep.) that the mean length of utterance does not systematically increase during the process of L2 development. Rather, there is a great deal of variation in the MLU values which cannot be related to different developmental stages. Consequently, simple quantitative measures of increasing length are not illuminating, on the whole, at least as far as *L2* development is concerned.

A second group of quantitative measures which might be used as grading devices are generalized mean scores of grammatical development, such as the Syntax Acquisition Index (SAI) which is calculated in the Bilingual Syntax Measure (cf. Burt *et al.*, 1975) or the "syntactic index" used in the Heidelberger Projekt Pidgin-Deutsch (cf. Klein & Dittmar, 1979). The SAI indicates "how much of the grammatical structure that the child offered was well-formed" (Dulay & Burt, 1974:47), and the "syntactic index" attempts to describe four successive stages in migrant workers' natural L2 acquisition of German. One of the major problems of such procedures concerns the hypothesis that development is uniform, which is, at least implicitly, assumed in these studies. It is taken for granted that all parts of the learners' grammar which are included in the score develop uniformly. If this were not the basic assumption, one could not claim that a mean score consisting of different grammatical features indicates an overall level of L2 proficiency.

However, several results on L2 acquisition suggest that development does not progress uniformly along a straight line from zero to the target variety. Rather, one has to distinguish between different groups of learners who may follow different paths on their way to acquiring the target language. Pienemann (1981), Nicholas (1984), and Meisel *et al.* (1981) have shown, for example, using results from longitudinal studies, that some of the grammatical features included in the "syntactic index" of Klein & Dittmar (1979), such as the deletion of the copula, cannot be regarded as developmental stages of L2 acquisition, thus suggesting that this measure is not a reliable index of L2 development.

A second danger of generalized mean scores is that they conceal differences of L2 achievement in the individual, i.e. intra-subject variation. Given the fact that a mean score is meant to summarize the crucial grammatical features of the whole interlanguage under evaluation, it does not allow one to assess an individual learner's strength or weakness in particular areas of the L2. Finally, quantitative measures are only useful if a significant number of empirically based comparative norms are available. As far as German L2 acquisition is concerned, we do not have at our disposal a sufficient data base which could be used to establish general quantitative norms of L2 achievement. In conclusion, I do not find quantitative measures to be especially helpful as a grading device of L2 proficiency. Rather, it seems necessary to develop qualitative measures specifying the *types* of linguistic structures used by the learners.

The most important requirement of the grading device, however, is that it must be "developmental", i.e. the measures should be based on the order of acquisition in natural L2 development. As mentioned before, this research has discovered, among other things, a set of ordered developmental sequences of L2 acquisition. I suggest that such sequences should be the primary grading device of an L2 assessment procedure. This approach corresponds to the interlanguage hypothesis which claims that L2 acquisition is a "creative construction process" during which the learners develop approximative systems of the target language. As opposed to arbitrary quantitative measures and to simply calculating the distance from the target norm, the developmental sequences approach allows one to reconstruct the learners' approximative systems at the various acquisitional stages.

A second argument for using developmental sequences as the primary grading device comes from recent research on tutored L2 acquisition. It has been shown that the principles of natural L2 development, at least in part, also apply to the formal learning of a language in a classroom setting. Despite the obvious differences between the two acquisitional types with regard to language-external learning conditions, Felix & Simmet (1981) and Hahn (1982) found a considerable number of structural parallels and similar learning strategies. In addition, Pienemann (1984) has shown, in an instructional experiment with 10 Italian migrant children learning German in a classroom setting, that particular target language phenomena can only be acquired under instruction if the learners have already reached a stage one step prior to the phenomena to be taught. These results suggest that "there is no way to leave out a stage of the developmental sequence in formal teaching" (cf. Pienemann, 1984:1).

Such findings have important consequences with regard to assessment. If, as suggested by the above-mentioned results, teaching must be based on the developmental sequences and processes of natural L2 acquisition (cf. Pienemann, this volume), then the teacher needs to determine the acquisitional stage reached by the learners before he can introduce new learning objectives. In order to solve this problem, an assessment procedure is required which allows the teacher to evaluate the developmental stage of an individual interlanguage in terms of the natural order of acquisition.

Finally, a third argument supporting the present proposal to use the sequences of natural L2 development should be mentioned. It is necessary for us to keep in mind that L2 development of those migrant workers who are attending language classes does not come to a standstill outside of school. Even these learners acquire a considerable amount of their L2 proficiency in everyday interactions, i.e. outside the classroom. Thus, these learners' L2 proficiency is a product of both natural and tutored learning processes. Provided the teacher is willing to adapt the learning objectives to the learners' linguistic knowledge, it is necessary for him to determine what they are acquiring outside the language class. In managing this task, an assessment procedure which is based on the natural order of acquisition may certainly be helpful.

As far as I know, such an assessment procedure is not yet available. In particular, we do not have a test or an evaluation procedure which could be applied to assess migrant workers' L2 achievement of German in terms of the natural order of acquisition. Instead, arbitrary procedures such as distance from the target norm, simple quantitative measures and the like have been suggested as grading devices. As a result of the previous discussion, we may conclude that the procedures cannot be regarded as adequate assessments of the developmental level of an interlanguage. The main objection to the currently available procedures is that they have completely ignored the bulk of research on L2 development. This research, however, provides us with the empirical basis necessary for developing an L2 assessment procedure. Consequently, we should look for a methodological framework which allows us to integrate these results into an assessment procedure. As mentioned before, the profiling approach provides such a framework, and I suggest that we should try to develop a linguistic profile of the acquisition of German as a second language.

The profiling approach

The notion of linguistic profiles has been developed for use in the assessment and treatment of language disorders, particularly with regard to grammatical disabilities in children. Recently, the profiling approach has been applied to languages other than English (cf. Berman et al., 1982) and to phonological, prosodic, and semantic disorders (cf. Crystal, 1982). In addition, Crystal (1979) has summarized routine clinical practice in working with profiles.

The initial motivation of the profiling approach was to provide a detailed linguistic assessment of grammatical disability and to suggest a remedial approach. It must be emphasized, however, that linguistic profiles should not be confused with (i) language tests or (ii) language teaching programmes (cf. Crystal, 1982 : 2f.). As opposed to language tests, profiles are informal evaluation procedures of language behaviour which attempt to be comprehensive in the linguistic domains under investigation. With regard to remediation, profiles are only concerned with establishing potential teaching goals and possible courses of action, but they do not constitute a teaching programme consisting of a fixed set of teaching materials and an underlying syllabus. Profiles do not touch upon the development of remedial programmes, but, on the other hand, they may provide the linguistic evidence needed to suggest possible remedial approaches.

The most well-known profile currently available is directed towards the analysis of grammatical aspects of language disorders. It came to be known as LARSP, the Language Assessment Remediation and Screening Procedure. According to Crystal & Fletcher (1979:169) the salient characteristics of LARSP are threefold: *descriptive*, *developmental*, and *interactional*. With the descriptive framework used in LARSP it is possible to analyse the whole range of adult syntactic structures in English. A distinction is made between different levels of grammatical organization (word, phrase, clause). At each level, the utterances are analysed into combinations of constituents or inflectional endings without, however, considering the order of elements. On the whole, LARSP provides for an exhaustive grammatical analysis of all the utterances gathered in a sample of an individual patient's spontaneous speech. Crystal (1982:4) insists on the principle of descriptive comprehensiveness, because, as he states, it is not possible to decide in advance which syntactic or morphological aspects to omit from consideration.

The second characteristic of the procedure is that the linguistic categories are graded developmentally, i.e. in terms of their emergence in normal child language acquisition. Based on a descriptive synthesis of the L1/English acquisition literature, a set of seven age-related developmental stages is suggested. At each stage, the profile gives the most commonly used structures. Thus, LARSP is not just a descriptive framework for analysing disordered language, but, more importantly, the procedure provides a way of identifying the developmental level of language acquisition an individual patient has achieved.

Finally, linguistic profiles may be characterized as "interactional". The assessment is based on a sample of spontaneous speech gathered in an unstructured conversation, using whatever stimuli are likely to facilitate the interaction (cf. Crystal, 1982:14). Then, a sample of approximately 30 minutes duration has to be transcribed "in order to check the validity of

one's findings, and to suggest explanations of curious patterns" (p.10). All
the utterances found in an individual patient's sample are transferred onto
the profile chart. Apart from the grammatical structures, the profiles also
contain categories for analysing certain aspects of the interactional setting
in which the conversation has taken place. For example, a distinction is
made between the patient's spontaneous and reactive utterances, the
therapist's utterances are classified as to whether they are questions or not,
the type of the patient's responses is analysed, and so on. This part of the
profile is meant to identify salient characteristics of an individual patient's
interactional strategies.

Coming back to L2 assessment, I would advocate development of an
L2 assessment procedure within the profiling approach. This proposal is
motivated by the fact that the criteria I used to evaluate L2 assessment
procedures are fulfilled in linguistic profiles: (i) profiles focus on a patient's
oral language production (=A); (ii) the data base consists of a sample of
spontaneous speech (=B); (iii) profiles provide for an exhaustive linguistic
description of a patient's language (=C); (iv) profiles are primarily
concerned with syntax and morphology (=D); (v) profiles include a
developmental grading device (=E). Adapting the profiling approach to
L2 assessment, however, requires some preparatory work. It is not
possible simply to translate the profile chart, since (i) most of its categories
are specific to the grammar of English and (ii) the developmental stages of
the LARSP chart are meant to describe the way monolingual English-
speaking children acquire their knowledge of grammar. Thus, what is
particularly needed before we can try to establish a profile chart of German
L2 achievement is a generalized developmental sequence of the acquisition
of German as a second language. In the next section, some of the results of
recent research on German L2 acquisition by migrant workers will be
summarized. These results suggest that the development of certain syntactic structures of German can be described in terms of a strictly ordered
developmental sequence. This sequence may be used as the empirical basis
for establishing a profile chart of German L2 achievement.

Some results with regard to German L2 development

In spite of the relevance of individual differences, it is now generally
acknowledged that children pass through an ordered set of developmental
stages on their way to acquiring their native language (cf. Brown, 1973).
Such sequences have been a necessary prerequisite to establishing profile
charts such as LARSP. Recent research on L2 development has shown that

there are developmental sequences in natural L2 acquisition as well (cf. Wode, 1981; Felix, 1982; Clahsen et al., 1983). Some examples of sequences in L2 development will be mentioned below. It must be emphasized, however, that L2 acquisition should not be seen as a linear process in which each systematic difference between two learners may be interpreted as a developmental stage in the direction of the target variety. Rather, different groups of learners may follow different paths on their way to acquiring the target variety. On the other hand, such differences, i.e. inter-subject variations, do not conflict with the possibility of describing L2 acquisition in terms of a developmental sequence. Thus, L2 development should be regarded as a bidimensional process consisting of acquisitional sequences *and* patterns of inter-subject variation within each stage of the sequences.

As mentioned before, profile charts only include the invariant aspects of the acquisition process, i.e. those linguistic features representing developmental stages. Thus, establishing a profile chart of L2 acquisition requires a method of identifying those features which are not affected by inter-subject variation. In recent L2 acquisition research, the method of implicational scaling has been used as a criterion for determining developmental stages (cf. Hyltenstam, 1977; Meisel et al., 1981). Thus, only those developmental sequences which have been justified by the implicational criterion will be included in the profile chart. In addition, language acquisition researchers generally call for longitudinal studies as the data base best offering convincing evidence of developmental sequences. Thus, only those stages which have been verified in a longitudinal study should be included in a profile chart of L2 development.

As far as the acquisition of German as L2 is concerned, it has been shown that word-order phenomena are especially qualified for establishing developmental sequences. The most detailed work on German L2 word order development has been done in the ZISA projects (cf. Clahsen et al., 1983, Clahsen et al., in prep.). The ZISA projects ("Zweitspracherwerb *i*talienischer, *s*panischer und portugiesischer *A*rbeiter") gathered natural language data in its combined cross-sectional and longitudinal study of the acquisition of German as a second language by Italian, Spanish, and Portuguese migrant workers.[1] The cross-sectional data consists mainly of informal interviews and unstructured conversations with 45 adult learners from age 15 to age 65. In the longitudinal study, the linguistic development of 12 adult learners is being investigated over a period of approximately two years starting as soon as possible after their arrival in Germany. One of the major results of these studies was a general developmental sequence of German L2 word-order acquisition. Without consideration of several details, the sequence regarding verb placement can be described as follows:

(i) None of the standard word-order rules is applied, and the linear order of constituents is: NP (AUX/MOD) V (NP) (PP)

(1) ich *ankomme* hier an Wuppertal.[2]

"I arrive here in W."

(ii) Learners use a rule which has the effect of moving non-finite parts of verbal elements to sentence-final position (PARTICLE).

(2) mit mein bruder ich *habe* sieben monat *gewohnt.*

"with my brother I have seven months stayed."

(iii) (Subject-Verb)–INVERSION is applied.

(3) in die große schule *kann man* englisch lerne.

"in the big school can one English learn."

(iv) A rule is used which only applies in embedded clauses and moves the finite verb into final position (V END).

(4) aber früher habe ich viel gesäuft, wie ich meine
sorgen *gehabt habe.*

"but earlier have I much drinked, as I my sorrows
have had".

Each of these word-order rules marks just one developmental stage. Note from the examples that the learner belonging to a stage x_i defined by a rule r_i also applies all of the rules r_{i-1}, $r_{i}-2$, ..., r_{i-n} characterizing the previous stages and does not use any of the rules r_{i+1}, r_{i+2}, ..., r_{i+m} which would define the subsequent stages. This is what we mean by the implicational criterion when trying to define an ordered developmental sequence. Since other cross-sectional as well as longitudinal studies on the acquisition of German word order [3] confirm these stages, it might be concluded that the sequence represents the way in which German verb-placement rules are acquired, at least by learners with a Romance-language background.

Consider as a second example of a developmental sequence the placement of adverbial phrases. According to the results of the ZISA studies, two developmental stages must be distinguished:

(i) Adverbial phrases, i.e. adverbs and prepositional phrases, are moved into sentence-initial position (ADV PREP):

(5) un *einmal* die war in garderobe

"and once she was in the closet"

(ii) Adverbial phrases are placed between the finite verb and the object (ADV VP):

(6) die bringen *jedes jahr* ein wunderbares zeugnis

"they bring every year a wonderful report card"

The longitudinal study has shown that ADV PREP is used quite early, whereas sentence-internal placement of adverbial phrases is only acquired at comparatively advanced stages. In addition to that, it has been demonstrated (cf. Clahsen, 1980) that all the learners who apply ADV VP also have ADV PREP, whereas learners who apply ADV PREP need not necessarily also use ADV VP, thus suggesting that the implicational criterion also holds for the development of adverbial placement rules.

Finally, let us consider the acquisition of negation. The results of the ZISA studies focus on the placement of the negator in relation to the verb. Essentially, the development sequence suggested in the ZISA study may be summarized as follows (cf. Clahsen, 1981):

Stage I: variable NEG placement
The learners use a rule which moves the negator to a position adjacent to the verb; in most cases, preverbal NEG placement is preferred.
(7) warum *nich* sprechen die zwei?
    "why not speak the two?"
    (= Why don't the two of them talk to each other?)
(8) *nich* gehen in schule
    "not go to school"
    (= [She] doesn't go to school.)

Stage II: postverbal placement
The rule of (I) is constrained to the extent that NEG is placed only postverbally. This also applies to structural contexts where Standard German requires separation of the negator from the verb.
(9) ich weiß *nich* die andere seite
    "I know not the other side"
    (= I don't understand the rest of the page.)
(10) ich kenne *nich* die welt
    "I know not the world"
    (= I don't know the world at all.)

Stage III: separation of NEG
The learners acquire a rule which has the effect of separating the negator from the finite verb in main clauses.

(11) sie kennen sie sowieso *nich*
    "you know it anyway not"
    (= Anyway, you don't know it (= the name of my hometown),
(12) wenn ich a eine andere fabrik gehen dann geben mir diese geld *nicht*
    "If I to another factory go then give me this money not"
    (= If I go to another factory, I won't get as much money.)

This sequence is supported in studies of the acquisition of German by learners with English as L1 (cf. Felix, 1982), thus suggesting that we have not merely discovered coincidences but that the sequence reflects general properties of the acquisition process.

Developmental sequences such as the three examples mentioned above should now be entered into a profile chart of German L2 acquisition. The problem we are confronted with, however, is that the suggested sequences are separated from each other. As mentioned above, a profile chart consists of general stages referring to different aspects of grammar. Thus, what is needed is an attempt at relating the different developmental sequences to one another, in order to arrive at just one generalized sequence.

In a recent paper, I tried to establish such a sequence on the basis of the ZISA studies (Clahsen, 1984). The comparison of the various sequences has shown, for example, that the adverb preposing rule (ADV PREP) is used very early, before the learners have acquired any other German word-order rule. At that time, the dominant verb-position pattern is SVO. This also holds for the initial stage of the negation sequence: As long as the learners have not acquired any of the verb-placement rules, the negator always appears next to the verb, in most cases in preverbal position. As far as clause-internal placement of adverbial phrases (ADV VP) is concerned, it has been demonstrated that the frequencies of application for this rule change in a similar manner to the applications of Subject-Verb Inversion, i.e. approximately at the same time. Thus, we might hypothesize that the acquisition of both rules might be the result of a single language-learning process. Finally, it has been shown that the separation of the negator from the finite verb is acquired simultaneously with Inversion and ADV VP. From these results we may conclude that the development of verb and adverbial placement, as well as of negation may be described in terms of four general developmental phases:

	verb placement	adverbial placement	negation
I	SVO	ADV PREP	NEG next to Verb
II	PARTICLE		
III	INVERSION	ADV VP	NEG sep. from Verb
IV	V END		

Thus, what appeared to be separate sequences of L2 development can be reduced to just one in terms of general developmental phases. This result led me to suggest that development in L2 acquisition might be better defined in terms of a developing mastery of processing heuristics than in terms of arbitrary syntactic rules. This is to say that the use or the abandonment of certain language-processing strategies by the learner may result in the ability to produce a number of superficially different (syntactic) operations. For example, as soon as the learner is ready to separate underlying units such as verb-complement structures and separable verbal elements, several syntactic structures appear within a relatively short period of time. They did not appear previously, as they would have violated the principle not to separate underlying semantic units. Similar explanations also hold for the other developmental phases, thus suggesting that the whole sequence is explicable in terms of a developing mastery of language-processing strategies. Such generalized developmental sequences should provide the empirical basis for establishing profile charts of L2 achievement. As a first step toward this aim, I will present a preliminary profile of the acquisition of German in the next section.

A preliminary profile of German L2 development

The profile chart presented in the following is based on the empirical results of L2 acquisition research. It should be emphasized that the present version is only a preliminary one which cannot yet be used in practice. The chart (cf. Appendix) is meant merely as a first step towards developing an L2 assessment procedure within the profiling approach.

The basic idea of linguistic profiles is to analyse a corpus of one learner's spontaneous speech in order to reconstruct the linguistic rules of his/her interlanguage and in order to assess the developmental stage he/she has already reached. This is to say, methodologically, that all the learner's utterances have to be analysed in the chart, since each utterance may contribute information to the final assessment. Even the use of imitations, repetitions, and/or unintelligible utterances may be important in this regard. The upper part of the profile, i.e. sections A, B, and C, give a preliminary classification of such utterances. These sections of the chart provide a selective description of some pragmatic-conversational aspects of the learners' utterances including the use of imitations, repetitions, and the like. As these categories are language independent, sections A, B, and C are virtually the same as in the original LARSP and the Hebrew adaptation.

Section A

When the learner uses an utterance which cannot be understood because of outside noise and the like, it is not analysed in terms of its syntactic structure. Rather, it is simply registered in section A under UNINTELLIGIBLE . The same applies to utterances which have not been completed by the learner, for example, because of interruptions; these utterances are registered under INCOMPLETE . Finally, when an ambiguous utterance occurs and it is not possible to resolve its ambiguity on the basis of intonational cues and conversational context, then the utterance is registered under AMBIGUOUS . The utterances registered in section A are not further analysed in the chart.

Section B

At the present stage of the adaptation, section B (= RESPONSES) contains only an extract of the original LARSP profile chart. A distinction is made between

(i)	IMITATIONS	:	when the learner repeats an utterance or parts of an utterance that was made by the interviewer
(ii)	ELLIPTICAL	:	when the learner uses an incomplete utterance because of pragmatic-conversational reasons, for example, answering a question
(iii)	FULL	:	when the learner uses a complete sentence as a response to a question or a command of the interviewer
(v)	MINOR	:	simple responses such as "yes", "no", "mhm", etc.

The response types (i), (ii), and (iii) are further classified according to the number of constituents. A distinction is made between utterances consisting of one constituent (= "1"), two constituents (= "2"), and three or more constituents (= "3+"). Imitations and minor responses will not be further analysed on the chart; elliptical responses are further classified within the phrase-level analysis of the developmental chart, and with full responses a complete (phrase- and clause-level) analysis can be made.

Section C

This section is concerned with the description of the learners' spontaneous utterances. Provided that good sampling methods have been used, this section should be the main corpus for the grammatical analysis of the developmental chart. Firstly, all spontaneous sentences are classified under OTHER in section C. Then, utterances in which the learner repeats his/her immediately preceding utterance, or a part of it, are classified under

REPETITIONS . The number of constituents is also given, similarly to section B. In addition to that, section C contains two minor categories:

(i) STEREOTYPES : when the learner uses a formulaic routinely used sentence

(ii) SOCIAL : when the learner uses phrases for greeting, thanking, vocatives, and the like.

Only the utterances belonging to OTHER of section C are further analysed on the developmental chart; utterances belonging to REP, STEREO or SOC will not be considered for the grammatical analysis.

The developmental chart

The part of the chart which is located below the double black line focuses on the area of syntax, i.e. the combination of words and phrases into sentences. The analysis takes place at two levels:

(i) *Phrase-level*: refers to the internal structure of major constituents, such as noun phrases (NP), verb phrases (VP), and adverbial phrases (AP).

(ii) *Clause-level*: refers to the combination of major constituents such as subject (S), object (O), adverbials, and verbs to form sentences.

In addition, the sentence structures are further classified according to three main sentence types: STATEMENT, QUESTION, and NEGATION. There are three kinds of questions:

(i) *Information questions* begin with a "wh" pronoun (Q), require INVERSION of S and V and ask for specific information about location, place, time, etc.

(ii) *Yes/No questions* require INVERSION in Standard German and simply ask whether something is or is not the case.

(iii) *Indirect questions* have the form of subordinate clauses, i.e. they require clause-final placement of the finite verb in German, and may be further divided into *indirect yes/no questions* introduced by *ob* (= whether) and *indirect information questions* which are introduced by a "wh" pronoun.

With regard to the negatives, a distinction is made between (i) propositional and (ii) constituent negation. The first type of negation requires postverbal placement of the negator (NEG) in Standard German, at least in main clauses. Constituent negation, however, requires the negator to be placed immediately before the element which is negated. All the sentence structures will be analysed according to (i) the type and the number of complements and (ii) the order of elements in the learners' utterances. With regard to the complement structures, a distinction is made between clauses containing

    (i) two or more adverbials
    (ii) an object and one or more adverbials
    (iii) an indirect and a direct object.

The analysis of the complement structures has to be carried out irrespective of the order of elements in the sentence. The description of the word-order patterns has to be made as a second step of the analysis. The word-order categories will be explained below.

Each of the different phrase and clause structures have been assigned to the developmental phase in which they most typically emerge in natural L2 acquisition of German. Four phases in the acquisition of grammar are recognized, each characterized by the main grammatical structures which seem to be operating within it. The phases are defined in terms of the generalized developmental sequence (I–IV) already described (see pp.294–99).

Phase I: Phrase-level analysis

Research on L2 acquisition has shown that adult L2 learners do not pass through a stage characterized by the exclusive use of single-word utterances. Rather, these learners produce elementary sentence structures even at the beginning of the acquisitional career. In addition, it has been demonstrated that, with the exception of auxiliaries and modal verbs, the major constituents may already be used during the initial developmental phase:

1. Noun Phrases   NP
   A noun phrase may consist of a single noun $\boxed{N}$, e.g. *milch* (= milk), a pronoun $\boxed{Pron}$, or a whole phrase. "Pron" is further classified according to whether it is a personal pronoun $Pron^P$, e.g. *ich, du* (= I, you) or "other" pronoun $\boxed{Pron_O}$, e.g. demonstratives, interrogatives, and the like. Noun phrases may contain a determiner $\boxed{DN}$ such as an article, a possessive pronoun, or the like. Finally, noun phrases may consist of a noun and an adjective in attributive function $\boxed{Adj\ N}$, e.g. *schlechtes wetter* (= bad weather).
2. Adverbial Phrases   AP
   An adverbial phrase may consist of a single adverb $\boxed{Adv}$, e.g. *hier* (=

here) or a prepositional phrase $\boxed{\text{Prep NP}}$, e.g. *in diesem land* (= in this country). The NP included in the prepositional phrase has to be analysed separately with respect to the subcategories of noun phrases.

3. Verb Phrases   VP

A distinction is made between simple verbs $\boxed{\text{V}}$, e.g. *gehen* (= go), *essen* (= eat), copulas $\boxed{\text{Cop}}$, e.g. *Er* IST *ein Metzger* (= He is a butcher), verbal elements containing a prefix $\boxed{\text{V Ptcl}}$, e.g. *zurückkommen* (= come back), and adjectives in predicative function $\boxed{\text{Adj}}$, e.g. *Die aufgabe ist* SCHWIERIG (= The task is difficult). The use of some form of *haben* (= have) or *sein* (= be) together with a participle and the use of modal verbs with an infinitive is analysed in Phase II: $\boxed{\text{Aux}}$, $\boxed{\text{Mod}}$.

In addition to these major constituents, adult L2 learners can be seen to use coordinated and subordinated sentences quite early. From the results of the ZISA studies (cf. Clahsen *et al.*, 1983:150), it has been concluded that there is no developmental stage which is characterized by the sudden appearance of embedded sentences. On the contrary, some learners use embedded sentences even during the initial developmental phase. Clauses which are introduced by a coordinating or subordinating conjunction are analysed under $\boxed{\text{Conj}_\text{C}}$ and $\boxed{\text{Conj}_\text{S}}$ in Phase I of the profile chart.

Phase I: Clause-level analysis

The description of the sentence structures focuses on the order of elements in the learners' utterances. As already mentioned (see pp.294–99), the empirical results of L2 acquisition research suggest that learners with a Romance language as L1 prefer verb-second patterns during the initial developmental phase, i.e. all verbal elements, even those for which Standard German requires discontinuous word order, are placed in sentence-second position. The category "VP" used in the various sentence structures of Phase I is meant to indicate that the learners do not distinguish between the order of the different verbal elements. The use of verb-second patterns even holds for subordinate clauses where clause-final placement of finite verbal elements is required in Standard German. Thus, the order of elements in main and subordinate clauses may be analysed using the same set of sentence structures in Phase I.

As far as complement placement is concerned, adverbial phrases may appear in clause-initial position before the subject (cf. ADV PREP, pp.294-99). However, the rule of Subject-Verb Inversion, required in German after preposed complements, is not adhered to. Thus, during Phase I the following typical sentence structures may occur:

1. Subject-Verb Sentences
   This type of sentence includes a subject in addition to a verb. If the verb is intransitive, or if the object has been deleted, the sentence can be simply $\boxed{\text{SVP}}$ in form:

   (13)   ich versteh
          "I understand"

   If the utterance contains an object and/or at least one adverbial phrase (in addition to a subject and a verbal element), it will be analysed under $\boxed{\text{S VP X (AP)}}$

   (14)   wir haben keine schwierigkeiten
          "we have no problems"
   (15)   ich war hier auch zwei jahre in die schule
          "I was here also two years in school"

   If one of the complements has been preposed to clause-initial position, the sentence has the form *X S VP (Y)*

   (16)   vielleich ich bleiben hier
          "perhaps I stay here"

2. "Verbless" Sentences
   These sentences do not contain a verbal element; the subject, however, is present. Again, utterances with preposed complements should be distinguished from the neutral order of elements, in which the subject appears in clause-initial position:

   (17)   wir keine lokal spanier $\boxed{\text{S X (Y)}}$
          "we no pub Spanish"
          (= We don't have a Spanish pub.)

   (18)   dann wir keine Probleme $\boxed{\text{X S (Y)}}$
          "then we no problems"
          (= Then we don't have any problems.)

3. "Subjectless" Sentences
   These sentences do not contain an NP functioning as the subject; a verbal element, however, is present:

   (19)   un nachher en paar worte lernen $\boxed{\text{(X) Y VP}}$
          "and then a few words learn"
          (= And then, I learned a few words.)

   (20)   elf jahre bezahle in weizen $\boxed{\text{X VP Y}}$

"eleven years pay in wheat"
(= Eleven years ago, they paid in wheat.)

(21)   arbeiten im fabrik sechs monate   VP X (AP)
"work in the factory six months"
(= I've been working in the factory for six months.)

4. Sentences without Subject and Verb
Sentences in which the subject and the verb phrase have been deleted
are analysed under (X) Y Z

(22)   kontakt con deutsch so en AOK jetz
"contact with German in AOK now"
(= Now, I have some contacts with Germans in the AOK.)
(The AOK is a German health insurance company)

5. Questions
During the initial developmental phase, the learners do not apply the
inversion rule in interrogatives. Questions are either marked by "wh"
pronouns or by intonational cues (cf. Clahsen *et al.*, 1983:115–18). In
addition, it has been found that "wh" pronouns are always placed in
clause-initial positions. Thus, we may distinguish two types of questions
in Phase I:

(23)   warum du nix zu sag?   Q X Y (Z)
"why you not to say"
(= Why don't you say anything to that?)

(24)   deine mutter deine vater nix arbeit   X Y (Z)
"your mother your father not work"
(= Don't your mother and your father work?)

6. Negation
As mentioned earlier (cf. pp.294–99), the learners tend to prefer
preverbal negation, even in those cases where postverbal NEG placement is required in German:

(25)   und das *nich* verstehn   (X) NEG VP (Y)
"and this not understand"
(= And that, I don't understand it.)

Contrary to such utterances, which are deviant in terms of German
syntax, NEG is placed in the correct position in cases of constituent
negation:

(26)   dann wir *keine* probleme (cf. 18)   (X) NEG NP (Y)

(27)   vielleich denken von mir *nich* gut   (X) NEG AP (Y)

"perhaps think of me not well"
(= Perhaps they don't have a good idea of me.)

(28) Wuppertal *nis* schön $\boxed{\text{(X) NEG Adj (Y)}}$
      "W. not nice"

As a second step of the analysis, the negatives as well as the interrogatives of Phase I have to be analysed again as if they were affirmative declarative sentences (cf. p.304 (1.) to (4.)).

Phase II

Research on natural L2 acquisition has shown that the types and number of complements are systematically extended as the learners proceed on their way to acquiring the target variety (cf. Clahsen *et al.*, 1983:102–14). It has been demonstrated, for example, that the learners use more and more adverbial phrases as soon as they enter the second developmental phase. In the profile chart, we will focus on the following main types of complement structures (recall that this part of the analysis is carried out irrespective of the order of elements in the sentence):

1. Two complements
   (29) arbeiten in fabrik sechs monate $\boxed{\text{VP AP AP}}$
         (cf. example 21)
   (30) un nachher ein paar worte lesen $\boxed{\text{VP O AP}}$
         (cf. example 19)

2. Three complements
   (31) jetzt zwei jahre mache schon $\boxed{\text{VP AP AP AP}}$
         "now two years make already"
         (=Now I've been doing this job for two years already.)

   (32) vielleicht denken von mir nich $\boxed{\text{VP O AP AP}}$
         gut (cf. example 27)

The main criterion, however, for establishing the second developmental phase comes from the area of word order. The learners can now be seen to separate correctly the non-finite elements of complex verb phrases from their finite parts. The following cases will be distinguished:

   (33) ich *habe* einen vertrag über die
         firma *gekricht* $\boxed{\text{(X) Aux Y Part}}$
         "I have a contract by the company got"
         (= I got a contract through my employer.)

(34) *wollt* is damals *heiraten* (X) Mod Y Inf
      "wanted I at that time marry"
      (= I wanted to marry at that time.)

(35) *fängt* der auch noch mit der wirt *an* $(X)\ V_f\ Y$ Ptcl
      "starts he also with the innkeeper on"
      (= He even starts making trouble with the employer.)

(36) die fabrik *ist* für mich nich *schwer* (X) Cop Y Adj
      "the factory is for me not difficult"
      (= Working in the factory is no problem for me.)

In these cases, both finite and non-finite parts of the complex verbal elements have been produced by the learners. In addition to such examples, there are a considerable number of utterances in which the finite verb has been deleted and the non-finite verbal element appears in clause-final position, e.g.

(37) und dann ich immer alleine hier *gewesen* $(X)\ (S)\ Y\ V_i$
      "and then I always alone here been"
      (= And then I was always alone here.)

Such examples do not belong to Phase I because of the correct final placement of the participle: all verbal elements appear in sentence-second position during Phase I.

Simultaneously with PARTICLE, i.e. the rule of separating non-finite verbal elements, the learners acquire a preliminary version of the rule of Subject-Verb INVERSION. This rule has been described in detail in Clahsen (1981). It has the effect of extraposing the subject to clause-final position after preposed complements and in interrogatives:

(38) jetzt hat mir gesagt *das lehrerin* $(X)\ V_f\ Y\ (V_i)\ S$
      "now has me told the teacher"
      (= Now the teacher has told me.)

(39) maken die foto *du* ↑   Question
      "make the picture you" $(X)\ V_f\ Y\ (V_i)\ S$
      (= Did you take the picture?)

Similarly to Phase I, the learners do not use any specific word-order patterns for subordinate clauses during the second phase. Thus, the same set of sentence structures may be used to describe the order of elements in main and in subordinate clauses.

As far as negation is concerned, the learners can now be seen to more frequently replace the preverbal patterns of Phase I with postverbal negation. However, the negator still appears adjacent to the finite verb, even in those cases where Standard German requires separating NEG from the verb, e.g.

(40) ich kenne *nich* die welt $\boxed{\text{(X) V}_f \text{ NEG (Y)}}$
      (cf. example 10)

In addition to such examples, there are cases in which complex verbal elements have been negated. It has been shown in various publications (cf. Meisel, 1983; Clahsen *et al.*, 1983: 124 f.) that NEG is correctly placed immediately before the non-finite parts of complex verbal elements as soon as complex verbs are used, e.g.

(41) dann kann das *nich* verstehn $\boxed{\text{(X) (Mod) Y NEG Inf}}$
      "then can that not understand"

(42) aber damals habe ich noch *nich* gehört $\boxed{\text{(X) (Aux) Y NEG Part}}$
      "but at that time have I yet not heard"
      (= But at that time, I had not yet heard about it.)

Phase III

The third developmental phase is characterized by the acquisition of three rules of German syntax: (i) Inversion of subject and verb, (ii) ADV VP, i.e. placement of adverbial phrases between the finite verb and the object, and (iii) separation of NEG from the finite verb. As far as (i) is concerned, a distinction is made between the following structural contexts:

1. after preposed adverbial phrases
   (43) hier *wohnen* ich $\boxed{\text{AP V}_f \text{ S (X)}}$
         "here live I"

2. after topicalized objects
   (44) dialetten *haben wir* nix in Portugal $\boxed{\text{O V}_f \text{ S (X)}}$
         "dialects have we not in P."

3. after topicalized embedded clauses
   (45) was meine schwester und meine schwager $\boxed{\text{CL V}_f \text{ S (X)}}$
         hast gemacht in polizei. *hast Frau*
         Narciso auch gemacht
         "what my sister and my brother-in-law have done in
         police have Mrs. Narciso also done"
         (= First my sister and my brother-in-law and now

Mrs. N. have made arrangements with the police
[to get a residence permit for me].)

4. in "wh" questions
    (46) wieviel *kostet alles?* $\boxed{\text{Q } V_f \text{ S (X)}}$
          "how much costs everything"
          (= How much is that all together?)
5. in yes/no questions
    (47) fliegen sie ↑ $\boxed{V_f \text{ S (X)}}$
          "fly you"
          (= Are you going to fly?)

In regard to ADV VP, the following distinction is made:

1. Prepositional phrases between verb and object

    (48) ich habe *in die ganz papier* $\boxed{\text{(X) } V_f \text{ PP O (Y)}}$
          fünf november
          "I have in all papers five november"
          (= [The date of birth recorded] in all my papers is the
          fifth of november.)
2. Adverbs between verb and object
    (49) hab *hier* keine eltern $\boxed{\text{(X) } V_f \text{ Adv O (Y)}}$
          "have here no parents"
          (= [My friend's] parents aren't here.)

Again, as in the previous phases, we can use the same set of sentence
structures for main and subordinate clauses, given the fact that the learners
do not produce word-order patterns specific to subordinate clauses.

With regard to negation, the learners can now be seen to separate the
negator from the finite verb, thus having acquired the Standard German
rule for NEG placement in main clauses:

(50) dies ton gefiel mir *nich* $\boxed{\text{(X) } V_f \text{ Y NEG (Z)}}$
     "this tone pleased me not"
     (= I didn't like their tone [of voice].)

Phase IV

The last phase of the suggested developmental sequence is characterized by the acquisition of a rule which has the effect of placing the finite
verb in clause-final position in embedded sentences. In addition, the
learners produce sentence structures containing two object phrases: an
indirect and a direct object. With regard to such sentences, the following
distinctions are made:

1. Two complements

    (51)   Herr Stader sacht ich zu ihm $\boxed{\text{VP O}_i \text{ O}_d}$
          "Mr. S. said I to him"
          (= I called him Mr. S.)

2. Three complements

    (52)   kann sie mir mal ein arzt empfehlen $\boxed{\text{VP O}_i \text{ O}_d \text{ AP}}$
          "can you me just a doctor recommend"
          (= Can you just recommend me a doctor?)

    As far as verb placement in subordinate clauses is concerned, we will distinguish between the following types of embedded clauses:

1. Adverbial clauses
These clauses tell about time, reason, place, or manner in which an event or an action took place; they are introduced by a subordinating conjunction, e.g.
    (53)   wenn jetzt die papiere *kommen* $\boxed{\text{Conj}_S \text{ X V}_f}$
          ich muß in die berufsschule gehen
          "when now the papers come I must to the technical school go"
          (= If the papers arrive I will have to go to tech. school.)

2. Relative clauses
These clauses modify a preceding noun phrase. They are introduced by a relative pronoun, such as *der*, *die* (= who), *das* (=which), etc., e.g.

    (54)   hier in Cronenberg gibts ein $\boxed{\text{Relpron X V}_f}$
          deutsches frau die gut italienisch
          sprechen *kann*
          "Here in C. is there a German woman who well Italian speak can"
          (=... who speaks It. well.)

3. Complement clauses
These clauses function as the object of the matrix verb. One type of complement clause is introduced by the conjunction *daß* (=that); the second type, which is sometimes called the "infinitive clause", is not introduced by a subordinating conjunction. In both types, however, clause-final placement of the verb is required, e.g.

    (55)   hat noch nix gemerkt daß ich mit $\boxed{\text{daß X V}_f}$
          ne Rockefeller zu tun *hab*
          "has not yet realized that I with a R. to do have"
          (= [I] have not yet realized that I'm dealing with a rich man.)

(56) un is für mich etwas leichter   ☐ X V ☐
      gewesen eine arbeit zu *finden*
      "and is for me a bit easier been a work to find"
      (= And it has been a bit easier for me to find a job.)

4. Indirect questions
   Indirect questions may be regarded as a specific type of complement
   clause. However, as in the previous phases, questions will be separately
   analysed on the present profile chart. We distinguish between indirect
   "wh" and indirect yes/no questions.

   (57) ich weiß nich was jetz besser *wäre*   ☐ Q X V$_f$ ☐
         "I know not what now better would be"
         (= I don't know what would be better [to do] now.)
   (58) ich wisse nich ob ich hier pensioniert werde   ☐ ob X V$_f$ ☐
         "I know not whether I here retired will be"
         (= I don't know whether I'll retire here.)

   As far as negation is concerned, the learners correctly place the
negator before the finite verb in subordinate clauses. Recall that during the
previous developmental phases no distinction was made between the
domain of application of the acquired rules, i.e. all the syntactic rules are
applied in main as well as in subordinate clauses. This regularity also holds
for negation. In Phase IV, however, the learners make a distinction
between the placement of NEG in main and in subordinate clauses. In the
latter, NEG appears before the finite verbal element:

(59) wenn jetzt eine erste mal *nit* begreifen   ☐ X NEG V$_f$ ☐
      "if now one first time not comprehend"
      (= Now, if one [of my children] doesn't understand the first time
      [what the teacher says] ....)

   The present profile chart may now be used to analyse a sample of one
learner's spontaneous speech. As a result of such an analysis we would be
able to (i) assess the developmental level which the learner has reached. In
addition, we would be able to (ii) identify certain linguistic problems of an
individual learner with those aspects which are recognized in the profile
chart. Finally, the procedure provides a description of an individual
interlanguage which enables the analyst to (iii) reconstruct the syntactic
rules an L2 learner is using. There are, however, two major problems with
the present version of the chart. The first concerns the fact that the chart
does not provide for a *complete* analysis of all the aspects of German
grammar. Contrary to the original LARSP and the Hebrew adaptation

HARSP, the present chart does not, for example, include a word-level analysis dealing with morphological endings such as number and case affixes. This limitation simply stems from the fact that the L2 development of morphology has not yet been sufficiently investigated for a reasonably detailed developmental sequence to have emerged. But once such empirical results are available, it should be possible to integrate a word-level analysis into the present chart. The profile chart described above may thus be regarded as a preliminary descriptive framework which has to be worked out in more detail as soon as more empirical results on German L2 development are available.

A second limitation of the present chart concerns the data base which has been used to establish the suggested developmental sequence. It has already been mentioned that the chart is based only on research studies dealing with adult learners with a Romance-language background. Thus, in order to establish a *general* L2 assessment procedure within the profiling approach, it is necessary to compare the suggested developmental sequence with the acquisition of German by learners from a different language background.

Such a comparative study has been carried out in Clahsen & Muysken (1983). Learners from a Romance-language background were compared with Turkish learners with regard to the initial developmental phase of their acquisition of German word order. The main result of the comparison is that even the Turkish learners prefer verb-second patterns during the initial phase, despite the fact that Turkish is an SOV language and is thus typologically different from the Romance languages. In addition, it has been demonstrated that the dominant use of verb-second patterns also applies to subordinate clauses in spite of the fact that verb-final placement is suggested by the target language and the Turkish learners' L1. From these observations it might be hypothesized that L2 learners, probably irrespective of their first-language background, tend to assume that German has an SVO word-order system, thus suggesting that at least the first developmental phase of the profile chart may be regarded as representing the general starting point of German L2 word-order acquisition.

As far as the subsequent developmental phases are concerned, it will be necessary to eventually refine the chart on the basis of a much wider range of data before it can be used as a general L2 assessment procedure. Currently, however, we do not have such data at our disposal. Thus, the domain of application of the present chart is restricted to Romance learners, i.e. we will assume, until evidence to the contrary has been presented, that the present profile chart correctly describes what happens in the process of the acquisition of German syntax by adult learners with a Romance language as L1.

Applying the profile chart: an example

In the following, I will analyse two transcripts from the ZISA longitudinal study. This analysis is intended to illustrate the use of the suggested profile chart as an L2 assessment procedure. I chose transcripts from *Giovanni* because a grammatical description of this learner's acquisition of word order, which is based on large parts of the whole period of observation, has already been published (Clahsen, 1982). Thus, it is possible to compare the grammatical analysis with the results of the profile chart in order to ascertain whether the chart provides a reliable description of Giovanni's L2 proficiency.

Giovanni

He was born in June, 1955, in a village close to Catania, Sicily. After elementary school and high school, he studied medicine for two years in Sicily. Then, after breaking off his studies, he followed his parents to Wuppertal in 1978, where he started to work as a grinder. His parents had forced him to earn money and to immigrate to Germany. G is still living together with his family in a small flat which is located in the immigrants' ghetto of Wuppertal. G does not have any private contacts with German colleagues or friends. He occasionally attended language classes, but very soon after his arrival in Germany he gave them up, because he felt that these classes were not helping him to learn German.

The first transcript (T1) which has been chosen for the profile analysis represents the initial period of G's L2 development. In T1, he had been in Germany for seven weeks. The second corpus (T2) is taken from an interview which was made approximately one year after T1: in T2, G had been in Germany for 63 weeks. The two transcripts are based on recordings of unstructured conversations between G and two German interviewers. One of the interviewers spoke only German, the other had a rudimentary knowledge of Italian. The first recording was made at G's home and the second at the home of one of the interviewers, where G had been invited to have tea with the interviewer's family. During the period of observation, a very friendly relationship developed between G and the two German interviewers. In both recordings, the topics of conversation developed quite naturally and dealt with the immigrants' situation in

Germany and in their home countries. Each recording lasted for about 60 minutes. After the recording sessions, transcripts were made, consisting of 110 consecutive utterances for T1 and 107 for T2. These transcripts, which were double-checked, provide the data base for the subsequent profile analysis.

The profile charts for T1 and T2 are shown in the Appendix. Let us first look at the upper part of the profiles. Section A shows that nearly 10% of the utterances of T1 cannot be further analysed on the chart, because they are unintelligible, incomplete, or ambiguous. In T2, however, there are only very few examples of unanalysable utterances. Consider the following example from T1, which was analysed as an incomplete utterance because G was interrupted by one of the interviewers:

(60) un tisch. ich
        I: was machst du in der fabrik?
     'an table I.
        I: what are you making in the factory?"

With regard to the major utterance types, sections B and C do not demonstrate significant differences between T1 and T2, and, in particular, the frequency of spontaneous utterances in relation to responses is approximately the same in T1 and T2. From this observation, we may conclude that there are no dramatic changes from T1 to T2 as far as those interactional aspects recognized in the profile chart are concerned.

As already mentioned, the utterance types recognized in sections B and C are also classified according to the number of constituents. With regard to this aspect, i.e. utterance length, the profiles display certain differences between T1 and T2. Whereas spontaneous utterances consisting of two constituents are dominant in T1, the profile of T2 shows some increase of three-constituent and a decrease of one-and two-constituent utterances. On the whole, the utterances of T2 are longer than those of T1. As I will attempt to demonstrate in the subsequent description, the increase in utterance length is the result of certain acquisition processes between T1 and T2.

Let us now consider the phrase-level analysis. The profile of T1 shows that G has at his disposal all the word classes recognized in the chart with the exception of complex verbal elements (cf. Cop, V Ptcl, Aux, and Mod). These verbal elements, which consist of a finite and a non-finite part, have been acquired in T2 (cf. the second profile). The following examples are taken from the second recording:

(61)   ich *bin* falsch
       "I am wrong"

(62)   *muß* Chiasso bleiben ungefähr fünfzehn minute
       "must Ch. stay approximately 15 minutes"
       (= You have to stay in Ch. for about 15 minutes.)

Thus we may conclude from the phrase-level analysis of T2 that G has reached Phase II of the proposed developmental sequence, whereas the phrase structures of T1 correspond to the characteristics of Phase I.

The frequencies shown in the phrase-level analysis display G's preference for the use of certain word classes. With regard to *noun phrases*, for example, the profiles of T1 and T2 demonstrate G's preference for "nominal reference". This is to say that approximately 80% of the NP's are nominals, whereas only about 20% are pronouns. The predominantly used *adverbial phrase* in T2 is the adverb, whereas in T1 there is no marked preference for either prepositional phrases or adverbs. As already mentioned, the *verb phrases* in T1 consist only of simple verbs (V) or predicative adjectives. In T2, "expanded" verb phrases consisting of finite and non-finite parts are used (cf. examples 61, 62).

With regard to *connectivity*, i.e. the linking of phrases and clauses to one another, it can be seen from the profile of T1 that G is already using co-ordination as well as subordination in the first recording. The co-ordinating conjunctions used in T1 are *und* (=and), *oder* (=or), and *aber* (=but). The same set of conjunctions is also produced in T2. Consider the following examples from T1:

(63)   bus *oder* zug
       "bus or train"

(64)   *aber* meine stadt
       "but my town"
       (= But there is a theatre in my hometown. (After a negative answer to the question whether he had ever been to the theatre.))
(65)   *un* mein vater
       "and my father"
       (= My father is also working.)

Thus, there appear to be no significant differences in the use of coordinating conjunctions between the earlier and the later sample. As far as subordination is concerned, however, the profiles demonstrate certain differences between T1 and T2. In T1, subordinating conjunctions have been deleted in most cases; there is only one example of an embedded clause introduced by a conjunction:

(66) *warum* arbeit funf person
"why work five person"
(=... because five persons are at work. (Note that Standard German
requires *weil* (=because) instead of *warum* (=why) in this sentence.
But *perchè* (Italian) = why, because))

In contrast to T1, most of G's embedded sentences in T2 contain a
subordinating conjunction; in most cases *wenn* (= if, when) is used, e.g.

(67) *wenn* mit zug in Italien
"when by train to Italy"
(= When you go by train to Italy,...)

We will now turn to the analysis of sentence structures. Consider first
the use of *complement structures*. The profile of T1 shows that nearly all of
the sentences contain only one complement. G uses only 6 expanded
structures containing either two adverbial phrases ("VP AP AP") or an
object and one adverbial phrase ("VP O AP"). In other words, only 12%
of the sentences of T1 consist of expanded complement structures, e.g.

(68) aber in Deutschland besser arbeite
"but in Germany better work"
(= It is better to work in Germany.)

(69) ich sprechen deutsch allein hier
"I speak German only here"

In T2, the relative frequency of such complement structures is twice
that in T1. There are, however, no examples of sentences containing two
objects. Such complement structures have been said to be typical of the
final developmental phase. Thus, we may conclude from the complement-
structure analysis that the sentences of T2 display the characteristics of the
second developmental phase, whereas most of the sentences of T1 are
typical of Phase I.

The next part of the analysis is directed towards certain *deletion*
phenomena. In addition to the description of word order, the sentence
structures of the profile chart also allow us to analyse missing elements at
the clause level. The profile of T1 shows, for example, that the VP has
been deleted in 24 cases (cf. S X (Y), X S (Y), (X) Y Z). That is to say,
about 50% of all the sentence structures do not contain a VP. Consider the
following examples from T1:

(70) meine stadt Catania
"my town C."
(= The town I come from is called C.)

(71) aber ausländer nee gut
"but foreigners not good"
(= I don't like the tourists.)

In T2, the frequency of VP deletion is significantly smaller; in only 13 cases, the complete VP is missing, i.e. VP deletion has decreased to approximately 25%.

The profiles also show that the deletion of major constituents (VP and subject) may depend on structural features of the sentences. The crucial feature affecting the deletion of these constituents is the position of complements. The profiles demonstrate that, if complements have been preposed to clause-initial position, major constituents will be favoured for deletion. Note that in such cases, i.e. after preposed complements, Inversion of subject and verb is required in Standard German. Recent research on L2 acquisition suggests that this rule is difficult to acquire, and that the learners develop certain simplification strategies in order to avoid having to apply the rule (cf. Pienemann, 1981; Meisel *et al.*, 1981). One of these strategies is the deletion of the major constituents which are affected by Inversion. Consider the following examples:

(72) in mein haus Sizilien meine oma meine mutter (T1)
"in my house Sicily my grandma my mother"
(= My grandmother and my mother lived together with me in S.)

(73) nur eine jahr fahre in Deutschland mit führerschein italienisch (T2)
"only one year drive in Germany with driving licence Italian"
(= I can drive with the Italian driving licence in G. only for one year.)

In T1, there is no example in which the subject and the VP have been realised after preposed complements (cf. X S VP (Y)). In the sentences with initialized complements, either the VP (cf. X S (Y)) or the subject (cf. (X) Y VP) has been omitted. In T2, the picture that emerges from the profile is quite similar: there are only two examples with preposed complements in which both the subject and the VP are produced, but 17 utterances in which one of the major constituents has been deleted after preposed complements (cf. X S (Y), (X)Y VP, X VP Y). Thus, as far as these deletions are concerned, there seem to be no significant differences between T1 and T2.

We will now turn to the description of the *order of elements* in G's utterances. The most important part of the word-order analysis concerns the position of verbal elements. As can be seen from the profile of T1, there are no examples of discontinuous verb placement in the first sample, i.e. verbal elements are not separated. In addition, G does not make a distinction between the placement of verbal elements in main and in subordinate clauses. Finally, there are no cases of Subject-Verb Inversion after preposed complements or in interrogatives. Rather, the dominant word order is the verb-second pattern. Out of the 50 sentence structures of T1, there are only two utterances (cf. "Other") which cannot be unequivocally described as SVO or as being derived from SVO:

(74) ich allein essen
     "I alone eat"
     (= I'm eating by myself.)

(75) besser kollege deutsch
     "better colleague German"
     (= German colleagues are better.)

On the whole, then, we may conclude that verb placement in T1 is typical of the initial developmental phase suggested in the profile chart.

Most of the sentence structures of T2 can also be described in terms of the categories of Phase I. Even in T2, G does not distinguish between verb placement in main and in subordinate clauses:

(76) wenn ich *habe* eine führerschein italienisch
     "if I have a driving licence Italian"

(77) wenn *sehen* meine führerschein italienisch
     "if [they] see my driving licence Italian"

G similarly uses SVO patterns in subordinate clauses even though clause-final placement is required in Standard German. In addition, G does not apply Inversion in T2 apart from three interrogatives (cf. V_f S (X)) to which we will come back later. Thus there appear to be no significant differences between T1 and T2 with regard to (i) the dominant word-order pattern, (ii) the use of Inversion, and (iii) verb placement in subordinate clauses. Contrary to T1, however, we find some examples of discontinuous verb placement in T2, e.g.

(78) ich *habe* schon *gesagt*
     "I have already said"

(79) *hast* du schon *gemacht* ↑
   "have you already done"

On the other hand, there is some evidence for the claim that G has not yet fully acquired the rule of separating verbal elements. Rather, it seems to be the case that he is in the process of acquiring that rule. First, there are three examples in which the finite verbal part has been deleted after moving the non-finite part to clause-final position, e.g.

(80) sofort wasser rein
   "immediately water in"
   (= Then, you should immediately fill in water.)

The deletion of the finite verb in such cases may have the same function as the omission of major constituents after preposed complements, i.e. avoiding the application of complex syntactic rules such as discontinuous verb placement. Second, the rule of separating complex verbal elements has not been applied in all the relevant contexts, although this rule is obligatory in Standard German. The phrase-level analysis of the profile shows that G uses two verbal elements containing separable prefixes, six auxiliaries, one modal verb, and one Cop+Adj structure. In all these structural contexts, discontinuous verb placement is required in German. This rule, however, is only applied in three cases, as can be seen from the profile of T2. Third, there are two utterances in which discontinuous verb placement has not been applied correctly (cf. "Other"):

(81) muß Chiasso *bleiben* ungefähr fünfzehn minute
   (cf. example 62)

(82) hast du *gemacht* ein seminar ↑
   "have you made a seminar"

Note that German requires clause-final placement of *bleiben* and *gemacht* in these sentences. Obviously, G has only acquired a preliminary version of the rule of discontinuous verb placement, a rule which allows him to have just one constituent between the two verbal elements. Recall that there is only one constituent interrupting the verbal elements in those examples where discontinuous verb placement was applied (cf. 78, 79). From these observations we may conclude that G has now (i.e. in T2) reached the second developmental phase but that he has not yet fully acquired the Standard German rule of discontinuous verb placement, since for him only one constituent can be placed between the two verbal elements.

The second part of the word-order analysis is concerned with the *placement of complements*. As mentioned before, G is able to prepose complements even in T1 (cf. examples 68, 72, 73). There is only a quantitative difference between T1 and T2 with regard to the application of this rule: whereas only 8% of the sentence structures of T1 contain preposed complements, the relative frequency of such sentence structures is about 16% in T2. In addition, the profiles show that there is no example, neither in T1 nor in T2, in which an adverbial phrase has been placed between the finite verb and the object. Such sentence structures (cf. (X) V_f Adv O (Y), (X) V_f PP O (Y)) have been said to be typical of the more advanced developmental phases (= III). Thus, we may conclude that the position of complements in G's utterances displays the characteristics of the early developmental phase suggested in the sequence.

Finally, we will be concerned with the analysis of the *negatives* and the *interrogatives*. The profiles do not show any significant differences between T1 and T2 in G's use of negated utterances. In both recordings, G follows the semantically motivated strategy NEG+X according to which the negator is placed immediately before the constituent to be negated (cf. Meisel *et al.*, 1981). This strategy provides for the correct position of the negator with regard to constituent negation, e.g.

(83) aber unter *kein* metallröhre ↑
     "but under no metal tube"
     (= But is there a metal tube under the machine?)

(84) *kein* arbeit in Sizilien
     "no job in S."
     (= There are no jobs in S.)

The NEG+X strategy, however, does not provide for the correct placement of the negator as far as propositional negation is concerned. Contrary to Standard German, which requires postverbal placement, NEG appears immediately before the verb in these cases, e.g.:

(85) *nich* gucken theater jetzt
     "not look theatre now"
     (= I'm not going to the theatre now.)

(86) viel schallplatten *nich mehr* kaufen
     "many records no more buy"
     (= I don't buy many records any longer.)

Thus, the placement of the negator in G's utterances, in T1 and T2, is typical of the first developmental phase. The profile of T1 shows that G does not use any specific syntactic rules for interrogatives. Rather, he applies the rules of the declarative sentence to interrogatives as well. In particular, there is no interrogative in T1 in which the Inversion rule has been carried out. Thus, the questions of T1 display the characteristics of the first developmental phase. The fact that G only uses Yes/No questions in T1 might be attributed to the small number of interrogatives in the whole recording. In T2, most of the interrogatives are typical of Phase I as well, i.e. no distinction is made between the syntactic rules of declarative and interrogative sentences.

(87) aber wo finden diese gummi?
"but where find this rubber?"
(= But where do I find this rubber?)

There are, however, three cases in which Inversion of subject and verb has been applied:

(88) hast du schon gemacht ↑
(cf. example 79)

(89) hast du gemacht ein seminar ↑
(cf. example 82)

(90) hast du gemacht ↑
"have you made"

Given the fact that these utterances are completely identical as far as the verb forms and the subjects are concerned, it might be concluded that they are stereotypes, i.e. fixed formulaic expressions which cannot be said to be internally analysed.[4] In particular, such stereotypes do not allow one to conclude that G has already acquired the Inversion rule. Rather, it seems more appropriate to assume that there are no significant differences between T1 and T2 with regard to the syntactic rules of the interrogatives.

Summarizing the previous profile analyses, we may conclude that G's utterances of T1 correspond to the characteristics of the first developmental phase, whereas in T2 he has already begun acquiring certain parts of Phase II. In particular, the development of (i) discontinuous verb placement, (ii) expanded complement structures, and (iii) complex verbal elements is emerging in T2. The complete grammatical analysis of the whole period of observation led us to the same conclusion (cf. Clahsen *et al.*, in prep.; Clahsen, 1982), thus suggesting that the profile chart may provide for a reliable assessment of L2 learners' proficiency in German syntax. In addition, I hope to have shown that the profile chart enables the analyst to identify the linguistic problems Giovanni has with certain aspects of German syntax. Finally, it has been demonstrated that the profile chart allows the analyst to reconstruct an L2 learner's interlanguage. The next step would be to suggest explanations for the acquisitional strategies Giovanni is using. Among such explanations are strategies such as language transfer, overgeneralization, simplification, etc. This, however, requires another paper, given the fact that the search for theoretical explanations involves a wide range of socio-psychological and linguistic variables which it is the business of L2 acquisition research to explicate. In contrast, linguistic profiles are merely descriptive devices which attempt to provide the sufficiently detailed analysis necessary for empirically based explanations of L2 development.

Acknowledgements

A preliminary version of the present paper was presented at the "Institut für Deutsch als Fremdsprache" ("Department of German as a Foreign Language") at the University of Munich in October 1982. I want to thank Harald Weinrich and the other members of the department for their corrections and helpful remarks. I am also grateful to Jürgen Meisel, Harald Mispelkamp, Frank Müller, Howard Nicholas, Helmut Zobl and the editors of the present volume for comments on an earlier version of the paper, and to Constance Guhl for lending me her English language competence.

Notes to Chapter 12

1. During the period when the research on this paper was carried out, ZISA consisted of four researchers and myself. I want to thank Jürgen Meisel, Howard Nicholas, Klaus-Michael Köpcke and Maryse Vincent for the very interesting discussions and the pleasant time we have had. The ZISA group was supported by two research grants to Jürgen Meisel (principal investigator). 1977/78, the cross-sectional study was funded by the "Minister für Wissenschaft und Forschung des Landes Nordrhein-Westfalen". Part of the work on the cross-sectional study, as well as the longitudinal study were supported by a grant from the "Stiftung Volkswagenwerk", 1978–1982.

2. All the examples used in the present paper come from the learners studied in the ZISA research projects. The examples will be translated literally into English; the glosses are in inverted commas under the original utterance. Where necessary, a Standard English translation or additional information about the situational context is given.

3. A survey of the research studies on the acquisition of German word order is presented in Clahsen & Muysken (1983). In conclusion, it is suggested that certain parts of the proposed developmental sequence hold even for L2 learners from a different language background. We will return to this issue in pp.299–313 of this chapter.

4. If that description turns out to be correct, it is, of course, necessary to transfer the three sentences (88), (89), and (90) to the "Stereotypes" of section C.

References

Berman, R., Rom, A. & Hirsch, M. 1982, *Working with HARSP-Hebrew adaptation of the LARSP language assessment remediation and screening procedure*. Ms. University of Tel-Aviv.

Brown, R. 1973, *A first language: The early stages*. Cambridge, Mass.

Burt, M., Dulay, H. & Hernández-Chávez, E. 1975, *Bilingual Syntax Measure*. New York.

Clahsen, H. 1980, Psycholinguistic aspects of L2 acquisition: word-order phenomena in foreign workers' interlanguage. In S. Felix (ed.), *Second language development: trends and issues*, 57–79.

—— 1982, Autonomy and interaction in (second) language acquisition: evidence for an integrativist position. In C. Pfaff (ed.), *Cross Linguistic Studies of Language Acquisition Processes*.. Rowley, Mass.

—— 1984, The acquisition of German word order: A test case for cognitive approaches to second language acquisition. In R. Andersen (ed.), *Second Languages*. Rowley, Mass.

Clahsen, H., Köpcke, K.-M., Meisel, J. & Vincent, M. in preparation, *Sprachentwicklung in der zweiten Sprache*.

Clahsen, H., Meisel, J. & Pienemann, M. 1983, *Deutsch als Zweitsprache. Der Spracherwerb ausländischer Arbeiter*. Tübingen.

Clahsen, H. & Muysken, P. 1983, The accessibility of move alpha and the acquisition of German word order by children and by adults. Ms. Universities of Düsseldorf and Amsterdam.

Crystal, D. 1979, *Working with LARSP*. London.
—— 1982, *Profiling linguistic disability*. London.
Crystal, D. & Fletcher, P. 1979. Profile analysis of language disability. In Ch. Fillmore, J. Kempler & W. Wang (eds), *Individual differences in language ability and language behavior*. New York, pp.167–88
Crystal, D., Fletcher, P. and Garman, M. 1976. *The grammatical analysis of language disability*. London.
Dulay, H. & Burt, M. 1974, Natural sequences in child second language acquisition. *Language Learning*, 24, 37–53.
Felix, S. 1982, *Psycholinguistische Aspekte des Zweitsprachenerwerbs*. Tübingen.
Felix, S. & Simmet, A. 1981, Der Erwerb der Personalpronomina im Fremdsprachunterricht. *Neusprachliche Mitteilungen*, 3, 132–44.
Göbel, R. 1978, Zur Möglichkeit der Messung kommunikativer Fertigkeiten. *Deutsch lernen*, 2, 21–26.
Hahn, A. 1982, *Fremdsprachenunterricht und Spracherwerb*. Diss. University of Passau.
Hatch, E. 1974, Second language learning- universals? *Working Papers on Bilingualism*, 3, 1–17.
Hegele, I. 1981, Deutsch als Zweitsprache: Sprachstandsdiagnose und Sprachförderung von Ausländerkindern. *Deutsch lernen*, 4, 41–56.
Hyltenstam, K. 1977, Implicational patterns in interlanguage syntax variation. *Language Learning*, 27, 383–411.
Ihssen, W. 1978, Psychologie, Linguistik und Primärsprachdiagnostik, *Studium Linguistik*, 5, 89–98.
—— 1980, Probleme der Sprachentwicklungsdiagnose bei Ausländerkindern, *Praxis Deutsch*, 80, 40–42.
Klein, W. & Dittmar, N. 1979, *Developing grammars*. New York.
Luchtenberg, S. 1983, Sprachbarrieren verstehen und überwinden. Überlegungen zur Sprachstandsdiagnose ausländischer Kinder im Vorschulbereich. *Ausländerkinder in Schule und Kindergarten*, 1, 33–36.
Luchtenberg, S., Neumann, H.-J. & M. Wespel 1982, Informeller Test zur Sprachstandsdiagnose bei ausländischen Kindern und Jugendlichen. In U. Coburn-Staege *et al.* (eds), *Türkische Kinder in unseren Schulen- eine pädagogische Herausforderung*. Stuttgart. 134–76.
Ludwig, G. 1982, Ausländerkinder und Sonderschultests. *Ausländerkinder*, 11, 23–33.
Meisel, J. 1983, Strategies of second language acquisition. In R. Andersen (ed.), *Pidginization and creolization as language acquisition*. Rowley, Mass.
Meisel, J., Clahsen, H. & Pienemann, M. 1981, On determining developmental stages in natural second language acquisition, *Studies in Second Language Acquisition*, 3, 109–35.
Molony, C. 1977, 'Ich bin sprechen Deutsch aber': The sequence of verb and word order acquisition of an American child learning German. In C. Molony, H. Zobl & W. Stölting (eds), *German in contact with other languages – Deutsch im Kontakt mit anderen Sprachen*. Kronberg/Ts., 274–95.
Nemser, W. 1971, Approximate systems of foreign language learners, *IRAL*, 10, 9, 115–23.
Nicholas, H. 1984, 'To be or not to be': is that really the question. Developmental sequences and the role of the copula in the acquisition of German as a second language. In R. Andersen (ed.), *Second Languages*. Rowley, Mass.

Nicholas, H. & Meisel, J. 1983, Second language acquisition: The state of the art. In H. Wode & S. Felix (eds), *Language development at the crossroads*. Tübingen.

Pienemann, M. 1981, *Der Zweitspracherwerb ausländischer Arbeiterkinder*. Bonn.

—— 1984, Psychological constraints on the teachability of languages. *Studies in Second Language Acquisition* 6, 186–214.

Portz, R. & Pfaff, C. 1981, *SES- Soziolinguistisches Erhebungsinstrument zur Sprachentwicklung*. Berlin.

Scherzinger, A. & Scherzinger, G. 1981, Sprachstandsdiagnose für die schulische Förderung von Ausländerkindern. *Ausländerkinder in Schule und Kindergarten*, 2, 18–22.

Selinker, L. 1972, Interlanguage, *IRAL*, 209–31.

Wode, H. 1981, *Learning a second language*. Tübingen.

Appendix

Name: Age: Duration of stay:

A. Unanalysed
   1. Unintelligible   2. Incomplete   3. Ambiguous   4. Other

B. Responses

	1	2	3+	Minor
Imitations				
Elliptical				
Full				

C. Spontaneous

Repetitions				Stereotypes	Social
Other					

	Phrase		Sentence Structures
Phase I	DN	Prep NP	**STATEMENT** SVP SVPX(AP) XSVP(Y) SX(Y) XS(Y)
	AdjN	Adv	main
	N	V	sub.
	$Pron_O^P$	V Ptcl	(X)YVP XVPY VPX(AP) (X)YZ Other main
	$Conj_c$	Cop	sub.
	Other	Adj	QUESTION ┆ NEGATION
		$Conj_s$	QXY(Z) XY(Z) ┆ (X) NEG VP (Y) (X) NEG NP (Y) ┆ (X) NEG AP (Y) (X) NEG Adj (Y) ┆ Other

	Phrase	Sentence Structures
Phase II	Aux Mod	VPAPAP VPOAP VPAPAPAP VPOAPAP Other

		STATEMENT
		   (X) Aux Y Part (X) Mod Y Inf (X)V_f Y Ptcl
		main
		sub.
		   (X) Cop Y Adj (X) (S) Y V_i (X)V_f Y (V_i) S Other
		main
		sub.

		QUESTION NEGATION Q V_f X (V_i) S (X) V_f NEG (Y) (X) (Aux) (Y) NEG (X) V_f Y (V_i) S Part (X) (Mod) (Y) NEG Inf Other Other

Phase III		STATEMENT
		   $APV_f S(X)$ O V_f S(X) $CIV_f S(X)$ (X) V_f PP O (Y)
		main
		sub.
		   (X) V_f Adv O (Y) Other
		main
		sub.

		QUESTION NEGATION Q V_f S(X) V_f S(X) Other (X) V_f Y NEG (Z) Other
Phase IV		$VPO_i O_d$ $VPO_i O_d$ AP Other
		STATEMENT $Conj_s$ XV_f daß XV_f Relpron XV_f XV Other sub.
		QUESTION NEGATION Q XV_f ob XV_f Other X NEG V_f Other sub. sub.

Name: *Giovanni*   Age: *23 years*   Duration of stay: *Seven weeks*.

A. Unanalysed
   1. Unintelligible *5*   2. Incomplete *2*   3. Ambiguous *2*   4. Other

B. Responses

	1	2	3+	Minor
Imitations	*7*			
Elliptical	*21*	*4*		*13.*
Full		*3*		

C. Spontaneous

Repetitions	*1*			Stereotypes	Social
Other	*15*	*31*	*16*	*4*	

	Phrase	Sentence Structures
Phase I	DN *36* Prep NP *20* AdjN *10* Adv *19* N *33* V *25* Pron P *14* O *2* V Ptcl Conj_c *21* Cop Other Adj *9* Conj_s *1*	STATEMENT SVP SVPX(AP) XSVP(Y) SX(Y) XS(Y) main *1* *10* *16* *4* sub. *1* (X)YVP XVPY VPX(AP) (X)YZ Other main *4* *6* *4* *2* sub. *2* - QUESTION | NEGATION QXY(Z) XY(Z) | (X) NEG VP (Y) *3* (X) NEG NP (Y) *6* *4* | (X) NEG AP (Y) *1* (X) NEG Adj (Y) | Other

	Phrase		Sentence Structures

Phase II	Aux	Mod	VPAPAP ⅋ VPOAP ⅋ VPAPAPAP VPOAPAP
			Other
			
			STATEMENT
			   (X) Aux Y Part (X) Mod Y Inf (X)V_f Y Ptcl
			main
			sub.
			   (X) Cop Y Adj (X) (S) Y V_i (X)V_f Y (V_i) S Other
			main
			sub.
			
			QUESTION | NEGATION
			Q V_f X (V_i) S | (X) V_f NEG (Y) (X) (Aux) (Y) NEG
			(X) V_f Y (V_i) S | Part
			             | (X) (Mod) (Y) NEG Inf Other
			Other

Phase III			STATEMENT
			   APV_fS(X) O V_f S(X) ClV$_f$S(X) (X) V_fPP O (Y)
			main
			sub.
			   (X) V_f Adv O (Y) Other
			main
			sub.
			
			QUESTION | NEGATION
			Q V_f S(X) V_f S(X) Other | (X) V_f Y NEG (Z)
			                          | Other

Phase IV			VPO$_i$O$_d$ VPO$_i$O$_d$AP Other STATEMENT Conj$_s$ XV_f daß XV_f Relpron XV_f XV Other sub. QUESTION | NEGATION Q XV_f ob XV_f Other | X NEG V_f Other sub. | sub.

Name: *Giovanni*   Age: *24 years*   Duration of stay: *63 weeks*

A. Unanalysed
1. Unintelligible *2*   2. Incomplete *1*   3. Ambiguous   4. Other

B. Responses

	1	2	3+	Minor
Imitations	*13*			
Elliptical	*23*	*6*		*23*
Full		*3*	*1*	

C. Spontaneous

Repetitions	*2*			Stereotypes	Social
Other	*11*	*24*	*20*	*3*	

	Phrase	Sentence Structures
Phase I	DN *20* Prep NP *14* AdjN *21* Adv *35* N *19* V *35* Pron$_O$ *12*$_6$ V Ptcl *2* Conj$_c$ *21* Cop *1* Other Adj *8* Conj$_s$ *8*	STATEMENT SVP SVPX(AP) XSVP(Y) SX(Y) XS(Y) main *3* *3* *1* *4* *6* sub. *2* *1* (X)YVP XVPY VPX(AP) (X)YZ Other main *5* *5* *4* *2* sub. *1* *1* *1* QUESTION NEGATION QXY(Z) XY(Z) (X) NEG VP (Y) *1* (X) NEG NP (Y) *2* *2* *2* (X) NEG AP (Y) (X) NEG Adj (Y) *2* Other

	Phrase	Sentence Structures
Phase II	Aux *6* Mod *1*	VPAPAP *8* VPOAP *3* VPAPAPAP *1* VPOAPAP Other
		STATEMENT (X) Aux Y Part (X) Mod Y Inf (X)V_f Y Ptcl main *3* sub. *1* (X) Cop Y Adj (X) (S) Y V_i (X)V_f Y (V_i) S Other main *3* *2* sub.
		QUESTION | NEGATION Q V_f X (V_i) S | (X) V_f NEG (Y) (X) (Aux) (Y) NEG (X) V_f Y (V_i) S | Part | (X) (Mod) (Y) NEG Inf Other Other |
Phase III		STATEMENT APV_fS(X) O V_f S(X) ClV_fS(X) (X) V_fPP O (Y) main sub. (X) V_f Adv O (Y) Other main sub.
		QUESTION | NEGATION Q V_f S(X) V_f S(X) *3* Other | (X) V_f Y NEG (Z) | Other
Phase IV		VPO$_i$O$_d$ VPO$_i$O$_d$AP Other
		STATEMENT Conj$_s$ XV_f daß XV_f Relpron XV_f XV Other sub.
		QUESTION | NEGATION Q XV_f ob XV_f Other | X NEG V_f Other sub. | sub.

13 Pedagogical implications of direct second language testing: A Canadian example

SHARON LAPKIN

The Ontario Institute for Studies in Education, Toronto, Canada

"Undoubtedly the most serious criticism of direct tests is that they are time-consuming and, where large numbers of learners are involved, simply impracticable for that reason." (Ingram, this volume, p.225)

If language testing can be viewed as an integral part of the curriculum, integrated into the ongoing day-to-day activities of the classroom, direct language testing may be time well spent and may provide teachers with creative suggestions they can exploit in their curriculum planning. This chapter is intended to exemplify one such attempt at second language testing that is productive not only for purposes of assessment and diagnosis, but also for subsequent exploitation as curriculum content.

The most radical innovation in Canadian second language pedagogy during the last twenty years is undoubtedly the widespread implementation of French immersion programmes for English speaking students. Based on 1983–84 enrolment figures, approximately 100,000 Canadian students have spent or will spend from one to nine years of their elementary schooling studying all school subjects through the medium of French, their second language. The success of the immersion approach has been established through testing programmes designed to demonstrate that instruction through the medium of a second language has no long-term negative effects on measured IQ, the normal development of first language (English) skills or general academic achievement. Until it was conclusively demonstrated that there were no such long-term negative effects (e.g. Lambert & Tucker, 1972; Swain & Lapkin, 1982), the question of what level of French proficiency immersion students may expect to attain received somewhat less research attention.

Since the mid-seventies, educators, parents and researchers have increasingly been concerned with describing the second language proficiency of immersion students. The focus of test development activity has shifted from evaluating the receptive skills of French listening and reading comprehension and assessing French achievement (i.e. grammar) through indirect tests of the discrete point variety. Tests for immersion students in the eighties are more integrative and communicative, with emphasis on evaluating second language speaking and writing skills used in real-life situations. (A chronology of second language test development for the French immersion context can be found in Green & Lapkin, 1984 and Lapkin, 1984.)

In this paper an experiment in communicative second language test development will be described, and the implications for second language teaching and learning explored. The "French language evaluation units" developed for this purpose represent an attempt to come as close to the "direct" extreme of the indirect-direct language testing continuum as possible. The units test speaking and writing skills only, since it is known that by the end of elementary school, the measured second language comprehension skills of French immersion students are close to those of their unilingual French speaking peers (living in Quebec).

In 1982, the Department of Education of Saskatchewan contracted with the Modern Language Centre of the Ontario Institute for Studies in Education to prepare an assessment package for the evaluation of French immersion and French minority language programmes in that province. Two distinct programmes have been established, one for the francophone student population (who are bilingual, living for the most part in an English dominated environment), and one for anglophones wishing to become functionally bilingual through their school experiences. The specifications for the assessment package were defined by Department of Education officials, working in conjunction with an Advisory Committee of educators and administrators representing both types of French language programme in Saskatchewan.

The target grades were 3, 6 and 9 (students of approximately 8–9, 11–12 and 14–15 years of age), and the tests were to measure the collective communicative competence of the class as a group, rather than individual performance. The evaluation units were to be designed for use by teachers, so that teachers could administer the tests, score them reliably according to criteria outlined in the Teachers' Guides, and interpret the results.

The goal of French immersion programmes is to produce second language skills which are as close to the first language skills of native French speaking students as possible. It was agreed that an appropriate reference group for defining native-like proficiency in French would be unilingual French speaking students of the same age and grade level attending schools in Quebec, the only Canadian province in which French is the majority language. In order to describe the nature of their language proficiency, a theoretical framework of communicative competence developed by Canale & Swain (1980; see also Canale, 1983) was used as a starting point.

The framework identifies four major components of communicative competence: grammatical, sociolinguistic, discourse, and strategic competence. Grammatical competence refers to knowledge of the language code itself, including the rules of word formation, vocabulary, pronunciation, spelling and sentence formation. Knowledge of the code is framed in terms of understanding the literal meaning of utterances. Sociolinguistic competence addresses the extent to which utterances are produced and understood appropriately in different sociolinguistic contexts depending on such factors as topic, status of participants and purposes of the interaction. Discourse competence refers to the rules and conventions of combining grammatical forms and meanings to achieve unified spoken or written texts in different genres, such as narrative, a business letter, recipe, or scientific report. This unity of text is achieved through cohesion in form and coherence in meaning. Cohesive devices include pronouns, synonyms, conjunctions and parallel structures which help to link individual utterances and show the logical or chronological relations among a series of utterances. Coherence refers to the logical sequencing of the ideas in a text. Strategic competence relates to the mastery of communication strategies used by a speaker either to enhance the effectiveness of communication or to repair breakdowns in communication. These breakdowns may result from insufficient competence in one or more of the other components of communicative competence, or they may be attributed to limitations of the actual communicative event (for example, having to speak loudly or repeat oneself when a telephone connection is poor).

With these broad categories in mind, a set of evaluation units was developed. It was agreed that the materials should draw on students' ability to carry out such activities as talking to peers in an informal setting as well as conducting oneself in a semi-formal interview with an adult; and the ability to write in both formal and informal styles, depending on the intended audience and the purpose. By working from goal to method, the functions to be tested and scored were defined in terms of the hypothesized components of language proficiency, and the types of tasks requiring such functions were constructed accordingly. The theme chosen for the grade 9 unit related to fictitious summer employment projects for youths across Canada fifteen years and older in two francophone communities in Canada. The title "À vous la parole" was taken from a letter by a young Montrealer included in a booklet in which he claims that youths face discrimination in the job market and suggests that it is time for adults "to let us have our say" in decision-making that affects youth. The booklet also includes information about job qualifications, the nature of each job, and working and living conditions. In order to motivate students further, a list of government agencies which offer and organize real summer employment opportunities for youth is provided so that students can write for more information if they wish.

The second component of the evaluation unit consists of a series of six communicative tasks that any mature speaker should be able to handle: writing a letter, a note, a composition and a technical exercise (involving putting "point-form" information into continuous text in an expository style). The two oral tasks are participating in an informal discussion with other students and in a formal job interview with an adult.

The third component, a Teachers' Guide, provides instructions on how to administer and score the tests, and how to interpret the results.

The grade 6 unit deals with the theme of summer camp ("Bienvenue au Camp de la Gélinotte".) The illustrated booklet which constitutes the basis of the unit depicts an imaginary camp near Prince Albert National Park in northern Saskatchewan. The booklet offers basic information about camp activities, and informs students about the National Park and some of its features. The written tasks include a short-answer exercise focussing on preposition use, a factual cloze passage related to bears in the park, a writing exercise requiring students to transform information about camp activities from point form into prose, and a short composition in which students describe from photographs a friend they met at camp. The unit has two oral tasks: retelling a taped story from pictures depicting a fish that got away, and a campfire tale in which four students continue the story a sentence at a time, round-robin style.

The grade 3 unit consists of a slide show with a soundtrack on cassette. The items include a story-retelling task based on selected pictures from the slide show, five short-answer questions, a composition starter and a cloze task. There is also a sentence repetition task with 20 sentences containing such constructions as reflexive verbs, object pronouns, prepositional phrases and impersonal constructions (*il faut, il y a*). All of the tasks are based on the slide show, which tells the story of a French Canadian boy visiting his cousin's school and having an adventure involving a runaway guinea pig.

All three evaluation units were prepared using four guiding principles of communicative test development. Swain (1983) describes these as (1) start from somewhere, (2) concentrate on content, (3) bias for best and (4) work for washback.

"Start from somewhere" refers to the principle of building on existing theoretical knowledge and practical experience to determine what aspects of speech and writing should be assessed. In the case of the projects described, the constituent components of communicative competence formed the basis of the design of the tasks and decisions about what each task is to be scored for.

The second principle, "concentrate on content", refers to at least four characteristics we have striven to achieve in designing the evaluation instruments. The materials had to be motivating, substantive, integrated and interactive. For example, before deciding on the theme of the Saskatchewan grade 9 evaluation unit, members of the team met with high school students over lunch to find out what interested them. The materials subsequently developed reflect students' expressed interest in travel, music, and care of animals, among others. We have become increasingly more attentive to the design of the materials. They are colourful and as attractive as our budget permitted, and the tasks were developed to approximate the kinds of real-life language activity students would have to engage in after leaving school. Moreover, they provide substantive information, some of which is new to the students. In this way, developing good tests is analogous to developing good curriculum materials. The choice of a unifying theme provides an integrated content, maximizing the possibility of using clues from the larger context in completing any task. The final aspect of "concentrating on content" is the interactive nature of the materials: using the grade 9 materials as an example, students interact with an absent peer, Eric, in the letter task, and with each other in the group discussion.

The third principle, "bias for best" refers to an attempt to elicit the students' best performance. Thus we believe that as far as possible, the testing should allow for as much time as necessary to accommodate the students' different paces in completing each task. The testing occurs over a three- to five-day period, so that students have several opportunities to make changes or additions. Dictionaries are made available for the written tasks, and suggestions are provided to students as to how to respond to each task.

The fourth principle is to "work for washback", that is, to involve teachers in the testing and possibly to influence them to provide greater opportunities for productive language use in their classrooms. In part, this has been accomplished by working with an advisory committee of educators to obtain feedback on the materials. In most cases, teachers themselves carry out the testing, and even the scoring. In the process, they become informed about the purposes of the evaluation and the framework underlying the test development. Further, through the use of comprehensive scoring manuals rich in example and explanations, teachers become familiar with different approaches to scoring productive language skills. Ideally such materials will serve an in-service function, to inform teachers about the relative strengths and weaknesses in the collective communicative competence of their classes, and to encourage them to provide as many varied contexts for language use as possible in their teaching.

The fourth principle is particularly relevant to the topic of this chapter. The pedagogical implications of the grade 6 evaluation unit, "Bienvenue au Camp de la Gélinotte", will be explored by examining the tasks, scoring procedures and results obtained in field trials of the test materials carried out in May 1983. The reason for selecting grade 6 is that complementary data are available from another project in the OISE Modern Language Centre. The Development of Bilingual Proficiency (1983), a research project funded by the Social Sciences and Humanities Research Council of Canada, also used a grade 6 French immersion population to generate second language performance data to test a model of bilingual proficiency based on a modified Canale and Swain framework.

The Teachers' Guide is structured so that it presents step-by-step instructions on how to administer and score the tests, how to interpret the results (in relation to the all French immersion and French minority language classes in Saskatchewan tested at grade 6 in 1983). Comparative data from unilingual francophones living in Quebec are also provided for the teachers' information. The Guide provides a rationale for the test materials including a statement of objectives, and a description of the theoretical framework underlying the materials. The exploitation of the evaluation unit for *instructional* rather than assessment purposes is not addressed in the existing version of the Guide; however, we hope to produce a set of pedagogical suggestions at some future date.[1]

The objectives of "Bienvenue au Camp de la Gélinotte" are stated as follows:

- To provide (immersion) teachers with materials that will assist them in assessing the French speaking and writing skills of their students.
- To introduce teachers to evaluation procedures that reflect current research about language proficiency.

For practical reasons, it is suggested that a representative sample of eight students be selected at random from any given class. Although all students may do the written exercises, it is usually not feasible to test up to 30 students on an individual basis. (Individual testing is required for one of the oral tasks, the retelling of a taped story.) A flow chart presenting a suggested timeline and procedure for administering the tests is shown in Figure 1.

The set of written and oral tasks, taken together, require students to make use of each component of communicative competence. Figure 2 shows the chart provided in the Teachers' Guide to display the specific aspects of each area of communicative competence assessed in each exercise. These aspects were chosen in the light of earlier work using the grade 9 test materials in another project. For that study, entitled "Second Language Maintenance at the Secondary School Level" (Lapkin & Swain, 1983), data were collected in a small number of early immersion and late immersion classes, as well as bilingual and unilingual francophone comparison classes. These were analysed in considerable detail, using many more linguistic categories. Decisions about which aspects to focus on for the Teachers' Guides were based on the following criteria:

1. Did a given measure (or scoring procedure) produce significant differences between second language learners (immersion students) and first language comparison groups?
2. To what extent do particular measures distinguish between high achievers and low achievers across programme groups. (To identify high achievers and low achievers, an independent cloze test was given and global ratings of students' writing were used.)

In developing the Teachers' Guide, the next step was to operationalize the scoring categories so that they could be scored reliably by teachers. This process is ongoing, since the timespan of the research project did not permit field testing of the scoring procedures. We have very limited

FIGURE 1 *Flow-Chart: Based on use of kit with two groups of four students*

Day	Teacher	Group	Procedure	Time*	Outcome (for later assessment)
1	Teacher A	Groups 1 and 2	Introduction of student booklet	10 minutes	
			Supervision of students' perusal of booklet	5 minutes	
			Administration of «Où est la gélinotte?» exercise	15 minutes	Written sentences
			Administration of «Les activités quotidiennes»	25 minutes	Written technical exercises
2	Teacher A	Groups 1 and 2	Administration of «Décris ton ami(e)» exercise	20 minutes	Written compositions
	Teacher A	Group 1	Recording of «Autour du feu de camp» exercise, in another room	20 minutes	Recorded group stories and written cloze tests
	Teacher B	Group 2	Administration of «Le camping» exercise, in the classroom		
	Teacher A	Group 2	Recording of «Autour du feu de camp» exercise, in other room	20 minutes	
	Teacher B	Group 1	Administration of «Le camping» exercise, in the classroom		
3	Teacher A (while Teacher B stays with class)	Groups 1 and 2, one student at a time	Presentation and recording of «Le concours de pêche» exercise, in other room	10 minutes each	Recorded individual stories

* The time periods shown for each activity are approximate, as *these are not timed tests*. In setting up a timetable for testing, one should allow an additional five minutes a day for mechanical activities, such as handing out booklets, moving from one room to the other, etc.

FIGURE 2 *Scoring-procedure chart*

	Grammatical competence		Sociolinguistic competence	Discourse competence	Strategic competence
	Vocabulary items	*Rules of grammar and pronunciation*			
WRITTEN					
Sentence writing		– use of prepositions (error count)			
Technical exercise		– word formation and grammatical spelling ("oral") error count	– appropriateness of style (2-point scale)		
Composition	– variety of vocabulary (verb count) – sophistication of vocabulary (verb count)			– basic task fulfilment (check list) – tense sequence (error count)	
Cloze test	– overall language proficiency (exact response scoring)				
ORAL					
Individual story retelling		– pronunciation (4-point scale)		– tense sequence (error count)	
Group story telling					– communicative strategies (3-point scale)

information on the consistency with which *teachers* will score test data; we do have inter-rater reliability calculations for our own scoring teams, however.

As an example of how scoring categories were operationalized, consider the case of "word formation and grammatical spelling". This involves assessing non-homophonous morphological errors, that is forms which "sound" wrong in oral language. Figure 3 is an extract from the Grade 6 Teachers' Guide consisting of instructions on how to score for this aspect of grammatical performance.

One desirable outcome of focussing teachers' attention on forms which *sound* wrong (as opposed to forms which *look* wrong, e.g. *allé* for *aller*) is to suggest that these are more serious errors than homophonous morphological errors. By "serious" we mean that these errors are more likely to impede communication, and also to irritate native-speaker interlocutors (Lepicq, 1980).

It has been our observation that teachers (and, at least to some extent, researchers working in the area of language assessment) feel most comfortable in evaluating grammatical aspects of language use. We suggest that some of the scoring procedures designed to assess the other components of communicative performance will lead teachers to focus on

FIGURE 3   *Excerpt from the Grade 6 grammatical scoring procedures for teachers*

Scoring:

1.1. *For word formation and grammatical spelling ("oral")*
Starting with the first word *the student* has written for each technical exercise, count off fifty words and bracket this segment as indicated in the samples below. Remember that "c'est", "l'artisanat", "d'équipe", etc., are each two words and should be counted as such. Also counted as individual words are those separated by a hyphen, as in "après-midi". Abbreviations to indicate time, such as "15h15" or "17h00", should just be treated as one word.

Underline all misspelled grammatical forms in the first fifty words that involve any one of the following:
1) *number* (singular, plural) — e.g. "on doit débarrasser les table." or "il y a des jeux d'équipes";
2) *gender* (masculine, feminine) — e.g. "il faut aller au réunion pour les activités des jours suivantes" or "on peut faire la ski nautique";
3) *verb endings* — e.g. "il faut allé à une réunion" or "on jouent au volleyball".

Go back over the grammatical spelling errors you have underlined. This time, use an X to indicate whichever of these forms would also be incorrect if used in oral communication. This can be determined easily by reading each of the relevant words aloud. If the word, or word ending *sounds* correct — "on jouent au volleyball", for example — it should not be marked as wrong. If it does *not* sound correct — "on peut faire la ski nautique", for example — it should be marked with an X: "on peut faire X ski nautique".

discourse, sociolinguistic or strategic skills as well. Thus, for example, aspects such as "basic task fulfilment" were included in the discourse measures. This category was developed in the context of a project referred to earlier, the Development of Bilingual Proficiency (DBP). It addresses the question of how well each composition fulfils the basic semantic requirements of the particular discourse task. Thus, for this exercise entitled "Décris to ami(e)" the student must identify (from four photographs provided in the illustrated booklet) which one was his or her special friend at camp. The wording of the task instructions requires that a reason for this choice be stated, that the friend's personality be described, and so on. Figure 4 presents the scoring instructions for this task.

Such a procedure may suggest to teachers that fulfilling the *discourse* requirements for different communicative tasks is an important dimension of writing or speaking ability. The fact that the written and oral tasks are quite varied may encourage teachers to incorporate a wider variety of communicative activities in their curriculum.

In each case instructions such as those presented in Figures 3 and 4 are accompanied by authentic examples of students' work. This may offer the opportunity for teachers to judge to what extent their students resemble representative students from the grade 6 population. In many cases, it may prove reassuring to teachers to realize that the writing or speaking skills of their students are similar to those of other students of the same age and grade level in their province.

In the "Interpreting the Results" section of the Teachers' Guide, teachers find out how to situate the performance of their class in relation to that of other grade 6 classes in Saskatchewan. Figure 5 presents a sample frequency table with an accompanying explanation for teachers, and the specific instructions for interpreting scores on the "grammatical spelling" measure (discussed above).

Similar information is provided about all measures (or scoring procedures) shown in Figure 2. A quick glance at the final "Communicative Competence Results Chart" on which teachers record their assessments (below average, average, above average) for each aspect evaluated enables teachers to identify areas of strength and weakness in the collective communicative competence of their classes.

The data from Quebec, also provided in the Teachers' Guide (see the second excerpt in Figure 5), enable teachers to focus on areas of similarity or difference between bilingual students (i.e. French minority language or French immersion groups in Saskatchewan) and a small sample of unilingual French-speaking comparison students in Quebec.

FIGURE 4　*Excerpt from Grade 6 discourse scoring procedures for teachers*

2.1 *For basic task fulfilment*

Reread each composition to see whether the student has fulfilled the basic requirements of the task by including all the relevant points of information outlined in the instructions. The five different points of information required are listed on the chart provided below, from which a copy can be made for scoring. This chart also includes eight columns, so that you can write the students' names at the top, and then place a tick beside all points of information that are put across coherently in each of the eight exercises. These points may be presented in *any order*, and the sentences used to convey them may contain various grammatical errors, but *their meaning must be clear* before they can be ticked off.

Points of information in the composition	S t u d e n t s							
1. Which one of the four young people shown on page 5 of the *Bienvenue au Camp de la Gélinotte* booklet has been chosen as the student's friend.								
2. Why the student has chosen this person as his or her friend.								
3. Description of the friend's personality.								
4. Description of the friend's interests.								
5. Description of what the student and his or her friend have done together at camp.								

Note re points 1, 2, 3 and 5:

Point 1. Although stylistically it would be better to use a complete sentence, starting out with a simple "A", "B", "C" or "D" does fulfill the basic task requirement for the first point of information and can therefore be ticked off, as it has been for the "Leane D." sample shown below. If no specific reference has been given, this point can still be ticked off if the student has provided a physical description that *clearly* identifies his or her friend from among the four photographs (see the "Roland B." sample below).

Point 2. Remember that students have been asked to say "why", not "how" they became friends with "A", "B", "C" or "D". The words "La raison...", "parce que", "car" or "c'est pourquoi" must therefore accompany an appropriate point of information before a student can be considered to have successfully fulfilled this basic task requirement.

Point 3. "Il/elle est gentil(le)" is acceptable as a description of the friend's personality.

Point 5. In describing what they and their friends have done together at camp, students must give at least one specific detail. "On a fait beaucoup de choses ensemble" does *not* provide sufficient information to fulfill this basic task requirement.

Count the number of check marks for each student's composition ("3" and "4" for the following samples) and enter the scores on your "Results Chart" (see page 46).

FIGURE 5 *Excerpts from the Grade 6 "interpreting the results" section of the teachers' guide*

One example will serve to illustrate the basis on which we assigned the ratings "below average", "average" and "above average". The following table presents the distribution of Saskatchewan classes' average scores for "pronunciation":

FREQUENCIES OF SCORES OBTAINED FOR "PRONUNCIATION"

Score (max=3)	Number of Classes Obtaining Each Score	Percentage of Classes Obtaining Each Score	
1.25	2	12.5	
1.50	3	18.8	31.3%
1.63	1	6.3	
1.67	1	6.3	
1.71	1	6.3	37.7%
1.88	3	18.8	
2.0	4	25.0	
3.0	1	6.3	31.3%

Approximately one third of the classes tested were assigned the score of 1.25 to 1.50 (out of a possible 3.0), one third scored 1.63 to 1.88, and the top third got 2.0 to 3.0. The following information will enable you to determine if your class average falls in the lower third (below average), the middle third (average) or the upper third (above average) in relation to the performance of all grade 6 Saskatchewan classes tested in 1983.

Look at the class average for "grammatical spelling" (technical exercise) and assess your class as follows:

1.14 or more grammatical spelling errors – BELOW AVERAGE
0.88 to 1.13 grammatical spelling errors – AVERAGE
0.87 or fewer grammatical spelling errors – ABOVE AVERAGE

Enter this assessment in the appropriate place on your Communicative Competence Results Chart. For your information, the average number of grammatical spelling errors made by Saskatchewan grade 6 students was 1.16, while Quebec students made fewer (0.17) such errors on the average.

Thus, teachers learn that the discourse skills of their students are comparable to those of unilingual students, for example. Saskatchewan students lag behind their Quebec counterparts on several aspects of grammatical competence. The sociolinguistic measures, involving an assessment of the ability to maintain an impersonal style in the technical exercise, revealed no differences between bilingual and unilingual students. An examination of the use of communicative strategies in the group story telling task suggests that while Quebec students encounter no communication difficulties in this exercise, the bilingual students do have some problems. In general, however, they are able to invoke coping strategies to get around any problems in communicating.

These findings are particularly interesting in the light of data from the DBP project mentioned above. The latter study is more theoretical in its orientation, and the test items were more rigorously conceived for the purposes of testing a model, rather than forming part of a thematically unified evaluation unit for classroom use. Swain (in press) summarizes the DBP findings as follows:

> "...the results of a series of tests administered to grade 6 immersion students indicate (in spite of seven years of comprehensible input in the target language) their grammatical performance is not equivalent to that of native speakers. Immersion students, however, perform similarly to native speakers on those aspects of discourse and sociolinguistic competence which *do not rely heavily on grammar for their realization.*" (emphasis added)

With some qualifications, these findings seem to apply to the Saskatchewan results also. The DBP findings apply only to immersion rather than minority language students. The DBP study did not include a consideration of strategic competence. In spite of these limitations, the overall pattern of grade 6 results from Saskatchewan (where French immersion students show few differences from French minority language students in their test scores) is strikingly similar.

From these results, we may infer that improving grammatical competence would have a positive effect on the development of the other areas of communicative competence. One danger is that teachers will interpret this to mean that they must focus on the explicit teaching of isolated grammatical rules and vocabulary items. Through the nature of the test materials themselves, we hope to convey to teachers that significant improvements in grammatical and other areas of competence will occur if students can be provided with enriched exposure to the second language and ample opportunities to use French in meaningful communicative situations.

Acknowledgements

I wish to thank Daina Green, Birgit Harley and Merrill Swain for their valuable input to this paper.

Notes to Chapter 13

1. Such pedagogical suggestions could be quite varied. For example, material in the student booklet of "Bienvenue au Camp de la Gélinotte" could be exploited for

geography or natural history lessons. (The booklet contains a map of Saskatchewan showing the location of Prince Albert National Park and some information about the topography of the park.) Immersion programmes are based on the principle of developing second language skills through subject matter instruction. The French language Evaluation Units reflect this principle: on the one hand, they serve to test productive second language skills, while on the other, their substantive content can be used as an integral part of the curriculum.

References

Canale, M. 1983, From communicative competence to communicative language pedagogy. In J. Richards & R. Schmidt (eds), *Language and Communication*. London: Longman Group Ltd.

Canale, M. & Swain, M. 1980, Theoretical bases of communicative approaches to second language teaching and testing, *Applied Linguistics*, I, 1, 1–47.

Development of Bilingual Proficiency: Second Year Report. Toronto: The Ontario Institute for Studies in Education, 1983 (mimeo).

Green, D.Z. & Lapkin, S. 1984, Communicative Language Test Development: Where we are and how we got there. *ELT Documents*, No.119, 129–48.

Lambert, W.E. & Tucker, G.R. 1972, *Bilingual Education of Children*. Rowley, Mass.: Newbury House.

Lapkin, S. 1984, How well do immersion students speak and write French? *Canadian Modern Language Review*, 40(4), 575–85.

Lapkin, S. & Swain, M. 1983, Second language maintenance at the secondary school level: Final report for Year 2. Toronto: The Ontario Institute for Studies in Education (mimeo).

Lepicq, D. 1980, Aspects théoriques et empiriques de l'acceptabilité linguistique: Le cas du français des élèves des classes d'immersion. Ph.D. thesis, University of Toronto.

Swain, M. 1983, Large scale communicative language testing: A case study. *Language Learning and Communication*, 2(2), 133–47.

—— in press, Communicative competence: Some roles of comprehensible input and comprehensible ouput in its development. In S. Gass & C. Madden (eds), *Input and Second Language Acquisition*, Rowley, Mass.: Newbury House.

Swain, M. & Lapkin, S. 1982, *Evaluating Bilingual Education: A Canadian Case Study*. Clevedon, Avon: Multilingual Matters.

14 On the validity of second language tests

LILIAN FRIED

Zentrum für empirisch pädagogisch Forschung, Rheinland-Pfalz, West Germany

Diagnosing the level of language achievement among foreign children is absolutely essential as a prerequisite and basis for subsequent pedagogic steps. This is generally accepted in theoretical discussions as well as in practice. However, there is no clear consensus of opinion concerning methodological approaches.

Until now there have been very few attempts made in Germany to measure L2 achievement. One noticeable aspect of these projects is the fact that they do not reflect the latest developments in pedagogic diagnostics, i.e. that basic and important aspects of diagnostics are often given no or too little attention. This becomes especially evident when viewed in light of the much more advanced stage of discussions on first language diagnostics (cf. Grimm, 1978; Ihssen, 1978a; Heidtmann, 1981; Fried, 1982). In the same way, Ingram's discussions (this volume, Chapter 10) indicate that the stage of development of L2 diagnosis in Germany is not very advanced in comparison.

Validity as a Criterion of Efficiency

This article takes up the aspect of validity as one of a great number of weak points concerning this subject. Ingram's article deals with this aspect in a rather unsystematic manner, as he himself admits. For this reason, special attention will be drawn here to this important test criterion.

The following example is one way of explaining what we mean by validity (cf. Birkel, undated). The test criterium "validity" is concerned

349

with the question of whether the test actually measures what it is meant to measure. Let us suppose we want to know how many litres of wine a jug contains and that the measuring instrument we use for this purpose is a set of scales. We can begin the measuring process with the scales, have many different people carry it out, and always obtain the same result. The measuring result is highly reliable, but it doesn't give us the information we require. Only when the measuring result is obtained with a measuring instrument which actually measures what we want measured can we evaluate the result. In other words, we can only obtain a reliable *and* valid measuring result if we measure the contents of the jug with a litre measure.

The same principle also applies to language tests; only in this latter case, there is the added difficulty that we must first reach agreement over what we mean by the term "language". This question has been and still is the subject of innumerable discussions and will not be pursued further here. What is required of the group of language tests which concern us here, is that the test problems are able to "translate" a *language learning theory* in such a way that the *language structures measured* represent an *actual advance in the learning of the language*. If this is so, then the language test can be considered to produce valid measurements.

Selected preconditions for valid language measurements

The test criterium "validity", defined in this way, brings with it extremely complex requirements which can only be touched upon within the scope of this paper. The following discussion deals with only a few of the great many points which have to be observed before we are able to claim that a measuring procedure actually gives valid information on the language level of a child.

The validity of a measuring procedure is determined by a great number of factors. Among others, it is dependent on criteria related to the efficiency of measuring procedures. In this case, the main criteria to be named are objectivity and reliability.

By the term *objectivity* of a language measuring procedure, Lienert (1969) means the degree of independence of results (with respect to the language level of a child) achieved by the examiner (for other definitions cf. Rauchfleisch, 1980). Depending on the different phases of the measurement procedure we must differentiate between objectivity of performance, of evaluation, and of interpretation.

Example: In a language measuring procedure which, according to its conception, defines dialect forms as errors, the examiners, who themselves are dialect speakers, and the standard speakers must achieve the same results.

If the "profile chart" introduced by Clahsen in this volume permits objective measurement, then language researchers as well as practitioners should obtain the same measurement results with it.

By the term *reliability* of a language measuring procedure, Lienert (1969) means the degree of accuracy with which this instrument measures the language behaviour of a child. This is a matter concerning the formal accuracy of the description of language achievement.

Example: If the language test for a child with a reliable measuring instrument has indicated a comparatively low level of language development, then a repetition of the test (with another examiner, naturally) must lead to the same results. At the same time, it becomes apparent that the test criterion "reliability" is directly related to the test criterion "objectivity".

Besides the test criteria, there are also two determining factors concerning the criterium "validity" which should be mentioned at this point (it would be possible to add countless other aspects to this list).

One of these is the *test situation*. In the case of standardized language tests, this is often an "unnatural and extremely asymmetrical communicative situation" (Heidtmann, 1981:345 see also Biere, 1980). A rather positive exception can be found in Götte's (1976) language test. She succeeds very well in producing diagnostic game situations. For example, the child may enter into playful competition with the diagnostician. Since the child's success is to be anticipated, this "game" is especially enjoyable for pre-school children.

The problem of acquiring appropriate *language samples* is also a serious one.

The test situation is, of necessity, restricted to one possible communication situation. Accordingly, the preliminaries of the test situation have important consequences with respect to the validity of the language test. Thus the proof that a given test situation actually represents natural language behaviour is of great importance; i.e. practically all possible communicative situations must be represented in the test situation. This is unquestionably an extremely exacting standard.

Neuland (1982) refers to these problems also in her analysis of existing German vocabulary tests. Using one vocabulary test as an example (Anger *et al.*, 1971a), she attacks, among other things, the preponderance of technical and foreign terms. "These tests mainly examine knowledge which often can only be acquired during the formal education process" (p. 264). Besides this, the author is annoyed by the fact that a number of archaic words are used.

In her opinion, this means that the conclusions drawn from the test results on the active command of the terms and their practical application in everyday speech are at best speculative (p. 268).

Types of validity

It has now become clear that the task of developing truly valid language tests is a very complex and demanding one. The next question of interest is how it is possible to ascertain whether or not the attempt to conceive a valid instrument has been successful.

Again, the scope of this paper does not permit description of all the many different ways and complicated methods employed to ascertain the validity of an instrument. Therefore, we will give a brief description only of those methods which are of significance within the context of existing German language L2 tests (For the types of validity cf. Rauchfleisch, 1980). The various types of validity are of differing standards.

The *concurrent validity* can be expressed in terms of a simple correlation coefficient (measurement of relationship). It can always be calculated in cases where a test already exists which for its part, measures with sufficient reliability and validity the feature which the new test is also designed to measure, or where some other external criterium exists which is plausibly related to the feature measured by the test.

Whoever devises an intelligence test will check to what extent the measuring results of this test concur with other intelligence tests, or how well they concur with, for example, performance in school or in life in general, as it is reasonable to assume that intelligent behaviour will express itself in success at school or in life in general. The extent of concurrence is expressed by a correlation coefficient. This aspect of validity is also dealt with in connection with Ingram's measuring instrument in this volume.

The *predictive validity* of a test can also be expressed in the form of a correlation coefficient. It should be calculated wherever a prediction of future behaviour is to be made on the basis of a test result. German children, for instance, are allocated differing forms of further education on the basis of their school marks upon termination of primary education. We expect this allocation process to be carried out in such a way that as few children as possible have problems in the course of their further education. Thus a prediction is made of the subsequent learning behaviour of the children in further education on the basis of their school marks. We know, however, that a relatively large number of children fail in further education and thus that the predictive validity of school marks is not very great. The predictive validity of intelligence tests and school performance tests is considerably greater than that of school marks, but still by no means great enough to prevent false decisions. The predictive validity is calculated as the correlation between the test performance and, for instance, the subsequent performance at school. The question of predictive validity will be dealt with again in connection with the German language L2 test discussed here.

Pawlik (1976) introduced the concept of *ecological validity*. According to this concept, a language test situation is only ecologically valid if it actually represents all the language situations relevant for the child. This concept takes on particular significance if the child's learning environment (e.g. the school environment) is to be changed following test diagnoses. I am of the opinion that this (admittedly demanding) concept will be of growing significance in the future.

A further very demanding criterium is *construct validity* (theoretical validity). This aspect is concerned with how well a test concurs with the theory on the basis of which it was devised. If, within the framework of a personality theory, we make statements on some personality feature which we, naturally, cannot observe, we attempt to devise a measuring instrument which can register this feature. When we have devised such a test, we can try to verify the statements contained within the framework of the theory. As regards the personality feature "anxiety" for instance, we can, within the framework of an anxiety theory, make specific statements about how "anxious people fail examinations more often than people with only a little anxiety". It should then be possible, in investigations in which a test expected to measure the anxiety of a person is used, to prove that it is true that people with a high score in the anxiety test, i.e. anxious people, fail in examinations more often than people with a low score. Construct validity is not expressed in the form of a correlation coefficient; rather, the test author reports on the investigations he has carried out in order to confirm construct validity.

The procedure for checking the construct validity of L2 tests will be dealt with in more detail at a later stage in connection with Clahsen's diagnostic concept (this volume, Chapter 12).

The discussion up to this point clearly demonstrates just how demanding a test criteria "validity" is. Several selected points have served to demonstrate the demands a valid language test has to meet, the differing angles from which the validity of a test can be observed, and the methods with which it is possible.

It is now time to look more closely at the (to my knowledge) existing L2 language tests in areas where the German language is the dominant one, together with the preliminary concepts of Clahsen and Ingram (this volume). For this purpose, I shall present a survey of the tests and an analysis of the procedures used.

The validity of L2 tests

The linguistic disorders of foreign children challenge our sense of responsibility in education. The need for pedagogic help, however, cannot be attended to so easily. Educational steps are made difficult because (among other things) teachers are overburdened by the task of measuring L2 achievement precisely. Accordingly, Ihssen (1980:40) draws attention to the fact that an extensive and systematic analysis of the individual language ability of the children is most probably a rare exception in the case of compensatory language courses for foreign children.

At any rate, there have already been a few attempts made in Germany to substantiate language analyses with the help of more or less developed models of diagnosis. These first experiments can only be characterized as rather tentative in nature. It is obvious that this is an effort to finally deal with the "predicament in reality".

The evaluation of existent diagnosis approaches for L2 achievement must take this stage of development into consideration. An additional problem is presented by the fact that these less than adequate techniques are not at all standardized with respect to their objectives, their reference to age, their methodological approaches, or their theoretical reference point.

However, what must be demanded of the existing procedures is that they allow valid measurement of language level, because only then can the practitioners rely on the measuring results and direct their practical efforts in the right direction.

Survey of L2 language tests

Attempts to construct a fundamental basis for the diagnosis of the L2 language level have their roots in educational practice. This explains why the development and the application of *standardized instruments to assess language* are still in the pioneer stage. This is partially a result of the high requirements set on developing such instruments, as well as the fact that many educators have reservations concerning standardized tests.[1]

Standardized language tests are those instruments for assessing language which permit the comparison of individual test results against the standard "language behaviour of a representative sample group or their standard group". In addition to such comparisons, which may be used effectively for assessment and decision-making processes, standardized instruments make an *objective* and *reliable* estimation of ability possible. The advantages of such instruments in contrast to conventional performance evaluation (such as grades) (see Ingenkamp 1971, 1981), as well as the limitations of standardized instruments (see Ihssen, 1978a), must be taken into consideration. Problems may arise out of the fact that the *testing situation* is simultaneously a communicative situation. Further critique concerns *the language samples*.

Two methods of utilizing standardized language tests are possible. First, one may apply available language tests with a mother-tongue orientation for L2 language level measurement.[2] Of course, this will require that sufficiently tested native language instruments are adapted for the purpose. This would necessitate standardizing such instruments for testing foreign children, conducting a review of the item analysis, etc. (Ihssen, 1980 points out the dangers of such methods).

Mitzschke (1978) tested standardized test material in form of a reading test (Anger *et al.*, 1971b) in connection with a "preparatory vocational programme for foreign adolescents" (1977). The test was applied in its original form. Mitzschke admits that certain sources of error are bound to be present as a result, but believes he can deal with this. By using this standardized instrument, the author attempts to assess "passive language ability". He believes that this aspect cannot be registered via spontaneous language analysis (for example, analysis of teacher-student conversations). The author comes to the preliminary conclusion that a standardized reading test represents an adequate aid in decision-making for classification purposes.

On the other hand, it is of course possible to develop totally new standardized L2 language tests (such projects are just being started, e.g. Fliegner *et al.*, 1980). Some of the instruments now available are *informal tests* (cf. Gaude *et al.*, 1971; Standop, 1972; Wendeler, 1972; Heller, 1974; Ingenkamp, 1975). Such tests have not, however, been standardized. These instruments do not allow comparison, or they only offer a means of comparison to be used within a specific class. On the other hand, such tests do show higher objectivity as compared to the more traditional evaluation instruments such as grades. The comparatively higher objectivity of informal tests is assured by precisely established procedural regulations as well as by an answer and rating key designed beforehand. Additionally, there are computation hints available which permit estimates of *reliability* and *validity* to be made (cf. Wendeler, 1972).

Informal tests have the advantage that they stem directly from classwork and that such tests may be utilized to refer back to lessons. The fact that the teacher may develop such instruments him/herself is also a benefit. This means that diagnosis and educational measures can be co-ordinated. However, one must not forget that developing and constructing such test instruments entails a great deal of time and effort (cf. Rosemann, 1974). For this reason, informal tests have been unable to establish themselves firmly in practical teaching. Furthermore, the usage of available informal tests for assessing foreign students is complicated by the fact that the L2 groups are distinctly heterogeneous.

Informal language level tests have been introduced by Fliegner *et al.*, 1980; Fleßa & Kopp, 1980; Luchtenberg *et al.*, 1982; and the Academy for the Advanced Training of Teachers in Dillingen.

These endeavours have differing goals. For example, Fleßa & Kopp accentuate the process-oriented character of language in their learning progress tests. Luchtenberg *et al.*, on the other hand, limit themselves explicitly to verbal communication. These tests also differ in that they are constructed for different age groups. Fliegner *et al.* concentrate on foreign children first entering school. The Academy for the Advanced Training of Teachers in Dillingen has specialized on fourth-graders. The other authors believe they can assess a broader age group (grade-school students through vocational school students). The common concern of all authors is *objectivity*. The quality of their results varies, however. Whereas the testing procedures are all described and constructed relatively well in a step-by-step manner by all the authors (This applies explicitly to Fliegner *et al.* 1980; Luchtenberg *et al.*, 1982), the evaluation guidelines are quite vague (for example, see Fleßa & Kopp, 1980). In some cases, instructions for interpreting the data are inadequate.

In all the procedures, it appears that the aspect of *reliability* is almost disregarded (See Rosemann, 1974). Overall, it appears that too much is expected of all the informal language level tests. This pronounced "optimism" also becomes apparent when it is claimed that these instruments can evaluate children within a broad age-span (preschoolers through vocational school students!). It would be more realistic to employ tests developed for specific language areas and to lower the expectations of what such test instruments are capable of measuring.

It is interesting to note that most authors of informal tests attempt to standardize their instruments. Endeavours to obtain objectivity are still inadequate; more efforts must be made if objectivity and reliability are to be attained.

Other authors have chosen to use *error analysis* for diagnosing language problems of foreign students (For example, see Eichler 1977). This form of diagnosing deficiencies (for example, Schwarzer, 1979) deals with tracking down sub-standard language performance or language gaps. This demonstrates the similarities to the findings and the diagnostic problems of pathological language disorders. The dimension of "error-laden language differences between L1 and L2 language" must also be included in the L2 language level analysis.

Representatives of error analytic diagnosis accentuate the fact that these methods may give the teacher useful pointers for planning and executing specific steps for helping and promoting these children. However, this diagnostic approach is still at an early stage of development. This is also the reason why the application of error analysis has largely been confined to specific, relatively well-structured areas of language.

Kuhs *et al.* (1980); Hegele (1981; see also 1979) give useful information regarding error-analytic language level measurement. Both approaches underline the emphasis of this diagnostic form on helping and promoting the child. Kuhs *et al.* explain the conversion into compensatory education in an exemplary way. The *language samples* in both error analyses are written text problems. The objective is to assess spelling problems in the first approach (Kuhs *et al.*, 1980) and weaknesses in the area of morphosyntax in the other. Unfortunately, the two articles do not offer enough aid for the planning and implementation of error analysis. However, the authors do make reference to appropriate basic literature.

Both of these approaches demonstrate the high standards and value of the error analysis method of diagnosis. Problems in this area call to mind similar problems arising in the field of special-education language diagnosis. As long as detailed aids are not offered, the educator will be incapable of applying this method in an objective and reliable manner.

Other diagnostic methods may be categorized as *spontaneous language diagnosis*. Spontaneous language diagnosis attempts to analyse spontaneous language behaviour in a natural communicative setting (Ihssen, 1978a). The advantages of this approach may be seen in the possibilities of assessing the natural productive usage of language in children. On the other hand, the fact that passive language competency cannot be appraised must not be forgotten.[3]

Also, as a result of the simple structure of the *testing situation*, a considerable degree of error is present which may influence the measuring process. In addition, there is no guarantee that the test results obtained through spontaneous language diagnosis can be used for comparative purposes.

Nevertheless, it seems that in educational practice it is often the case that more or less elaborated forms of spontaneous language diagnosis are utilized. There is no objection to this as long as the limitations of these methods are made known to the user. Of course, it would be advisable to heighten the relevance of such measurement by employing structured patterns (such as elaborated categories of analysis which may be used on type recordings) and by including these in studies with more objective data (cf. Ihssen's example LARSP). Such attempts to heighten the relevance of and to verify the correctness of spontaneous language diagnostic data require a considerable amount of time and effort.

Luchtenberg (1983) and Neumann *et al.* (undated) offer suggestions and models for spontaneous language diagnosis. The reference groups are quite different: Luchtenberg is interested in foreign pre-school children, while Neumann *et al.* seek to diagnose female Turkish students in preparatory vocational schools. As a result, the methodical approaches differ. Luchtenberg emphasizes the arrangement of the *testing situation* as a play situation. She believes that story books are suitable as a conversation-opener. Neumann *et al.* attempt to assess the complete range of language behaviour by choosing three different *communication situations* (playing, school lessons, group work). The structuring devices offered in both approaches have not been given enough thought to be used as the foundation for analysis. A positive fact is that both diagnostic approaches are process-oriented. As far as educational measures are concerned, this possibility of following up language development with a means of diagnosis is quite important.

In addition to listing available German L2 language level instruments, the severe limitations regarding the prerequisites for valid language level measurements must be described. Even when the present stage of development of L2 language level diagnosis and its associated limitations are taken into consideration, it is startling to see the tentative and incomplete character of the various approaches offered. The user must pay attention to this fact since the limitations which must be taken into consideration, such as test *objectivity* and *reliability*, are generally not stated explicitly.

The problem of random language testing is also dealt with in differing manners. When choosing language samples there is a tendency to select specific areas of language whose structure has already been developed and refined to a relatively satisfactory level, the same applied to first language diagnostics e.g. vocabulary, syntax (surprisingly, this does not apply to the area of phonetics). This trend is opposed to the stipulation that practical language usage is of central importance. Prior structuring of the language sample context leads to the obvious assumption that language related to the lessons will be recorded (for example, Neumann *et al.*, undated). The fact that some of the approachers consider the developmental aspect of language seems promising (for example, Fleßa *et al.*, 1980). Other problems arise in language tests which aim to measure overall language behaviour and which give varying weights to individual areas of ability without sufficient reason (for example, listening comprehension and speaking in Fliegner *et al.*, 1980, see also Pienemann, 1982). It is questionable whether or not a combination of specific language abilities observed in isolation from each other can reflect the entire scope of behaviour.

Not enough efforts have been made to verify the representativeness of the *language samples*, or at least to attempt this. The chosen language samples do not reflect the current level of language acquisition research (for example, see Ihssen, 1978b; Biere, 1980; Jäger, 1980 and others).

At any rate, some of the test authors did centre their attention on the test situation and influences related to it. Many authors point out the influence that the behaviour of the tester may have (for example, Fliegner *et al.*, 1980). Some authors express their concern in reference to the structure of the test situation (for example, Fleßa *et al.*, 1980; Luchtenberg *et al.*, 1982). On the other hand, the picture material used in most tests seems to represent less of a problem (for example, Fliegner *et al.*, 1980; Hegele, 1981). Obviously the authors do not seem to be aware of this potential source of error. Only Luchtenberg (1983) points out the importance of test material being suitable for the child. Still, there has been no examination conducted of the possible sources of error inherent in the test situation.

Validity in the L2 language tests

It has become clear that the efforts of the authors of the existing L2 language tests in regard to the preconditions of valid tests (of which only a few selected examples have been mentioned here) are by no means satisfactory. This lack of care becomes even more striking if we look at the efforts the test authors have made to ensure the validity of their various procedures. In the following section I will, above all, look at the ways in which the authors of the tests check the validity of their instruments.

When one does this, one rapidly comes to the conclusion that the efforts made to ensure validity are so rudimentary that it is extremely difficult for a critical appraisal even to find a point of departure. As concerns this group of tests, it so happens that not in one single case were calculations made in order to check for *concurrent validity*. This is so, even though this aspect of validity is relatively easy to check. In the same way none of the authors makes an effort to verify the *ecological validity* of his approach. It must be said, however, that this is a very demanding task.

At least the Academy for the Advanced Training of Teachers in Dillingen (no year) made an effort as regards the *predictive validity* of their procedure. This attempt, however, cannot be seen as having provided sufficient evidence of validity, and I will look at it more closely. The procedure was tested on 34 foreign school children. However, care was not taken to ensure that the pupil sample was made up in such a way as would permit generalization of the results. Rather, this sample was composed of a randomly compiled group of school children from widely differing guest worker nationalities with "relatively good knowledge of German", from totally different classes. Apart from the fact that the selection of pupils was very small and in no way representative, the test was carried out and evaluated by the respective teachers. With this by no means optimally objective and reliable procedure, therefore, we must also expect there to be a corresponding influence of the diagnostician on the test itself, i.e. the comparability of the respective test results is questionable.

The checking procedure for "predictive validity" was as follows: the respective German teacher gave a prediction concerning success or failure of the foreign child in a German class, expressed in plus or minus, without knowing the test results. A positive connection was established by means of this method. However, the predictive validity was not verified against the actual subsequent success or failure at school and therefore cannot be indicated.

The authors of the existing L2 tests did not give any information on the question of *construct validity* either. In this case, however, it is possible to draw several conclusions. The theoretical linguistic foundations are of decisive significance in this respect. It is generally true that none of the authors fulfils the demand made at the beginning of this paper: namely, that a language learning theory should be "translated" in such a way that the language structures measured represent an actual advance in the learning of the language.

There are many shortcomings in this area. This is especially true of instruments which are claimed to be able to measure overall language behaviour. Traditional methods of structuring, such as are evident in conventional grammar lessons, are singled out as being specific aspects of grammatical competency and are applied, in a generalization, upon the entire spectrum of language behaviour (for example, see Neumann *et al.*). In the cases where more differentiated language structuring is presented, theoretical deduction and reasoning seem to be lacking (for example, Fleßa *et al.*, 1980; Academy for the Advanced Training of Teachers, Dillingen etc.). Clahsen's efforts (this volume) to establish a differentiated linguistic basis are an encouraging example.

Apart from this, there are some aspects of language which are completely ignored even though the instruments available for measuring are quite accurate, one good example of this being the case of phonetics. And foreign children, especially, are the ones who have considerable difficulties with such elementary language capabilities (see Ihssen, 1980). If one considers the relationship between mastering phonetics and acquiring reading and writing skills (for example, see Andresen, 1979; Hohensee *et al.*, 1982) or the interaction between articulatory disorders and reading or spelling problems (for example, see Angermaier, 1976; Blumenstock, 1979), then there should be no reason for this.

The more specialized approaches to language measurement tend to reveal more highly developed conceptions (e.g. Hegele, 1981). The fact that specific aspects of language are treated with priority must be stated here (such as syntax, vocabulary and spelling). The users of such tests are forced to estimate the validity of available instruments regarding their theoretical linguistic aspects. This would necessitate familiarization with the present level of research concerning children's language. But this cannot be the task of a professional educator. This shortcoming is again evident in the case of a further aspect.

Special problems arise in the diagnosis of communicative competency. Most of the test authors are of the opinion that communicative abilities are of prime importance. Nevertheless, this concern is not visible in their diagnostic concept. For example, the goal of Hegele's diagnostic approach is for children to become capable of applying their knowledge of language to solve their problems in different concrete communicative situations. A diagnostic approach which seeks to register word endings and sentence structure patterns by means of written text problems cannot reach this goal. The attempt by Neumann *et al.* to measure communicative capabilities cannot be realized through deliberate and specific observation of "behaviour when writing" or of "language usage in critical situations".

The procedures advocated by Ihssen (1980) and Luchtenberg (1983) show a better course of action. Recording spontaneous verbal communication on tape, particularly, can be of help. On the other hand, it must be admitted that methods of analysing communication have been slow developing.

It is not very helpful or encouraging for teachers to learn that people such as Göbel (1978) challenge the idea that it is possible to measure communicative abilities using present research knowledge. It is true, though, that efforts to measure these abilities are seldom rewarded by satisfying results. Constructive suggestions for structuring communicative competency, such as Heringer's (1974), seem to be on the right track.

None of the test authors discuss the question of disturbed L2 language acquisition processes, although "at least the same percentage" of L2 speakers "show linguistic disorders" as L1 speakers do (see Ihssen, 1980:42).

The question of exactly what the available L2 language tests measure (construct validity) cannot be easily answered. Several first-language tests can be of use to show the course of further action in L2 language diagnosis, although they, of course, do have their limitations.[5] Certainly it would also be a step in the right direction if test authors could resolve to submit their conceptions to strict empirical and statistical examinations more often.

Clahsen's concept

Here, again, it is only possible to take up a few points. Clahsen demonstrates (this volume, Chapter 12) how much time and effort are necessary to obtain *construct validity* in general. In order to establish valid developmental stages for his "developmental chart", it was necessary to comb through an entire research field for information. Despite his extensive efforts, there are several restrictions which must be placed upon his claim of construct validity (i.e. limitations in regard to morphosyntax; Romance L1: adults). Empirical verification of construct validity for this instrument has not yet been carried out, since the development of this test is still at an early stage.

Accordingly, calculations regarding the *concurrent validity* of Clahsen's instrument (this volume) cannot be expected to furnish high coefficients. This is due to the fact that there is no test in existence in the German-speaking area capable of assessing L2 language level with comparable accuracy while taking the developmental aspect into consideration.

In contrast, I would tend to see Clahsen's instrument under a more critical light as regards the aspect of *ecological validity*. Clahsen's objective is a detailed description of the individual strengths and weaknesses in performance. Therefore, he has decided in favour of the so-called "medical model" within the context of deficit diagnosis; a model which, in the meantime, has become outdated, especially in the fields of clinical psychology and special education. In other words, more recent diagnostic approaches do not only take account of the child, but they also evaluate weaknesses in performance within the context of an "interaction model" as a disturbance in the pedagogic communication process as a whole. If we transfer this principle to the area in question, i.e. diagnosis of the language capability of a foreign child, then analysis should not be limited solely to the language performance aspect, but should also take into account the whole interaction process within the classroom, for example.

This is admittedly a very great demand to make, and it in no way denigrates Clahsen's meritorious efforts as regards the construct validity of this procedure. In spite of criticisms made, therefore, it should be said in connection with Clahsen's diagnostic approach that I consider his concept to be extremely fruitful and significant. I am impressed by the care with which theoretical perceptions are "translated". At the same time, however, I am aware of the limitations which are an inevitable consequence of this intensive approach. His efforts up to the present represent an abundance of intensive preliminary investigatory work, carried out in exemplary fashion. This preliminary approach is an important step on the way to the development of a profound diagnostic instrument.

Ingram's concept

Ingram's concept (this volume, Chapter 10) can of course not be counted together with the German language L2 tests. As it is described in great detail in this volume, however, I would like to take up one or two points.

Calculations concerning *concurrent validity* constitute the central feature in Ingram's efforts to establish validity. Ingram seeks to prove concurrent validity in his research work by comparing the ASLPR with other instruments. This cannot be accepted, however, without some criticism: it is gratifying to see that the correlations between the ASLPR and other instruments are very close, but unfortunately these are based on data from a small population sample. In such cases, it is absolutely necessary that, for the sake of credibility, confidence intervals are specified. This would enable the reader to evaluate precisely how reliable the results of such findings are. A demonstration is offered in the following example:

Ingram established a correlation of r=0.86 between ASLPR-listening and CELT-listening. This corresponds to a confidence interval of 0.65 — 0.95 for the correlation coefficient (for a sample of N= 18 and a 95% confidence interval). In other words, the actual relationship between ASLPR-listening and CELT-listening may amount to 0.65 or 0.95 with a probability of 95%. This puts Ingram's optimistic findings in a more relative light.

Apart from this, various aspects of validity may even tend to act inversely to one another; i.e. the increased importance of one aspect may result in the decrease of another. For example, construct and concurrence validity may differ when a newly developed language test with a more differentiated theoretical foundation differs (of necessity) from already existing instruments with global foundations.

For this reason it is to be expected that Ingram's ASLPR (this volume) will not correspond all that closely with other instruments (for example, dictation). After all, it is claimed that ASLPR assessments of L2 language levels are much more valid than those of other instruments.

Ingram's comments regarding the *construct validity* of the ASLPR (in this volume) are also interesting. The question arising here concerns the basis on which the decisions for 9 (maximum 12) evaluation levels was made. Such a restriction must be theoretically supportable and, if possible, empirically validated. Ingram (this volume) does not furnish any information in this regard.

At the same time, it is absolutely necessary that the problem areas are pointed out in regard to the rating scales. Of course, rating scales are the choice method for assessing the behaviour of persons in a natural setting. Still, it must be pointed out that evaluation scales suffer limitations in regard to *objectivity* and *reliability*. For this reason, raters should be specially trained for research work when such scales are utilized. Satisfactory and reliable measurement is possible only in this manner.

The possibility of applying such additional precautionary measures are limited in actual practice. In other words, the practical utilization of such scales must be evaluated with care. The user must be made conscious of the fact that measuring with rating scales will not be very objective and, inevitably, will be neither reliable nor valid under certain circumstances, as long as no additional measures are taken to guarantee the objectivity of the diagnosis.

The scope of this paper does not permit further discussion of the instrument, the advantages of which Ingram, justifiably, clearly emphasizes in his contribution to this volume.

A final note on Ingram's (and Clahsen's) concept: here are two exemplary tests or test approaches which, in spite of their shortcomings, constitute important stages in the further development of German language L2 tests.

Conclusion

It is not the aim of this survey to discourage the educator, who is the potential L2 language test user, from utilizing these instruments. The discussions surrounding L2 language diagnosis, still in the early stages of development, may have perplexed him/her. It is true that the instruments currently available in the German-speaking area may be criticized quite strongly. However, the question of whether or not these diagnostic approaches may be of value after all remains unanswered.

Following the evaluation samples to rate the language level of foreign children proposed by Luchtenberg (1983) is not necessarily to be recommended (for example, "Tuncay understands almost everything" etc.). This demonstrates that teachers constantly conduct L2 language level diagnosis more or less consciously, which is inevitable anyway. The educator cannot forestall judging the language level of his foreign students, especially in regard to teaching methods. But without the appropriate aids, such implicit diagnoses conceal the dangers of naive and generalizing spontaneous evaluations. The practical relevance of this problem area may become particularly clear as decisions are made concerning the delegation of children to preparatory or regular class, or concerning the approval of residence permits (see also Dederichs, 1979).

For this reason, even these not yet perfected L2 language tests do have an important function. Undoubtedly, the differentiated criteria for analysis of these instruments, in comparison to lump-sum evaluations, may induce a sensibilized perception of language in the educator, and lead him to use appropriately differentiated compensatory methods. This refers to differentiating and individualization measures, as well as to the measurement of learning success.

The development of instruments which allow for the practical implementation of combined diagnosis and remedial measures is desirable. For example, it is of utmost importance to know how to treat each diagnosed weakness in the best possible manner when administering deficit-oriented tests. It is equally important to know which measures are the most adequate for a specific language developmental stage.

Nevertheless, the existing L2 language tests are capable of improving remedial language training. One requirement is that the utilization of such instruments be accompanied by an adequate amount of discriminating reserve. This will ensure that the high standards attributed to these tests are seen in the appropriate light. The test authors do not offer a good example in this respect. Therefore, it is of the utmost importance that the educator sees his own goals clearly. It is easier for him/her to choose the appropriate instruments if it is clear which crucial points characterize his teaching assignments. For example, if problems concern deficit-oriented work, a different test will have to be chosen than for raising the competency of communicative abilities. It is also a question of how much time and effort one is willing to invest.

The imperfections of the L2 language tests currently utilized cannot be ameliorated simply by critical application and modification of expectations; the combination of various measuring methods is of the utmost importance as well. It should be possible to allocate the most appropriate diagnostic instruments to the different aspects of language (for example: spelling — error analysis; communicative competence — spontaneous language diagnosis; vocabulary — informal tests). I believe that the use of first language tests involves too much uncertainty. Some tests, particularly ones which have a solid foundation in linguistic theory, may be of profit when applied in the diagnostic phase (For example, see Hegele, 1981). In such cases, too, the educator must decide when the time and effort expended in such diagnoses have reached their limits.

The lack of environmental orientation[6] seems to me to be far more problematical than the absence of linguistic theory in the L2 language tests. Many of the problems of foreign children are the result of the fact that they must first orient themselves in a strange environment. Language problems are only one aspect of this.

Important tasks are awaiting future diagnosis concepts. Unfortunately, primary language diagnosis cannot be of any help. And it has still not been possible to find ways to deal with dialect and sociolect problems in tests. Therefore, orientation toward the current learning test discussion may be helpful for further development (For example, Wiedl *et al.*, 1978).

At the same time, Abudarham's (1980) approach should be taken into consideration. The solution to the diagnostic problem lies in process-oriented diagnostic measures. Such tests which consider the dynamics of ability should be capable of assessing language learning potential in children. The practical relevance of this approach is obvious.

Abudarham believes he is able to solve the difficult problem of assessing the L2 language level as well as the child's total language repertoire with the aid of such instruments. There is an interesting relationship between such tests and current developments in the area of intelligence diagnosis. The static concept of intelligence and corresponding intelligence tests are becoming things of the past. Learning tests which reflect the dynamics of intellectual abilities are given preference. The goal of these instruments is to assess interindividual differences in the processing of stimuli in learning situations (for example, Wimmer *et al.*, 1977).

Future tasks may be seen in reference to disturbed language processes. Ihssen (1980:42) believes that "staking the boundary between normal and disturbed language acquisition in children growing up in a two or more language environment may be one of the most difficult problems to solve in language diagnostics".

This aspect of the problem may be solved at present by utilizing primary-language, special-education methods embedded in specific language structure comparisons. Abudarham gives important consideration to this matter. He approaches the problem by differentially assessing the total linguistic repertoire, which may consist of a merger of both languages. Similar possibilities are offered by Clahsen (this volume). It seems feasible to compare the individual L2 developmental stage with the corresponding L1 developmental stage. Analyzing these discrepancies may provide younger language learners especially with important and useful points of reference.

Notes to Chapter 14

1. Neuland (1982:259) also observes this fact: "... in daily practice of teaching German, language tests remain a side issue".
2. Such a procedure requires theoretical premises regarding L2 acquisition; for example, in form of an "identity hypothesis" (see Bausch *et al.*, 1979).
3. Cf. Borstel, who was able to ascertain significantly better language competency than was first expected (based on observations of colloquial speech employed) by using a standardized language test.
4. The diagnosed stage of development of the first language must be considered. The present problem of measuring communicative competence has not yet been solved.
5. For example Angermaier, 1974 (even though his language-theoretical foundation must be regarded as outdated) or Grimm, 1978 (with a generally accepted differential linguistic foundation).
6. Important developments in current educational diagnostics is also ignored here.

References

Abudarham, S. 1980, The Problem of Assessing the Linguistic Potential of Children with Dual Language Systems and their Implications for the Formulation of a Differential Diagnosis. In F.M. Jones (ed.), *Language Disability in children*. New York: Univ. Park. 231–46.

Akademie für Lehrerfortbildung Dillingen (eds.) o. J.: Deutschunterricht für Kinder ausländischer Arbeitnehmer. Ein Fortbildungsmodell. Donauwörth: Auer.

Allen, J.P.B. & Davies, A. (eds.) 1977, *Testing and Experimental Methods*. Oxford: University Press.

Andresen, H. 1979, Die Bedeutung auditiver Wahrnehmungen und latenter Artikulation für das Anfangsstadium des Schriftspracherwerbs. *Osnabrücker Beiträge zur Sprachtheorie*, 4, 28–56.

Anger, H. *et al.*, 1971a, Wortschatztest WST 5–6. Weinheim: Beltz.

—— 1971b, Verständiges Lesen VL 5–6. Weinheim: Beltz.

Angermaier, M. 1974, *Psycholinguistischer Entwicklungstest PET*. Weinheim: Beltz.

—— 1976, *Legasthenie*. Frankfurt: Fischer.

Bausch, K.-R. *et al.* 1979, Der Zweitsprachenerwerb: Möglichkeiten und Grenzen der "großen" Hypothesen. *Linguistische Berichte*, 64, 3–34.

Birkel, P. undated, Glossar wichtiger, testtheoretischer Begriffe. Unveröff. Manuskript (mimeo).

Biere, B.U. 1980, Kindersprache, kindliche Kommunikation und Spracherwerb. *Zeitschrift für Germanistische Linguistik*, 8, 236–51.

Blumenstock, L. 1979, *Prophylaxe der Lese- und Rechtschreibschwäche*. Weinheim: Beltz.

Borstel, M. 1981, Erste Untersuchungsergebnisse mit dem Heidelberger Sprachentwicklungstest (H-S-E-T) bei sprachlich retardierten Kindern. Sprache-Stimme-Gehör, 5, 137.

Brack, U.B. 1982, Psychologische Sprachdiagnostik im Vorschulalter. Sprache-Stimme-Gehör, 6, 20–26.

Buse, L.; Massing, H. & Pirsich, V. 1978, Faktoren und Bedingungen sprachlicher Leistungen im Vorschulalter. *Zeitschrift für Entwicklungspsychologie und Pädagogische Psychologie*, 10, 217–28.

Caillieux, M. *et al.* (eds) 1974, *Probleme des kommunikativen Sprachunterrichts*. Stuttgart: Klett.

Dederichs, E. 1979, Nachweis "einfacher" und "ausreichender" Deutschkenntnisse. Die Erlasse der Bundesländer. *Deutsch lernen*, 1/79, 88–92.

Eichler, W. 1977, *Sprach-, Schreib- und Leseleistung*. München: Fink.

Fleßa, G. & Kopp, G. 1980, Lernfortschrittstests. In A. Schorb & G. Simmerding (eds), *Ausländische Kinder in der Schule*. München: TR-Verlagsunion, 258–81.

Fliegner, J. *et al.* 1980, *Sprachstandsmessung bei Schulanfängern*. Düsseldorf: Pädagogisches Institut.

Fried, L. 1978, Entwicklung von Verfahren zur Diagnose von Lautbildungs- und Lautunterscheidungsdefiziten. Unveröff. Diplomarbeit Landau (mimeo).

—— 1979, Entwicklung eines Lautbildungs- und Lautunterscheidungstests für Kinder im Vorschulalter. *Zeitschrift für empirische Pädagogik*, 3, 309–26.

—— 1981, *Lautunterscheidungstest für Vorschulkinder LUT*. Weinheim: Beltz.

—— 1982, Sprachdiagnose im Vorschulalter. In K. Ingenkamp *et al.* (eds), *Tests und Trends 1982*. Weinheim: Beltz, 43–69.

Fried, L. & Ingenkamp, K. 1982, Vorbeugende Maßnahmen bei Kindergartenkindern – Diagnose und Förderung der Lautbildungs- und Lautunterscheidungsfähigkeit. *Die Sprachheilarbeit*, 4, 184–96.

Gaude, P. *et al.* 1971, Objektivierte Leistungsmessung in der Schule. Frankfurt: Diesterweg. 2nd edition.

Göbel, R. 1978, Zur Möglichkeit der Messung kommunikativer Fertigkeiten. *Deutsch lernen*, 2, 21–26.

Götte, R. 1976, *Landauer Sprachentwicklungstest für Vorschulkinder LSV*. Weinheim: Beltz.

—— 1981, Ein Meßinstrument für Sprachentwicklung. Unveröffentl. Manuskript. Landau (mimeo).

Grimm, H. 1977, *Psychologie der Sprachentwicklung*. Volume 1 and 2. Stuttgart: Kohlhammer.

—— 1978, Sprache. In K.J. Klauer (ed.), *Handbuch der Pädagogischen Diagnostik*. Volume 2. Düsseldorf: Schwann, 355–66.

Grimm, H. *et al.* 1978, *Heidelberger Sprachentwicklungstest H-S-E-T*. Braunschweig: Westermann.

Grimm, H. & Kaltenbacher, E. 1982, Die Dysphasie als noch wenig verstandene Entwicklungsstörung: Sprach- und kognitionspsychologische Überlegungen und erste empirische Ergebnisse. *Frühförderung interdisziplinär*, 1, 97–112.

Hegele, I. 1979, *Lerndiagnose und Sprachförderung*. Bochum: Kamp.

—— 1981, Deutsch als Zweitsprache: Sprachstandsdiagnose und Sprachförderung von Ausländerkindern. *Deutsch lernen*, 4, 41–56.

Heidtmann, H. 1981, Sprachdiagnostik. Eine kritische Reflexion. *Die Sprachheilarbeit*, 26, 341–48.

Heller, K. (ed.), 1974, *Leistungsbeurteilung in der Schule*. Heidelberg: Quelle & Meyer.

Heringer, H.-J. 1974, Tests. In M. Caillieux *et al.* (eds), *Probleme des kommunikativen Sprachunterrichts*. Stuttgart: Klett, 45–72.

Hohensee, I. *et al.* 1982, Zur Bedeutung der Vorausartikulation beim Lesenlernen. *Zeitschrift für Entwicklungspsychologie und Pädagogische Psychologie*, 14, 236–44.

Ihssen, W.B. 1978a, Psychologie, Linguistik und Primärsprachdiagnostik. In D. Wunderlich *et al.* (eds), *Studium Linguistik*. Volume 5. Königstein: Scriptor, 89–98.

—— 1978b, Linguistik, Kindersprachforschung und Pathologie der Kindersprache. *Linguistische Berichte*, 6, 62–70.

—— 1980, Probleme der Sprachentwicklungsdiagnose bei Ausländerkindern. Praxis Deutsch, Sonderheft 80, 40–42.

Ingenkamp, K. (ed.) 1971, *Die Fragwürdigkeit der Zensurengebung*. Weinheim: Beltz.

——1975, *Pädagogische Diagnostik*. Weinheim: Beltz.

——(ed.) 1981, *Wert und Wirkung von Beurteilungsverfahren*. Weinheim: Beltz.

Jäger, L. 1980, Einführung in die Sprachtheorie. *Linguistik und Didaktik*, 41, 1–29.

Jones, R.L. & Spolsky, B. (eds) 1975, *Testing Language Proficiency*. Arlington: Center for Applied Linguistics.

Kastner, M. 1979, Spezielle Probleme von Schulreifetests. *Psychologie in Erziehung und Unterricht*, 26, 13–21.

Kleber, E.W. 1973, Der Einfluß äußerer Faktoren auf die Konzentration und Belastbarkeit bei Vorschülern. *Psychologie in Erziehung und Unterricht*, 20, 235–43.

Kornmann, R. *et al.* 1982, Untersuchungen zum Versuchsleiter – Einfluß bei der Prüfung der auditiven Diskriminationsfähigkeit. *Diagnostica*, 28, 273–84.

Kuhs, K. *et al.* 1980, Rechtschreibprobleme türkischer Schüler. Fehleranalyse und Unterrichtsvorschläge. Praxis Deutsch. Sonderheft 80, 55–61.

Lienert, G.L. 1969 Aufl.: Testaufbau und Testanalyse. Weinheim: Beltz.

Luchtenberg, L. 1983, Sprachbarrieren verstehen und überwinden. Überlegungen zur Sprachstandsdiagnose ausländischer Kinder im Vorschulbereich. *Ausländerkinder in Schule und Kindergarten*, 4, 33–36.

Luchtenberg, S. *et al.* 1982, Informeller Test zur Sprachstandsdiagnose bei ausländischen Kindern und Jugendlichen. In U. Coburn-Staege *et al.* (eds), *Türkische Kinder in unseren Schulen – eine pädagogische Herausforderung.* Stuttgart: Klett, 134–76.

Mitzschke, M. 1978, Probleme der Eingruppierung ausländischer Jugendlicher im Deutschunterricht. *Diskussion Deutsch*, 9, 77–81.

Neuland, E. 1982, Sprachtests. Möglichkeiten und Grenzen standardisierter Sprachleistungsmessung. *Diskussion Deutsch*, 13, 256–80.

Neumann, U. *et al.* undated, Materialien zur Einstufung türkischer Schülerinnen im Berufsvorbereitungsjahr (erste Schulwoche). Materialien der Regionalen Arbeitsstelle zur Förderung ausländischer Kinder und Jugendlicher. Essen.

Nickel, H. 1981, Schulreife und Schulversagen: Ein ökopsychologischer Erklärungsansatz und seine praktischen Konsequenzen. *Psychologie in Erziehung und Unterricht*, 28, 19–37.

Oksaar, E. 1980, Sprachbarrieren. In W. Spiel (ed.), *Die Psychologie des 20. Jahrhunderts.* Volume 11. Konsequenzen für die Pädagogik. Zürich: Kindler.

Pawlik, K. 1976, Ökologische Validität: Ein Beispiel aus der Kulturvergleichsforschung. In G. Kaminski (ed), *Umweltpsychologie. Perspektiven, Probleme, Praxis.* Stuttgart: Klett, 59–72.

Pienemann, M. 1982, Psychological Constraints on the Teachability of Languages. *Studies in Second Language Acquisition*, 6.3.

Rauchfleisch, U. 1980, *Testpsychologie.* Göttingen: Vandenhoeck & Ruprecht.

Ritsert, J.; Stracke, E. & Heider, F. 1976, *Grundzüge der Varianz- und Faktorenanalyse.* Frankfurt: Campus.

Rosemann, B. 1974, Konstruktion und Einsatz von informellen Tests zur Leistungsbeurteilung (Lernkontrolltests). In K. Heller (ed.), *Leistungsbeurteilung in der Schule.* Heidelberg: Quelle & Meyer, 182–221.

Scholz, H.-J. 1970, Von der Notwendigkeit linguodiagnostischer Verfahren für die Zeit der Sprachentwicklung. Die Sprachheilarbeit, 15, 97–103.

Schwarzer, C. 1979, *Einführung in die Pädagogische Diagnostik.* München: Kösel.

Seitz, W. 1981, Der Heidelberger Sprachentwicklungstest (HSET) von H. Grimm und H. Schöler. *Psychologie in Erziehung und Unterricht*, 28, 54–57.

Singh, S. & Lynch, J. (eds) 1978, *Diagnostic Procedures in Hearing, Speech and Language.* Baltimore: University Park Press.

Standop, E. (ed.) 1972, *Objektive Tests im Englischunterricht der Schule und Universität.* Frankfurt: Athenäum.

Tiedemann, J. 1974, Die Problematik der Schuleingangsdiagnose unter entscheidungstheoretischem Aspekt. *Zeitschrift für Entwicklungspsychologie und Pädagogische Psychologie*, 6, 124–32.

Überla, K. 1968, *Faktorenanalyse.* Berlin.

Wendeler, J. 1972, Aufl.: Standardarbeiten. Weinheim: Beltz. 4th edition.

Wiedl, K.H. 1978, Ökologische Aspekte der differentiellen Prognosegültigkeit von Lern- und Intelligenztests. *Psychologie in Erziehung und Unterricht*, 25, 369–71.

Wiedl, K.H. & Herrig, D. 1978, Ökologische Validität und Schulerfolgsprognose im Lern- und Intelligenztest: Eine exemplarische Studie. *Diagnostica*, 24, 175–86.

Wiedl, K.H. *et al.*, 1982, Situative Veränderungen von Leistungsangst, Selbstbild und Situationsbewertung bei Anwendung von Lerntestprozeduren. *Psychologie in Erziehung und Unterricht*, 29, 206–11.

Wimmer, R. 1974, Das Konzept der kommunikativen Kompetenz. In M. Caillieux *et al.* (eds), *Probleme des kommunikativen Sprachunterrichts*. Stuttgart: Klett, 8–26.

Wimmer, H., Ziegler, H. & Roth, E. 1977, Die Entwicklung eines Tests intellektueller Lernfähigkeit für Vorschulkinder. *Diagnostica* 23, 74–83.

15 Second language proficiency: An interactive approach

Free University, Amsterdam, The Netherlands

This chapter addresses the following question: what is "second language proficiency", is it a unitary construct, or does it consist of several subskills, and, if so, what is their number and nature? It will be argued that for an adequate understanding of the notion of second language proficiency, two types of theories need to be combined in what will be called an interactive approach. The question then is how various skills, specified by information-processing theories and linguistic theories of language proficiency, are influenced by, i.e. interact with, various background variables, specified by social-psychological and educational theories.

The cognitive perspective

In the last 25 years or so, a great number of scholars have studied the processes of listening, speaking, reading and writing on the basis of new hypotheses, derived from information-processing theories. All of these theories account for language proficiency in terms of extremely complex systems involving many elementary processes. For example, the production of even a simple sentence is considered to involve the determination of the message, the selection of lexical items, the planning of the syntactic and morphological structure, as well as the execution of the sentence plan by the speech organs. The system in which these processes are integrated is thought to be based on principles of incremental and parallel processing, allowing the various planning and execution stages to influence each other (Bock, 1982).

A second example of how information-processing theories have led us to conceive of linguistic skills as composed of many components may be derived from the extensive literature on reading. Most scholars would now agree that the comprehension of a sentence or a text may be arrived at by partly different, alternative routes. There are currently three main complementary cognitive approaches to understanding verbal comprehension (Sternberg & Powell, 1983): (a) the bottom-up approach, which focusses on information-free, mechanistic processes of letter perception and word recognition (b) the top-down approach, focussing on expectation driven, inferring processes, and (c) the knowledge-based approach studying the structuring influences of old, prestored knowledge (expertise) in the acquisition of new knowledge.

So far, we have illustrated the complexity of verbal skills in the competent, skilful individual. Let us now briefly look at the acquisition of these skills. During the acquisition period, the number and nature of the processes involved change, along a developmental path, from controlled to automatic processing, thus further complicating our understanding of "language proficiency". In the first stages of acquisition, procedures can only be carried out, or programmes can only be constructed when the individual pays attention to their components and critical features; these are controlled processes (Shiffrin & Dumais, 1981). For instance, the pronunciation of a particular sound combination or the recognition of a particular syntactic structure may first require a great deal of attention. But when the individual carries out these procedures again and again, they become implemented as ready made programmes in long term memory. When triggered, these programmes run off automatically. It is important to note that the establishment of a skill may involve a qualitative change in the processing procedure. Thus, automatic processing may involve the integration of bottom-up processes with top-down processes. For instance, skilled readers do not actually take in every letter of a word, nor every word of a sentence. Thus, the sequence of information-processing events may be different for skilled readers as compared with unskilled readers. Hence, skill acquisition is a matter of creating efficient superordinating routines rather than speeding up the execution of a series of controlled processes.

What conclusions can be drawn from these points for our discussion of the notion of language proficiency? First, since cognitive theories focus on the elementary processes and their integration into routines and strategies, they tend to proliferate the number of hypothesized skills and subskills that play a role in speaking, listening, reading, and writing. Therefore, it is not very likely that such information-processing theories will conceive of language proficiency as a unitary construct, but rather as composed of many skills and subskills, the nature and number of which being dictated by the theory. For instance, Guilford's Structure of Intelligence Model contains a taxonomy of 120 theoretically unique abilities, 30 of which dealing with semantic information (Guilford & Hoepfner, 1971). Similarly, Sternberg's componential subtheory of human intelligence identifies quite a few 'components' (i.e. elementary information processes) differing in function and level of generality (Sternberg, 1980). Second, different processes and strategies may lead to the same behavioural result. Therefore, if two individuals exhibit what appears to be the same overt behaviour, they may have arrived at this result by different strategies and their corresponding processes. Hence, a task or a test, while purporting to elicit the ability to produce a certain kind of overt behaviour, may not necessarily measure the same underlying strategies and their corresponding processes for all individuals. Also, as a corollary of this, if two individuals fail to perform a particular task, this may be due to deficiencies in different skills. For instance, there is no single cause of reading difficulties across all readers — some readers may be lacking in decoding ability, others in vocabulary, and still others in inference or comprehension abilities (Sternberg & Powell, 1983).

The linguistic perspective

It is not surprising that the issue of the number and nature of language proficiency components has primarily been addressed by linguists and psychologists dealing with the following practical problem of language testing: if we have to validly assess people's mastery of a language, how many and what kind of tests do we have to administer? For many years, the answer to this question was found in classifications derived from structural linguistics: testers operated with the traditional framework consisting of phonology/orthography, syntax, and vocabulary, crosswise linked with speaking, listening, reading, and writing. Later, in an often quoted paper, Carroll (1968) provided this framework with a psychological foundation by extending it with various "performance abilities" pertaining to diversity of response, complexity of information processing, and awareness of linguistic competence. At about the same time, Cooper (1968) suggested some elaborations to account for the notion of communicative competence, i.e. the ability to use situationally appropriate language registers. Since then, similar communicative models have been proposed. Among the more recent ones, the Canale & Swain (1980) framework has attracted considerable attention. This model of communicative language use identifies four components: grammatical, sociolinguistic, discourse, and strategic competence (see also Canale, 1983).

Language proficiency: How many composing skills?

So far, we have dealt with universal, or invariant processes in language proficiency. These processes, however, tend to be invariant only at the level of elementary tasks. For more complex tasks, i.e. tasks that require the combination and integration of various subroutines, performance will tend to differ across individuals. Let us use the word "skill" to refer to the ability to perform a task that has been found to elicit individual performance differences. If an information-processing theory predicted that two tasks demand the utilization of different processing procedures, an empirical investigation would have to reveal whether individuals do indeed perform differently. This need not necessarily be so. Meuffels (1981) argues that it is conceivable that someone with a high score on a task such as "recognition of implicit relations in a text" would also achieve a high score on the task "recognition of explicit relations in a text". The principle of parsimony would now force us to reduce the number of tasks differentiated by the theory (skill candidates) to the number of tasks that have been shown to elicit individual differences (real skills). Thus, the basic question "is language proficiency a unitary construct or does it consist of several subskills, and, if so, what is their number and nature?" is an empirical problem that cannot be resolved in an exploratory, inductive fashion, in the absence of theoretically based hypotheses. We need theories from which we can predict that certain tasks involve different skills. In empirical research we can then attempt to sustain or disconfirm such claims. Assuming that hypothesized skills have been appropriately operationalized and thus been made susceptible to empirical investigation, we can conceive of several possible outcomes.

Let us first consider the case when two tasks (tests) are not found to discriminate between individuals. There are two possible reasons for this: we may have been testing either on a too elementary, below-skill level, or on a too complex level, above the single skill. In the former case, there may still be good theoretical reasons to distinguish the two tasks (processes). In Meuffels' hypothetical example: recognition of explicit versus implicit relations in a text may not be found to differentiate individuals. We would then conclude that they belong to the same skill, but we continue to distinguish these two processes on the basis of our theory at a below-skill level. In the latter case, i.e. testing above the single skill level, there may also be good theoretical or practical reasons for distinguishing the two tasks, but these tasks may turn out to overlap considerably in terms of the elementary skills involved. For instance, a dictation test and a reading test, although clearly different, may still share a number of elementary skills. This partial commonality between the two tests may thus still create high correlations between the two sets of scores.

Let us next consider the case that two tasks (tests) are indeed found to discriminate between individuals. Here, we may have been testing exactly on the single skill level and thus been successful in finding empirical support for the existence of two different skills, as predicted by our hypothesis. However, we could still conceivably have been testing above the single skill level. For instance, what we assumed to be two single skills A and B, may later be found to be complex skills, e.g. when A is found to comprise two separate skills C and D. It has to be emphasized that such is the normal, fruitful course of theoretically based empirical research. At the same time, however, it should be clear that we cannot attach great value to differences which were found between tasks or tests, not as the result of a theoretically based prediction, but as it were, accidentally.

Methodological issues

During the last ten years or so, a substantial number of factor-analytic studies have been conducted in attempts to settle the issue whether second-language proficiency must be considered as a unitary or a multicomponential construct. Recently, Oller (1983) edited a book that provides the reader with an overview of these studies. (The controversies that are in evidence in this book are similar to the quarrels between proponents of unitary and multicomponential theories of intelligence.) Many empirical investigations turn out to have been hampered by the lack of strong theoretical hypotheses, so that, in the absence of claims which are theoretically justified, the application of factoranalytic techniques has limited value (Vollmer, in press; Vollmer & Sang, 1983). Some studies have attempted to define second language proficiency by way of an exploratory, inductive method, whereas other studies analysed the scores of only a small range of tests (thereby creating a bias in favour of a unitary construct).

Another methodological problem concerns the complexity of the task that a test requires the testees to perform. For example, the components in a framework such as the one proposed by Canale & Swain (1980) are characterized on a fairly high level of task complexity, They will therefore easily overlap. The more "simple skills" are shared by two competencies or "macroskills", the higher the correlation will be between the scores on the tasks that purport to measure these macroskills, and hence there will be less room to provide empirical support for their independence by means of correlational methods.

A third methodological problem bears upon the homogeneity of the sample of the L2 learners tested. If we want to demonstrate that two tasks elicit different skills or competencies, then the more homogeneous the sample of tested individuals is in terms of background variables (e.g. age, mother tongue, amount and type of L2 input in and outside the classroom), the higher the chance that we will obtain high correlations between the two sets of scores, and the less room there is to support our claim.

The integrated, interactive approach

So far, we have discussed cognitive and linguistic approaches to a theoretical understanding of language proficiency. We have seen that both types of theories aim at distinguishing the components in language proficiency below, at, and above the single skill level. Thus they both tend to account for the existence of commonalities rather than differences between individuals. For an adequate theory of second language learning, however, it is just as important to account for the differences in second language proficiency between individuals (Cziko, 1982). Let us take as an example the following, hypothetical study. A battery of L2 tests has been administered to a number of L2 learners; the learners' performance on these tests has been scored and the scores have been submitted to a factor analysis. Let us further assume that this analysis has yielded two factors, which have been labelled by the researchers "grammatical competence" (G) and "sociolinguistic competence" (S). Among other things, this means that among these L2 learners, some performed well on G-items and poorly on S-items but that others performed poorly on G-items and well on S-items. If we were only interested in the construct of language proficiency, we would concentrate on the issue whether knowledge of grammar rules and knowledge of sociolinguistic rules must be conceived of as independent or as related components. But for a broader view on L2 learning, we would have to answer the equally relevant question why it is that some learners do better on G-items and others on S-items. Furthermore, it might be important to investigate whether the relationship between G and S skills for each of these two groups of learners has remained and will always remain the same during the entire L2 acquisition process or whether G-skills have dominated at one stage of development, and S-skills at another. When a researcher wants to answer this kind of questions, a factor analysis will not constitute the end point of his investigations (as in so many current studies), but the starting point. He or she will further analyse the results of the factor analysis and try to predict and determine the influence of input and background variables on the factors found (in this example: on the G- and S-factor). He will, for example, want to find out what amount of L2 instruction the tested learners had received, what teaching method had been applied and which skills had been emphasized in class, how much and what sort of L2 input the learners had received from native speakers outside class, what sort of learning strategies they had employed, which language skills they themselves had considered essential, what kind of beliefs and attitudes they had maintained towards the L2 community and their place in it. Obviously, in this kind of research, too, one would prefer to test theoretically based predictions, rather than conducting exploratory "fishing expeditions".

In conclusion, for a second language proficiency theory to account for all these possibly confounding variables adequately, it is mandatory that not only information-processing and linguistic approaches be taken into account, but the language-pedagogy and social-psychological approaches as well. It is only by specifying how cognitive and linguistic variables interact with social, psychological, and educational variables, that we can arrive at a less incomplete understanding of the notion of second language proficiency. This approach may appropriately be called an interactive approach on second language proficiency

References

Bock, J.K. 1982, Toward a cognitive psychology of syntax: Information processing contributions to sentence formulation. *Psychological Review*, 89, 1–47.

Canale, M. 1983, On some dimensions of language proficiency. In J.W. Oller Jr. (ed.), *Issues in Language Testing Research*. Rowley, Mass.: Newbury House.

Canale, M. & Swain, M. 1980, Theoretical bases of communicative approaches to second language teaching and testing. *Applied Linguistics*, 1:1–47.

Carroll, J.B. 1968, The psychology of language testing. In A. Davies (ed.), *Language Testing Symposium: A Psycholinguistic Approach*. London: Oxford University Press.

Cooper, R.L. 1968, An elaborated language testing model. In J. Upshur & J. Fata (eds), *Problems in Foreign Language Testing, Language Learning*, 28, 57–65.

Cziko, G.A. 1982, Developing Models of Communicative Competence: Conceptual, Statistical, and Methodological Considerations. Paper presented at the 1982 TESOL Conference, Hawaii. Published, in revised form, as Some Problems with Empirically-based Models of Communicative Competence. *Applied Linguistics* 5 (1984): 23–38.

Guilford, J.P. & Hoepfner, R. 1971, *The Analysis of Intelligence*. New York: McGraw Hill.

Meuffels, B. 1981, Taalvaardigheden en processen; een poging tot theoretische en empirische integratie. *Tijdschrift voor Taalbeheersing*, 3, 14–31.

Oller, J.W. Jr. (ed.) 1983, *Issues in Language Testing Research*. Rowley, Mass.: Newbury House.

Shiffrin, R.M. & Dumais, S.T. 1981, The development of automatism. In J.R. Anderson (ed.), *Cognitive Skills and Their Acquisition*. Hillsdale, N.J.; Erlbaum.

Sternberg, R.J. 1980, Sketch of a componential subtheory of human intelligence. *The Behavioral and Brain Sciences*, 3, 573–614.

Sternberg, J.R. & Powell, J.S. 1983, Comprehending verbal comprehension. *The American Psychologist*, 38, 878–93.

Vollmer, H.J. in press, The structure of foreign language competence: The state of the art. In A. Hughes & D. Porter (eds), *Current Developments in Language Testing*. London: Academic Press.

Vollmer, H.J. & Sang, F. 1983, Competing hypotheses about second language ability: A plea for caution. In J.W. Oller, Jr. (ed.), *Issues in Language Testing Research*. Rowley, Mass.: Newbury House.

16 Language assessment as a social activity

WILFRIED STÖLTING

Universität Oldenburg, West Germany

"One half of our population is constantly engaged in testing the other half." – (director of a local office of state examinations)

Introduction

The contributions by Ingram (this volume, Chapter 10) and Clahsen (this volume, Chapter 12) underline the social responsibility of language testing and the possibility of test abuse. These aspects of language assessment have a special appeal to the present writer, who lives in a country of factual, but not officially recognized immigration from the Mediterranean area. Here, a restrictive policy regarding the so-called "foreigners" makes use of language tests for the purpose of deciding about the right of permanent rèsidence and about school careers. This chapter will first give some examples of such bureaucratic testing for selection, then proceed to discuss language assessment as a socially mediated interpretive activity, and, finally, review some tests of German as a second language for migrant children.

Testing scenes from the German West

For German as a *foreign* language, there exist a limited number of established tests (the certificates of the Goethe-Institut, the language diplomas of the Kultusministerkonferenz for German schools abroad, the language examination of university entrance for foreign students of the

Westdeutsche Rektorenkonferenz, the certificate of the Volkshochschule /adult further education/ and the threshold level of the council of Europe). Although a small proportion of migrants attend courses leading up to the two last-mentioned certificates, these are not designed for migrants acquiring German as a *second* language. They are certainly not applicable to migrants of school age.

So the school authorities have started looking for an instrument to select migrant pupils according to their command of German. This selection is essential to a school system which, on the one hand, expects migrants to adapt to the requirements of German national classes (of the submersion type) — thus ensuring a continuous gap between language needs and language learning possibilities of the socially disadvantaged migrant — and, on the other hand, relegates the predictable amount of unsuccessful migrants to "special classes" of various descriptions (only not of the language shelter type). Clahsen, in his introduction, mentions the Berlin case. In September 1982, the Berlin House of Representatives passed a law that states:

> "(4) The command of German on the part of the foreign pupils may be determined by a special procedure at the time of enrolment in the Berlin school and in the second half of year 4."
> (Gesetz- und Verordnungsblatt für Berlin, 38. Jahrgang, Nr. 51 12.10.1982, p.1807; my translation)

This innocuous-sounding provision acquires political relevance in connection with article 2 of the same law:

> "(2) The proportion of foreign pupils in classes with German pupils may not exceed 30% in the years 1 and 7 at the beginning of the school-year, or 50% if more than one half of the foreign pupils can follow instruction without language difficulties. (...) Also in the remaining years, the proportion of foreign pupils in classes with German pupils, as a rule, shall not exceed 50%."

The development of a "special procedure" mentioned by the law was commissioned by a group of applied linguists who declaredly work on a *diagnostic* instrument based upon oral German production and focussed on syntax and morphology for evaluation (Bruche-Schulz et al., 1983). A protest letter by eight professors of German as a second language to the school's senator in April 1982 denied any value to this test as a basis for educational decisions and concluded by saying:

> "The proposed cut-off point beyond which a foreign child is no longer considered to know 'enough German for integration' is

> no measure of his command of the language. It only allows valid
> conclusions about the amount of money which you are prepared
> to spend on the educational promotion of foreign children."
> (Menk, 1982; my translation)

Not surprisingly, this appeal did not prevent the passage of the law five months later. Political pressure of the majority (the concern of German voters about their children becoming a minority in regular classes) prevailed.

Another controversy has developed about the assessment of migrant adults' German by the German authorities once a migrant applies for an unlimited residence permit ("unbefristete Aufenthaltserlaubnis") after 5 years of residence, or the right to reside permanently ("Aufenthaltsberechtigung") after 8 years of residence. The legislation concerning foreigners requires, among other things, the ability to "make oneself understood in German in a simple way" for the first case and a "sufficient command of German" for the second (Dederichs, 1979). The criteria for these language requirements and for their assessment are left to each *Land* (administrative region) and, in practice, to the local authorities.

The bi-monthly publication of the metal workers' union, in July 1983, brought to light the wildly diverging practices of the authorities. Assessment of sufficient command of German ranges from "simple questions about personal circumstances" to written dictations; sometimes, a certificate of a language school is required. In one spectacular case, where a 15-minute dictation was given to a Turkish worker after 14 years of residence, the application for the right to permanent residence was dismissed on the grounds of missing dots over the i's, non-application of capital letters to nouns and insecurity in the handling of inflected pronouns. The district authorities justified the dictation by referring to "latest (scientific) knowledge" (Kandel, 1983). After this publication, the government of Lower Saxony revoked language assessment by means of dictation and ordered the local authorities to conduct detailed conversations ("vertiefende Gespräche") instead. The dependency of the migrant applicant on the individual official's impressionistic views on what sufficient command of German means, and how it can be assessed, remains unchanged.

Such instances of bureaucratic testing have led to two kinds of reaction on the part of applied linguists and language teachers in the country. There is the voiced hope for standardized test procedures for the German language assessment of migrants in the future (Scherzinger & Scherzinger, 1981:18; Hegele, 1981:42) in order to preclude such wilfulness and subjectivity of testers. There is also the wide-spread opinion that at least communicative skills cannot be validly tested and that irreversible decisions (about the right to permanent residence, school careers, etc.) may never legitimately be based upon tests (Göbel, 1978:25). Both lines of thinking agree that language testing must remain a secondary concern, and that attention should be focussed on improving social communication between migrants and the majority population as well as language learning conditions in schools and courses. It is the shared opinion of socially-committed language professionals in West Germany that in these respects migrants are subjected to a "swim-or-drown"-programme of the host society (Barkowski, 1982: chapter 1; Januschek & Stölting, 1982). If assessment of the migrants' German is to be approached at all, the development of diagnostic instruments is of prime importance. Clahsen's profile analysis, in its motivation, is representative of this conviction.

"The intuitive ability to judge proficiency"

Contrasting with the popular belief in the objectivity of tests, is the enlightened specialist's awareness of the limitations of testing and of its presuppositions, as Ingram so clearly demonstrates. While I propose to take the following points for granted, their general acceptance is still being awaited.

- General ability to communicate in a language cannot be tested as such,
- language command is more than the sum of its parts and must not be judged by one of its components,
- the sheer complexity and redundancy of language and its development make a single test for all purposes impossible; instead, the purpose of testing influences the choice of the test (and even of the underlying linguistic theory?) and limits interpretation of the test results,
- objective (indirect) tests rest on a series of subjective decisions,
- academic success is also determined by non-language factors and therefore cannot be predicted by language tests.

Ingram then proceeds to develop the position that, in sum, the testing of single components of language by indirect methods may be appropriate for attainment and diagnosis, but that overall language proficiency can best be assessed by summative tests relying on the inter-subjective consistency of experienced testers. Hauling down language testing from the heights of irreproachable objectivity, he establishes it as a controlled social process by ascribing degrees of language command. While sympathizing with this liberal standpoint as opposed to earlier and current test fetishism, I want to consider some of its implications by pushing the social aspect even farther.

Auer (1981), in an investigation into lay assessment of bilingual competence among Italian children in Germany, compares lay and professional assessment from the view-point of ethno-methodology, a study which has inspired much of my argument. Let us begin with the statement that self-assessment of competence, which would seem to be of prime importance because the person in question is nearest to and most experienced with himself, is not accepted as reliable in our culture. Division of social rôles and of labour, competition and mutual distrust may account for this. So other-assessment is given more credit in advance. In peer-groups, as Auer shows in detail, assessed persons can react to other-assessment, making the ascription of competence negotiable. Competence ascription as a negotiable process allows a good intuition for language assessment to build up, a concept which Ingram so frequently invokes as a basis for subjective testing. Part of the negotiation may be the refusal to undergo an informal test situation: putting equals into such a situation may result in self-compromise on the part of the tester and in discrediting the testee.

> "Thus, tests may be carried out without questioning the identi-
> ties of the parties involved between teacher and pupils, between
> parents and their children, in short, wherever the remnants of
> authority may be found, and in all these cases, they will
> contribute to the maintenance of these unequal relationships."
> (Auer, 1981: 20)

It seems to me that we have here the most fundamental distinction of language assessment as a social activity: equal relationships that allow for negotiation and unequal relationships that impede it. Into the latter category fall both lay (parents) and professional assessers (teachers) — a secondary distinction. Discrimination arising from subjective, uninformed and inaccurate assessment of another's language skills presupposes unequal relationships, and it is in these relationships that the concept of "judging" becomes appropriate. I recall my first activities as a "judge" of foreign students' German and the elated feeling it gave me; my experience in judging may have grown since, but my intuition may have deteriorated due to the exclusion of important aspects of communication in the unequal situation.

Division of labour in our societies has led to a "duplication" of lay persons' assessment by linguists who administer ex officio. The decisive difference from lay assessment is the linguist's claim to analyse the same phenomenon (i.e. language skills) as lay persons by using better techniques. Now the logic of science tells us that in developing theories/models, we disengage ourselves from immediate reality in order to reconstruct it by definable concepts, categories and relationships. In empirical science a model is a construct serving as an analogy for the object hidden from immediate observation. Setting up constructs and hypotheses about their relationships may require other criteria (e.g. those of productiveness and simplicity) than the principles governing "real life". A point in question concerns the various concepts of language proficiency, which are derived from the lay notion of proficiency that is close enough to reality ("intuitive") and at the same time sufficiently diffuse to continuously stimulate concept formation of the professionals. Ingram's discussion makes it quite clear to what extent approaches to defining proficiency are shaped by traditions and aims of linguistic enquiry and language teaching. The concept of proficiency advocated by Ingram — "the learner's behaviour as he attempts to carry out receptive and productive communication tasks" — is incompatible with Clahsen's who only considers the developmental aspect, and a developmental stage does not correlate to how efficiently a learner exploits the currently available linguistic means for communicative tasks. Other constructs would (and will) emerge when developed within the context of, for example, Soviet psychology of the Vygotskian tradition or Freudian psychology. Accordingly, tests based upon different concepts of proficiency will fail different individuals. This does not make them invalid as long as construct-validity is concerned. It is obvious, however, that the social sphere of (language) sciences is continually transporting its own constraints and contradictions upon the object it investigates, thereby transforming the object and re-shaping it even in the conscience of lay-persons.

As for the scientific techniques of assessing language, we have to take into account the scientific urge to put testees quasi into a social vacuum in order to reduce intervening factors to a controllable number. This de-personalization transforms the subject into an artefact of scientific discourse (Auer, 1981:24), and the old sociolinguistic dilemma arises: How can we know to what extent the utterances of testees are a product of experimental procedure? Auer gives a beautiful critique of the word association test designed to measure proficiency in domains:

"The numerous contextual relations in which and for which we produce a lexical item in unprompted contexts *cannot* be reproduced in a test situation which is specifically designed to *control* and *reduce* the number of contextual dependencies to a manageable minimum." (Auer, 1981:25)

A post-hoc correlation of context-free linguistic data with language-free sociological/psychological data will not solve the problem.

So, due to the constraints of construct formation and because language proficiency is not neutral to the methods employed to capture it, we have to conclude that

"the more professionals succeed in 'improving' lay ascription practices, the more they move away from the object of these ascriptions, so that their original intent to give competent (and, of course, superior) ascriptions eventually amounts to descriptions of a different competence." (Auer, 1981:6–7)

This should not be taken as a value judgment: Distortion of the "real thing" (language proficiency as a pre-scientific concept) exists on both lay and professional sides for possibly very good reasons — reductionism on the professional's; affect, prejudice and lack of clarity on the lay person's. Distortions cannot be avoided because the task of ascertaining the degree of language proficiency has to do with a highly organized quality of human behaviour which is not comparable to features like height or weight. The endeavour to get at the bottom of this complexity is bound to bring into focus the assesser himself. Ascription of language proficiency, then, is a socially-mediated interpretive activity where social relationships and interpretive patterns are at work.

Within the scope of this paper I can only hint at two interpretive patterns, common with lay-persons and professionals alike, where the social nature is obvious: (1) the idea that there *is* a language to which we gain access rests upon the Saussurean concept of langue which may well be a myth because, perhaps, there is no code external to and more permanent than the users of the code (LePage, 1969:144–46). National language policies with their reference books on standardized language have put this notion into our heads. (2) The idea that language competence/proficiency is an inherent and measurable personal property may be the result of another process of reification which dislocates interactive experiences into the "heads" of persons we want to "characterize" (Auer, 1981:43–44). The interaction model of diagnosis, mentioned by Fried (this volume, Chapter 14), may be a step forward in resisting this process.

So, reservations must be made whenever professional language assessment, because of the social prestige it enjoys and the unequal relationships it maintains, transgresses the limitations imposed by construct formation and data gathering methods in order to pass judgements on phenomena outside these limitations (e.g. equating language proficiency with general intelligence and as a prediction for school achievement), or where reductionism in construct formation will have negative social consequences for the party assessed. A striking example of how language policy, monolinguistic tradition and de-personalization combine to ultimately describe a "different competence" is the almost total absence in Ingram's and Clahsen's contributions and, indeed, in the conception of this book of *bilingual* competence/proficiency. The bilingual is reduced to how one monolingual group — not accidentally the socially dominant one — experiences him. The purpose of assessment is not to do justice to what the bilingual can do with the whole of his language repertoire, but to measure to what extent he meets the expectations of the monolingual group in power. Linguists, for their part, should have agreed by now that (social) bilingualism is neither "exprimer la réalité de deux façons différentes au moyen d'un double fond linguistique" nor "'traduction-en-deux-idiomes' d'une langue universelle, idéale, préexistant à l'expression, autrement dit, d'un langage intérieur" (van Overbeke, 1972:23), which would allow the assessment of the mental and interactional abilities of bilinguals through one language only. Bilingualists agree about the broad hypothesis that the bilingual's languages interact within a general bilingual competence. It follows for language assessment that

> "If compared with a monoglot whose totality of linguistic experience is enjoyed in one language, the bilingual may well reveal differentiated behaviour on verbal tests since his total linguistic experience is spread over two languages." (Baetens Beardsmore, 1982:92)

In other words: It makes a substantial difference (e.g. in decisions about schooling, streaming, even occupation) if the person assessed can handle language only to the extent indicated by a monolingual test, or if he has at his disposal another, dominant language for cognition, interaction and intrapsychic development. Even if one accepts the politically conditioned monolingual proficiency measurement of bilinguals, a strictly monolingual assessment of social bilinguals for diagnostic purposes falls beyond the possibilities even of the linguistic sciences.

Ingram, aware of the dilemmas of the scientific approach to language assessment, seeks to resolve them by recommending subjective assessment which reduces as little as possible language complexity and the personality of the assessed. The improvement in comparison to lay authorities' assessment lies in overcoming impressionism through the combined experience of linguists (language teachers) and the development of inter-subjective criteria. The tester, his training, understanding and skill become the pivots of assessment; his individuality is bound up in the social body of accredited testers, and as even judges can err there is the provision of a court of appeal. This model acknowledges the social character of professional language assessment and provides some safeguards against gross misjudgement. For all practical purposes, its introduction to the present writer's country, alongside a replica of the ASLPR, would be a considerable step forward.

Nevertheless, some reservations have to be made. Unification of language proficiency concepts and methods of assessment among testers strengthens prevailing opinions at the expense of deviant new developments; social bodies of testers are susceptible to political pressure; unequal relationships between the assessed and the assessers are maintained; the slotting-in of learners to the point where their proficiency falls in the rating scales is not exactly a model of jurisdiction where everybody deserves individual treatment and consideration of their personal circumstances. Such reservations may be of considerable weight in a country whose leading politicians are determined to discourage the migrants' aspirations. In this atmosphere, it is unlikely that migrants will not experience anxiety in an oral interview that has a bearing upon their further lives.

Migrants' German testing as a compensatory movement

Section 1 of this paper was concerned with the authorities' interest in language testing of migrants in West Germany; this section will try to show how an inflexible and irresponsible school system forces pedagogues and linguists to bring the sins of the system to bear on the migrants.

In the 70's (and even today), there was a marked stress on contrastive analysis and error analysis to find out problem areas of migrants' acquisition/learning of German (cf. e.g. Meyer-Ingwersen et al., 1977). Publications on the assessment of migrant pupils' German started to appear in 1980. On the linguists' part, these were stimulated by the universals/

interlanguage-oriented approach (Clahsen, this volume; Portz & Pfaff, 1981). Pedagogues claimed that it was not enough to be informed about the so-called typical errors of Turks, but that we must know the deficiencies of the individual pupil. The direction of the growing demand of teachers for assessment instruments became apparent when test authors had to caution against misunderstanding their preliminary results as a basis for decisions about school careers (Fliegner & Gogolin, 1982:2).

The proposals for language assessment instruments, published in this short span of time, have several characteristics in common. First, they all decline to offer absolute solutions and more or less explicitly invite the teacher/tester to provide feedback reports. Next, they are without exception monolingual (L2 German), although some authors state the desirability of bilingual assessment (Ihssen, 1980:42; Luchtenberg, 1983:36). Monolingual orientation is especially remarkable in the SES ("Soziolinguistisches Erhebungsinstrument zur Sprachentwicklung" by Portz & Pfaff, 1981) which takes the "Bilingual Syntax Measure" for a model. Assessment procedures of previous, bilingually-oriented sociolinguistic studies of migrant children (e.g. Stölting et al., 1980; Auer, 1981) are not discussed within the narrower frame of testing for school purposes. There is no proposal on the market for an assessment of the migrants' command of their languages of origin, although mother-tongue instruction is offered on a voluntary basis in some Länder (administrative regions) under the auspices of the German school system (here the introduction of the languages of origin as a first or second "foreign language" might bring about further developments). This state of affairs is clearly due to the professed language policy of the school system, as characterized in section 2; it contains the tacit consent that no bilingually-oriented or bilingually-based German language courses (along the lines of the Bilingual Method) are feasible or even desirable — which takes us a step further to the connection between the proposed instruments and the principles on which classes are to be formed and streaming done.

What are the purposes of the instruments available? These are not so easily ascertainable as might be desired, according to Ingram (pp.256–67). The generally professed purpose is diagnosis of the migrant's deficiencies and abilities in German, generally labelled "level of language capability" (Sprachstand) in dangerous analogy to "level of the sea" (Wasserstand). Hints as to the possible exploitation of the diagnostic information for placement and streaming keep cropping up (Fliegner & Gogolin, 1982:15; Hegele, 1981:41; Luchtenberg et al., 1982:134; Scherzinger & Scherzinger, 1981:18). An explicit statement like

> "the proposed diagnosis through kindergarten-specific media serves exclusively the purpose of language training (...) Streaming into groups of learners or even placement of pre-school children into definite forms are not possible on the basis of the proposed diagnosis". (Luchtenberg, 1983: 36; my translation)

is the exception.

There may be several reservations about the immediate translation of diagnostic results into placement/streaming decisions. Language capabilities by themselves are too weak a predictor of educational success and must be supplemented by non-linguistic information (Fliegner & Gogolin, 1982:16–17). Homogeneous grouping may not result in optimal learning processes (Göbel, 1981 describes in detail the possible advantages of heterogeneity in language classrooms) and may rather serve the purpose of selection. Next comes the disregard of Ingram's principle (this volume, p.264) that

> "for streaming purposes, the basis on which the classes are to be formed and the streaming done must be determined and then one can decide what are the most appropriate test instruments to use"

It is naive to expect that once the learners' deficiencies have been diagnosed, the contents of courses and classes are established. Regular classes, preparatory classes for migrants, remedial German language courses all have their own pedagogic dynamics and aims (content matter learning, help with homework, promotion of social integration etc.) and have a bearing on school careers: preparatory classes prolong social segregation from the mainstream system, remedial language courses often make children miss lessons in the regular class. So the deficiencies diagnosed lead to children being placed into classes and courses where these deficiencies may not be worked upon at all.

The main fault, of course, is the absence of established syllabi for the language education of migrant pupils, which leaves almost everything to the teacher (commercial language teaching materials are a help but cannot substitute a syllabus). It goes without saying that the diagnostic assessment of the pupils' German, as well as contrastive and error analysis, gives important information to be considered in establishing these syllabi; but I find it a doubtful procedure to extract such information with the help of a diagnostic instrument which, at the same time, serves to make placement decisions about the individual pupil.

The case against the use of diagnostic results for other purposes appears even stronger when we look at the selection of items to be measured by the proposed instruments. Morphology and syntax are at the centre of the authors' attention, with elementary lexis and listening comprehension thrown in (Fliegner & Gogolin, 1982; Luchtenberg et al., 1982). Clahsen (this volume) summarizes the arguments for this approach. Without challenging them, I would like to point out that linguistic tradition (preoccupation with morpho-syntax and applicability of the interlanguage hypothesis), the native German speaker's and the teacher's preoccupation with "correct language" without much communicative relevance (e.g. verb-placement rules), and the treatment of lexical items as "spare parts" to be fitted into a syntactically generated terminal chain may play a part in the authors' decision. In any case, they strengthen these traditional convictions among educators.

The main point, however, is the one Ingram makes (this volume, p.234) that for the practical purposes teachers have in mind, findings concerning morphology and syntax have to be related to the language tasks that a learner can carry out. We are still very far from this step. Even with regard to L2 diagnosis, I think the authors would agree that we are still at the beginning. The evaluation tables given in Hegele (1981) and Portz & Pfaff (1981), to take the more explicit examples, simply list incorrect and correct utterances according to the traditional system of morpho-syntactic categories: possessive pronoun — adjective — definite article etc./local prepositions- temporal prepositions — prepositions to indicate the indirect object etc. When we consider the "monoflexive co-operation" of the parts of the German nominal system or adopt valence theory (as most modern descriptive grammars of German do), we are no longer sure under which of the traditional headings to enter an utterance. In other words, the categorization gives little advice for therapy. A diagnosis of the learner's strengths and weaknesses has to be rooted in a cohesive structural description of the language or, better still, in a psycholinguistic theory of development of the items under consideration.

This is what Clahsen intends to give for a limited set of syntactic regularities. Compared to the instruments mentioned above, his proposal is an excellent example of scientific approach in that he clearly states his criteria for assessment, describes the embedding developmental theory, writes the required portion of grammar, and details the process of evaluating spontaneous speech. Of course, this profile analysis, too, constructs its own reality (cf. Auer, 1981; 12–13, for a critique of cutting down a conversation to analyzable phrases), but there is no harm in this as long as the instrument keeps within the limits of developing and refining linguistic theory. Outside the scientific field, the resulting regularities can sharpen the language awareness of teachers and make them want to adjust instruction to the learners' needs. Clahsen does not propose to derive decisions about placement and streaming from his results. Will the teacher adhere to this limitation, given the pressures of the school system? If not, Ingram's remarks about "the too-ready application of psycholinguistics to testing" apply, as does the criticism of morpho-syntax as a basis for assessing proficiency in Ingram's understanding of this concept. Several of my migrant acquaintances "misplace" the German verb after adverbal clauses or in dependant sentences quite regularly, without endangering a mutually satisfying exchange of language acts; sociolinguistically, a deviant rule has emerged among them which I must try hard not to imitate. "Correct" verb placement for them is neither a target rule nor a requisite for successful communication.

Within the German context, one area of testing seems to have been lost from view in the multiple activities of assessing the individual migrant pupil and which would assess the instruction migrants are given: the evaluation of a second language programme (Ingram, this volume, p.265). This omission is significant and in line with my remarks on the present state of syllabi for migrant pupils. Given the alternatives: to study the interaction of the pupils with teaching materials and teachers (including the teachers' silent assumptions about language learning), or: to study language proficiency of the individual migrant as a personal property, professionals still prefer the second one. The educational system is the invariant and the migrant the dependent factor, not just in a statistical sense.

Hopefully, the contradictions and inconsistencies of this initial phase of L2-testing with migrants will open up a broader perspective where the interactional quality of ascribing language proficiency is recognized. Evaluation problems have already led to a more fundamental reflection of the rôle of teachers in L2-testing. As can be expected, much of the variance in test results can be accounted for by how teachers administer and evaluate the instruments. Gogolin (1984), one of the first to take up this issue in the field of migrant testing, makes it clear that no substantial progress can be made without simultaneous linguistic training of teachers. This is not just a question of standardizing the handling of test instruments. Ultimately, such training should promote awareness of the dilemmas and choices in language assessment as sketched on pp.384–89 of this chapter.

Acknowledgements

My thanks to Delia Krause, Antje-Kathrin Menk and Manfred Pienemann for help with this paper.

References

Auer, J.C.P. 1981, *Bilingualism as a members' concept: Language choice and language alternation in their relation to lay assessments of competence*. Research papers of the Sonderforschungsbereich 99 Linguistik Universität Konstanz, no. 54. Konstanz.

Baetens Beardsmore, H. 1982, *Bilingualism: Basic principles*. Clevedon, Avon: Multilingual Matters.

Barkowski, H. 1982, *Kommunikative Grammatik und Deutschlernen mit ausländischen Arbeitern*. Königstein/Ts.

Bruche-Schulz, G. Hess, H.-W. & Steinmüller, U. 1983, *Sprachstandserhebungen im Grundschulalter. Ein Projektives Linguistisches Analyseverfahren (PLAV)*. Senator für Schulwesen, Jugend und Sport. Berlin.

Dederichs, E. 1979, Nachweis 'einfacher' und 'ausreichender' Deutschkenntnisse: Die Erlasse der Bundesländer. *Deutsch lernen*, 1, 88–92.

Fliegner, J. & Gogolin, I. 1982, *Sprachstandsmessung bei Schulanfängern*. Pädagogisches Institut Düsseldorf. Düsseldorf.

Göbel, R. 1978, Zur Möglichkeit der Messung kommunikativer Fertigkeiten. *Deutsch lernen*, 2, 21–26.

—— 1981, *Verschiedenheit und gemeinsames Lernen. Kooperative Binnendifferenzierung im Fremdsprachenunterricht*. Königstein/Ts.

Gogolin, I. 1984, Lehrer als 'Tester'. In H.H. Reich & F. Wittek (eds), *Migration – Bildungspolitik – Pädagogik*. Berichte und Materialien der Forschungsgruppe ALFA 16. Essen/Landau, 151–69.

Hegele, I. 1981, Deutsch als Zweitsprache: Sprachstandsdiagnose und Sprachförderung von Ausländerkindern. *Deutsch lernen*, 4, 41–56.

Ihssen, W.B. 1980, Probleme der Sprachentwicklungsdiagnose bei Ausländerkindern. *Praxis Deutsch '80*, 40–42.

Januschek, F. & Stölting, W. (eds) 1982, *Handlungsorientierung im Zweitsprachenerwerb*. Osnabrücker Beiträge zur Sprachtheorie 22. Osnabrück.

Kandel, N. 1983, Diktat für Ausländer. *metall, 14*, 16–17.

LePage, R.B. 1969, Session 3/Commentaries. In L.G. Kelly (ed.), *Description and measurement of bilingualism*. Toronto, 142–47.

Luchtenberg, S. 1983, Sprachbarrieren verstehen und überwinden. Überlegungen zur Sprachstandsdiagnose ausländischer Kinder im Vorschulbereich. *Ausländerkinder in Schule und Kindergarten*, 1, 33–36.

Luchtenberg, S., Neumann, H.-J. & Wespel, M. 1982, Informeller Test zur Sprachstandsdiagnose bei ausländischen Kindern und Jugendlichen. In U. Coburn-Staege *et al.* (eds), *Türkische Kinder in unseren Schulen – eine pädagogische Herausforderung*. Stuttgart, 134–76.

Menk, A.-K. 1982, Offener Brief an die Senatorin für Schulwesen, Jugend und Sport Berlin (13.4.1982), unpublished.

Meyer-Ingwersen, J. Neumann, R. & Kummer, M. 1977, *Zur Sprachentwicklung türkischer Schüler in der Bundesrepublik*, Vols. 1,2. Kronberg/Ts.

Portz, R. & Pfaff, C. 1981, *SES-Soziolinguistisches Erhebungsverfahren zur Sprachentwicklung.* Pädagogisches Zentrum Berlin.

Scherzinger, A. & Scherzinger, G. 1981, Sprachstandsdiagnose für die schulische Förderung von Ausländerkindern. *Ausländerkinder in Schule und Kindergarten,* 2, 18–22.

Stölting, W., Delić, D., Orlović, M., Rausch, K. & Sausner, E. 1980, *Die Zweisprachigkeit jugoslawischer Schüler in der Bundesrepublik Deutschland.* Berlin.

van Overbeke, M. 1972, *Introduction au problème du bilinguisme.* Bruxelles–Paris.

Index